On Mao's Political Ideology: Reviewing Chinese and Global Studies 1940-2007

Yang Fengcheng

Translated by Zhu Yanhui

CANut

Originally published as A General Review of Studies of Mao Zedong Thought in 2004 by China Renmin University Press.

Original Chinese Edition Copyright © 2004 by Yang Fengcheng
ISBN: 978-7-300-03930-5

On Mao's Political Ideology: Reviewing Chinese and Global Studies 1940-2007
ISBN: 978-3-942575-03-4

Published by
Canut International Publishers
Yorck Street. 66
10965 Kreuzberg
Berlin-Germany

Canut International Publishers
12a Guernsey Road E11
London 4BJ-England-U.K.

URL: http//www.canut.us
E-Mail: canut@aol.com

Acknowledgments

This book is a reference book for students learning Mao Zedong Thought in universities and colleges in China and for theoreticians and researchers studying it in Party schools, theoretical publicity bodies and academic research institutes. It offers an objective, equitable, and comprehensive introduction and assessments on the past and latest achievements in the study of Mao Zedong Thought in China and foreign countries and on the controversial issues in the study. When deciding on the English edition of this book, we have aimed to deliver the global reader a complete picture on how Mao Zedong and Mao Zedong's ideology is evaluated and studied in today's China. It is a representative book of its kind and also reflects how the mainland Chinese scholars have evaluated foreign studies on Mao Zedong. Thus we hope the book will encourage more exchanges on Mao Zedong studies worldwide. The book also offers a comprehensive and systematic study material and factual information for those interested in the history of Marxism in China.

The book was written by a team work and young and middle-aged scholars teaching and studying Mao Zedong Thought and the history of the Communist Party of China at the Department of History of the Communist Party of China in Renmin University of China, have contributed to the chapters of it.

Here we would like to thank them for the valuable work they have realized and present their contribution for the English reader.

Pan Huanzhao: "Chapter 1: The Historical Process in the Study of Mao Zedong Thought" and "Part 1 of the chapter 2: Study on the History of Development of Mao Zedong Thought"He Husheng: "Chapter 3: Mao Zedong Thought as a Scientific System" and Part 4 of the chaper five: On the Theory of the People's Democratic Dictatorship"

Liu Hui: "Part 1 of the chapter 4: The Theory of the New-Democratic

1

Revolution" and "Part 1 of the chapter 5: On the Theory of a New-Democratic Society"

Wang Yunsheng: "Part 2 of the chapter 4: The Theory of Encircling the Cities from the Countryside"

You Guoli: "Part 4 of the chapter 4: The Theory of the United Front" and "Chapter 8: Study on the of Living Soul of Mao Zedong Thought,"

Wu Meihua: "Part 5 of the chapter 5: The Theory of Party Building"

Li Yongfeng: "Part 3 of the chapter 4: The Theory of People's Revolutionary War" and "Part 2 of the chapter 5: The Theory and Policy on the Peasant Problem and Agrarian Reform," and also "Chapter 7: The Theory of Socialist Construction"

Xin Yi: "Part 3 of the chapter 5: The Thinking on Building Revolutionary Bases"

Wang Xiaoming: "Chapter 6: The Theory of Socialist Revolution"

Wen Lequn: "Chapter 9: Studies on the Relationship between Mao Zedong Thought and Deng Xiaoping Theory"

Yang Fengcheng wrote the chapters related to foreign studies on Mao Zedong Thought. And, Wang Shunsheng has compiled those excerpts from the documents and speeches of the three generations of CPC Collective Leadership, and the CPC leading bodies, who have evaluated Mao Zedong and Mao Zedong Thought.

Yang Fengcheng as the chief compiler has also contributed to the general design and the style of the book. We owe special thanks to Professor Wang Shunsheng, director of the Department of History of the Communist Party of China in Renmin University of China, who supported and helped us in this project. The book was translated to English by Zhu Yanhui, through translation and editing of this book we have overcome many difficulties with him, Yang Fengcheng and China Renmin University Press. We express our gratitude to all of them for the creation of this edition.

Walter Meyer
Berlin

Contents

Part Two   Studies on Mao Zedong Thought in Foreign Countries

Part Three   Authoritative Assessments and Documents on Mao Zedong and Mao Zedong Thought

Part One

Studies on Mao Zedong Thought in China

Chapter 1

The Historical Process in the Study of Mao Zedong Thought

Mao Zedong Thought is a guiding ideology founded by Chinese Communists with Comrade Mao Zedong as their chief representative to lead the Chinese revolution and construction. Its destiny is closely tied to the destiny of the Communist Party of China (CPC) and of China's revolution and construction. Therefore, Mao Zedong Thought is a political theory of great value for practice. The study on Mao Zedong Thought is often closely related to the learning and publicity on it, and senior and middle-rank Party cadres and Party members working in the fields of theory and publicity have been the main participants in the study and publicity of it from the very beginning. At the same time, the study and publicity of Mao Zedong Thought is inseparable from the study and publicity of Mao Zedong and his thought because he is personally the chief leader of the Party and the principal founder of Mao Zedong Thought.

Mao Zedong Thought has a forming and developing process and different development stages; correspondingly, the study on it also has a developing process and different development stages. With regard to the historical process in the study of Mao Zedong Thought at home, the years over half a century beginning from the 1940s can be divided into two major historical stages, each of which can be further divided into several historical periods according to the different features in the study of Mao Zedong Thought.

1.1 Brief Introduction to the Study of Mao Zedong Thought before the Third Plenary Session of the Eleventh Central Committee of the CPC

The study of Mao Zedong Thought before the Third Plenary Session of the Eleventh CPC Central Committee can be divided into three historical periods: 1941-1949, the preliminary period; 1950-1965, the developing period; 1966-1978, the setback period.

1.1.1 The Preliminary Period in the Study of the Thought (1941-1949)

1.1.1.1 The Historical Background of Studies on Mao Zedong Thought

Generally, when a thought or theory comes into being, the study on it will emerge correspondingly. Therefore, along with the emergence and formation of Mao Zedong Thought, the study on it had emerged.

During the period from the late 1920s to the early 1930s, Mao Zedong's some specific works were printed and distributed within CPC members, such as his "Report on An Investigation of the Peasant Movement in Hunan," which was generally accepted as his concentrated exposition on peasant problems in the days of the Great Revolution (1924-1927)[1] and was prefaced

---

[1] The Great Revolution, which lasted from 1925 to 1927, was a revolutionary movement of the Chinese people against imperialism and feudalism.

by Qu Qiubai who had fully affirmed the report and the ideas it elaborated. In the latter half of the 1930s, some biographies on Mao Zedong's life emerged, and what produced the profoundest influence were *Autobiography of Mao Tse-tung* edited by Edgar Snow based on interview speech with Mao Zedong and *Brief Biography of Mao Zedong* published by the CPC delegation to the Communist International. While introducing the life and deeds of Mao Zedong, these biographies had also introduced or commented on his thought. However, such introductions and comments were separate and exceptional, far from common or systematic. From 1938 on, in the anti-Japanese base areas under the leadership of the CPC, studies and publicizing Mao Zedong's "On Protracted War," "On the New Period" and some other separate writings were started, but their study and publicity were targeted on specific questions and were also not systematic or comprehensive.

Studies on Mao Zedong Thought in the true sense had emerged in the late 1930s and the early 1940s due to conditions both inside and outside the Party and both at home and abroad. At that time Mao Zedong's concepts and theories were proved correct along with the successful completion of the Long March campaign of the Red Army, and his leading position in the Red Army and in the Party was confirmed and was recognized by the Communist International. During that period, study on Mao Zedong's theories about China's revolution developed greatly, leading to the publication of his several works "Problems of Strategy in China's Revolutionary War," "On Practice," "On Contradiction," "On Protracted War," "On the New Period," "Introducing *The Communist*," "The Chinese Revolution and the Chinese Communist Party," "On New Democracy" and some other writings. All this indicates that Mao Zedong was becoming increasingly mature in theories and was getting high prestige in theoretical studies among Party members. With the launching of the Yan'an rectification movement in 1942, the entire Party ushered in an upsurge in studying the theories of Marxism-Leninism and summing up the historical experience in the Chinese revolution, and many Party members and theoreticians came to realize that the theory and practice of the CPC with Mao Zedong as its chief representative were exactly the example of the integration of Marxism with the practice of the Chinese revolution and should be correctly judged and given a proper name. From the winter of 1939 to the spring of 1940, the Kuomintang (KMT) launched its first anti-Communist campaign, mobilizing all its publicity machines for propagandizing "one party, one doctrine, one leader" in addition to military offensive and attacks. Under this situation, to confirm Mao Zedong's leading position in politics and authority in ideology became vital for the efforts of the CPC to fight back the enemy on the ideological fronts and wage a publicity war against the KMT. In addition, the dissolution of the Communist International had set higher requirements on the CPC for its ability to independently solve problems of the Chinese revolution and created an objective requirement for the CPC to raise its own ideological flag.

The above facts indicated that both the subjective and the objective conditions were ripe for publicizing Mao Zedong and his thoughts and theories, so the emergence of the concept of "Mao Zedong Thought" and the affirmation of Mao Zedong Thought as the guiding ideology of the CPC were just natural. Therefore, the 1940s became extremely important for the publicity and study of Mao Zedong Thought.

1.1.1.2 The Emergence of the Concept of Mao Zedong Thought and the Affirmation of Its Guiding Position

Mao Zedong suggested at the Sixth Plenary Session of the Sixth CPC Central Committee to "apply Marxism concretely in China" in October 1938 and advanced the fundamental ideological principal of "integrating the theory of Marxism-Leninism with the practice of the Chinese revolution" in the "Introducing *The Communist*" in October next year. The above two cases were of great importance for the formation and formulation of Mao Zedong Thought.

The Party's theoretician Zhang Ruxin had published in early 1941 an article "On Bolshevist Educators," in which he had made the earliest wording as "Thought of Comrade Mao Zedong." He had commented that Mao Zedong's words and writings were results of typical integration of the theory of Marxism-Leninism with the practice of the Chinese revolution and that educators of the Party should devote themselves to the thoughts of Lenin and Stalin as well as to the thought of Comrade Mao Zedong. He had also argued that theoreticians should study Mao Zedong's writings and "learn how he applies the basic tenets of Marxism-Leninism to the specific circumstances of China and develops Marxism in a creative way," which indicated that theoreticians like him had got a rational understanding of Mao Zedong Thought and were starting to learn, study and publicize it consciously.

In February 1942, Zhang Ruxin had published in the *Liberation Daily* an article "Study and Grasp Mao Zedong's Theories and Tactics," advancing that Mao Zedong's theories and tactics represented the application and development of the theories and tactics of Marxism-Leninism, in colonial, semi-colonial and semi-feudal China and were China's Marxism-Leninism. He had also stressed that Mao Zedong's theories and tactics, being consistent, systematic and complete in both history and logic, could be divided into three parts relatively and conditionally for the convenience of elaboration and study, i.e., ideological line or thought way, political line or science, and military line or science. Deng Tuo, another theoretician of the Party who had made great contribution to publicizing Mao Zedong Thought in the 1940s, had published in the *Jinchaji Daily* on July 1, 1942 an editorial "The Entire Party Should Study to Grasp Maoism on July 1 at the 21st Anniversary of the Founding of the Communist Party of China," in which he used the term "Maoism," holding that Maoism was a unified and complete system of theories and tactics of the CPC in leading the Chinese revolution and represented new, creative development of Marxism-Leninism. I can say that the Party had started to attach great importance to the learning, publicity and study of Mao Zedong Thought, and theoretical preparations had been made for the emergence of the concept of Mao Zedong Thought and for the affirmation of its guiding position.

Along with the launching of the rectification movement in Yan'an in 1942, the entire Party got a further understanding of Mao Zedong Thought, which created the necessary theoretical environment for large-scale learning, publicity and study of it. Besides, with the consent of Mao Zedong himself, the concept "Mao Zedong Thought" formally came into being and was widely used to summarize all of Mao Zedong's thinking, theories and principles. On July 8, 1943, Wang Jiaxiang had published in the *Liberation Daily* an article "The Road of the Communist Party of China and Chinese National Liberation," affirming that Mao Zedong Thought was "Marxism-Leninism, Bolshevism and Communism in China," "formed on the basis of the theory of Marxism-Leninism after studying the realities in China and drawing on experience from the Party's twenty-two years of difficulties and struggles both inside and outside the Party," and "is the result of integrating Marxism-Leninism with the practice and experience of the Chinese revolution." This indicates that Wang Jiaxiang had reached a new level in understanding Mao Zedong Thought and in refining its theories. Although the article confused Mao Zedong Thought with the thought of Mao Zedong, it represented a new development since it had integrated Mao Zedong Thought with the Party's twenty-two years of experience. It could be said that the article was of pioneering significance to the publicity and study of Mao Zedong Thought and greatly inspired and influenced later researchers. Thereafter, the term "Mao Zedong Thought" was more often used and expounded in the Party's documents and in speeches of Party leaders.

The Seventh National Congress of the CPC in 1945, was of vital importance for the study mode on Mao Zedong Thought. The Party decided in its Constitution at its Seventh Congress to take Mao Zedong Thought- the integration of the theory of Marxism-Leninism with the practice of the Chinese revolution- as the ideology guiding all its works. Furthermore, Liu Shaoqi, in his presentation "Report on the Revision of the Party Constitution", allocated a whole section titled "Concerning the Guiding Ideology of Our Party" to expound the theoretical problems concerning Mao Zedong Thought, such as its meaning and basic ideas, the necessity for its emergence, its relation with the Party, its social foundation and theoretical source, the reasons why Mao Zedong created such a body of scientific theories about the Chinese revolution, and the significance of its emergence and development. "Special attention should be given to judgments on Mao

Zedong Thought such as "it is a perfect example of applying Marxism in China" and "a complete body of theories of the Chinese people on revolution and national development," which fully affirm its theoretical and practical significance." His comment under "Mao Zedong has remarkably and successfully" applied Marxism in China answered the question why the theories about the Chinese revolution were named by his name. For the first time in the history of the CPC, the detailed ideas and basic components of Mao Zedong Thought were summed up in nine aspects and gave a rather complete summarization. In addition, the entire Party was called to learn and publicize Mao Zedong Thought and various corresponding measures were taken to promote the study, publicity, learning and spread of it. With regard to whether Mao Zedong Thought belonged to Mao Zedong himself or to the collective wisdom of the entire Party, Liu Shaoqi had affirmed both but had generally expressed that it belonged to Mao Zedong himself, which was common in the studies of Mao Zedong Thought in the 1940s and also in a rather long period, afterwards.

The affirmation of Mao Zedong Thought as the Party's guiding ideology at the Seventh Congress had marked the formal beginning of conscious and systematic study of Mao Zedong Thought and made it a focus of discussion in the Party's domain of ideological and theoretical study. Besides, Liu Shaoqi's report to the Congress had not only introduced the newest progress in the study of Mao Zedong Thought but also promoted the further development of the study.

Right before and after the Seventh Congress, Party leaders including Chen Yi, Bo Gu, Deng Xiaoping, Chen Yun and Zhou Enlai had elaborated Mao Zedong Thought for many times in their speeches. Many theoreticians of the Party wrote articles and books to propagandize and discuss it from different angles and at different levels, and some books with great influence: *Mao Zedong Thought and Work Style* (September 1946) by Zhang Ruxin, and *Political Thinking in Mao Zedong Thought* (August 1949) and *Thought Way in Mao Zedong Thought* (July 1949) by Huang Qian were published.

1.1.1.3 Publication of Mao Zedong's Works

Mao Zedong's works and speeches are the concentrated embodiment of Mao Zedong Thought. With the formation and development of Mao Zedong Thought and the progress in its learning, publicity and study, the CPC naturally put the publication of Mao Zedong's works on its agenda. As a result, many of Mao Zedong's writings in off prints, treatises and selections were published. This was very important for the publicity and study of Mao Zedong Thought at that time and provided favorable conditions for further studies as well.

The offprints of Mao Zedong's works had emerged as early as in the late 1920s and increased after the War of Resistance Against Japan broke out. The covers of some off prints were disguised[1] in order to be transported to or published in enemy-occupied areas and in Kuomintang-controlled areas. The publication of Mao Zedong's treatises began after the Lugouqiao Incident in July 7, 1937. The two collections of Party documents *Before the Sixth National Congress* and *Since the Sixth National Congress* were edited and published by the Secretariat of the CPC Central Committee in the early 1940s which included Mao Zedong's most important and representative works at the time. The publication of the off prints, treatises and collections had not only publicized the political position of the CPC and the people it represented but had also prepared necessary conditions for introducing and elaborating the ideas of Mao Zedong Thought and facilitated editing and publishing selected works of Mao Zedong.

Different editions of selected works of Mao Zedong were published in the liberated areas from 1944 on. The earliest edition, five-volume *Selected Works of Mao Zedong* published by *Jinchaji Daily* in 1944, collected Mao Zedong's twenty-nine writings with a total of about 450,000 characters. Categorized by content, these five volumes respectively focused on the

---

[1] There are such off prints with disguised covers collected at the National Library of China: some names on the covers read *General Account on Literature and History* or *Treatise on Awakening Mahayana Faith*, while the contents are "On Protracted War," "On the New Period" and "On New Democracy."

basic theories and political system of the new-democratic revolution, the question of the united front, war and military problems, issues on economy and finance, and Party building. The publication of this edition of selected works was aimed at systematically propagandizing Mao Zedong Thought and promoting the Party's theoretical development. Since the CPC had raised its own ideological flag at its Seventh National Congress, it became an important work for it to appeal to all its members to systematically study Mao Zedong's works and grasp the basic ideas of Mao Zedong Thought, so it was just necessary to publish selected works of Mao Zedong in all base areas and liberated areas. The Soviet-Chinese Publishing House, the Xinhua Bookstore in Shandong, the Xinhua Bookstore in Bohai, the Northeast Bookstore and the Shanxi-Hebei-Shandong-Henan Central Bureau of the CPC Central Committee had all published their editions of selected works of Mao Zedong, although their layouts and selection of writings were different. *Selected Works of Mao Zedong* published by the Soviet-Chinese Publishing House was a special one among them. The preface "On Mao Zedong Thought" to this edition was written by eighteen Party leaders including Zhu De, Zhou Enlai and Liu Shaoqi, who elaborated a number of issues concerning Mao Zedong Thought such as the conditions for its emergence, its meaning, basic ideas and theoretical and practical significance, and assessment of Mao Zedong.

Due to objective restrictions, these editions, were different in layouts, and failed to include some important writings of Mao Zedong and also had some errors because they had not been checked by Mao Zedong or the central authorities before being published. Nevertheless, those editions and publication of selected works of Mao Zedong reflect how editors and Party and government organs in the base areas understood and summarized Mao Zedong Thought and how they had attempted to elaborate it by publishing these works, in those days. These selected works were very important for publicizing Mao Zedong Thought and helped studies made by senior and middle-rank Party cadres and Party members working in the fields of publicity and theory.

1.1.1.4 The Basic Features in the Study of Mao Zedong Thought

Generally speaking, the principle line guiding the CPC during that period was affirming and elaborating the correctness of Mao Zedong Thought, while the study on it had focused mainly on its meaning, features, position and role, the conditions for its formation, and the preliminary summarization of its contents.

Here are the main features in the study of Mao Zedong Thought during that period:

First, the mode of the studies. After Mao Zedong Thought was regarded as a concept and was affirmed as the Party's guiding ideology, participants in the study had expanded from single individuals to the entire Party, and the study had upgraded from unconscious and separate mode to conscious and systematic mode.

Second is the emphases of the studies. Perceptual cognition had outweighed rational cognition. Although researchers had begun to stress theoretical problems concerning Mao Zedong Thought, yet the study still tended to affirm and publicize the Thought politically and theoretically and focused on emphasizing the meaning of applying Marxism in China.

Third is in the products of the study. More historical materials than theoretical analyses were produced. Although monographs had begun to appear, they were often short and were restricted to certain issues concerning general introduction, political thinking and thought ways. There were less studies focusing on special topics.

Fourth is the object of the study. Mao Zedong Thought was generally regarded as the thought of Mao Zedong due to insufficient understanding and pressing political needs.

Fifth is the aim of the study. The aim was to raise an ideological flag for the CPC and make Mao Zedong Thought a guiding ideology in the thinking of the Party and the people.

Sixth is the territory in which the study was conducted. The study was mainly conducted in the base areas and liberated areas under the leadership of the CPC, and was beginning to appear in Kuomintang-controlled areas and enemy-occupied areas or even in faraway Hong Kong.

Seventh is the methods of the study. Special emphases were placed on the integration and unity of Mao Zedong Thought with Marxism and on the basic characteristic of Mao Zedong Thought asserting the idea that it is the result of the integration of Marxism with the practice of the Chinese revolution.

The visible limitations in the study and publicity during that period was that Mao Zedong Thought was equated with the thoughts of Mao Zedong himself. Here are the reasons.

First, the outstanding contributions in opposing dogmatism and applying and developing Marxism in China were made by Mao Zedong himself and was commonly recognized by the entire Party.

Second, the Marxism-Leninism, which is the theoretical source of Mao Zedong Thought, was also regarded as the theoretical ideas and thinking systems of Marx, Engels and Lenin personally, and the concept as "collective wisdom" was not formed yet.

Third, the complete body of Mao Zedong's theoretical viewpoints concerning the Chinese revolution had proved correct at the time. It was after the "cultural revolution" and test of practice that the question of distinguishing Mao Zedong Thought from the thought of Mao Zedong was raised.

Fourth, due to understanding limitations at the time, the possible harm of equating the Party's guiding ideology with the ideology of a leader was neglected.

1.1.2 The Developing Period in the Study of Mao Zedong Thought (1950-1965)

1.1.2.1 The Reasons for Wide Publicity and Study

The reason that Mao Zedong Thought was widely publicized and studied during that period was that the Chinese revolution had gained the victory under the leadership of the great banner of Mao Zedong Thought.

First, with the victory of the Chinese revolution, Mao Zedong Thought became a dominant ideology in social thought and developed from an ideology guiding the acts of the Party to an ideology guiding the acts of the whole people. As the social system had changed fundamentally after the founding of the People's Republic of China, drastic changes had occurred in ideology, social thought and culture. It was just natural for the CPC to make its guiding ideology an ideology guiding the whole nation so that it could govern and construct new China in its own way. As a result, Mao Zedong Thought irreversibly began to influence every aspect of society, and the study on it was no longer the exclusive work of senior and middle-rank Party cadres and Party members working in the field of theory.

Second, Mao Zedong Thought had proved to be a scientific truth by the victory of the Chinese revolution and was becoming the intellectual destination for all the revolutionaries and the masses. The Chinese people who were liberated and were heading to prosperity admired Mao Zedong and the CPC as their liberator, believed in Mao Zedong Thought, and were willing to know and study it. So there were favorable conditions in the society for studying Mao Zedong Thought.

Third, after the victory of the democratic revolution, the CPC was faced with a new, challenging task of socialist revolution and construction, and it needed a spiritual motivation to hold all the people together in accelerating social progress. As a result, ever since the founding of New China, the Party has been attaching great importance to the learning, publicity and study of Mao Zedong Thought in the social, political and cultural life of the people and has adopted various methods to educate them in Marxism and Mao Zedong Thought.

Fourth, the wide publication of Mao Zedong's works had facilitated intensive learning and study of Mao Zedong Thought. Due to the fact that the versions of selected works of Mao Zedong published in liberated areas in the 1940s were confusing in layouts and contained some mistakes and therefore could not meet the current requirements, *Selected Works of Mao Zedong* in four volumes that had been checked by Mao Zedong himself were published during the period from 1951 to 1960 including his major writings during the democratic revolution. In addition, some of his works and speeches during the socialist era were frequently published in newspapers or in offprints, and some collections of his works on special topics were published as well. As a result, there were plenty of material for Party cadres and the people to learn Mao Zedong Thought and for academicians and theoreticians to study it.

Owing to the above factors, the seventeen years after the founding of New China witnessed a greater development in the study and publicity of Mao Zedong Thought than the 1940s.

However, the CPC did not use the term "Mao Zedong Thought" in its Constitution at its Eighth Congress in 1956. Instead, when defining its guiding ideology, it had only stated: "The Communist Party of China takes Marxism-Leninism as its guide to action." There were several considerations for this choice. The first was that the practice of socialist construction was short, and Mao Zedong's theories on socialist construction were not systematic and had not been tested by practice. The second was that solidarity among socialist countries could be better enhanced if the revolutionary parties in these countries would affirm Marxism-Leninism instead of the thought of their leaders as their guiding ideology. The third was that Mao Zedong was very vigilant against personality cult due to the lesson of Stalin and was highly cautious about publicizing Mao Zedong Thought, and had demanded that theoreticians should "use the term as few as possible." As a result, during the four years, from 1956 when the CPC held its Eighth Congress to September 1960, the term "Mao Zedong Thought" was seldom found in newspapers or books published. Generally, the term was substituted by "works of Comrade Mao Zedong" as required by Mao Zedong himself. In September 1960, Mao Zedong Thought was formally raised again by the CPC Central Military Commission at its enlarged meeting, which had called the People's Liberation Army to "hold high the red banner of Mao Zedong Thought." Thereafter, the term "Mao Zedong Thought" was again often seen in newspapers. The main reason for this change was that the CPC and the Communist Party of the Soviet Union (CPSU) began to show dramatic difference in ideology and could not continue their cooperation in politics and economy, so the CPC had decided to raise Mao Zedong Thought again to show its resolute attitude in regard to ideology or Marxism and Leninism. Secondly, the CPC believed that China had gathered considerable experience in socialist construction, and this was also a reason for the change. But, whether the term "Mao Zedong Thought" was applied or not, Mao Zedong Thought has always been the guiding ideology of the CPC ever since its Seventh Congress, and the learning, publicity and study of it had never ceased.

1.1.2.2 Basic Issues in the Study of Mao Zedong Thought

With the rapid development in the studies of the Thought, a lot more books and writings in this regard were published, and the scope of study was greatly widened. Studies on concrete aspects of Mao Zedong Thought were carried out rapidly, and more and more books and writings on special topics concerning Mao Zedong Thought were published. Covering issues in the sphere of philosophy, literature and art, military affairs, education, economy and politics, these books and writings reflect how the people in the early days of New China understood and studied Mao Zedong Thought and what subjects they had focused on.

Focusing on Mao Zedong's "On Practice" and "On Contradiction," the study on his philosophical thought has always been of overriding importance. Ever since they were published in 1950 and 1952, the two essays have become the focus of study and research. All the major newspapers across the country published articles to introduce and elaborate them, and almost all well-known theoreticians, such as Li Da, Ai Siqi, Feng Youlan, Hu Sheng, Li Qi, Chen Boda, Wang Ya'nan and Shen Zhiyuan, have written articles or books on them. According to incomplete statistics, during those several years between 1951 and 1956, nearly 140 articles on learning "On Practice" and fifty articles on learning "On Contradiction" were published by newspapers of the municipal or higher levels, and twenty-five books on learning "On Practice" and eight books on learning "On Contradiction" were published.[1]

---

[1] Han Rongzhang et al., *The Study on Mao Zedong Thought in China*, Chongqing Publishing House, Chongqing, 1993, p. 53.

Among them, Li Da's "Explication to 'On Practice'" and "Explication to 'On Contradiction'," Li Qi's "Intepretation on 'On Practice'" and "Elementary Introduction to 'On Contradiction'," and Zhang Ruxin's *Mao Zedong's Contribution to Marxist Materialism* and *Mao Zedong's Contribution to Marxist Dialetics* had produced great influence. But generally, all these books and writings have focused on explaining Mao Zedong's "On Practice" and "On Contradiction."

The study on Mao Zedong's thinking on literature and art and on education was another focus in the study of Mao Zedong Thought after the founding of New China. The study in this sphere had concentrated mainly on Mao Zedong's "Talks at the Yan'an Forum on Literature and Art," and dealt with issues such as the development orientation of literature and art, standards of criticism on literature and art, the relation between politics and literature and art, the creation of literature and art, and the argument that literature and art should serve workers, peasants and soldiers. The study on Mao Zedong's thinking on education was centered on his "On New Democracy" and "On the Correct Handling of the Contradictions Among the People" to explain his education principles of establishing a national and scientific education for the broad masses, letting education serve proletarian politics, promoting the combination of education with productive labor, and enabling everyone receiving an education to develop morally, intellectually and physically and become a worker with both socialist consciousness and culture.

At the core of study on Mao Zedong's military thinking was the idea of people's war and its strategies and tactics. Generals and officers such as Lin Biao, Zhang Zhen, Mo Wenhua, Liu Yalou and Xiao Jinguang all wrote articles to study Mao Zedong's military thinking. In particular, Guo Huaruo's "Study Mao Zedong's Military Thinking" had made a comparatively systematic summarization of the developing progress, basic components and features of Mao Zedong's military thinking. On June 7, 1959, the Academy of Military Science had published an important paper in the *Liberation Army Daily* after discussing Mao Zedong's military thinking extensively, which had argued that Mao Zedong's military thinking includes the idea of people's war, the idea of building the people's army, and operational tactics under the people's war.

In a fairly long period of time, the study on Mao Zedong's economic thinking had focused on theories concerning the transition from new-democratic economy to a socialist economy. The studies had mainly explored Party's general line for the transition period. A great number of writings were published in the mid-1950s to analyze the basis, principles and steps for cooperative transformation of agriculture and the Party's class line in rural areas. These writings discussed how Mao Zedong's ideas in this regard had developed the Marxist economic theory.

The study on Mao Zedong's political thought had focused on his theories about the new-democratic revolution, people's democratic dictatorship and the correct handling of two types of contradictions differing in nature.[1] On June 28, 1951, Chen Boda published in the *People's Daily* a long article titled: "Mao Zedong Thought Is the Integration of Marxism-Leninism with the Chinese Revolution," in which he had made a detailed interpretation of Mao Zedong's theory on the new-democratic revolution. This article represented the research level at that time. In the late 1950s, more and more theoreticians came to elaborate on Mao Zedong's contributions to Marx's theory on the dictatorship of the proletariat, while at the same time spread a wide discussion of Mao Zedong's ideas of "let a hundred flowers blossom, let a hundred schools of thought contend" and of the two types of contradictions differing in nature. In the 1960s when China's socialist construction was confronted with difficulties, theoreticians began to pay closer attention to Mao Zedong's ideas as "proceeding from reality and stressing investigation and study, adhering closely to the mass viewpoint, and of being independent and self-reliant".

1.1.2.3 Basic Features in the Study on Mao Zedong Thought

Basic features in the studies during that period can be summarized as

---

[1] "We are confronted with two types of social contradictions—those between ourselves and the enemy and those among the people. These two are totally different in nature."

follows:

First, the central aim of the study was to serve the spread of Mao Zedong Thought. As a result, many of the study results were just explanations of Mao Zedong Thought or discussions about how to learn it and help the people understand it.

Second, the studies had produced many longer writings. But most of them were still pamphlets or collections of papers which focused on sharing study experience or making comments or explanations, while there were few independent, academic works. In addition, these writings had contained more citations rather than debating.

Third, after Mao Zedong stressed class struggle at a working conference of the CPC Central Committee meeting at Mount Lushan in 1959 and at the Tenth Plenary Session of the Eighth CPC Central Committee in 1962, the "Left" tendencies began to rise in the country's political life again. The study on Mao Zedong Thought began to exaggerate Mao Zedong's theories on class struggle, and there were more and more areas and topics that researchers and theoreticians could not discuss. In short, the study was negatively affected, and scientific studies in the real sense were rarely conducted.

Fourth, personality cult had begun to emerge in the study of Mao Zedong Thought. After Lin Biao, who was in charge of the work of the Military Commission at the time, had advocated "to learn and apply Mao Zedong Thought in a creative way", this combined by other effects had directed people to recite apothegms in Mao Zedong's works, and the study of Mao Zedong Thought was simplified and became one-sided.

In conclusion, the study on Mao Zedong Thought in this period was quite far from scientific, mature or academic, the focus was rather learning and publicity and not a real research. Mao Zedong Thought was still considered as identical to Mao Zedong's thoughts. Although Mao Zedong Thought was widely studied, only few works of other revolutionaries of the older generation were published or studied, and little attention was paid to the important documents of the Party.

1.1.3 The Setback Period in the Studies (1966-1978)

The reason that the study on Mao Zedong Thought suffered setbacks during this period was that the people came to deify Mao Zedong and believe that every word of his thought was absolutely correct.

Due to the ultra-Left tendencies prevalent in the country's political theories and in people's values and ways of thinking as well as the widespread personality cult in the "cultural revolution" (1966-1976), the study on Mao Zedong Thought ran into irrational fanaticism. First, theoretical studies were substituted by large-scale political publicity that flooded newspapers, meetings, *dazibao* [big-character poster, prevalent during the "cultural revolution"—*Tr.*], leaflets and all through people's activities. There were almost no study results other than the words of workers, peasants and soldiers about how they had learned and applied "Mao Zedong's works in a creative way" or some shoddy guidance material.

Second, no real objective and scientific study results were produced. The "study" and publicity of Mao Zedong Thought were dogmatic and full of formalism, idealism and pragmatism. Words and sentences in Mao Zedong's works were quoted and believed to be absolute truth while their meaning was understood only partially and out of context. Booklets with quotations from Mao Zedong should be carried personally and read everyday.

Third, the study on Mao Zedong Thought was closely connected to the "cultural revolution." The theory of "continuing the revolution under the dictatorship of the proletariat" was considered a new development in Mao Zedong Thought, and the study and publicity of Mao Zedong Thought had become a tool of Lin Biao and Jiang Qing to promote personality cult and scheme to usurp power. The idea of class struggle was totally dominant.

The "cultural revolution" was ended in October 1976, but its influence on ideology and theoretical studies did not stop immediately. The study on Mao Zedong Thought was still harmed by two factors. First, the influence of personality cult was still there. An ideological line known as the "two whatevers" [the notion that after the death of Chairman Mao Zedong, whatever policy decisions he had made should be firmly upheld and whatever instructions he had given should be followed unswervingly.—*Tr.*] was put forward, and the study on Mao Zedong and his thought was still heavily influenced by dogmatism and idealism. Second, on the reverse side there were a handful of individuals who tended to wrongly depreciate or even deny Mao Zedong and his thoughts totally. These two factors were surely quite negative for understanding Mao Zedong Thought and study it in a realistic way.

In short, the study on Mao Zedong Thought during this period had suffered severe setbacks. Although the publication of Mao Zedong's works had reached an unprecedented level[1], the scientific study of Mao Zedong Thought sank to the bottom. Mao Zedong Thought was still considered the thoughts of Mao Zedong himself; it was not easy to elevate Mao Zedong Thought to the collective wisdom of the Party because a large number of revolutionaries of the older generation and Party leaders were supressed.

1.2 Developing Period after the Third Plenary Session of the Eleventh Central Committee of the CPC

Although the introduction, publicity and study of Mao Zedong Thought had lasted half a century, the academic research of it in the real sense began only after the Third Plenary Session of the Eleventh CPC Central Committee. The study of Mao Zedong Thought after the Third Plenary Session of the Eleventh Central Committee can also be divided into three historical periods: from 1978 when the CPC held the Third Plenary Session of its Eleventh Central Committee to 1981 when it held the Sixth Plenary Session. This was

---

[1] According to rough statistics, a total of 86.4 million copies of *Selected Works of Mao Zedong* (Volumes 1-4) with different editions were published during 1966-1978, which amounted to 7.5 times of those published in the fifteen years before the "cultural revolution." Also published during this period were 47.5 million copies of *Selection of Mao Zedong's Works*, 57 million copies of *Poems of Mao Zedong*, 350 million copies of *Quotations from Mao Zedong*, and off prints of Mao Zedong's works too numerous to be counted.

a period in which the study of Mao Zedong Thought was set to the correct direction. From 1981 to 1991, the 70th anniversary of the founding of the CPC, a period in which the study of Mao Zedong Thought registered great achievements. And third, from 1991 till present, a period in which the study of Mao Zedong Thought has achieved deeper results.

1.2.1 The Period in Which the Study Was Set to the Correct Direction (1978-1981)

At the Third Plenary Session of its Eleventh Central Committee in December 1978, the CPC has restored the ideological line of seeking truth from facts, criticized the idea of "two whatevers," and requested the whole Party and all the people to study the scientific system of Mao Zedong Thought correctly and as an integral whole. Since then, ideological and theoretical studies in the country were gradually freed from personality cult and dogmatism, and the study of Mao Zedong Thought got rid of the erroneous ideas and was set to the correct orientation. But, the CPC had not yet answered certain major theoretical problems, such as how to assess the historical role of Mao Zedong and Mao Zedong Thought, how to define Mao Zedong Thought, how to treat the mistakes Mao Zedong made in his later years, and how to understand the relation between Mao Zedong's personal works and comments and Mao Zedong Thought. As a result, the study of Mao Zedong Thought had just made a start in the correct direction. Most of the study results were generally some political comments, rewievs to introduce Mao Zedong's life or to commemorate him, or elaborations on some of his individual ideas; thus academic, theoretical or comprehensive novel results were still rare. In short, the study of Mao Zedong Thought was still limited both in depth and in scope.

1.2.2 The Period with Great Achievements (1981-1991)

1.2.2.1 The Emergence of a Fever for Studying Mao Zedong Thought

At the Sixth Plenary Session of its Eleventh Central Committee, the

CPC had passed "the Resolution on Certain Questions in the History of Our Party Since the Founding of the People's Republic of China"(See Appendix), in which Mao Zedong Thought was summarized for the second time in the history of the Party after 1945. The Resolution scientifically appraised the merits and demerits of Mao Zedong and his historical role, declaring that Mao Zedong Thought is a body of correct principles and a summary of experience as well as the crystallization of the Party's collective wisdom and giving an in-depth elaboration on its theoretical system. As a document guiding the whole Party to correctly understand Mao Zedong and Mao Zedong Thought and as well as a major theoretical result scientifically evaluating the Mao Zedong Thought, the Resolution has greatly guided and paved the way for future study of Mao Zedong Thought. Since then, the study of Mao Zedong Thought began to make novel achievements, and a fever for study has began to rise.

Firstly, a lot of books were published to summarize and elaborate the basic theoretical issues of Mao Zedong Thought. Books published in the first two years were *An Elementary Introduction to Mao Zedong Thought* by Ma Qibin and Chen Dengcai, *A Basic Elaboration to Mao Zedong Thought* by Xiong Fu, and *A Guide to Principles of Mao Zedong Thought* prepared and edited by the CPC Central Committee Party School.

Secondly, substantial attention was paid to the history of development of Mao Zedong Thought, and this sphere became a new subdiscipline in the studies on Mao Zedong Thought. Earlier works on this subject included *History of Mao Zedong Thought (The New-Democratic Revolution Period)* and *History of Mao Zedong Thought (The Socialist Construction Period)* by Zheng Derong and his study group. and *A Brief History of Development of Mao Zedong Thought* by Liu Mengyi.

Thirdly, special studies on the components of Mao Zedong Thought were carried out. The study on Mao Zedong's thinking on economy, Party building, the united front, journalism, ethics, aesthetics and law which had rarely drawn attention before has made visible progress. The studies on Mao Zedong's philosophical thought that had always led and dominated the study of Mao Zedong Thought have produced numerous results: many works were published to introduce, brief or research Mao Zedong's philosophical thoughts or introduce its history of development.

Fourthly, more and more academies and institutions have published magazines and journals to study Mao Zedong Thought, and the influential ones were *Trends in the Study of Mao Zedong's Philosophic Thinking* (1982 in Shanghai), *Research of Mao Zedong Thought* (1983 in Sichuan), and *Forum on Study of Mao Zedong Thought* (1988 in Hunan). Social science institutes, research centers in universities and colleges, and national and local academic associations have intensified their studies on the Thought. The periodical *Mao Zedong Thought* edited by the books and periodicals center in Renmin University of China has transmitted and embodied the latest trends and focuses in the study of Mao Zedong Thought.

1.2.2.2 Progresses in Study of Mao Zedong Thought

1.2.2.2.1 Progresses in the general study of Mao Zedong Thought

First, the basic tenets of Mao Zedong Thought were scientifically defined, and its dialectical relations with Marxism-Leninism, with the Chinese revolution and construction, and with the struggle and collective wisdom of the CPC and the Chinese people were correctly expounded.

Second, the scientific system and complete content of Mao Zedong Thought were given a detailed account. In addition, certain points were made clearer. For example, Mao Zedong as a revolutionary and a leader of the people did not start theoretical activities with the purpose of creating a system of thinking; on the contrary, he was determined to develop theories in order to lead China's revolution and construction, and the theories he had produced are systematic, complete and integrated.

Third, the living soul of Mao Zedong Thought was analyzed deeper. Researchers explained the reason why seeking truth from facts, the mass line, and self-reliance are the three basic points of the living soul of Mao Zedong Thought, and they generally agreed that the three basic points had begun to take shape in Mao Zedong's essay "Oppose Book Worship."

Fourth, researchers have expounded explicitly the contributions made by the collective leadership of the CPC on the Mao Zedong Thought, which reflected the crystallization of collective wisdom of the Party. Although, these study results were stiil remained in the frame of the Resolution on Certain Questions in the History of Our Party Since the Founding of the People's Republic of China, they have undoubtedly progressed in understanding Mao Zedong Thought.

1.2.2.2.2   Progress in the historical development of Mao Zedong Thought

Studying the history of development of Mao Zedong Thought to understand its course of development has always been a major focus in the efforts to study Mao Zedong Thought. After the Resolution on Certain Questions in the History of Our Party Since the Founding of the People's Republic of China was passed and promulgated, a large number of scholars have focused their study efforts on the historical development of Mao Zedong Thought and established an initial framework for that study. They have made encouraging progress in basic research of the development of Mao Zedong Thought, such as the historical stages in its development and the symbols and fundamental features of different stages, and analyzed the historical conditions of its formation and as well as the logical connection between stages. Besides, they have reviewed and described the historical course for the formation of the idea of "Mao Zedong Thought" and generally tended to argue that Mao Zedong Thought has more than one theoretical source.

1.2.2.2.3 Progress in studying Mao Zedong's theory of New Democracy

Study in this area has started earlier and made a lot of breakthroughs after the Third Plenary Session of the Eleventh CPC Central Committee. In addition to some detailed, systematic elaborations to Mao Zedong's ideas on the united front and armed struggle and on the basis and process for the emergence of Mao Zedong's theory of New Democracy, researchers have made great achievements in two major areas. The first is about the road of Chinese revolution. Researchers have generally argued that "establishing independent regimes of the workers and the peasants by armed forces" and "encircling the cities from the countryside" are two ideas that are closely connected to each other and at the same time distincted from each other. They have also reviewed the course in which the idea of "encircling the cities from the countryside" formed and developed.

The second is about new-democratic society. Researchers have suggested that the new-democratic society had enabled a smoother transition from the new-democratic revolution to socialist revolution and had greatly enriched the theory of scientific socialism. They have also pointed out that the theory on the new-democratic society has vagueness and temporary and contained a duality related major contradictions in that society and lacked a clearr central task.

1.2.2.2.4 Progress in studying Mao Zedong's theory of socialist transformation

There were heated arguements and disagreements in this area, and more attention was given to this theory and certain progress was achieved. They have estimated the influence of the general line formulation related to the transition period which was then defined as: "the transition period refers to the period from the founding of the People's Republic of China to the basic completion of socialist transformation", and most of them have argued that "a sudden transformation occuring in the future" and "a gradual transformation starting from present" have some common elements (such as goals, tasks and transformation methods) as well as some different elements (such as policies on private sectors of the economy, the beginning date of transformation and transformation steps). They have comprehensively revealed the Party's several debates on cooperative transformation in agriculture during the socialist transformation, pointing out that the debates were in essence about concrete issues such as the starting, consolidation and speed of the transformation, and not about working principles. In addition, they have comprehensive reviewed and produced fair evaluations on the theories and practice of socialist transformation, debating on both achievements and mistakes.

1.2.2.2.5 Progress in studying Mao Zedong's theory of socialist construction

Researchers have discovered some of Mao Zedong's ideas that they before barely knew or those which was rarely noticed. They have suggested that Mao Zedong has made great theoretical contributions to many concepts, such as basic social contradictions, focuses of the country's political activity, shift of focuses in governmental work, principles for development of democratization, guidelines for cultural development, path of industrialization, political restructuring, commodity production and distribution, social development stages, idea of four modernizations [modernization of industry, agriculture, national defense and science and technology—*Tr.*] and Party building, and that he has laid an ideological foundation for China's reform after the Third Plenary Session of the Eleventh CPC Central Committee. They have also carefully analyzed the mistakes Mao Zedong made in his theoretical exploration, arguing that the utopian idea of economic development divorced from realities and expansion of class struggle were the two major theoretical mistakes he had made.

1.2.2.3 Basic Features in Study of Mao Zedong Thought during This Period

There are some basic features in the study of Mao Zedong Thought during this period:

First, many of the research results were guided by "the Resolution on Certain Questions in the History of Our Party Since the Founding of the People's Republic of China" when discussing and evaluataing Mao Zedong and his thoughts. This resolution was the general frame of the studies and has become the foundation of studies on Mao Zedong Thought.

Second, many books and writings began to debate and elaborate Mao Zedong Thought or some of its components in a more comprehensive way, paying attention both to particular and general issues and evaluated Mao

Zedong Thought as an integral body.

Third, as more and more works of Zhou Enlai, Liu Shaoqi, Zhu De, Deng Xiaoping, Chen Yun and other Party leaders were published, researchers have published many books and articles to study their works. As a result, the idea that Mao Zedong Thought is the crystallization of the Party's collective wisdom has reached a deeper cognition.

Fourth, many foreign books studying Mao Zedong and his thoughts were introduced into China, such as *Mao Tse-tung* by Stuart R. Schram, which has broadened the horizons of domestic researchers and academic exchanges with foreign scholars have begun to share their newest study results.

Fifth, in addition to concentrated efforts on studying Mao Zedong's correct ideas, researchers also studied his incorrect ideas and began to shift their attention to studying his thought and theories in the period of socialist construction that have great significance for guiding practice.

Sixth, looking politics from a cultural perspective, a certain number of researchers discussed the influence of traditional Chinese culture on Mao Zedong Thought to emphasize its national character.

1.2.3 The Period of Deeper Studies After 1991

In 1991, the 70th anniversary of the founding of the CPC and the centenary of birth of Mao Zedong, a new fever for studying Mao Zedong occurred, and the study of Mao Zedong Thought was deepened.

1.2.3.1 Many Important Books and Writings Were Published

First, works and writings of Mao Zedong were prepared more systematically for publication. The publication of a thirteen-volume *Writings of Mao Zedong after the Founding of the People's Republic of China* was finished in 1998, which included an enormous wealth of Mao Zedong's writings after the founding of the People's Republic. This collection was designed to serve the study of Mao Zedong Thought, so it included both his judgments and ideas that had been proved correct by practice and judgments and ideas that had been proved incorrect or not entirely proved correct by practice. The publication of an eight-volume *Collected Works of Mao Zedong* was finished in 1999 to collect many of Mao Zedong's important writings, speeches and talks that were not included in the four-volume *Selected Works of Mao Zedong*. A six-volume *Collection of Mao Zedong's Military Writings* were published to include Mao Zedong's over 1,600 writings, telegraphs, instructions and speeches on military affairs from 1927 to 1972, most of which were published for the first time. This Collection gave a systematic elaboration to Mao Zedong's military thinking including his thinking on military dialectics. In addition, *Collection of Mao Zedong's Annotations to Chinese Classic Literature and History*, *Collection of Mao Zedong's Writings on Foreign Relations*, *Report and Speeches of Mao Zedong at the Seventh CPC National Congress* and *Poems of Mao Zedong* were also published. All these books have great theoretical value and are important material for the study of Mao Zedong Thought.

Second, collections of works of Zhou Enlai and Liu Shaoqi as well as collections of writings of other revolutionaries of the older generation were published, which offered rich material for the study of Mao Zedong Thought.

Finally, the edition and publication of collections of important documents of the CPC Central Committee, biographies and memoirs of major Party and government leaders and chronicles of their lives, and other documents related to Mao Zedong Thought also has provided valuable material for the study of Mao Zedong Thought.

1.2.3.2 A Number of Study Results of Higher Theoretical Value Were Published

The study on how the CPC's two generations of collective leadership had theoretically developed the Marxist theory entered a new stage after many books and writings in this area were published, such as Hu Qiaomu's *How The Communist Party of China Developed Marxism*. The book *Hu Qiaomu's Reminiscences of Mao Zedong* made a concentrated review on Mao Zedong's theoretical exploration and practice during the period of the War of Resistance against Japan, representing a great achievement in the study of

Mao Zedong's thought during that period. The book *The Hard Exploration by Mao Zedong* by Shi Zhongquan was published twice with revisions and supplements in the 1990s, and its many original ideas attracted close attention from theoretical researchers. The *Chronicle of Mao Zedong's Life from 1893 to 1949* edited by the Party Literature Research Center has included not only historical material but also theoretical study results. It analyzed the scientific intellectual system of Mao Zedong from the multi-perspectives of theoretical ideas, strategic thinking, policies and tactics, and principles for ideological and governance work, and it also revealed the course in which Mao Zedong's thought developed. The *Biography of Mao Zedong (1893-1949)* published in 1996 included large amount of reliable first-hand material about Mao Zedong such as his manuscripts, telegraphs, letters and speech excerpts and depicted his life as a revolutionary, thus having great value for reference.

1.2.3.3 Many Hot Topics Attracting Wide Attention from Theoretical Researchers

Many scholars began to pay close attention to the study of the system of Mao Zedong Thought. In addition to the study results believing that Mao Zedong Thought includes his theories on philosophy, literature and art, education, Party building, economy, and military affairs and that seeking truth from facts, the mass line, and self-reliance are its living soul, many new ideas and topics for discussion have emerged in the 1990s. Some researchers have argued that the main components of Mao Zedong Thought include Mao Zedong's thinking on politics, military affairs, economy, and culture and his ideas on seeking truth from facts, the mass line and self-reliance. Others believed that the framework of Mao Zedong Thought is composed of Mao Zedong's theory on New Democracy, Deng Xiaoping's theory on new socialism, and Mao Zedong's methodology (such as Mao Zedong's principles of independence, seeking truth from facts, practice, contradictions, and overall interests and Deng Xiaoping's ideas on respecting the principal position of the people, achieving substantive results, progressing in a gradual and orderly way, thinking dialectically, and taking overall picture into consideration). Still others have advanced that the system of Mao Zedong Thought is a systematic, organic whole with multi-levels that is philosophically based on Mao Zedong's philosophical thought, and is mainly composed of the two theories formed during its two major development periods, i.e., the theory of the new-democratic revolution and the theory of building socialism with Chinese characteristics, and includes thinking in various fields such as politics, economy, armed forces, foreign relations and Party building. At the same time, many scholars pointed out that Deng Xiaoping Theory has developed into an independent theoretical system and should no longer be included in Mao Zedong Thought because it had been formally formulated by the CPC as early as at its Fifteenth National Congress and has become another guiding ideology of the Party in addition to Mao Zedong Thought.

The theoretical sources of Mao Zedong Thought was another focus among researchers. Some of them believe that it has one source, others, two, and still others, three. One-source believers hold that Marxism is the sole source. Although traditional Chinese culture has facilitated the formation and development of Mao Zedong Thought, its effect can not be compared with Marxism. Two-source believers consider that in addition to Marxism, which is an undoubted source, traditional Chinese culture is also a source because it has produced an irreplaceable impact on Mao Zedong Thought. Three-source believers are divided into two groups. One group believes that the universal truth of Marxism, the concrete practice in Chinese revolution and the quintessence of traditional Chinese culture are the three theoretical sources of Mao Zedong Thought, while the other group believes that in addition to Marxism, which is the fundamental source, traditional Chinese culture and Sun Yat-sen's Three People's Principles [the Three People's Principles were the principles and programs put forward by Sun Yat-sen on the questions of nationalism, democracy and the people's livelihood—*Tr.*] are two important sources as well. Generally speaking, most researchers tend to believe that traditional Chinese culture is indeed a theoretical source of Mao Zedong Thought.

Soon after the *Collection of Mao Zedong's Military Writings* was published, researchers studying theories about army building have paid close attention to studying Mao Zedong's military thinking. After producing many study results on special issues in specific stages, they began studying it in a comprehensive, systematic way. Study on the new developments of Mao Zedong Thought was also started, and a surge in study of Deng Xiaoping Theory has appeared. Mao Zedong's theories and practice in his later years also drew close attention from researchers who have analyzed the reason for the mistakes he made in his later years and his attempts to explore an outlook and path for socialism. They also discussed many related issues, such as China's strategy of modernization, unbalance in the country's economic development, the efforts of the first generation of the Party's leadership to explore a path for socialist development, Jiang Zemin's speech on the Three Represents, and thoughts of the older generation of revolutionaries.

1.2.3.4 A Summarization of Study Efforts: A Comprehensive Review on the Study of Mao Zedong Thought

The Party Literature Research Center under the CPC Central Committee held a seminar entitled "A Review of Studies on Mao Zedong" in Beijing in December 1991, at which over seventy scholars and researchers teaching or researching Mao Zedong Thought gave an overall review on the study of Mao Zedong himself and Mao Zedong Thought over the past half a century. They have centered on the history of study of Mao Zedong and Mao Zedong Thought, the study of its development in different historical stages, and the study on its major theories and principles. After the seminar, the Party Literature Research Center edited and published the book *A Review of Study on Mao Zedong*, using four parts to sum up and review every single important research achievement in the study of Mao Zedong and Mao Zedong Thought. The first part concentrated on how Mao Zedong Thought was studied in different historical stages, what were its basic features, and how it was developed in the new period. The second part assessed some major research efforts such as those on how Mao Zedong changed his worldview in his young years; how he carried out activities and developed his thinking before and after the CPC was founded; how he had developed his theories and thinking about proletarian leadership, peasant problems, path of China's revolution, establishment of revolutionary bases, the united front, the new-democratic revolution, agrarian revolution, socialist transformation, and socialist construction; and why he made the mistakes in his later years. The third part focused on the living soul of Mao Zedong Thought and its thought ways, his theories about military affairs, Party building and people's democratic dictatorship, his thinking on economy, education, news and literature, his poems, and the influence of traditional Chinese culture on him. The fourth part reviewed the publication of Mao Zedong's works as well as books and writings researching his life, and the study of Mao Zedong in foreign countries.

Thereafter, books such as *A Brief Introduction to the Study of Mao Zedong Thought in Half a Century* edited by Hu Weixiong and Jiang Rubin, *The Study on Mao Zedong Thought in China* by Han Rongzhang et al., *The Study on Mao Zedong Thought in Fifty Years* edited by Han Rongzhang, Xiao Decai and Shao Heping, and *History of Study on Mao Zedong Thought* by Zhou Yiping, and many analytical papers have all made research efforts in this area. In these books and papers, researchers made a comprehensive review of their research efforts and results. After the review, they shifted their focuses to weak areas and explored new areas for research.

1.2.3.5 New Field for Study: A Start to Research Different Editions of Mao Zedong's Works

It is commonly believed by scholars that new editions of Mao Zedong's works with detailed notes should be used in learning of Mao Zedong Thought because they are more convenient for general readers, and original editions can be better used in theoretical study because they reflect more on the conditions under which the author wrote these works. For that reason, researchers began to compare different editions, and many of them have left taking the *Selected Works of Mao Zedong* published by the People's Publishing House as the sole standard edition. When publishing Mao Zedong's works, editors have paid much attention to examination, comparison and selection of editions of works. They compared different editions of Mao Zedong's "Analysis of Socialist Classes in China," "On Practice," "On Contradiction" and some other writings, making their study of Mao Zedong's works, thought and historical activities and research of development of Mao Zedong Thought more scientific. In particular, the book *Introduction to Different Editions of Mao Zedong's Works* written by Liu Yuejin in 1999 gave an all-round review and introduction of the many editions of Mao Zedong's works. Although the examination, introduction and study of different editions of Mao Zedong's works were just started and were far from systematic, they have opened up a new field and were of great significance for the study of Mao Zedong Thought.

1.2.3.6 Features of Study: Comparative Study Being Widely Adopted

In addition to horizontally comparing the thinking and ideas of Mao Zedong with that of other members of the first generation of the Party's leadership, researchers vertically compared the theories and practices of the Party's two generations of leadership respectively with Mao Zedong and Deng Xiaoping at their cores. They have also compared Mao Zedong with great thinkers in Chinese history and with famous foreign Marxists. By comparison, they have broadened their understanding on Mao Zedong and his thought. After the three-volume *Selected Works of Deng Xiaoping* were published in 1993 and 1994, the comparison between Mao Zedong Thought and Deng Xiaoping Theory has become a trend. Researchers compared not only theories of the two systems but also some specific issues such as views on life and values, thought ways and work methods, development strategies and analyses on China's conditions.

After Deng Xiaoping Theory was established as the Party's guiding ideology, scholars and researchers have paid close attention to discussing its relationship with Mao Zedong's theory of socialist construction. Some scholars have approached to the difference between Mao Zedong's thinking and Deng Xiaoping's thinking from their difference in philosophical methods, believing that Mao Zedong and Deng Xiaoping were different in understanding the features of socialist economy and in deciding the means, ways and methods for socialist construction because Mao Zedong had stressed the struggle of the aspect of a contradiction while Deng Xiaoping had stressed the identity of the aspect of a contradiction. Other scholars believed that the exploration of a road for socialist construction with Chinese characteristics was started by Mao Zedong and completed by Deng Xiaoping.

Finding out and sorting out documents about judgments of leaders on each other could greatly help researchers better and more correctly understand the relationship between their thinking. For that reason, many researchers have made efforts to collect related material and wrote to study the judgment of Mao Zedong and Deng Xiaoping on each other.[1]

1.2.3.7 **Form of Research Results: More Comprehensive Research Results in Multi-Volumes or Series Were Produced**

Although some of such book series were just a mediocre cobbled together from some random material by authors who were not rigorous in scholarship, some exact scholars did produce many works and reference books that not only have great academic and theoretical value but are very readable such as the seven-volume *Complete Collection of Studies of Mao Zedong Thought* compiled under the charge of Chen Zhili, *Series of Books on Continuation and Development of Mao Zedong Thought* edited by Zheng Bijian, and *Trilogy of Study on Mao Zedong* written by Li Junru.

---

[1] Li Junru, "History: Mao Zedong's Opinions on Deng Xiaoping" and "Nowadays: Deng Xiaoping's Opinions on Mao Zedong," *Study of Mao Zedong and Deng Xiaoping*, 1997 (1) and 1997 (2).

1.3 Assessment and Prospects

1.3.1 General Appraisal of Studies on Mao Zedong Thought in the Twentieth Century

A general survey into the historical course of study of Mao Zedong Thought shows that the study efforts have undergone a process of progress and development, just like Mao Zedong Thought itself has a process of formation and development.

During the war years, more efforts were made to publicize rather than to study Mao Zedong Thought, which was required by revolutionary needs. During that stage, Mao Zedong Thought was greatly affirmed and publicized.

After the founding of the People's Republic of China, Mao Zedong was regarded by the Chinese people as their savior. They believed in and extolled Mao Zedong and his thought, and theoretical researchers began their study with publicizing and praising Mao Zedong Thought. Greatly influenced by emotional and political factors, the study on Mao Zedong Thought were quite unscientific or irrational but had produce some research results, and they have enabled Mao Zedong Thought more accessable and understandable for more people.

During the "cultural revolution," Mao Zedong was deified and his works became bible words that every person should be able to recite. Mao Zedong Thought was interpreted dogmatically, and no study in the real sense was carried out.

The wide discussion of the criterion for testing truth has ceased the practice of deifying Mao Zedong and his thoughts, and the study on Mao Zedong Thought has flourished and began to focus on more profound issues. That was due to a fundamental change in the people's ideas. In the past, people had unconsciously believed that Mao Zedong Thought should not be researched scientifically like other thoughts, theories or doctrines, because it was a flag and was the guiding ideology of the Party ever since the Party's Seventh National Congress and the dominant ideology guiding the whole country after the People's Republic was founded. As a result, the study on Mao Zedong Thought had always been about explanation and study experience, far from being objective or profound. After the Third Plenary Session of the Party's Eleventh Central Committee, however, researchers began to generally believe that Mao Zedong Thought can be both a guiding ideology and an object for research. This change in thinking has greatly promoted the study of Mao Zedong Thought. Researchers have opened up many new areas for research, making the study of Mao Zedong Thought a new, independent discipline. Their research results in the twenty years thereafter surpassed the total previous research results, and the width, depth and height as well as methods and influences of these results have improved greatly. They have paid more attention to research of Mao Zedong Thought than its publicity, carried out many profound research activities and produced many academic achievements. They have made the study of Mao Zedong Thought a focus in international cultural exchange. So, those twenty years have been a mature stage in the study of Mao Zedong Thought.

In conclusion, during the historical course of study of Mao Zedong Thought, Party members including high-ranking leaders and ordinary cadres as well as researchers who are or are not Party members and who are from the revolutionary ranks or are from various social strata have devoted themselves to the research efforts. In this course, they have shifted their focus from a part of Mao Zedong Thought to the whole and constantly opened up new areas for research. They have studied both easy and difficult and both apparent and profound issues and produced more and more mature research results.

Although significant progress has been made in the study of Mao Zedong Thought in the recent twenty years, problems and shortcomings were not not totally overcome.

First, the fields of research are still limited, and many issues under study are redundant. Many research results are similar in content and fail to produce any fresh ideas or opinions from any novel viewpoint.

Second, some researchers were restless and were eager to produce quick results. Under the market economy, researchers tend to finish certain tasks and keep a closer eye on hot topics. For that reason, some of them fail to dig deep into the issues under research or produce penetrating results because they do not spend enough time digesting and understanding literature and material that had been already published or utilizing existing research results.

Third, generally researchers do not have enough debate and discussion over different academic opinions. Although some researchers have voiced some different opinions, they do not debate or debate hard over these opinions.

Fourth, research methods are rather simple, which greatly influences the depth and efficiency of research efforts. Researchers have just started to understand the theoretical sources and ideological content of Mao Zedong Thought by investigating into the theoretical works, practice, ways of thinking, backgrounds, habits and hobbies of its creators.

Fifth, the collection and compilation of literature and documents fail to meet the needs of research. There is still no complete collection of Mao Zedong's works published in China. Consequently, researchers sometimes had to quote phrases or sentences from Mao Zedong's works published in foreign countries (for instance, the *Collection of Mao Zedong's Works* published in Japan).

1.3.2 Prospects for Study of Mao Zedong Thought in the New Century

Mao Zedong Thought, having profoundly influenced China's historical course in the twentieth century, continues to be a core ideology in China that will offer researchers numerous topics for research in the twenty-first century, because it is a guiding ideology of the Party and represents the country's ideological orientation, and fundamentally because it has a rich content and great influence. After taking into consideration the current conditions of research, we have every reason to believe that the study of Mao Zedong Thought could probably progress in the following aspects in the near future.

1.3.2.1 The Study of Mao Zedong Thought Can Cover More Areas and from More Plural Viewpoints

At present, researchers focus more on Mao Zedong's theories about the new-democratic revolution and socialist revolution and construction, not paying enough attention to the other aspects of Mao Zedong Thought. So, they need to better understand the relations and interactions between different components of Mao Zedong Thought and its profound influence on Chinese society. With the introduction of a socialist market economy in China and a plural attitude toward culture, people will read and understand Mao Zedong Thought from a variety of viewpoints. As a result, researchers can make more efforts to research areas that they have not explored before and achieve newer results.

1.3.2.2 Researchers Can Futher Focus on Knotty Issues in the Study of Mao Zedong and His Thoughts

Generally, knotty issues are issues that need to be considered both academically and politically, which make them even more difficult to understand and research. At the same time, they are also the issues that are of great significance for the overall study of Mao Zedong Thought and are often related closely with the reality. Consequently, researchers always pay close attention to them. They include issues such as the big difference between Mao Zedong's pursuit for ideals and his practice in his later years, his success and failure in dealing with class struggle, his thinking during the "cultural revolution," the relation between the mistakes he made in his later years and his thought in his early years, and the influence of traditional Chinese culture on his thought and personal character. Although some researchers have analyzed these issues to some extent, there is much room for further research.

1.3.2.3 Mao Zedong's Ideas on Chinese Modernization Need Further Studies

To realize modernization as early as possible is still the main theme of the times in the new century. The first generation of leaders of the Party represented by Mao Zedong had made relatively thorough theoretical analyses on a series of issues about how a country like China which had started later than it could catch up others in the race for economic development and can move towards an advanced modernization. Thus prerequisites, basic goals, development strategies and overall arrangement for an advanced modernization were the questions they have dealt earnestly. Although failing to completely solve those problems, they have left valuable ideas and ways for solving these problems to their successors as guides on the path to China's modernization. Their errors and limitations are also landmarks in China's course to modernization. So, research in this sphere needs to be enhanced.

1.3.2.4 Study on Mao Zedong's Life and His Achievements Can Become More Comprehensive

The studies on Mao Zedong's life, career and practice has registered remarkable achievements. For example, the *Chronicle of Mao Zedong's Life* and the *Biography of Mao Zedong* are both definitive works that contain the whole process how Mao Zedong has applied Marxism in China and developed his thoughts. It is a pity that elaborations in the two books include only his career and achievements before 1949 while they have not said a word about his major theories and practices after 1949 which arouses much more interest among the people. But, with the passage of time, more documents and literature will be declassified, and researchers will have the chance to make great progress in studying Mao Zedong's life and achievements.

1.3.2.5 Study on Different Editions of Mao Zedong's Works Will Play an Important Role in the Study of Mao Zedong Thought

Some books and papers studying editions of Mao Zedong's works have been published, and elaborations in some of them were affirmed as conclusions. But, still more efforts need to be made to study all of the different editions from an overall viewpoint. Because the manuscripts of Mao Zedong's some works are classified, only few researchers have the opportunity to compare the printed editions with the original manuscripts.

However, in future study of editions of Mao Zedong's works, his original manuscripts, transcripts of talks, tapes of speeches and other original material should play a unique and important role. To collect all editions of Mao Zedong's works and classify them in a scientific way to form an organic database could form not only a fundamental project in studying his editions of works but also the part of work guaranteeing that the studies on Mao Zedong Thought and its development progresses in the correct direction. Therefore, study in this area will attract more and more attention from researchers.

1.3.2.6 Comparative Study of Mao Zedong Thought and Deng Xiaoping Theory Will Be Flourishing for a Long Time to Come

Mao Zedong Thought and Deng Xiaoping Theory are the two major theoretical achievements the Chinese people have made in applying Marxism in China in different historical stages for development and social progress. Although created to address problems in different historical periods, they are interconnected and based on the same ideological belief and share the same common goal. So, a comparative study of the two will continue to be a key focus in the study of Mao Zedong Thought in the twenty-first century.

References

Shi Zhongquan (ed.), *A Review of Study on Mao Zedong*, the Central Party Literature Press, Beijing, 1992.

Han Rongzhang et al., *The Study on Mao Zedong Thought in China*, Chongqing Publishing House, Chongqing, 1993.

Han Rongzhang, Xiao Decai, and Shao Heping (eds.), *The Study on Mao Zedong Thought in Fifty Years*, Hubei People's Publishing House, Wuhan, 1993.

Zhou Yiping, *History of Study on Mao Zedong Thought*, East China Normal University Publishing House, Shanghai, 1996.

Liu Yuejin, *Introduction to Different Editions of Mao Zedong's Works*, Beijing Yanshan Publishing House, Beijing, 1999.

Yang Sansheng, "Century-End Review of and Prospect for Study on Mao Zedong Thought," *Journal of Shaanxi Normal University*, 1996 (4).

Dong Zhongqi, "A Review of Major Issues in the Study of Mao Zedong Thought," *Research of Mao Zedong Thought*, 1997 (6).

Kong Xiangyu and Zhu Zhimin, "A Review of Study of Mao Zedong Thought in China in the 1990s," *Teaching and Research*, 1999 (1).

Zeng Changqiu, "Progress and Development: Study on Mao Zedong Thought in China in the Sixty Years," *Journal of Wuling*, 1999 (1).

Shi Zhongquan and Tang Zhouyan, "Analyses of Features in the Study of Mao Zedong Thought Since 1993," *Study of Mao Zedong and Deng Xiaoping*, 2000 (5).

Chapter 2

Studies on the History of Development of Mao Zedong Thought

After the Resolution on Certain Questions in the History of Our Party Since the Founding of the People's Republic of China was promulgated, a considerable number of scholars in China began to study Mao Zedong Thought vertically. They soon published numerous papers and a large number of highly influential books, making study in this area an important discipline in the study of Mao Zedong Thought. This has marked the beginning of researchers to study Mao Zedong Thought in a scientific and academic manner. The earlier books in this area includes *Lectures on the History of Development of Mao Zedong Thought (The New-Democratic Revolution Period)* (1983), *History of Mao Zedong Thought (The New-Democratic Revolution Period*" (1983) and *History of Mao Zedong Thought (The Socialist Construction Period)* (1985) edited by Zheng Derong and other professors at Northeast Normal University. The ones published later were *A Brief History of Development of Mao Zedong Thought* (1987) by Liu Mengyi,

Historical Development of Mao Zedong Thought (Vol. 1) (1987) by Miao Chuhuang, four-volume *History of Mao Zedong Thought* (1991-1993) edited by Yang Chao and Bi Jianheng, *Outline of History of Mao Zedong Thought* (1991) by Qin Yizhen et al., *History of Development of Mao Zedong Thought* (1993) edited by Jin Chunming and Chen Dengcai, *Historical Course for the Development of Mao Zedong Thought* (1993) by Fan Xianchao et al., and *Complete History of Mao Zedong Thought* (1995) compiled by the Institute of Marxism-Leninism Development in Renmin University of China.

In the last twenty years, important efforts were given to explore the laws and features of the development of Mao Zedong Thought, and researchers have basically found the thread of its development, set up a basic framework for the history of its development, and made significant progress in discovering the historical course, historical stages, landmarks and its development features in each step. In addition, they have basically reached agreement on some major issues such as the theoretical sources of Mao Zedong Thought, the historical conditions for its formation and development, its development in different historical stages, the interaction of ideas among Party leaders, the contribution of other Party leaders to its formation, and the logical connection of its development in different stages.

Their disputes and arguments are on the division of historical stages in the development of Mao Zedong Thought, on the landmark for each stage, and on Mao Zedong's thought in his early and later years.

2.1 Framework for the History of Development of Mao Zedong Thought

After making the study on the history of development of Mao Zedong Thought an independent discipline in the theoretical studies of Mao Zedong Thought in the 1980s, the number one concern for researchers was to establish a framework for the study and solve the major theoretical issues in the discipline. Researchers from the very beginning had declared that the history of development of Mao Zedong Thought is a history of an ideology, has its own features and is governed by its own laws. They have made great efforts in the following aspects.

2.1.1 Object and Tasks in the Study of the History of Development of Mao Zedong Thought and Nature of the Study

Researchers generally believe that to study the history of development of Mao Zedong Thought is to study the historical course of Mao Zedong Thought as a system of theories, viz. to study the complete process of formation and development of Mao Zedong Thought as well as the laws governing that process. They have studied in detail the course of formation and development of Mao Zedong Thought and its every theoretical component, its historical stages in development and their features, and also the theoretical contributions made by other thinkers, theoreticians and politicians. In conclusion, study in this area focuses on the dynamic historical process of Mao Zedong Thought, and not on Mao Zedong's certain works or specific theoretical aspects of the Thought.

The tasks are to explore the laws governing development of Mao Zedong Thought, explore the experiences and lessons in its development so as to promote its further development.

Researchers commonly believe that the history of development of Mao Zedong Thought as its nature is a development history of an ideology or a theory, so study on it should focus on its course of progress, completion and development. At the same time, because Mao Zedong Thought is an ideology guiding the Party and the people in China and has a unique political significance than ordinary ideologies, its history cannot be regarded as a history of pure isolated ideological or theoretical subject. For that reason, the study should also include the development history of Marxism and China's practices in revolution and construction.

2.1.2 Exploring the Sources of Mao Zedong Thought

Every thought has its source(s) because it originates from certain existing theoretical material. In studying the history of development of the Thought, researchers strive to discover its source(s). The idea of one-source has been dominant over a long period of time, believing that Marxism is the sole source of Mao Zedong Thought. Later, researchers tended to commonly agree that Mao Zedong Thought was affected by more than one source after they studied it from a wider cultural viewpoint. They suggest that Mao Zedong Thought was greatly influenced by both Marxism and traditional Chinese culture and consequently traditional Chinese culture was also an important source. The two-source believers base their argument on the fact that all creators of Mao Zedong Thought were influenced by traditional Chinese culture in different degrees and some of them were so well versed in Chinese national culture that they had even interpreted Marxism with it. The two-source believers argue that Mao Zedong Thought is an integration of Marxism with China's realities and China's traditional culture is an important part of its reality. They also argue that applying Marxism in China was an integration of Chinese culture with Western culture when observed from a cultural viewpoint. As researchers gradually broadened their understanding of the sources, some of them further advanced the idea of two sources with a clearer distinction—the primary source being Marxism and the secondary source being traditional Chinese culture. And, some researchers have suggested the idea of three sources. Discussion on this subject has become a focus among researchers, and they have made great efforts to elaborate how traditional Chinese culture had influenced the formation and development of the Thought. Some researchers have advanced that more attention should be attached to study how Marxism was spread in China because it was the main theoretical source of Mao Zedong Thought. They argue that although researchers have closely studied how Marxism was spread in China around the May 4th Movement, they have failed to carefully study how it was spread in China after the CPC was founded, how the Chinese Communists had studied it in various historical stages, and how the CPC had studied and accepted Marxist theories of philosophy, political economy and scientific socialism. By probing deeper into the above issues, researchers can better understand how Marxism was integrated with Chinese realities and how and in which way Mao Zedong Thought had developed Marxism.

2.1.3 Social and Historical Conditions for the Formation of the Mao Zedong Thought

Every thought reflects social existence. The formation and development of Mao Zedong Thought cannot not be separated from China's historical changes in society, politics, economy and culture. So, to study the history of development of Mao Zedong Thought, the most fundamental researchers do is to comprehensively investigate the social and historical conditions under which Mao Zedong Thought had emerged and developed. Why could the Chinese proletariat who was not so strong at the time be able to find the necessary social base to develop and spread its ideas in semi-colonial and semi-feudal China, while the bourgeoisie could not? Researchers needed to analyze China's social and historical conditions at that time to answer this question and to explain why Marxism could survive and flourish in China. Some researchers have suggested that the development of Mao Zedong Thought in every historical stage was subject to the influence and impact changes in China's politics, economy, culture and movements directly or indirectly and in this or that way. But, they have overlooked the importance of the historical conditions under which Mao Zedong Thought developed, although they did analyze the social and historical circumstances under which it emerged.

2.1.4 Other Ideas and Trends of Thought in and out the Party at That Time

Truth develops through its struggle against mistakes or subjectivism. This was how Mao Zedong Thought had developed. Mao Zedong Thought has developed in the struggle against erroneous ideas and trends of thought in and outside the Party. Consequently, researchers have started to carefully analyze the influence of other trends of thought on Mao Zedong Thought in their efforts to study its history of development. Debates on the thread of development of Mao Zedong Thought in isolation from other trends of thought is no different from study of Mao Zedong Thought in isolation from its social and historical conditions. In fact, other trends of thought, including the anti-Marxist or dogmatic ones, had promoted the development of Mao Zedong Thought. For instance, the "problem and doctrine" dispute around May 4 movement in 1920s had urged Chinese Communists to apply Marxism in China concretely, and criticism of dogmatism had facilitated the formation of Mao Zedong Thought.

2.1.5 Relation between Collective Wisdom and Personal Thought

Special attention needs to be paid on two issues. The first is that both the system of theories and thoughts of the thinkers who have invented the theories should be studied. Thinkers produce the thoughts. To study the thought, thoughts of the thinkers must be studied first. Recently, researchers have concretely analyzed the contribution of other thinkers, theoreticians and politicians on the Mao Zedong Thought when studying the history of its development. A comprehensive analysis of the contributions all the thinkers on the formation and development of Mao Zedong Thought have greatly helped researchers properly evaluate every stage in the development of Mao Zedong Thought and more comprehensively describe its history of development. They have also observed the conspicuous or potential limitations of the other contributers.

The second is that both the thought of the representative and the collective wisdom should be studied. On the one hand, every thought or theory has a representative representing it. The major representative of Mao Zedong Thought is Mao Zedong who has contributed the most to it. Consequently, his thought must be studied with higher priority. On the other hand, Party and state leaders, revolutionaries of the older generation and Party theoreticians have also contributed more or less to the development of Mao Zedong Thought. So, their thoughts and ideas should also be studied. Any attempts to study alone and solely the development of Mao Zedong's thought or to equate his thought with the development of Mao Zedong Thought will do no good for the study of Mao Zedong Thought. It is a significant theoretical matter to correctly elaborate the role Mao Zedong had personally played in forming and developing Mao Zedong Thought. Researchers have made great progress in this area and fundamentally changed people's limited understanding of Mao Zedong Thought which was prevalent in the past.

2.1.6 Stages in Development of Mao Zedong Thought

To recognise the stages in the development of Mao Zedong Thought is a key issue in the study of its history of development. Researchers commonly suggest that a thought or theory not only reflects social existence but also has its own laws and features in its development, and in certain circumstances it does not change in any phase with social, political or economic changes. Therefore, stages in development of Mao Zedong Thought should not be rigidly divided according to stages in CPC's development or periods in China's revolution, but should accord with the unique laws of that Thought. At the same time, special due attention should be given to the stages in the course in which Marxism was integrated with China's realities.

2.2 Historical Stages in the Development of Mao Zedong Thought

The assessment on Mao Zedong and Mao Zedong Thought made by the CPC at the Sixth Plenary Session of its Eleventh Central Committee was short, conclusive, and assertive, making no detailed or concrete elaborations. The Party had used only dozens of words to summarize its formation and development, asserting that it had developed and became mature during the later period of the War of the Agrarian Revolution and during the War of Resistance against Japan and had developed further during the War of Liberation and after the founding of the People's Republic. Naturally, such a brief summarization cannot not satisfy researchers, who make enormous efforts to further research the history of development of Mao Zedong

Thought and the historical stages in its development.

In their earliest research results, researchers have generally divided the historical stages in development of Mao Zedong Thought in accord with principles of the Sixth Plenary Session of the Eleventh CPC Central Committee. Ma Qibin and Chen Dengcai have published in October 1981 the article "A Brief Talk on Mao Zedong Thought," in which they have divided the history of Mao Zedong Thought into four stages.

The first stage was the initial stage, from July 1921 to July 1927. The Chinese Communists had set up the program of democratic revolution to fight against imperialism and feudalism, and advanced the idea of forming a democratic united front, and started to understand the importance of upholding proletarian leadership and relying on the peasants in the revolution.

The second stage was the formation stage, from July 1927 to January 1935. The Chinese Communists had formulated the general principles for launching the Agrarian Revolution and decided to employ armed forces to fight against the reactionary KMT, shifted their strategic focus from cities to the countryside, had established independent regimes of the workers and the peasants by armed forces, and creatively solved a series of major problems one of which was the road for Chinese revolution.

The third stage was the development stage, from 1935 to 1945. The Chinese Communists had politically developed the strategy of establishing an anti-Japanese national united front, and had unveiled the unique laws of China's revolutionary war, and formulated the strategy and tactics for China's revolutionary war. Components of Mao Zedong Thought had developed more comprehensively and were recognized by the entire Party.

The fourth stage was the continuation of the development stage, from 1946 to 1956. The Chinese Communists had further developed the Party's political and military strategies, achieved victory in the democratic revolution, successfully realized the transformation from armed struggle to economic development works and from the democratic revolution to socialist revolution, and had successfully solved the problems concerning transformation from the new-democratic to socialist society.

The two authors have also argued that Mao Zedong Thought had developed as well between 1957 and 1966 and that its basic tenets had developed further after the Third Plenary Session of the Eleventh Central Committee under the new historical conditions.

Thereafter, most research results have generally agreed with the above division of stages. Some have made supplements to that classification, holding that the "cultural revolution" period was a stage in which Mao Zedong Thought had developed amid twists and turns and that the period after the Third Plenary Session of the Eleventh Central Committee was a new stage for its development.

Other Ideas:

But, there are also other researchers arguing differently. For instance, after taking into consideration stages in China's revolution, Liu Mengyi has divided the history of development of Mao Zedong Thought into seven stages: the beginning stage—the period of the First Revolutionary Civil War (1924-1927); the formation stage—the period of the Second Revolutionary Civil Wa (1927-1934); the improvement stage (the period of the War of Resistance against Japan); the development stage—the period of the Third Revolutionary Civil War (1946-1949); the new development stage—the period of the socialist transformation (1953-1956); the stage of development amid twists and turns—the period of all-round socialist construction (1956-1978); and the stage of development after setbacks (the period after the Third Plenary Session of the Eleventh Central Committee). It is noticeable that he has not included the "cultural revolution" period as a stage.

Zhang Jingru and Ding Xiaoqiang suggest that the beginning stage should start from the May 4th Movement when Marxism was introduced and spread in China because Mao Zedong Thought is the product of the integration of Marxism with China's concrete realities, and that the formation stage should be from 1936 to 1940 when Mao Zedong Thought had become an independent system.[1]

---

[1] Zhang Jingru and Ding Xiaoqiang, "Several Problems in the Study of History of Development of Mao Zedong Thought," *Study of the History of the Communist Party of China*, 1988 (2).

Yang Fuxin has divided the stages as follows: the period from the founding of the CPC to the holding of the Zunyi Meeting in 1935 was the beginning stage; the period from the Zunyi Meeting to the victory in the War of Resistance against Japan was the formation stage; from the beginning of the War of Liberation to the publication of "On the Correct Handling of the Contradictions Among the People" had represented the first upsurge in the development of Mao Zedong Thought; from the launching of the uncontrolled combat against Rightists in 1957, to the Third Plenary Session of the Eleventh Central Committee was a stage in which Mao Zedong Thought had developed amid twists and turns and was under a gross distortion; and the period after the Third Plenary Session of the Eleventh Central Committee represents the second upsurge in the development of Mao Zedong Thought. He gave two supports as evidence for his argument on Mao Zedong Thought forming during the Yan'an period. The first is that the Yan' an period (1942-1945) had provided the necessary subjective and objective conditions for its formation: the Chinese Communists had better understood the features and laws of the Chinese revolution after their victories and failures in revolutionary struggles; the Chinese Communists had a chance to theoretically review and sum up their experiences in the revolutionary base areas, where there were favorable conditions for studying Marxism-Leninism; and books and writings written by many Party leaders during that period had contributed greatly to the formation and development of Mao Zedong Thought. His second was that the different systems of thinking in Mao Zedong Thought were formed during the Yan'an period: "Problems of Strategy in China's Revolutionary War" had marked formation of the scientific system of military thinking; "On Practice" and "On Contradiction" had marked the formation of the philosophical thoughts; "On New Democracy" and two other essays had marked formation of the theory of the new-democratic revolution; the theory of the united front and the thought of strategies began to take shape after the Wayaobao Meeting; and the doctrines of Party building were formed during the period of the Yan'an rectification movement[1].

Qin Yizhen and his study group has suggested that Mao Zedong Thought had begun to appear during the period of the Northern Expedition[2] in 1926-1927, and its formation was marked by the appearance of the thinking on China's democratic revolution.

In their book *History of Mao Zedong Thought*, Yang Chao and his study group have. asserted that Mao Zedong Thought had taken initial shape from the late 1920s to the early 1930s, was formed and had progressed from the middle 1930s to the middle 1940s, and developed amid twists and turns from the middle 1950s to the middle 1970s.

Li Ji has suggested that the period from the founding of the CPC in 1921 to the August 7th Meeting held in 1927 had been the initial stage.

Some researchers have not included the "cultural revolution" as a development stage, suggesting that it had not been a stage for development but a stage in which Mao Zedong Thought had been highly distorted.

2.3 Symbols of the Stages in the Development of Mao Zedong Thought

In the opinion of researchers, symbols and historical stages are closely connected. Different stages have different symbols, and even the same stage may have various symbols.. Disputes on the symbols have been raised on the symbols of the beginning, formation and maturity of Mao Zedong Thought.

---

[1] Yang Fuxin, "On the Formation of Mao Zedong Thought," *Study of the History of the Communist Party of China*, 1988 (3).

[2] The Northern Expedition was a punitive war against the Northern warlords launched by the revolutionary army which marched North from Guangdong Province in May-July 1926. The Northern Expeditionary Army, with the Communist Party of China taking part in its leadership and under the Party's influence, had gained a warm support of the broad masses of workers and peasants. In the second half of 1926 and the first half of 1927 it had occupied most of the provinces along the Yangtze and Yellow Rivers and defeated the Northern warlords. In April 1927 this revolutionary war had failed as a result of betrayal by the reactionary clique under Chiang Kai-shek within the revolutionary front.

2.3.1 Symbols of the Initial Stage

Many researchers suggest that Mao Zedong's works such as "Analysis of the Classes in Chinese Society" and "Report on An Investigation of the Peasant Movement in Hunan" had marked the beginning of Mao Zedong Thought. They have argued that the two reports had represented the initial achievements of the Chinese Communists in integrating Marxism-Leninism with China's realities, because they had given the initial answers to some basic problems in China's revolution such as its task, leadership, allies and prospects and had embodied the CPC's basic ideas on the new-democratic revolution.

Some researchers have advanced that the CPC's revolutionary program should be considered in studying how Mao Zedong Thought had begun to appear. They have argued that since Mao Zedong Thought was the product of the integration of the basic tenets of Marxism-Leninism with China's concrete realities and the crystallization of the collective wisdom of the entire Party, the study on how it had begun to emerge should not be limited to the ideas of Mao Zedong. Those events when the CPC had begun to integrate the basic tenets of Marxism-Leninism with China's realities should also be studied. Documents indicate that the CPC had formulated a program for a democratic revolution to fight against imperialism and feudalism and had set a series of policies and strategies to encourage their implementation at its Second National Congress in 1922. This indicates that the Chinese Communists had begun to integrate Marxism with China's realities at that Congress. Consequently, many researchers suggest that the formulation of the program to fight against imperialism and feudalism at the Second National Party Congress had marked the beginning of Mao Zedong Thought.

Other researchers have advanced that the initial formation of the theoretical system of the new-democratic revolution marks the beginning of Mao Zedong Thought. They suggest that the CPC, in its early years (1921-1927), had acquired an all-round understanding of a number of issues concerning China's democratic revolution, such as its target, motive forces, leadership, and nature, put forward some valuable ideas on the united front, armed struggle and Party building, and had created an initial theory of the new-democratic revolution. That was an initial fruit of the integration of Marxism with Chinese realities and therefore marks the beginning of Mao Zedong Thought.

Still other researchers have asserted that the period from late 1925 to early 1926 had marked the beginning of Mao Zedong Thought. Li Ji, has advanced some new opinions in his new book *New Opinions on the Beginning of Mao Zedong Thought* (Hunan People's Publishing House, 1998). He suggests that the beginning of Mao Zedong Thought should not be marked by any time point or any individual idea or essay, but should be marked by the period starting from the early winter of 1925 to the end of summer in 1927, in which Mao Zedong's six important writings were published. Li Ji, has not included "Analysis of the Classes in Chinese Society" in those six works; instead, he has suggested that "Answers to the Reorganizing Committee of Young China Association" which was published earlier should be included: He has asserted that the ideas in those the six writings form the initial stage.

2.3.2 Symbols of Formation: The Second Stage

This has been the most disputed and discussed issue in the studies. Yet, researchers have not reached an agreement over this stage. Before 1988 Researchers had generally agreed that the time when the Chinese Communists represented by Mao Zedong had charted the road of the Chinese revolution as encircling the cities from the countryside and eventually seizing political power nationwide should mark the formation of Mao Zedong Thought. This is the first view still being advocated. Their disputes are just about the most correct time and event. They cannot not reach an agreement on when the real creation of the road for the Chinese revolution was completely cleared. Some of them suggest that Mao Zedong's essay "A Single Spark Can Start a Prairie Fire" marks the formation of Mao Zedong Thought because it had put forward the theory of encircling the cities from the countryside and eventually seizing political power nationwide. But, other researchers have asserted that the essay had not solved all the theoretical problems related to the road for the Chinese revolution.

The second view has asserted that Mao Zedong's essay "Oppose Book Worship" marks the formation of Mao Zedong Thought because it had advanced the principle of integrating Marxism with the realities of the Chinese revolution and the three main ideas of seeking truth from facts, the mass line and self-reliance. Some researchers holding this view have further argued that the essay was a symbol in which Mao Zedong's philosophical thought had begun to take shape because it had embodied some propositions of the Marxist theory of cognition and Mao Zedong's some philosophical ideas.

The third view have argued that the solution of the two most basic problems in the Chinese revolution—the road of the Chinese revolution and political strategies for the new-democratic revolution—should mark the formation of Mao Zedong Thought. Therefore, the formation of Mao Zedong Thought should be evaluated as between 1930-1935 and marked by two symbols. Mao Zedong's "A Single Spark Can Start a Prairie Fire" in early 1930 can be a symbol because it had advanced the theory of encircling the cities from the countryside. The meeting of the CPC Central Committee in Wayaobao and Mao Zedong's "On Tactics Against Japanese Imperialism" in late 1935 can be other symbols because they had formulated the political strategy of establishing an anti-Japanese national united front and clarified the relationships between the enemy, alliances and the Party.

The Criteria for the Formation:

The fourth view has suggested that, firstly the criteria and prerequisites for the formation of Mao Zedong Thought should be considered. These researchers have argued that there are three criteria. The first is a comparatively complete content and normally as a complete system of theories, Mao Zedong Thought should include theories on every important aspect of the Chinese revolution and also should have developed a basic theoretical framework. "It is incorrect to assess that Mao Zedong Thought had formed solely because the problem of the road for the Chinese revolution had been solved.

Their second argument is that, although there were theories in the initial stage, the established Mao Zedong Thought should not be evaluated as specific experiences or policies, but it should be theories developed through review of experience in the Chinese revolution and summarization of laws and features of the Chinese revolution. Besides, its formation should have solid philosophical basis and include scientific worldviews and thought ways with Chinese features. "Oppose Book Worship" had not made a deep and sufficient logical argument on the philosophical questions it had dealt with, and philosophical questions in that essay were not enough to provide a philosophical basis for Mao Zedong Thought.

The third idea argues for a certain stability in the Thought. The basic tenets of an established Mao Zedong Thought can be supplemented and developed, but should not change fundamentally. But in the 1930s, some people still had not fully understand the basic condition in the Chinese revolution featured as "the enemy is strong and that we are weak."

The Prerequisites for the Thought:

There are four prerequisites. The first is that the established Mao Zedong Thought should fully reflect the laws and features of the Chinese society and revolution. The second prerequisite is that the Party should have gathered rich experiences in both victories and failures. The third is that the Party should independently be able to deal with its affairs and formulate its lines, principles and policies. The fourth is that some Party leaders should have produced some theories after profoundly reviewing their experience in the Chinese revolution.

After taking into consideration the above three criteria and four prerequisites, some researchers have argued that Mao Zedong Thought was formed during the period between December 1935 to July or August 1937, in which Mao Zedong had written a series of important works.

The fifth view has similarities with the above third and fourth views. They have argued that the reason researchers disagree with each other on the time points, symbols and prerequisites of formation of Mao Zedong Thought is that they take different criteria. The fifth view believes that the established Mao Zedong Thought should meet four criteria. The first is that it should have a roughly appropriate basic framework. The second is that it should have a set of central theories, which include the solution to the following problems: on the road of the Chinese revolution, correct analyses of the national bourgeoisie and other intermediate classes, and full embodiment of the living soul of Mao Zedong Thought. The third is that the Party's leadership should have accepted those theories. As a crystallization of collective wisdom of the entire Party, we cannot say it is definitely established if the Party had not recognized it as a guiding ideology. The fourth is that it should be comparatively stable. According to these criteria, the formation of Mao Zedong Thought had evolved during the period from the Zunyi Meeting of January 1935 to the late 1935, because Mao Zedong had solved a series of problems concerning the road of the Chinese revolution in 1930; the Fourth Army of the Red Army had solved a group of major problems concerning army building during its Ninth Party Congress in 1929; the Red Army had developed combat tactics in the resistance against the KMT's third campaign of encirclement; studies on the intermediate classes had reached a new high level in the late 1935; "Oppose Book Worship" had embodied the living soul of Mao Zedong Thought; "Left" and Right mistakes were criticized and Mao Zedong Thought was recognized as the Party's guiding ideology after the Zunyi Meeting in 1935. These researchers believe that Mao Zedong Thought was formed in the late 1935 when it had developed its framework, central theories and living soul. Thus, the fifth view overlaps with the third view on time point and with the fourth view on criteria.

The sixth view has opposed the criteria suggested by the fourth view. These researchers suggest that Mao Zedong Thought is a complete system of theories and main attention should be given to its most fundamental theories which can be the symbol of its formation. The problem of the road for the Chinese revolution and the idea of centering on countryside were the key to solving a set of significant issues such as regimes in the revolutionary bases, the Agrarian Revolution, the Red Army's strategies and tactics and Party building. So, the symbol of formation of Mao Zedong Thought should be the solution of the problem for the road of the Chinese revolution both in theory and in practice. They hold that the CPC had not only theoretically solved the problem of the road of the Chinese revolution but had attempted to solve a set of practical problems concerning Party building, army building, government building and the Agrarian Revolution in the early 1930s. So, that should be a symbol of initial formation of Mao Zedong Thought. Although Mao Zedong had not fully developed the idea of carrying out armed struggle in the countryside, accumulating strength and seizing political power nationwide when conditions were ripe, but this idea exactly indicates that Mao Zedong Thought was taking shape. That thought still was taking shape and could not be perfect so we should not judge it over-accurately. With regard to whether Mao Zedong Thought was strongly appreciated and recognized by the entire Party (mainly in the organs of the Central Committee) when it was taking shape, these researchers have argued that formation of the thought and its recognition by the Party are two issues that were related with each other and at the same time different from each other. They are related to each other because the formation and development of the thought cannot be separated from the Party's revolutionary practice; they are different from each other because recognition by the Party is not a necessary prerequisite for the formation of the thought. In fact, it had taken a long period of time for the Party's central leadership to judge and recognize Mao Zedong Thought—the CPC had discussed this problem in Yan'an rectification movement in 1942 and had formally established Mao Zedong Thought as its guiding ideology at its Seventh National Congress in 1945. Mao Zedong Thought was recognized by the entire Party when it became mature during the period of the War of Resistance against Japan. But, that was at a time when it had got mature, not it had taken shape.

The seventh view also believes that an important reason why researchers disagree with each other on the formation of Mao Zedong Thought is that they apply different criteria. According to these researchers: to judge that the Thought had taken shape by purely considering whether the basic tenets of

Marxism had been generally integrated with China's revolutionary practice generally overlooks the originality of Mao Zedong Thought because Mao Zedong Thought is the application and development of Marxism in China. On the other side, to judge the Thought had taken shape by solely considering whether the basic tenets of Marxism had been integrated with China's revolutionary practice and solving significant problems in the Chinese revolution overlooks the fact that Mao Zedong Thought is a scientific system of thinking. To judge that the Thought had taken shape by solely considering whether Mao Zedong's philosophical thought had taken shape overlooks the difference and relationship between Mao Zedong Thought and Mao Zedong's philosophical thoughts, and leads researchers to erroneously believe that "Oppose Book Worship," "On Practice" and "On Contradiction" are the symbols that Mao Zedong Thought had taken shape or become mature. Mao Zedong had stated in "Introducing *The Communist,*" "Therefore the united front, armed struggle and Party building are the three fundamental questions for our Party in the Chinese revolution. Having a correct grasp of these three questions and their interrelations is tantamount to give a correct leadership to the whole Chinese revolution."[1] Consequently, some researchers have argued that the solution of those three questions should be the criteria to judge the stages of development in Mao Zedong Thought. They have asserted that Mao Zedong Thought had begun to take shape at least before the Zunyi Meeting (1935) because that meeting had criticized the dogmatic military thinking and reviewed and affirmed Mao Zedong's military thinking, corrected the mistakes the Party had made in handling its relationship with the 19th Route Army, and improved the Party's understanding on the question of united front, and most importantly pointed Mao Zedong as the leader of the entire Party.

Besides, there are also views arguing that "Analysis of the Classes in Chinese Society" or the Yan'an rectification movement in 1942 should mark the formation of Mao Zedong Thought. But, most researchers believe that

---

[1] *Selected Works of Mao Tse-tung*, Eng. ed., FLP, Peking, 1965, Vol. II, p. 288.

they were either too early or too late. The former overlooks the nature of Mao Zedong Thought as a system, while the latter erroneously confuses Mao Zedong's mature works with those immature ones.

In conclusion, before 1988, researchers could not yet go beyond the conclusion made by the Resolution on Certain Questions in the History of Our Party Since the Founding of the People's Republic of China, and most of them have advocated that the Mao Zedong Thought had taken shape sometime during the 1920s and 1930s. But after 1988 some new opinions have appeared, suggesting that the Thought had taken shape later than the 1920s or 1930s.

2.3.3 Symbols Reflecting the Maturity of the Thought

In my opinion, at present, the following opinions make the mainstream:

Firstly, "On Practice" and "On Contradiction" symbolize that Mao Zedong Thought had become mature. There are two group of researchers holding this opinion. One group believes that the two essays had thoroughly criticized the "Left" dogmatism of Wang Ming and after twists and turns, had matured the theories of Mao Zedong Thought. The other group believes that the two essays were still the CPC's fresh understanding on the theory of the new-democratic revolution and other theories about the Chinese revolution, thus only after a thorough review of their successes and failures, can they be the symbols reflecting that the Mao Zedong Thought had entered a stage of maturity.

Second view argues that, "On New Democracy" marks the maturity of Mao Zedong Thought. These researchers assert that a large number of major theories concerning the Chinese revolution were solved in this essay.

Third view suggests that, "Introducing *The Communist*," "The Chinese Revolution and the Chinese Communist Party" and "On New Democracy" are the symbols reflecting that the Thought had become mature because they had given a complete, systematic elaboration on the theory of the new-democratic revolution.

Fourth view argues that, the Party's Seventh National Congress in 1945 marks the maturity of the Thought. The reasons are as follows. The Congress had systematically reviewed the lessons and experiences in the Chinese democratic revolution in the past twenty-four years and had given an all-round elaboration on the three aspects of the living soul of Mao Zedong Thought. At the Congress, the CPC had attained a correct and a deeper understanding of the three fundamental questions which have a direct bearing on the Chinese revolution and their interrelations: the united front, armed struggle and Party building. Besides, Mao Zedong Thought was formally established as the Party's guiding ideology, and its content was defined from nine aspects.

Fifth view asserts that, Mao Zedong Thought had needed to go through a historical process before getting mature. A complete and systematic elaboration on the theory of the new-democratic revolution should be the major symbol for its maturity. The CPC's Seventh Congress can also be another symbol that Mao Zedong Thought and the entire Party had become mature because the Congress had reviewed both the positive and negative experiences in the Chinese revolution and had fixed the Mao Zedong Thought as the Party's guiding ideology.

Besides, there are other opinions suggesting that the Mao Zedong Thought had become mature during its second historical transformation or during the Yan'an rectification movement between 1942-1945.

2.4 Mao Zedong's Thoughts in His Early and Later Years

The track of development in Mao Zedong's thoughts are closely connected to the formation and development of Mao Zedong Thought because he, himself is its chief creator and representative of the Thought. Therefore, the studies on development of his thoughts are very important for the efforts to study the history of development of Mao Zedong Thought.

The period from 1921 to 1956 was a period when Mao Zedong had produced his most illustrious works. Researchers commonly believe that all his theories and practice during that period were basically correct, and that his thoughts had developed and become mature during that period. In recent years, researchers have begun to focus on Mao Zedong's early years when he was not a Marxist and on his later years when he had gradually deviated from the scientific theory of Marxism.

2.4.1 Mao Zedong's Thoughts in His Early Years

Mao Zedong's early thoughts were connected at least with the appearance and emergence of the Mao Zedong Thought. Researchers have generally focused on his conceptions of society and history and his attitude toward ethics and education, on the influence of Chinese and Western cultures on his early thoughts, and on why, how and when he had become a Marxist. They have thoroughly studied his early thoughts from the viewpoint of culture. Some researchers believe that the traditional Chinese culture had produced a significant influence on his early thoughts, so they have made great efforts to study the ideological relation between his thoughts and the Confucianism, the Legalism, the Taoism, the Mohism, the neo-Confucianism in Song and Ming dynasties and the Concept of Real Learning in the Ming and Qing dynasties. Some researchers have studied his early thoughts from the perspective of relationship between folk culture and classical culture. Recently, there are researchers who have started to study how his early thoughts were influenced by thinkers in Hunan Province such as Wang Chuanshan, Zeng Guofan, Tan Sitong, Yang Changji and Xu Teli. With regard to the influence of Western culture on young Mao Zedong, some researchers have focused on the Darwin's theory of evolution while others, on anarchism or Atarashiki Mura (New Village Movement). Some researchers have also studied in what sequence Chinese and Western cultures had influenced young Mao Zedong. They believe that he was influenced mainly by traditional Chinese culture during the Shaoshan period and by both Chinese and Western cultures when he studied in Changsha, and that both traditional Chinese culture and modern Western culture had shaped his thinking with the latter playing a major role during the latter period in Changsha and during the May 4th Movement in 1919. Through these studies researchers can better analyze his early thoughts and have reached clearer conclusions on the theoretical sources of Mao Zedong Thought.

Transformation of His World-View:

The is a hot debate on when Mao Zedong had changed his world-view and what marks that change. It is generally argued that thoughts of young Mao Zedong had changed in two aspects: political view and philosophy. He was a general democrat who believed in the idealist philosophy before the new cultural movement in 1915. He had become a radical revolutionary democrat politically and had believed in mind-body dualism before the Xinmin Institute was established in 1918. He had transformed from a radical revolutionary democrat to a communist and his belief had changed from mind-body dualism to Marxist materialism before the CPC was founded in 1921. Researchers have debated on when he had changed to be a communist and a Marxist and what marks the change. Some have argued that the change had happened in the summer of 1920 because Mao Zedong had himself once commented on that. Others believe that the change had taken place in the winter of 1920 because the available historical material proves that fact, and that his two letters to Cai Hesen and another person on December 1, 1920 and January 21, 1921 and his two speeches at the Xinmin Institute Changsha Meeting on January 1 and 2, 1921 can be the symbols of that change. Still others believe that the change should take a longer process and a change in thinking can unlikely progress in a short period of time.

2.4.2 Mao Zedong's Thoughts in His Later Years

The study on Mao Zedong's thought in his later years is complex and more practical related to current problems, thus attracting much attention from researchers in the late 1980s and in the 1990s. Researchers have focused their studies mainly on Mao Zedong's ideas on socialism such as stages of development through socialist course, transformation to communism and the road of socialist construction, and on his theories of class struggle such as the reasons for the "cultural revolution" and the idea formulated as "continued revolution under the dictatorship of the proletariat". They have studied why he had changed and in some way tolerated or supported personality cult around himself and how he had erroneously applied the principle of democratic-centralism and the Party's unified collective leadership. In addition, they have also studied his ideas on "three worlds division" and on international united front to oppose super-power hegemony. Researchers have also studied the relationships between his later thoughts on the one side and the basic tenets of Marxism-Leninism and Mao Zedong Thought on the other.

The following three issues were much disputed among researchers.

2.4.2.1 Is the Terming "Mao Zedong's Later Thoughts" Scientific?

This issue is hotly debated among researchers. In drafting and preparation period of the Resolution on Certain Questions in the History of Our Party Since the Founding of the People's Republic of China, the Party had once considered using the term "Mao Zedong's later thought" to sum up his thoughts during the "cultural revolution" so that it could be distinguished from Mao Zedong Thought. But, because the term "later thought" is too limited and confusing, the term "Mao Zedong's later mistakes" was preferred in the final texting. Researchers have begun to use the term "later thoughts" in 1998, and the Party History Research Center under the CPC Central Committee has formed a special research group and held a seminar named "Mao Zedong's Later Thoughts." Thereafter, more researchers have begun to use this term. Generally, researchers have developed three definitions for Mao Zedong's later thoughts.

First, it refers to the thoughts and theories Mao Zedong had developed and applied in his exploration about the road for building socialism in China. Their fundamental direction was erroneous, but some specific ideas were correct.

Second, it mainly refers to his erroneous thoughts in his later years, so they are very different from the Mao Zedong Thought. It includes the mistakes he made in his later years but cannot only be restricted as mistakes.

Third, it refers to a system of contradictory theories he developed through his exploration about a suitable road for building socialism in China. They form a complex system that includes both mistakes and correct theories with mistakes gradually taking the lead.

But, some researchers have suggested different ideas. They have argued that the definition of Mao Zedong's Later Thought overlaps with that of Mao Zedong Thought because his correct thoughts and theories about socialism belong to both Mao Zedong's Later Thought and therefore also to the Mao Zedong Thought. They have also argued that if his correct thoughts and theories about long term socialist building and socialism are also incorporated into the definition of Mao Zedong's Later Thoughts (which mainly cover his mistakes in his later years) they cannot produce positive effects for the future generations. "They could produce more positive effects, if we include them in Mao Zedong Thought, and thus we can avoid them being confused with erroneous theories."

Some researchers have pointed out that "later" refers to a period of time and Mao Zedong's Later Thought, which is partial in time, cannot be separated from Mao Zedong Thought, which is complete in time. Some have argued that according to the meaning of words, "later thought" should include all Mao Zedong's theories and thoughts in his later years, so it would be inaccurate to place the mistakes he made in his later years under the term "later thought." Some researchers have argued that the "later years" should begin from the founding of the People's Republic, which leaves Mao Zedong Thought no other content than Mao Zedong's theoretical achievements during the democratic revolution. In conclusion, they generally agree that Mao Zedong's correct theories and thoughts in his later years should be incorporated into the definition and contents of the Mao Zedong Thought and mistakes could be called "Mao Zedong's mistakes in his later years," and there is no need to employ the terming as "later thoughts."

In addition, some researchers have pointed out that Mao Zedong's thoughts should be divided into the early, middle and later stages so that they will not be confused with the Mao Zedong Thought.

2.4.2.2 Periods and Stages in Mao Zedong's Later Thoughts

At present, there are three different views on when Mao Zedong's later thought had begun. The first argues that it had begun with the publication of "On the Ten Major Relationships" in April 1956 and after his investigations to explore the road of socialism. The second group argues that it can be started from the summer of 1957 when the combat against Rightists had gone out of control. The third group asserts that it can be started by May 1966 when the "cultural revolution" was declared.

Some researchers suggest that Mao Zedong's later thought can be divided into three stages. The first stage is from 1956 to the Tenth Plenary Session of the Eighth Party Central Committee in 1962, during which Mao Zedong had started to make mistakes and put forward the ideas of utopian socialism. The second stage is from 1962 to the eve of the "cultural revolution" in 1966, during which he had advanced the idea of taking class struggle as the key link and attempted to oppose and prevent revisionism through mass campaigns of education in socialism. The third stage is from 1966 to 1976, during which he had developed the "theory of continuing revolution under the dictatorship of the proletariat".

Other researchers have argued that the first stage should be further divided into two periods with 1957 as the boundary line. The former period includes mainly his theories on socialist democracy such as "the ten major relationships," "the two types of contradictions differing in nature" and "letting a hundred flowers bloom and a hundred schools of thought contend." The latter stage includes mainly his theories about utopian socialism such as the general line, the Great Leap Forward and on the people's communes.

2.4.2.3 Meaning and Content of Mao Zedong's Later Thoughts

Some researchers have suggested that Mao Zedong's later thoughts includes all the thoughts in his later years; others believe it includes only the mistaken ones he advocated in his later years; still others believe it only includes the theory of continuing revolution under the dictatorship of the proletariat. Some researchers hold that its content includes his ideas on socialism and his elaborations on socialist stages of development and on the road of socialist construction. Others believe that its content includes his ideas of utopian socialism reflected in the mode of people's communes, his economic development strategy as the "Great Leap Forward," and his theory of continuing revolution under the dictatorship of the proletariat.

References

Zheng Derong and Huang Jingfang, *History of Mao Zedong Thought (Revised)*, Gansu People's Publishing House, Lanzhou, 1990.

Yang Chao and Bi Jianheng (eds.), *History of Mao Zedong Thought*, Sichuan People's Publishing House, Chengdu, Vol. I-IV, 1991-1993.

Qin Yizhen and Jiu Yajun (eds.), *Outline of History of Mao Zedong Thought*, Shaanxi People's Publishing House, Xi'an, 1991.

Shi Zhongquan, (ed.) *A Review of Study on Mao Zedong*, the Central Party Literature Press, Beijing, 1992.

Jin Chunming and Chen Dengcai (eds.), *History of Development of Mao Zedong Thought*, the CPC Central Committee Party School Publishing House, Beijing, 1993.

Han Rongzhang, Xiao Decai, and Shao Heping (eds.), *The Study on Mao Zedong Thought in Fifty Years*, Hubei People's Publishing House, Wuhan, 1993.

The Institute of Marxism Development in Renmin University of China, *History of Mao Zedong Thought*, Renmin University of China Press, Beijing, 1995.

Zhou Yiping, *History of Study on Mao Zedong Thought*, East China Normal University Publishing House, Shanghai, 1996.

Li Ji, *New Opinions on the Beginning of Mao Zedong Thought*, Hunan People's Publishing House, Changsha, 1998.

Zhang Jingru et al., "Several Problems in the Study of History of Development of Mao Zedong Thought," *Study of the History of the Communist Party of China*, 1988 (2).

Yang Fuxin, "On the Formation of Mao Zedong Thought," *Study of the History of the Communist Party of China*, 1988 (3).

Li Hongkui, "A Review of Domestic and Foreign Studies on the Formation of Mao Zedong Thought," *Research of Mao Zedong Thought*, 1988 (2).

Feng Xiancheng, "Solution to the Problems of Revolutionary Road and Political Strategy Marks the Formation of Mao Zedong Thought," *Research of Mao Zedong Thought*, 1986 (4).

Zhang Xiuquan, "Some Opinions on the Criteria for the Formation of Mao Zedong Thought," *Research of Mao Zedong Thought*, 1989 (4).

Gao Jucun and Hu Changming, "Appearance of the Theory of the New-Democratic Revolution and the Beginning of Mao Zedong Thought," *Research of Mao Zedong Thought*, 1991 (4).

Kong Xiangyu and Zhu Zhimin, "A Review of Study of Mao Zedong Thought in China in the 1990s," *Teaching and Research*, 1999 (1).

Chapter 3

The Study of Mao Zedong Thought as a Scientific System

Researchers in China regard Mao Zedong Thought as a complete theoretical system. There has been many attempts to define it, what its main features are and how it was built up theoretically. I will summarize those works on these aspects.

3.1 Researches Aiming to Define Mao Zedong Thought

3.1.1 The Formation of Mao Zedong Thought and Its Scientific Definition

Researchers believe that, Mao Zedong Thought had formed its scientific definition during the course of China's progress in revolution and construction. According to research results of Pang Xianzhi and his study group, Mao Zedong Thought underwent a long process to form its scientific definition.[1]

Mao Zedong was the first to insist applying Marxism concretely in China. At the Sixth Plenary Session of the Sixth Central Committee of the CPC in October 1938, he had made a definite comment on that: "The theory of Marx, Engels, Lenin and Stalin is universally applicable. We should regard it not as a dogma, but as a guide to action. For the Chinese Communist Party, it is a matter of learning to apply the theory of Marxism-Leninism to the specific circumstances of China. Any talk about Marxism in isolation from China's characteristics is merely Marxism in the abstract, Marxism in a vacuum. Hence to apply Marxism concretely in China so that its every manifestation has an indubitably Chinese character, i.e., to apply Marxism in the light of China's specific characteristics, becomes a problem which it is urgent for the whole Party to understand and solve." In his essay: "Introducing *The Communist*" in October 1939, he had for the first time advanced the complete idea of applying the theory of Marxism-Leninism to the practice of the Chinese revolution.

The Party's theoretician Zhang Ruxin was the first to use the term "Thought of Comrade Mao Zedong" during the Yan'an period. In March 1941 he had published in the journal *The Communist* an article titled: "On Bolshevist Educators," in which he used the wording "Thought of Comrade Mao Zedong" and had argued that Mao Zedong's words and writings are results of typical integration of the theory of Marxism-Leninism with the practice of the Chinese revolution. He said, "Comrade Mao Zedong, on the basis of a review of the experience in China's long struggle and a deep understanding of the features of the Chinese society and the laws of the Chinese revolution, made un-ignorable achievements in using Marxism to creatively solve the problems of the Chinese revolution." He had also written

---

[1] Pang Xianzhi et al., "Mao Zedong's Place in Chinese History and Mao Zedong Thought," *Annotations to Resolution on Certain Questions in the History of Our Party Since the Founding of the People's Republic of China,* the People's Publishing House, Beijing, 1983. Their Research results are cited in the elaborations followed.

that educators of the Party should devote themselves to the thoughts of Lenin and Stalin as well as to the thought of Comrade Mao Zedong. In his another article "March on under the Flag of Mao Zedong" published in the weekly *Liberation* in April the same year, he had written: "As the leader of our Party, Comrade Mao Zedong is a typical example in creatively applying and developing Marxism in China." In his another article titled: "Study and Grasp Mao Zedong's Theories and Tactics" published in the *Liberation Daily* on February 18 and 19, 1942, he had pointed out, "Mao Zedong's theories and tactics represent the application and development of the theories and tactics of Marxism-Leninism in semi-colonial and semi-feudal China and are China's Marxism-Leninism." He had classified Mao Zedong's theories and tactics into three parts, i.e., ideological line or thought way, political line or science, and military line or science. He had argued that those organic three parts together constitute Mao Zedong's system of theories and tactics. In addition, he had used the term "Maoism" in his article.

On July 1, 1942, Zhu De had published an article in the *Liberation Daily* titled: "In Memory of the Party's Twenty-First Anniversary," advancing that the Party had become capable of making achievements in adapting Marxism to Chinese conditions to guide the Chinese revolution. He had written that the Party had accumulated extensive struggle experience, correctly understood the theory of Marxism-Leninism, and had successfully applied the basic tenets of Marxism-Leninism to the reality of the Chinese revolution. He had also written that the Party was under the lead of Comrade Mao Zedong who had a strong wisdom, knew well the theory of Marxism-Leninism and was capable of using the theory to steer the Chinese revolution towards victory.

Chen Yi had also written an article "The Greatest Twenty-One Years" to introduce how Chinese Communists led by Mao Zedong had creatively used the theory of Marxism-Leninism to solve problems in the Chinese revolution. He had evaluated Mao Zedong's ideas from five aspects: the nature of the Chinese society, the motive forces and prospects of the revolution, and revolutionary strategies and tactics; the revolutionary war; Soviet political power; Party building; and thought ways. He had written: "Mao Zedong has made impressive achievements in applying Marxism-Leninism to the Chinese conditions in a scientific manner and in integrating general theories of the world revolution with the practice in the Chinese revolution: thanks to his practice in the Autumn Harvest Uprising and guerilla operations in Hunan, Jiangxi, Guangdong and Fujian provinces and his investigations on Chinese society. A system of correct theories began to take shape."

In his article "Eliminate Menshevist Ideology Within the Party" written on July 4, 1943 to commemorate the twenty-second anniversary of the Party, Liu Shaoqi had said, "All cadres and all Party members should carefully study the experience gained by the Chinese Communist Party during these twenty-two years, carefully study and grasp Comrade Mao Zedong's theories on the Chinese revolution and other questions, arm themselves with the thought of Comrade Mao Zedong and use it to eradicate the Menshevist ideology in the Party."[1]

Wang Jiaxiang was the first in the Party to put forward the term Mao Zedong Thought and give a scientific definition on the Thought. In his article "The Road of the Communist Party of China and Chinese National Liberation" written on July 5, 1943 to commemorate the twenty-second anniversary of the Party, Wang Jiaxiang had put forward the term Mao Zedong Thought for the first time. He had written: "The only correct path for the Chinese national liberation—no matter in the past, at present or in the future—is the thought of Comrade Mao Zedong, viz.. the path Mao Zedong indicated in his works and practice. Mao Zedong Thought is Marxism-Leninism, Bolshevism and Communism in China. This correct path for the Chinese national liberation has come into being, has developed and become mature in the Party's struggles against domestic and foreign enemies and against erroneous ideological trends within the Party. The Chinese Communism represented by Mao Zedong Thought is formed on the basis of the theory of Marxism-Leninism after studying the realities in China and drawing on experiences from the Party's twenty-two years of difficulties and struggles both inside and outside the Party....It is a creative development of

---

[1] *Selected Works of Liu Shaoqi*, Eng. ed., FLP, Beijing, 1984, Vol. I, pp. 301-302.

Marxism-Leninism in China. It is Communism and Bolshevism in China."
He had also argued that Mao Zedong Thought was the result of integrating
Marxism-Leninism with the practice and experience of the Chinese
revolution and was a guarantee for the victory of the Chinese national
liberation and China's communism.

In a speech delivered on August 2, 1943, Zhou Enlai had also written:
"The twenty-two years of our Party's history have proved that the views of
Comrade Mao Zedong through the Party's entire history have developed
into a sinicized Marxist-Leninist line, that is, the communist line of China!"
"Comrade Mao Zedong's orientation is the orientation of the Chinese
Communist Party!" "Comrade Mao Zedong's line is the Bolshevik line in
China!"[1]

After Wang Jiaxiang, the term Mao Zedong Thought was gradually
accepted by more and more Party members. Many Party leaders began to
use the term and elaborate Mao Zedong Thought and defined it in Party
documents and in their speeches.

In his report on how to fight the enemy on November 10, 1943, Huang
Jing had said: "At present, our Party is built up on the basis of Mao Zedong
Thought, which is an integration of the theory of Marxism-Leninism with
China's practice."

In his speech in the meeting to mobilize cadres for rectification in the
Party School of the Northern Bureau on December 4, 1943, Deng Xiaoping
had not only used the term Mao Zedong Thought but had also definitely
pointed out that it should be used to guide the action of the Party and its
Central Committee. He had said, "Since the Zunyi Meeting of January 1935,
the Party, under the leadership of the Central Committee led by Comrade
Mao Zedong, has eradicated 'Left' and Right opportunism within the Party,
swept away subjectivism, sectarianism and stereotyped Party writing, and
placed the Party's cause entirely under the guidance of Marxism-Leninism
suited to Chinese conditions, that is, Mao Zedong Thought.... Indeed,
all the comrades, recalling the past bitter lessons under the leadership of

---

[1] *Selected Works of Zhou Enlai*, Eng. ed., FLP, Beijing, 1981, Vol. I, pp. 156-157.

opportunists, can see that they have been doing well over these years under the leadership of a Central Committee that has been guided by Mao Zedong Thought."[1] When giving a speech on December 18, the same year at the provincial assembly of organs directly under the general headquarters of the Eighteenth Group Army of the Northern Bureau, Deng Xiaoping had pointed out, "Just like the Party Central Committee has declared, the aim of rectification is to unite the entire Party under Mao Zedong Thought, which is China's Bolshevism, ideologically, politically and in action so that it can be able to fight better."

In December 18, 1943 Li Dazhang had published an article titled "An Investigation into Problems Put forward by the Comrades" in the fourth *Rectification Briefing* of the study committee for organs directly under the general headquarters of the Eighteenth Group Army of the Northern Bureau. He had held that Mao Zedong Thought was the thought of the Party. He said, "It became the thought of the Party not because Mao Zedong wanted so, but because it was recognized and supported by the entire Party and the people as a correct ideology suited to the Chinese conditions; and after the Party has launched the rectification movement to eradicate erroneous ideologies within the Party, more and more Party members have realized that Mao Zedong Thought is correct and have started to recognize it."

When reviewing achievements in carrying out ideological study and examining cadres' study efforts at the first department of the CPC Central Committee Party School on February 17, 1944, Peng Zhen, referring to the nature of the rectification movement, had put forward the idea that "Mao Zedong Thought is Marxism-Leninism suited to the Chinese conditions".

In his article "Study the Thought of Mao Zedong" in July 1944, Luo Ronghuan had written: "Mao Zedong has developed his thoughts by integrating the basic tenets of Marxism-Leninism with concrete realities in the Chinese revolution and inheriting China's history of revolution; thus Mao Zedong's thought should be used to guide the Party's action."

Xiao San had published the article "The Early Revolutionary Practices

---

[1] *Selected Works of Deng Xiaoping*, Eng. ed., FLP, Beijing, 1995, Vol. I, pp. 95-96.

of Comrade Mao Zedong" in the *Liberation Daily* on July 1, 1944. He had suggested that the term "Maoism" should be used to include all of Mao Zedong's thinking, thought ways, strategies, tactics and work styles related to Chinese revolution.

In his report on March 15, 1945, before the closing of the Seventh Plenary Session of the Sixth CPC Central Committee, Deng Xiaoping had urged every Party member to "study Marxism-Leninism and Mao Zedong Thought." That was the first time Mao Zedong Thought stood side by side with Marxism-Leninism, according to existing Party documents.

If I should conclude, the Party had pondered over the term "Mao Zedong Thought" for about four or five years before accepting it formally at the Party's Seventh Congress. Many Party leaders and theoreticians had elaborated it from different aspects and in different degrees. They have employed various terms such as "thought of Comrade Mao Zedong," "system of thinking of Comrade Mao Zedong," "Mao Zedong's thought" or "Chairman Mao's thought of Marxism-Leninism suited to the Chinese conditions". But generally the content was actually the same. For a long period of time after the term was accepted, both Mao Zedong Thought and thought of Comrade Mao Zedong was used alternatively.

3.1.2 The Position on Mao Zedong Thought at the Party's Seventh National Congress

The CPC had held it Seventh National Congress in Yan'an during April 23 to June 11, 1945. One of the significant achievements of the Congress was to give a complete summary of and systematic elaboration on the scientific definition of Mao Zedong Thought and establish it as the Party's guiding ideology. When discussing with other leaders on the report to be delivered to the Party's Seventh Congress at the Seventh Plenary Session of the Sixth CPC Central Committee on March 31, 1945, Liu Shaoqi had proposed that the General Principles are the prerequisite, starting point and important component of the Party Constitution and in order to improve unity among Party members, Mao Zedong Thought should be included in that part of the

Constitution. And the Party Constitution passed at the Congress read: "The Communist Party of China takes Mao Zedong Thought—the integration of the theory of Marxism-Leninism with the practice of the Chinese revolution—as the ideology guiding all its work." During the congress, Liu Shaoqi, in his Report on the Revision of the Party Constitution, had given a scientific definition and systematic elaboration on Mao Zedong Thought. He had said, "Mao Zedong Thought is the result of the integration of the theory of Marxism-Leninism with the practice of the Chinese revolution and is China's Communism and Marxism." "Mao Zedong Thought is the continued development of Marxism in the national democratic revolution in colonial, semi-colonial and semi-feudal China and is a perfect example of applying Marxism in China. It comes into being and develops in the revolutionary struggle of the Chinese nation and people. It is Marxism suited to the Chinese conditions." Mao Zedong Thought "is the Party's solely correct guiding ideology and solely correct general line," and "is a complete body of theories of the Chinese people for their revolution and national development." "These theories are to be found in Comrade Mao Zedong's writings and in many works of our Party literature. They include Comrade Mao Zedong's analysis of the present world situation and China's conditions and his theories and policies with regard to New Democracy, the emancipation of the peasantry, the revolutionary united front, revolutionary wars, revolutionary bases, the establishment of a new-democratic republic, Party building, culture, etc." This was a systematic and a scientific elaboration on the Thought.

3.1.3 The Position on Mao Zedong Thought at the Sixth Plenary Session of the Eleventh Central Committee

In the Resolution on Certain Questions in the History of Our Party Since the Founding of the People's Republic of China passed at the Sixth Plenary Session of its Eleventh Central Committee in June 1981, the Party gave Mao Zedong Thought a scientific definition from a historical viewpoint and with a higher level of understanding. The Resolution read: "The Chinese Communists, with Comrade Mao Zedong as their chief representative, made a theoretical synthesis of China's long experience in revolution to formulate a scientific guiding ideology that is in line with basic tenets of Marxism-Leninism and suitable for China's conditions, namely, Mao Zedong Thought." "Mao Zedong Thought is Marxism-Leninism applied and developed in China; it consists of a body of theoretical principles concerning the revolution and construction in China and a summary of experience therein, both of which have been proved correct in practice; and it represents the crystallized, collective wisdom of the Communist Party of China. Many outstanding leaders of our Party have made important contributions to its formation and development, and Mao Zedong's scientific works are its central manifestation." "Mao Zedong Thought is wide-ranging in content. It is an original theory which has enriched and developed Marxism-Leninism in the following respects: on the new-democratic revolution; on the socialist revolution and socialist construction; on the building of the revolutionary army and military strategy; on policy and tactics; on ideological and political work and cultural work; and on Party building." It also read: "The living soul of Mao Zedong Thought is the stand, viewpoint and method embodied in its component parts mentioned above. This stand, viewpoint and method boil down to three basic points: to seek truth from facts, the mass line, and independence." The Resolution also stressed, "Mao Zedong Thought is the valuable spiritual asset of our Party. It will be our guide to action for a long time to come. It is entirely wrong to try to negate the scientific value of Mao Zedong Thought and to deny its guiding role in our revolution and construction just because Comrade Mao Zedong made mistakes in his later years. And it is likewise entirely wrong to adopt a dogmatic attitude towards the sayings of Comrade Mao Zedong, to regard whatever he said as the immutable truth which should be mechanically applied everywhere, and to be unwilling to admit honestly that he made mistakes in his later years, and even try to stick to them in our new activities. Both these attitudes fail to make a distinction between Mao Zedong Thought—a scientific theory formed and tested over a long period of time—and the mistakes Comrade Mao Zedong made in his later years. And it is absolutely necessary that this distinction should be made. We should treasure all the positive experience obtained in the course of integrating the universal principles of Marxism-Leninism with the concrete practice of China's revolution and construction over fifty years or so, apply and carry forward this experience in our new work and enrich and develop Party theory with new principles and new conclusions corresponding to reality, so as to ensure the continued progress of our cause along the scientific course of Marxism-Leninism and Mao Zedong Thought."

3.2 Basic Features of Mao Zedong Thought

The Resolution on Certain Questions in the History of Our Party Since the Founding of the People's Republic of China passed at the Sixth Plenary Session of Eleventh Central Committee of the CPC had made an explicit elaboration on the basic features of Mao Zedong Thought. The Resolution had maintained that Mao Zedong Thought is Marxism-Leninism applied and developed in China; consists of a body of theoretical principles concerning the Chinese revolution and a summary of experience herein, both of which have been proved correct by practice; and represents the crystallized, collective wisdom of the Party. After this authoritative document, researchers have generally focused their studies on the above three points.

In his book *History of Development of Mao Zedong Thought* (Jilin People's Publishing House, 1990), Zheng Derong has expatiated on the basic features of Mao Zedong Thought from the following aspects:

Zheng Derong's Conclusions:

First, Mao Zedong Thought is Marxism-Leninism applied and developed in China. Based on the theory of Marxism-Leninism, it embodies the universal truth of Marxism-Leninism and is the result of applying and developing Marxism-Leninism in China. At the same time, it is not a simple application or development of Marxism-Leninism, but is developed Marxism-Leninism suited to Chinese conditions. It is the theoretical result achieved by the CPC, which, under the guidance of Marxism-Leninism, has analyzed the historical background of the Chinese democratic revolution and

China's social and class conditions, and correctly solved a set of fundamental problems of the Chinese revolution. It created the unique revolutionary road of encircling the cities from the countryside and seizing state power by armed forces; solved the problem of establishing a united front that included the bourgeoisie and the problem of carrying out armed struggle by relying on peasants; and found answers to the problem of Party building and to problems about the new-democratic revolution, which is a revolutionary road with Chinese characteristics. These theoretical principles and summary of experiences are Marxism-Leninism suited to Chinese conditions, belonging not only to China but also to Marxism-Leninism. It has greatly enriched and developed the theory of Marxism-Leninism and the worldview and methodology herein because it includes the unique stand, view and method of Chinese Communists.

Second, Mao Zedong Thought consists of a body of theoretical principles concerning the Chinese revolution and a summary of experience herein, both of which have been proved correct by practice. Mao Zedong Thought formed and developed on the basis of the practice in the Chinese revolution, which is its objective foundation and source of vitality. It is a scientific summary of the practice of the Chinese revolution in over half a century made by Chinese Communists who have raised their experience in the revolution to the level of theory. Without the concrete realities in China, without the rich experience the CPC has accumulated in leading the Chinese people in the revolutionary struggle, there would be no Mao Zedong Thought coming into being. Rooted and based on the Chinese revolution, it is the theory which was proved correct by the practice of the Chinese revolution. Marxism-Leninism is a powerful ideological weapon guiding the proletariat and oppressed nations around the world to fight for liberation. The Chinese revolution therefore could not achieve victory if not guided by Mao Zedong Thought, which is the result of integration of Marxism-Leninism with the practice of the Chinese revolution. It has been proved by history that the practice in China's revolution and construction will succeed and develop when it is under the guidance of Mao Zedong Thought and would fail and regress when divorced from the guidance of it. So, Mao Zedong Thought has been a powerful intellectual weapon leading the Chinese revolution into success. With the development and progress in Chinese revolution and construction and more experience accumulated, Mao Zedong Thought was enriched and developed as well. Marxism-Leninism has no end but continues to recognize and develop truth in practice. Therefore, we should never and ever take Marxism-Leninism or Mao Zedong Thought as dogmas under any conditions, but take them as a guide to action so that we can adhere to and develop Mao Zedong Thought under the new historical conditions.

Third, Mao Zedong Thought represents the crystallized, collective wisdom of the Party. This formulation focuses on how Mao Zedong as an individual and also how the entire Party had influenced the whole process of the formation and development of Mao Zedong Thought. Mao Zedong is the chief representative of Chinese Communists who created Mao Zedong Thought, which is the crystallization of the collective wisdom of the CPC.

Mao Zedong Thought absorbed the collective wisdom of the Party during its process of taking shape and developing. The rich and unique experience the CPC has accumulated during its long revolutionary struggle is the solid foundation for the formation and development of Mao Zedong Thought, which is a collection of theories developed on the basis of the great revolutionary practice of the CPC and the Chinese people. Although most of Mao Zedong's works were written by himself, they are a synthesis of experience of the CPC and the Chinese people in their practice in the revolutionary struggle, and represent the collective wisdom of the people and mark the victory of the CPC and the people in the revolution. Quite a number of Party leaders have also made great contributions to the formation and development of Mao Zedong Thought.

Mao Zedong's works are the central manifestation of Mao Zedong Thought; thus some of the works were documents or reports drawn up by Mao Zedong after discussion and approval of the Party Central Committee and related departments. Some were drawn up by related departments according to opinions of Mao Zedong and the Party Central Committee, were revised and approved by Mao Zedong. Others were written by Mao Zedong and other Party leaders, which were summed and reviewed by Mao Zedong. Still others were written by Mao Zedong after he absorbed the ideas and opinions of other Party leaders. Therefore, his many important works embody the collective wisdom of the entire Party. In addition, many works written by other brilliant Party leaders during their long revolutionary practice were also the result of the integration of the universal truth of Marxism with the Chinese revolution and are an important part of Mao Zedong Thought as well.

Mao Zedong had played an important and critical role in forming Mao Zedong Thought. As the chief representative of Party leaders, he led the Chinese revolution for as long as half a century and led New China in nearly thirty years. With his great insight and excellent leadership skills, he could always lead the Party and the people to victory at critical historical moments. He was the first to realize how necessary it was to integrate the universal truth of Marxism-Leninism with the practice of the Chinese revolution. To enable the CPC and the Chinese people to truly understand and master Marxism-Leninism, he had emphasized that Marxism-Leninism should be applied in line with China's concrete conditions. He wrote a large number of theoretical works during the long revolutionary struggle to lead the Chinese revolution and construction to victory. Consequently, it is just and practical to name Mao Zedong Thought under his name.

Fourth, Mao Zedong Thought should be separated from the mistakes Mao Zedong made in his later years. Mao Zedong was a great leader of the Party and the people of all ethnic groups in China and a great Marxist, proletarian revolutionary, strategist and theorist. He had made an indelible contribution to the founding and development of the CPC, to the launching and development of the people's War of Liberation, to the liberation of all ethnic groups in China, to the founding of the People's Republic of China, and to the development of China's socialist cause. He had also contributed greatly to the liberation of oppressed nations in the world and to human progress. Regretfully, he had made some mistakes in his later years. In particular, he had erroneously launched the "cultural revolution," which was a serious "Left" mistake that lasted a long period of time and produced severe consequences. However, Mao Zedong Thought and Mao Zedong's mistakes in his later years belong to different realms. Mao Zedong Thought is a body of theoretical principles concerning the Chinese revolution and a summary of experience herein, both of which have been proved correct by practice, and is the CPC's scientific guiding ideology. Therefore, Mao Zedong Thought does not include the mistakes he made in his later years. It would be a great failure to doubt the correctness of Mao Zedong Thought, or attempt to deny his great revolutionary practice or his glorious theoretical achievements or to deny the value of Mao Zedong Thought or its role in guiding China's revolution and construction. At the same time, we should also not understand his words and writings as dogmas, take his words as unquestionable truth to parrot every word he said, deny the mistakes he made in his later years or even copy these mistakes in practice.

Peng Chengfu's Ideas:

In his book *New Opinions on Mao Zedong Thought* (Xidian University Press, 1991), Peng Chengfu has explained the basic features of Mao Zedong Thought as follows.

First, Mao Zedong Thought is Marxism applied in China. The process, in which Mao Zedong Thought took shape, developed, got enriched and progressed, is the course of integrating the universal tenets of Marxism with the concrete realities in China's revolution and the course of applying Marxism in China. So, Mao Zedong Thought and Marxism cannot not be separated from each other, and it would not be correct to emphasize one of them while neglecting the other.

Second, Mao Zedong Thought is not the thought of Mao Zedong himself, but the crystallization of the collective wisdom of the CPC. Many brilliant Party leaders have made great contributions to its formation and development, it was named under Mao Zedong's name because he was the epitome of summarizing the experience in China's revolution and construction and has made the most part of the contribution to its formation and development. Although a certain number of brilliant Party leaders including Mao Zedong have made the most important contribution to its formation and development, it is neither the thought of Mao Zedong nor the thought of other brilliant leaders, but the thought of the entire Party. In understanding and studying Mao Zedong Thought, we should take it as the crystallized, collective wisdom of the entire Party and correctly handle the relationships between Mao Zedong, the outstanding Party members and the entire Party.

Third, Mao Zedong Thought is a summary of the correct practice in the Chinese revolution and construction. A prerequisite for adhering to and developing Mao Zedong Thought is to clearly separate it from the mistakes Mao Zedong made in his later years. Taking practice as the sole criterion for testing truth, the CPC, at the Sixth Plenary Session of its Eleventh Central Committee, has thoroughly examined and analyzed the theory and practice of Mao Zedong and the Central Committee with him at the core. At the Session, the proven theory, which is the result of the integration of Marxism with the Chinese realities, was called "Mao Zedong Thought," while the mistakes Mao Zedong made during the "cultural revolution" were called "Mao Zedong's mistakes in his later years." The idea of "taking class struggle as the key link" and the doctrine of "continuing revolution under the dictatorship of the proletariat" were judged as erroneous ideas, and were therefore excluded from Mao Zedong Thought. So, when we study Mao Zedong Thought, what we are to study is the theory that has been proved correct by practice in China's revolution and construction, excluding Mao's erroneous theories in his later years.

Other Articles:

In their co-article "On the Scientific Definition of Mao Zedong Thought" published in *Materials for Marxism Study* (No. 11), Zhu Chongru, Wang Guorong and Cheng Jiyao have argued that "the Resolution on Certain Questions in the History of Our Party Since the Founding of the People's Republic of China, in addition to giving Mao Zedong Thought a complete scientific definition, has outlined its three major features."

The three authors have suggested that there are three inseparable factors concerning the features of Mao Zedong Thought. One, "the result of the integration of the basic tenets of Marxism-Leninism with the practice of the Chinese revolution" which explains the theoretical source and objective conditions for its formation and development. Two, "the crystallized, collective wisdom of the entire Party" which explains that it is not a creation of Mao Zedong himself but a summary of experience of Chinese Communists represented by him in their long revolutionary struggle. Three, "central manifestation" which explains that works Mao Zedong had written during his hard theoretical exploration are the central manifestation of Mao Zedong Thought.

These researchers have raised an interesting question: "There is no doubt that Mao Zedong Thought is the result of the integration of the universal tenets of Marxism-Leninism with the practice in the Chinese revolution. But, do all the thoughts, theories and principles that are results of integrating the theory of Marxism-Leninism with the Chinese revolution belong to Mao Zedong Thought? We cannot think it that way. Around those years when the CPC was founded, many Chinese Communists and outstanding Party leaders had begun to explore the laws governing China's revolution, hoping to integrate the theory of Marxism-Leninism with the Chinese revolution. But, it was Mao Zedong who had actually integrated the theory of Marxism-Leninism with the Chinese revolution. For that reason, the system of theories about the Chinese revolution established by him was accepted by the CPC as its guiding ideology at its Seventh Congress. So, not all results of 'integration' made by other Party leaders during the process of the Chinese revolution could be called Mao Zedong Thought."

How to correctly and exactly understand that Mao Zedong Thought is the crystallization of the collective wisdom of the entire Party and that other outstanding Party leaders have also made great contributions to it? The three authors have argued that during the process of its formation and development, many Party leaders had also made careful theoretical explorations and produced some correct theories by integrating Marxism-

Leninism with the Chinese revolution. However, it was Mao Zedong who reviewed the hard struggle of the CPC and the Chinese people, absorbed correct theories of other Party leaders, and established a system of correct theories about China's new-democratic revolution and socialist revolution. So, "the collective wisdom of the Party" is the source Mao Zedong Thought, and term "crystallization" represents the efforts made by Mao Zedong to process theories of the Party and include them in his theoretical works. He has crystallized the Party's "collective wisdom," which was not simply a collection work, but he had organically integrated them to form a system. The theoretical contributions by other outstanding Party leaders made to the Chinese revolution were reflected in their contributions to Mao Zedong Thought. Their correct experience, theories, opinions and thoughts have all been absorbed by Mao Zedong and reflected in his works. In addition, they have carried out revolutionary practice and theoretical exploration in those fields under their charge. They have developed ideas and theories of their own during the process of revolutionary struggle of the Party and the people and have expressed them in their words and works.

If, Mao Zedong Thought embodies only to the correct theories and works, how should we treat Mao Zedong's other works and words and consider their relation with Mao Zedong Thought? Undoubtedly, the CPC had accepted that Mao Zedong Thought was closely related with all his works and words and his life when it established the Thought as its guiding ideology in 1945. At that time, there were no erroneous ideas of Mao Zedong which the Party should deem necessary to separate from Mao Zedong Thought. But, as the "cultural revolution" was ended, the CPC was confronted with the problem to decide how to treat the mistakes Mao Zedong made in his later years. It has solved the problem by making a resolution at the Sixth Plenary Session of its Eleventh Central Committee. It has separated the mistakes Mao Zedong made in his later years from the Thought, which should be a system of correct theories, and urged all its members to continue holding high the banner of Mao Zedong Thought. This solution accords with Marxism and is a continuation of Lenin's definition on Marxism and Stalin's definition on

Leninism. The resolution of the party has given Mao Zedong Thought a clear and complete definition, which was very important for clearing up confusion in thinking and for continuing to adhere to and develop Mao Zedong Thought. In conclusion, Mao Zedong Thought as the guiding ideology of the CPC refers to the correct theories in his works, while Mao Zedong's thoughts include all his works and practice and comments.

There have been also researchers who have questioned and disagree with the exposition of the scientific definition and basic features of Mao Zedong Thought in the Resolution on Certain Questions in the History of Our Party Since the Founding of the People's Republic of China. The paper "Reflections on the Definition of Mao Zedong Thought" published in *Research of Mao Zedong Thought* (No. 2) in 1989 has read: "The idea that Mao Zedong Thought does not include his mistakes but refers only to the theoretical principles and summary of experience that have been proved correct by the Chinese revolution and construction not only has theoretical shortcomings but also does not accord with the realities of Mao Zedong Thought. And the idea that Mao Zedong Thought does not embody the thoughts of Mao Zedong himself but the collective thought of Chinese Communists represented by Mao Zedong also needs further investigation." But, their conclusion was not logically supported with solid arguments.

In conclusion, Mao Zedong Thought has theoretical sources and objective foundations that are greatly different from other theoretical systems because it is the product of the integration of Marxism-Leninism with the concrete realities in the Chinese revolution as well as a summary of experiences of some outstanding Party leaders in the Chinese revolution. Mao Zedong's works were the central manifestation of that process of integration and summarization. We cannot consider Mao Zedong Thought in isolation from Mao Zedong personally and his unique contribution and works or without recognizing its correctness as a guiding ideology and a theoretical system.

3.3 The Structure of Mao Zedong Thought

In 1945, Liu Shaoqi, in the Report on the Revision of the Party Constitution at the CPC's Seventh Congress, had made a summary of Mao Zedong Thought from nine aspects: his analysis of the present world situation and China's conditions and his theories and policies with regard to New Democracy, the emancipation of the peasantry, the revolutionary united front, revolutionary wars, revolutionary bases, the establishment of a new-democratic republic, Party building, and culture. That was the first time for the CPC to expound on the components and structure of Mao Zedong Thought.

The Resolution on Certain Questions in the History of Our Party Since the Founding of the People's Republic of China passed at the Sixth Plenary Session of the Eleventh CPC Central Committee in June 1981 had summarized how Mao Zedong Thought had creatively developed Marxism-Leninism in six aspects: the new-democratic revolution; the socialist revolution and socialist construction; the building of the revolutionary army and military strategy; policy and tactics; ideological and political work and cultural work; and Party building. The Resolution had also declared that the living soul of Mao Zedong Thought has three basic points—seeking truth from facts, the mass line, and self-reliance. The Resolution's summarization and elaboration on the scientific system of Mao Zedong Thought has been widely recognized by researchers and scholars, which is often referred to when arguing on the composition of Mao Zedong Thought in their writings.

However, as China's reform and opening up and the socialist modernization had progressed and the theory of building socialism with Chinese characteristics has come into being, some researchers have questioned the Resolution's summarization on the contents of Mao Zedong Thought. They have argued that the six aspects and the three basic points for its living soul do not include all its contents. Some of them have argued that the complete system of Mao Zedong Thought could be studied from a macro point of view by dividing its basic content into three groups (or levels): experience, concrete theories, and worldview and methodology. They have proposed that the experiences from practice in China's revolution and construction, political and military struggles and economic and cultural development, belong to the first group, theories about the new-democratic revolution and the socialist construction, belong to the second group, and the philosophical and methodological issues belong to the third group.

Whether the theory of building socialism with Chinese characteristics is a component of Mao Zedong Thought or not was once a hot topic of argument among researchers. Quite a number of researchers suggest that the theory should be an important part of Mao Zedong Thought in line with the principles of the statement made by the CPC at the Fifth Plenary Session of its Thirteenth Central Committee in 1992. The statement read: "The series of ideas and theories advanced by Comrade Deng Xiaoping in line with the principle of integrating Marxism-Leninism with the Chinese realities are an important part of Mao Zedong Thought and its continuation and development under the new historical conditions, and are a treasure trove of intellectual wealth for the Party and the Chinese people." However, after the CPC had given a more systematic elaboration on this theory at its Fourteenth Congress and formulated Deng Xiaoping Theory at its Fifteenth Congress in 1997, researchers and scholars have started to generally agree that Mao Zedong Thought does not include the theory of Building Socialism with Chinese characteristics, which instead is a component of Deng Xiaoping Theory.

In the following paragraphs I will only introduce some basic theories of Mao Zedong Thought roughly; and in the later chapters I will expatiate on its every aspect more comprehensively.

3.3.1 Theory of the New-Democratic Revolution

Researchers have concluded several different opinions on this theory.

The first opinion suggests that Mao Zedong's theory of New Democracy had described the new-democratic revolution, in the era of imperialism and proletarian revolution, for the working class, the peasantry, the urban petty bourgeoisie and the national bourgeoisie opposing imperialism, feudalism and bureaucrat-capitalism under the leadership of the proletariat to establish a democratic coalition government, which to be led by the proletariat and participated by democratic classes; had introduced a two-step strategy for reaching socialism via the new-democratic revolution; formulated a set of corresponding political, economic and cultural programs; set out along the revolutionary road of encircling the cities from the countryside and seizing state power by armed forces; and had defined the three inseparable talismans for the Chinese revolution—the united front, armed struggle (a peoples' army) and Party building. This opinion is a correct summary of the CPC's theories and practice during the new-democratic revolution.

The second opinion offers a more conventional idea. It argues that China's new-democratic revolution took place in the new era when the Russian October Revolution had succeeded and the proletariat in China had awakened; was led by the proletariat and attended mainly by the working class and the peasantry and other social classes; and had opposed imperialism, feudalism and bureaucrat-capitalism; and aimed to establish a democratic coalition government, which is led by the proletariat and participated by democratic classes. This opinion describes the era, leadership, motive forces, targets and the tasks of the revolution.

The third opinion holds that the Chinese revolution contains four basic issues—its leadership, targets, motive forces and tasks.

The fourth opinion holds that the fundamental ideas of the general line for the new-democratic revolution were about the leadership, motive forces and targets.

3.3.2 Theory of the Socialist Revolution and Construction

Researchers have basically agreement on that the policies introduced by Mao Zedong and other Chinese Communists in line with the economic and political conditions for transition to socialism after victory in the new-democratic revolution—such as the principle of attaching equal importance to socialist industrialization and socialist transformation, and the policy of gradually transforming the private ownership of the means of production—

had solved the many thorny problems concerning establishment of a socialist system in China. After the socialist system was established in China, Mao Zedong had advanced the strategic idea of mobilizing all positive factors and uniting the people of all ethnic groups in China to build a strong socialist country, and had pointed out that the country was confronted with two types of social contradictions—those between ourselves and the enemy and those among the people—which were totally different in nature thus should be differentiated and dealt with correctly.

On this basis, researchers have generally focused on the following four issues:

The first is about contradictions in socialist society. Because Mao Zedong had made some mistakes in his later years, researchers have attached much attention to the study of the basic contradictions, principle problem and the two types of contradictions different in nature in socialist society and the motive forces for socialist development.

The second is about China's path of industrialization. Researchers have generally recognized Mao Zedong's theoretical contributions in this area and made a detailed narration on his line of thought and ideas, such as learning lessons from the Soviet Union, not blindly imitating other country's models, proceeding from China's realities, and correctly dealing with the relationship between heavy industry on the one hand and light industry and agriculture on the other.

The third is about properly handling all kinds of relationships comprehensively in socialist construction and maintaining overall balance. Researchers have expounded Mao Zedong's relevant ideas in his essay "On the Ten Major Relationships" and his speeches to explain the importance of these ideas and the process in which Mao Zedong had developed them.

The fourth is about the relationship between Mao Zedong's mistakes in his later years and the limitations in his theories of socialist construction.

3.3.3 Theory of Building the Revolutionary Army and Military Strategy

It is generally believed that Mao Zedong had made great contributions in this regard as follows. One, he had scientifically analyzed the features and laws of China's revolutionary war in line with realities in China. Two, he had put forward a set of systematic, fundamental principles for building a new army of the people. He had advanced the principle that the army should obey the leadership of the Party and take serving the people wholeheartedly as its fundamental purpose. "Our principle is that the Party commands the gun, and the gun should never be allowed to command the Party." Three, he had developed the idea of launching a people's war and created a complete set of strategies and tactics for the people's war by relying on the people's army, mobilizing the broad masses of the people and building rural base areas. Four, after the founding of New China, he had advanced that in addition to a powerful army, China also needs to build a powerful air force and a powerful navy, and develop other technical arms and modern national defense technologies.

The study on his thinking on building a people's army focuses on the following aspects. The first is about the nature of the people's army. Researchers have argued over two issues: what principles should be followed concerning its nature; and if the nature has changed or not under the new conditions after the CPC had seized power.

The second is about the purpose of the people's army. To serve the people wholeheartedly has always been its fundamental purpose. But, some researchers argue that this purpose could be developed somewhat under the new historical conditions.

The third is about functions of the people's army. The most argued issue is that if the people's army is still both a fighting force and a working force under the new historical conditions.

The fourth is about internal regulations of the people's army. There are three different opinions in this regard. The first is to give the highest attention to ideological and political work in the army. The second is to run the army with strict discipline. The third is to build the army in a democratic manner on the basis of self-discipline.

The fifth is about the target for building a people's army. Most researchers believe that the ultimate target is to build a strong army that is modern, standardized and revolutionary; others believe that the basic target is to build a "world-type" army.

There are two several hot topics in the study of Mao Zedong's thinking on strategies and tactics for the people's revolutionary war. The first is about its content, which is summarized in the book *Excerpts from Chairman Mao's Exposition of the People's Army and the People's War and Strategies and Tactics* which were published in twelve volumes, such as "taking an objective and all-sided view in studying the law of a war," "the characteristics of China's revolutionary war determine the line for guiding China's revolutionary war as well as many of its strategic and tactical principles," "advocating active defense and opposing passive defense," "concentrating a superior force and destroying the enemy forces one by one," and "to fight decisively win-able engagements and avoid non-win-able ones."

The second is about if Mao Zedong's strategic and tactical principles for the people's revolutionary war; are they capable of guiding the people's army to win in the future warfare, namely how to appraise their effectiveness under modern conditions of warfare.

3.3.4 Theory of Policies and Tactics

It is commonly believed that theories in this area include mainly four aspects. The first is about how to distinguish who are friends and who are enemies by employing the Marxist method of class analysis.

The second is about the idea that the revolutionary force, although weak in the beginning, can grow strong enough to defeat the reactionary forces with changes in both subjective and objective conditions, and about the necessity of despising the enemy strategically and taking full account of it tactically, and about the principle of focusing on the main target of the struggle and preventing from directing blows to all directions.

The third is about the strategy of dealing different enemies with different ways and splitting them; the policy of making use of contradictions, winning over the many, opposing the few and crushing our enemies one by one; coordinating between legal and illegal struggle in enemy-occupied areas and the practice of organizing well-selected cadres to work underground; the policy of offering members of the reactionary classes and reactionaries that had been overthrown a way out; and the principle of realizing unity through struggle and seeking independence and initiative within the united front.

The fourth is about the leadership of the proletariat in the revolutionary united front and the relationship between those who lead and those who are led.

3.3.5 Ideological and Political Work and Cultural Work

When studying the theory about the ideological and political work, researchers focus on the idea that the ideological and political work is the life-blood of the economic and other works. They have investigated Mao Zedong's "Talks at the Yan'an Forum on Literature and Art" when discussing his theories about the cultural work. They believe that Mao Zedong had creatively advanced the principle for the cultural work and emphasized the need to develop a new culture in China, which should be a national, scientific and popular culture guided by the Communism.

3.3.6 Theory of Building a Proletarian Party

Researchers have a high opinions on Mao Zedong's thoughts on Party building, and suggest that he had three major achievements in this aspect. One, he had emphasized the necessity of building the Party first ideologically and created a good way of educating all Party members in Marxism-Leninism through the rectification movements. Two, he had cultivated some fine traditions and work styles for the Party—the work styles of integrating theory with practice, forging close ties with the masses and practicing criticism and self-criticism. Three, he had advanced the idea of building the Party as a party in power after the victory of the revolution. He had called all the

Party members to resist the corrosive influence of capitalist ideas, oppose the bureaucratic practice of divorcing from the masses, and carry on the tradition of being modest and prudent and working hard while avoiding arrogance and rashness and impetuosity.

In recent years, Mao Zedong's thoughts on Party building have become increasingly popular among researchers and scholars. I can summarize the developments and research results as follows:

First, they have given a more accurate and comprehensive outline of the content in Mao Zedong's theory of Party building: strengthening the Party ideologically; strengthening the Party in line with its political line; stimulating the whole Party's enthusiasm through democratic-centralism; development of Party cadres and on lines and policies regarding cadres; improvement of the Party's work style; and principles and methods for inner-Party struggles.

Second, they have developed a better understanding on the symbol that marks the initial formation and development of Mao Zedong's theory of Party building. They generally believe that these theories began to take shape during the period of the War of the Agrarian Revolution because, then Mao Zedong had started to creatively integrate the Marxist-Leninist doctrine of Party building with the practice of the CPC during that period, and the symbol should be the resolution issued at Gutian Meeting in 1929.

Third, they have started to discuss stages in the development of Mao Zedong's theory of Party building. They have included the period of the democratic revolution as well as the period of the socialist construction when the Party was in power. Although there are some researchers who insist that Mao Zedong's theory of Party building is a unified whole and therefore should not be divided into stages, most researchers do believe that these theories should be divided into above two stages; because the Party's theories in leading the revolution were very different from its theories in leading the construction, and some of Mao's theories about Party building after 1949 apply only to a party in power.

Fourth, they have investigated the major feature of Mao Zedong's theory of Party building. Some believe that the major feature is the principle of "strengthening the Party ideologically," while others believe that it is a combination of the two as "strengthening the Party in line with its political line" and "giving top priority to ideological matters in Party building."

Fifth, they have made some progress in understanding the main content of Mao Zedong's theory of building the Party as a ruling party. They are some disagreements on this issue. In their book *History of Mao Zedong Thought*, Zheng Derong and other authors have asserted that Mao Zedong's theory of building the Party as a ruling party includes a five-aspect content: the socialist revolution and construction should be under the leadership of the CPC; carry on the fine traditions of persevering plain living and hard struggle and maintaining close ties with the masses, and combat subjectivism, sectarianism and bureaucracy; third, a party in power should be strict with its members and cadres; fourth, improve the party's democratic-centralism and develop intra-Party democracy; and lastly, rectification movement is an important way to strengthen the Party. Another book titled *Collection of the Party's Doctrines* believes that this Theory includes a six-aspect content: give top priority to ideological and education work and transformation of worldview; party building should be subordinate to and serve the central task of socialist economic development; the system of democratic-centralism should be improved; train a large number of socialist cadres; fifth, without good relations between the party and the masses, the socialist system cannot be established; and lastly, correct criticism and self-criticism are the motive force for pushing the Party forward.

Sixth, researchers have made remarkable progress on the theory of democratic-centralism. They generally agree that Mao Zedong has three important theories about democratic-centralism: democratic-centralism is a dialectical unity of democracy and centralism and is centralism on the basis of democracy and democracy under centralized guidance; the implementation of democratic centralism is a process of implementing the mass line of "from the masses, to the masses;" and the way to implement democratic-centralism within the Party is to stimulate the whole Party's enthusiasm through it.

References

Annotations to Resolution on Certain Questions in the History of Our Party Since the Founding of the People's Republic of China, People's Publishing House, Beijing, 1983.

Zheng Derong et al., *History of Development of Mao Zedong Thought,* Jilin People's Publishing House, Changchun, 1990.

Peng Chengfu et al., *New Opinions on Mao Zedong Thought,* Xidian University Press, Xi'an, 1991.

Zhang Jingru et al., "Several Problems in the Study of History of Development of Mao Zedong Thought," *Study of the History of the Communist Party of China,* 1988 (2).

Chapter 4

The Theory of New Democracy (First Part)

The theory of New Democracy is the most fundamental component of the theoretical system of Mao Zedong Thought. From a macro point of view, it consists of two major parts—the theory of the new-democratic revolution and the theory of a new-democratic society. From a micro point of view, it represents the theory, line, principle and policy advanced by Chinese Communists led by Mao Zedong to deal with problems in the Chinese revolution and society during the period of New Democracy and their experience in addressing these problems.

4.1 Theory of the New-Democratic Revolution

The theory of the new-democratic revolution includes theories about the general line, its path and three talismans for the new-democratic revolution in the broad sense, but in the narrow sense, it only includes the revolution's general line and its path. Researchers have long understood it in the narrow sense, even sometimes excluding theories about the revolutionary path from it. In fact, that understanding is too narrow. It is more reasonable and logical to understand and master it in the broad sense.

4.1.1 Introduction to Studies before the 1990s

Researchers have made visible progress in their studies on the theory of the new-democratic revolution both in width and in depth after the Third Plenary Session of the Eleventh CPC Central Committee. They have reached similarities on some issues, such as the targets, motive forces, goals and prospect of the revolution. However, they have also dissimilarities on the basic content of the theory, when it was formed and what marks its formation, and on some other issues such as the two-step strategy for the Chinese revolution.

4.1.1.1 Debates on the Formation, the Marks of Formation and on Its Content

Historically, there were different opinions on the time and symbol of the formation of the basic thinking on the new-democratic revolution. One opinion had argued that it was formed in 1925 when the CPC held its Fourth National Congress and another opinion held that it was formed in December 1925, when Mao Zedong had published his "Analysis of the Classes in Chinese Society". These arguments were prevalent before the "cultural revolution."

But, after the "cultural revolution," researchers have developed some new opinions. Some have argued that the core content of the basic thinking on the new-democratic revolution is the theory about the new-democratic political power, the formation of which is marked by a common consensus reached throughout the entire Party. Although Mao Zedong had put forward an initial theory about political power in his "Analysis of the Classes in Chinese Society" that theory had not been recognized by the entire Party. On the contrary, Chen Duxiu's idea of "second revolution" was the dominant ideology in the Party at that time. It was in the spring of 1927 when the CPC Central Committee's Political Bureau had passed the document "Explanations to 'The Resolution on the Chinese Question of the Seventh Enlarged Plenum of the Executive Committee of the Communist International'" to criticize the erroneous idea of "second revolution" and its harms and had given a comparatively complete elaboration on the theory about the new-democratic political power, that the entire Party got a clear understanding of the problems concerning democratic political power. Therefore, the basic thinking on the new-democratic revolution had taken shape in the spring of 1927.

Other researchers have argued that the basic thinking on the new-democratic revolution began to take shape when the CPC had formally raised the issue of encircling the cities from the countryside and seizing state power by armed force. Although Chinese Communists represented by Mao Zedong had made some contributions to its formation starting from the early 1925 to 1926, they had not grasped the issue of encircling the cities from the countryside and seizing state power by armed force. It was at an enlarged meeting of the CPC Central Committee's Political Bureau on July 4, 1927 that Mao Zedong in his speech had mentioned the idea of establishing independent regimes of the workers and the peasants by armed forces, which had laid an ideological foundation for the establishment of revolutionary bases in the Jinggang Mountains. Therefore, Mao Zedong's speech in July 1927 marks the formation of the basic thinking on the new-democratic revolution.

Obviously, the difference between the above two opinions lies in the criterion for judging the formation of the basic thinking. So, what criterion is more reasonable? To answer that question, I think another opinion needs to be introduced. According to this opinion, a solution to the issue of proletarian leadership should be the major criterion for affirming that the basic thinking on the new-democratic revolution had taken shape because proletarian leadership is the key to victory in the Chinese revolution, and the key what differentiates the new-democratic revolution from the old type democratic revolution, and is core content of the theory of the new-democratic revolution. Without a clear understanding on this problem, the CPC could not solve any other problems.[1] This opinion is based on a thorough and

---

[1] Zheng Derong and Dong Shiming, "A Review of Study on Mao Zedong's Theory of the New-Democratic Revolution," see Shi Zhongquan (ed.), *A Review of Study on Mao Zedong*, the Central Party Literature Press, Beijing, 1992. pp. 177-181.

complete understanding of the theory of the new-democratic revolution, and therefore has more advantages.

However, the argument is still not solved because researchers cannot not agree on when the theory of proletarian leadership was formed and what marks its formation. Before, it was generally believed that the CPC's Fourth National Congress marks its formation because the CPC had not only raised the issue of proletarian leadership at that Congress but had also formulated a set of policies on how the proletariat could achieve and establish its leadership and lead the revolution. But, some other researchers have argued that the theory was formed when Mao Zedong had published his essay "Analysis of the Classes in Chinese Society," which was later than the CPC's Fourth Congress, because the essay had given a scientific and all-round analysis of the classes in Chinese society and integrated the idea of proletarian leadership with the future of the revolution. Still other researchers suggest that the formation of the theory was still later than that because the CPC had not truly solved the issue of proletarian leadership although it had raised the issue at its Fourth Congress and had a better understanding on the issue after that Congress. After all, raising an issue is different from solving it. The issue was truly solved when the CPC had formed its theory of encircling the cities from the countryside and seizing state power by armed force—the key to solving the issue was to solve problems of armed struggle and the peasantry issue. Only after commanding revolutionary armed forces and leading the peasantry in launching the Agrarian Revolution, could the proletariat achieve victory in the Chinese revolution. Therefore, it was after the CPC had developed the revolutionary road (path) of encircling the cities from the countryside and formulated relevant theories; then the issue of proletarian leadership was truly solved. That is to say, the basic thinking on the new-democratic revolution was formed around 1930 when the theory of encircling the cities from the countryside had taken shape. This opinion seems more convincing than those above.

However, there is still room for discussion about when the issue of proletarian leadership was truly solved. It was not until the period of the

War of Resistance against Japan that Chinese Communists represented by Mao Zedong had fully understood the Chinese bourgeoisie and formulated a full set of policies and principles regarding this class. Without a clear understanding of the Chinese bourgeoisie, the proletariat could not find answers to the question of "whom should the proletariat lead" and "how to lead." In fact, it was also during the period of the War of Resistance against Japan that the idea of New Democracy was formulated. Therefore, it is more reliable and practical to believe that it took a long historical process for the theory of the new-democratic revolution to form. The CPC had formed the basic ideas of the new-democratic revolution during its exploration into problems about the Chinese revolution; throughout fourth national congresses, and Mao Zedong's "Analysis of the Classes in Chinese Society" and other essays had reviewed and developed these ideas, which was constantly enriched thereafter and lastly developed into a complete system of theories about the new-democratic revolution during the period of the War of Resistance against Japan.

The major reason researchers dispute on when the theory of the new-democratic revolution was formed is that their understanding on the content of the theory is different. Some conventionally believe that the five basic points—the era, leadership, motive forces, targets and prospect—constitute the basic thinking on the new-democratic revolution. And others believe that; what constitutes the basic thinking on the new-democratic revolution is the general line for the revolution, which includes leadership, motive forces and targets. In fact, these above two conventional opinions, still held by some researchers at present, are taken from Mao Zedong's essay "On New Democracy."

Researchers have advanced some new opinions after the 1980s. They have argued that the theory of the revolutionary road of encircling the cities from the countryside and seizing state power by armed force are also one of the contents of the basic thinking of the new-democratic revolution because the revolutionary road is of critical importance for the victory of the revolution. According to the realities in China at that time, the peasantry was the main force in the Chinese revolution, and their Agrarian Revolution was a basic part of the new-democratic revolution. If the road of encircling the cities from the countryside was not decided, the proletariat would have been unable to mobilize and organize the peasantry to launch the Agrarian Revolution and eliminate imperialism and feudalism and could have found no way to lead the revolution into a complete success. In some sense, the new-democratic revolution is a unique revolutionary path chosen by the Chinese revolution. Consequently, the theory of the new-democratic revolution is incomplete if it does not include the theory of the revolutionary road of encircling the cities from the countryside and seizing state power by armed force. At present, researchers generally agree that the theory of the new-democratic revolution is the core content of Mao Zedong Thought, and the theory of the revolutionary road of encircling the cities from the countryside marks the formation of Mao Zedong Thought. Therefore, it is unreasonable to exclude the theory of the revolutionary road of encircling the cities from the countryside, which marks the formation of Mao Zedong Thought, from the basic thinking on the new-democratic revolution. In addition, according to the internal logic of the theory of the new-democratic revolution, the theory of the three talismans in the new-democratic revolution should also be a part of it. For this reason, I can say that researchers have increasingly started to grasp it in the broad sense.

4.1.1.2 On the Two-Step Strategy for the Chinese Revolution

There are different views on this issue. One view believes that the two-step strategy had first appeared in the work titled "Program for Youth Movement in China" published in the organ of the Socialist Youth League of China on April 1, 1922. The paper read: "In order achieve success in our cause, the toiling masses need to struggle in two steps—the first is to overturn feudalism and make China a really independent country, and the second is to overthrow the bourgeois' political power and seize state power." Another view believes that the "Opinions on the Current Situation" promulgated by the CPC on June 15, 1922 had advanced the idea that the

Chinese revolution would develop in two steps—the democratic revolution and the socialist revolution. However, the above two views had not produced any big influence. Most researchers commonly believe that the two-step strategy for the Chinese revolution was formally advanced by the CPC at its Second Congress in 1922, during which the Party had defined its minimum program and maximum program. But, this opinion also had its limitations, which had been pointed out by some researchers in the 1980s. For instance, some researchers have pointed out that the CPC had not formed its two-step strategy at its Second Congress because it had neither defined the critical importance of proletarian leadership nor understood well the dialectical relationship between the new-democratic revolution and socialist revolution at that time. Although its minimum and maximum programs indeed had set a good starting point and laid a good foundation for the formation of the strategy, it was not until the period of the War of Resistance against Japan that the CPC had scientifically and completely put forward this strategy.

To reach a sound conclusion on when the two-step strategy was formed, we should first understand the contents it includes. In fact, it should include not only elaborations on the two revolutionary stages different in nature—the new-democratic revolution and the socialist revolution, and on their relationships—that the former is the basis for the latter, the latter is an inexorable development of the former and their ultimate goal is socialism and communism; but also statement that both of them should be under the leadership of the proletariat and proletarian Party, which indicates that proletarian leadership is also the important content of the two-step strategy. Therefore, the formation of the two-step strategy had also taken a long historical process—the CPC's Second and Fourth Congresses were landmarks in its development and Mao Zedong's "On New Democracy" and other essays in the middle period of the War of Resistance against Japan had given it a systematic expatiation.

4.1.2 The Studies after the 1990s

The studies on the theory of the new-democratic revolution have reached a new level after the 1990s. More researchers have started to understand and study the theory from a macro point of view, and discussed, analyzed and argued over some relevant opinions in China and foreign countries. In particular, they have conducted in-depth analysis and research on some basic issues as well as some definitions and conclusions that had been long used and accepted but need further discussion. For instance, Sha Jiansun in his book *Introduction to the Chinese New-Democratic Revolution* (Shandong People's Publishing House, 1993) has answered some key questions such as why the revolution fighting against imperialism and feudalism had embodied the character of bourgeois democracy, why the CPC as a proletarian Party had launched the bourgeois democratic revolution, and what role the proletariat had played in the democratic revolution.

4.1.2.1 Many researchers focus their study on how the theory of the new-democratic revolution has carried forward and developed Marxism-Leninism and the place of this theory in the theoretical system of Mao Zedong Thought.

It is generally believed that the theory had broadened the conventional assertion of Marx and Lenin that there are only two kinds of country—proletarian country and bourgeois country, and two kinds of revolution—proletarian revolution and bourgeois revolution by advancing the new idea and doctrine of new-democratic revolution and new-democratic country. The theory had answered the question of how to develop communism and establish socialist system in semi-colonial and semi-feudal China, built a bridge for transition from a semi-colonial and semi-feudal society to a socialist society, and solved the problem of the revolutionary road with Chinese characteristics. It had greatly carried forward and developed Marxism-Leninism-and upheld and developed Marx's principles of proletarian leadership in democratic revolution, violent revolution, class analysis and the dictatorship of the proletariat and Lenin's theory of the transition from capitalism to socialism.

Researchers argue little about the place of the theory of new-democratic revolution in Mao Zedong Thought. They unanimously believe that every ideological system contains a number of theories, one of which is the core one. A theory should meet two requirements to become the core of an ideological system. First, it should be a theoretical system itself. Second, it should be the basis of other theories, or it should trigger the development of other theories. The theory of the new-democratic revolution meets the two requirements and is therefore the core of Mao Zedong Thought.

4.1.2.2 Efforts to the study of problems concerning the formation of the theory of the new-democratic revolution and comparative study on the theory and the Three People's Principles of Dr. Sun Yat-sen.

In particular, how the theory drew upon and surpassed the Three People's Principles has become a hot topic ever since the 1990s. During studies, researchers have noticed and begun to emphasize such an idea and important fact that the thinking of Dr. Sun has also been an indispensable theoretical source of Mao Zedong Thought. Books and writings in this area include Dong Shiming's *A Comparative Study of the Theory of the New-Democratic Revolution and the Three People's Principles* (Northeast Normal University Press, 1995) and Chen Jinlong's "Thinking of Dr. Sun Yat-sen: An Important Theoretical Source of Mao Zedong Thought" (*Teaching and Research*, No. 8, 2000). Chen Jinlong believes that Mao Zedong had not only carried forward and developed the thinking of Dr. Sun in the aspects of politics, economy, armed force, culture, education and foreign relations but also had used Dr. Sun's terming on the new Three People's Principles to elaborate the theory of the new-democratic revolution. For instance, he had quoted Dr. Sun's words "The so-called democratic system in modern states is usually monopolized by the bourgeoisie and has become simply an instrument for oppressing the common people. On the other hand, the Kuomintang's Principle of Democracy means a democratic system shared by all common people and not privately owned by few." in defining the political program for New Democracy. Mao had commented, "These views of ours is completely in accord with the revolutionary views of Dr. Sun Yat-sen." In addition, he had quoted again Dr. Sun's words "Enterprises, such as banks, railways and airlines, whether Chinese-owned or foreign-owned, which are either monopolistic in character or too big for private management, should be operated and administered by the state, so that private capital cannot dominate the livelihood of the people: this is the main principle for the regulation of capital." when explaining industrial and commercial policies in the economic program for New Democracy, he said, "In the present stage, we fully agree with these views of Dr. Sun's on economic questions."[1] In short, Mao Zedong had carried forward the essence of the Three People's Principles, which consequently became an important theoretical source for Mao Zedong Thought. Although there were researchers mentioning this issue occasionally before, that was the first time researchers have conducted systematic research on the issue.

There was a mass enthusiasm among Party members for studying the Three People's Principles at the beginning of the War of Resistance against Japan, which was a noticeable ideological and cultural phenomenon. We cannot overlook that phenomenon when studying the formation of Mao Zedong Thought, especially its theory of New Democracy. Song Jin's *Exploration into the Treasure: the CPC's Study of the Three People's Principles during the War of Resistance against Japan* (Guangxi Normal University Press, 1994) is an important book to study that phenomenon.

4.1.2.3 Study on the influence of the Communist International on the formation of the theory of the new-democratic revolution.

The paper "The Communist International and the Formation of the Basic Thinking on the New-Democratic Revolution" (*Qilu Journal*, No. 3, 1996) by Dongfang Su has made an in-depth investigation and analysis of this issue according to a wealth of historical facts. In the paper he has pointed out that the CPC's early theorists had been under the guidance of Lenin's

---

[1] *Selected Works of Mao Tse-tung*, Eng. ed., FLP, Peking, 1965, Vol. III, pp. 280-281.

theory of revolution in a colonial country during their exploration into problems concerning the Chinese revolution and during the Great Revolution (1924-1927), and that the CPC's theoretical achievements at its Second National Congress were inseparable from the correct guidance of Lenin and the Communist International. It was under the influence of the Communist International that Chen Duxiu had decided to replace the original slogan of "democratic revolution" with the new slogan "national revolution," which profoundly influenced the revolution after the KMT-CPC cooperation. When the CPC was pondering on important problems concerning the Chinese revolution such as the status of the proletariat in the national revolution in different revolutionary stages and the worker-peasant alliance, discourses and directives of the Communist International had provided it with necessary ideological nutrients to help it understand these problems profoundly and comprehensively. Besides, the Communist International's assertion of "non-capitalist path" for the Chinese revolution had guided the CPC to consider the democratic revolution and the socialist revolution as an integrated whole and seek for a "non-capitalist path."

4.1.2.4 The Three People's Principles of Dr. Sun Yat-sen and the Communist International have both influenced the formation of the theory of the new-democratic revolution, but there is another factor that should not be ignored—the "modernization" trend.

The modernization trend:

In his "The Theory of New Democracy and Controversy over China's Modernization in the 1930s and 1940s" published in *Study of the History of the Communist Party of China* (No. 2) in 2000, Zhang Yong has tried to understand the theory of New Democracy in a broader context of controversies over China's modernization in the 1930s and 1940s, analyzing how the formation and development of the theory had been influenced by the multifarious modernization trends in the 1930s and 1940s. He has argued that researchers can never reach a scientific conclusion on the process of formation and development of the theory if they discuss it without considering these modernization trends, which were the concrete historical realities at that time. In fact, the Chinese modern intellectuals at that time had made quite a few pioneering and rational explorations into problems facing China's modernization. For instance, their dispute over the question of taking "industry" or "agriculture" as the foundation of the country in the 1930s and 1940s had induced them to further discuss problems of China's independent economic development, the fundamental position of agriculture, the relationship between industry and agriculture, the relationship between industrialization and democratization of political life, and the problems and difficulties confronting China's industrialization. Their dispute and discussion had greatly influenced Mao Zedong's thought on industry and economy in the theory of New Democracy. Zhang Yong has also pointed out that because both the theory of New Democracy and the multifarious modernization trends came into being in the 1930s and 1940s and were therefore confronted with the same national conditions and contradictions and restricted by the same social and historical circumstances, they naturally had possessed the same general features such as to consider China's problems as fundamentally a problem of culture, while often overlooking the problem of economic development; to naturally criticize capitalism, while ignoring its general feature of modernization; and they have both rarely considered China's modernization from the perspective of development of the productive forces. It should be said that to understand the theory of New Democracy by considering these modernization trends is very helpful to grasp its formation and meaning more profoundly.

4.1.2.5 With an upsurge in the 1980s to study culture, researchers began to study the thinking on new-democratic culture. Efforts to study the process and symbols of its formation and its content.

They generally believe that the formation of the thinking on new-democratic culture had undergone three stages: Li Dazhao, Chen Duxiu and other theorists had made the initial exploration during the May 4th Movement; Qu Qiubai and other theorists had pushed and deepened the thinking through their theoretical study on the new cultural movement after the founding of the CPC; and Mao Zedong had published "On New Democracy" in the early 1940s to mark its formation. However, some researchers have recently argued that the generally accepted conclusion of taking Mao Zedong's "On New Democracy" as the symbol of formation of the thinking on new-democratic culture is incomplete. They have argued that the paper "The New Cultural Movement since the War of Resistance against Japan and Future Tasks" by Zhang Wentian et al. is also a symbol, because the paper had fully embodied the feature of the thinking and reflected the collective wisdom of Party leaders in cultural problems and their ability to complement each other in ideological understanding. Besides, compared to Mao Zedong's principle of developing a national, scientific and mass culture, which had been widely accepted later, Zhang Wentian's principle of developing a national, democratic, scientific and mass culture had not only embodied the essential features of new-democratic culture more accurately and completely but also better reflected the common understanding of Party leaders on new-democratic culture before 1942.[1]

4.1.2.6 Efforts to compare the basic program of the new-democratic revolution with the basic program for the primary stage of socialism and ideas on their relationship and differences.

Researchers commonly believe that the two programs have the same long-term goal of realizing socialism and communism in China; they are both for transition—one for transition from New Democracy to socialism, while the other for transition from the primary stage of socialism to a prosperous, advanced and democratic socialist society; and they were both scientific programs for socialism rooted in the Chinese realities to realize the ideas

---

[1] Liu Hui, "New Opinions on the Symbol of Formation of the Thinking on New-Democratic Culture," *Journal of Renmin University of China*, 2001(2).

of Marx and Engels in *The Communist Manifesto* that "the capitalism will collapse and be replaced with socialism." The two programs are, in essence, theoretically the same: first, they are both scientific programs for socialism with Chinese characteristics, and two factors are needed to form Chinese characteristics—Marxist theory and Chinese realities, both of which have been included in these two programs; second, the latter is a continuation and development of the former. There are also researchers conducting comparative study of the thinking on new-democratic culture with the thinking on developing socialist culture with Chinese characteristics.

4.1.2.7 Efforts to study how the theory of New Democracy understands and deals with the Chinese bourgeoisie and the private capitalist economy.

"The Historical Development of Mao Zedong's Two Theories on the Chinese Bourgeoisie" (*Changbai Journal*, No. 1, 1996) by Wang Zhanyang and "A Brief Introduction to Mao Zedong's Thinking on Capitalism in New Democracy" (*Party Literature*, No. 1, 2000) by Zheng Derong and Liu Guoqing are two papers with great influence on this issue. In particular, special attention should be given to the latter one, which made a special investigation and analysis of Mao Zedong's ideas on "capitalism in New Democracy" which he had advanced at the CPC's Seventh Congress. The two authors of the paper hold that the idea applies only to the capitalist sector of the economy represented by the upper petite bourgeoisie and middle bourgeoisie, namely the capitalist economic sector of the national bourgeoisie, and not to capitalist economic sector in general or the bureaucratic-capitalist economic sector, and that it applies only to the capitalist economic sector under the state system or rule of New Democracy, and not to capitalist economic sector in all stages of the society. Such a capitalist economic sector would be permitted to exist and develop for a long time after victory of the new-democratic revolution, but its development should be restricted to prevent it from dominating or sabotaging the livelihood of the people. They also hold that Mao Zedong had developed his idea of capitalism in New

Democracy after learning from the success of the New Economic Policy in Russia after the October Revolution, critically assimilating the new Three People's Principles of Dr. Sun Yat-sen and drawing lessons from the CPC's "Left" errors in dealing with capitalism during the Agrarian Revolution (1928-1934). This idea, as an important component of the theory of New Democracy, accords with the principles of historical materialism and is a continuation and development of the idea of Marx and Engels on leaping over the capitalist stage. The practice of allowing existence and development of the private sector of the economy nowadays is an application and development of this thinking under the new historical conditions.

In addition, researchers also make great efforts to further study the theoretical exploration of Zhou Enlai, Zhang Wentian, Liu Shaoqi, Zhu De, Chen Yun and other Party leaders and their contributions to the formation of the theory of the new-democratic revolution. They published many articles and writings to elaborate on Zhou Enlai's theories about China's revolutionary road and the Chinese bourgeoisie, Zhang Wentian's division of five economic sectors under New Democracy, and Liu Shaoqi's theories about Party building. As a result, they have developed a better understanding on the theory of the new-democratic revolution.

4.2 Theory of Encircling the Cities from the Countryside

The theory of encircling the cities from the countryside is one of the most important components of Mao Zedong Thought. Researchers have begun to study the theory ever since the founding of the People's Republic. Up till today, their research has yielded a rich harvest.

4.2.1 Introduction to Study Efforts

Few writings on this theory was published before the end of the "cultural revolution." However, there has been an upsurge in study of this theory after the "cultural revolution" was ended. According to incomplete statistics, up till now a total of about 200 papers and some books have been published on this theory. These research results will be introduced in two groups—before and after the 1990s.

4.2.1.1 The First Period (Before the 1990s)

During this period, researchers have focused their study of the theory of China's revolutionary road on the following aspects.

4.2.1.1.1 The process for the formation of the theory of the revolutionary road of encircling the cities from the countryside

Many papers have pointed out that after the failure of the Great Revolution in 1927, Chinese Communists represented by Mao Zedong had made a thorough review of the lessons of the failure and gradually realized that they could lead the Chinese revolution into victory only by taking a revolutionary road suited to the Chinese realities. After unremitting explorations in both theory and practice, they had finally found a revolutionary road of encircling the cities from the countryside and seizing state power by armed force and had established a theory of revolutionary road with Chinese characteristics. This theory also had a process of formation.

First, the idea of "political power grows out of the barrel of a gun" was put forward. The August 7th Meeting held in 1927 was the beginning of Chinese Communists to find a revolutionary road in China. At the meeting, Mao Zedong had criticized Chen Duxiu's erroneous practice of surrender on the leadership of the revolution and advanced the famous idea that "political power grows out of the barrel of a gun." He said that the proletariat should command the leadership of the revolution to seize state power; the proletariat should launch the Agrarian Revolution to seek an ally when its forces are not strong; and the proletariat should have armed forces under its command to seize state power. Mao Zedong's idea that "political power grows out of the barrel of a gun" was based on his review of lessons of the failure of the Great Revolution and represented his beginning to explore China's revolutionary road.

Second, the idea of "establishing independent regimes of the workers and the peasants by armed force" had been advocated. Chinese Communists had understood that the principal form of struggle in the Chinese revolution was armed struggle, but they had not solved the problem of whether concentrating armed struggle in the cities or in the countryside. After considering the severe losses caused by the erroneous "Left" dogmatic idea of "concentrating armed struggle in cities", Chinese Communists represented by Mao Zedong proceeded from the Chinese realities and established and consolidated revolutionary bases in the countryside. After reviewing the experience of establishing revolutionary bases in Jinggang Mountains, Mao Zedong had advanced the idea of "establishing independent regimes of the workers and the peasants by armed force"—to establish rural revolutionary bases or Red political power under the leadership of the proletariat by carrying out armed struggle and leading the Agrarian Revolution and relying on revolutionary bases. As a development of the doctrine that "political power grows out of the barrel of a gun," the idea was a critical step taken by the CPC to shift its focus from the cities to the countryside and a great advance in its efforts to find a democratic revolutionary road with Chinese characteristics.

Third, the idea of "encircling the cities from the countryside" was formed. Mao Zedong had written a number of essays such as "Why is it that Red Political Power can Exist in China?" "A Single Spark Can Start a Prairie Fire" and "On Correcting Mistaken Ideas in the Party" in the late 1920s and early 1930s to expatiate on the idea that development of small rural areas under Red political power would bring about a revolutionary high tide. These essays embodied the idea of encircling the cities from the countryside and gave the initial shape to the theory of revolutionary road with Chinese characteristics. Although the theory of the revolutionary road of encircling the cities from the countryside was still not mature or systematic at that time, it had become "an idea of China's revolutionary road guiding the CPC to first establish Red political power in rural areas, encircle the cities from the countryside and seize state power when conditions become mature."[1] The theory of the road of encircling the cities from the countryside was further developed during the period of the War of Resistance against Japan. By steadfastly following the road of encircling the cities from the countryside in the revolution, CPC has led the Chinese revolution into victory.

4.2.1.1.2 Mao Zedong's outstanding contributions to the theory of the revolutionary road of encircling the cities from the countryside

Many writings pointed out that the theory of encircling the cities from the countryside and seizing state power by armed force was "a great creation of Mao Zedong, who made the most important contributions."[2]

First, Mao Zedong had developed the idea of "concentrating armed struggle in the countryside."

After the failure of the Great Revolution, the young CPC was confronted with a new task—how to build up and develop revolutionary forces under the objective condition that the enemy was strong and the CPC was weak. All Party members had explored ways to preserve and develop revolutionary forces under the new situation. The CPC's Central Committee, after making a review of experience and lessons from armed insurrections in different parts of the country, had realized that it could establish a large number of independent regimes of the workers and the peasants by armed force in order to carry on a guerilla war and establish state power of the workers and peasants, and that in order to seize big cities, it should first organize armed insurrections of peasants in surrounding counties to encircle the cities. After the famous judgment that "political power grows out of the barrel of a gun" at the August 7th Meeting in 1927 was advocated, Mao Zedong had led the Autumn Harvest Uprising and later established revolutionary bases in the

---

[1] *Chronicle of Major Events in the History of the Communist Party of China*, People's Publishing House, Beijing, 1987, p.74.

[2] Sun Jin'gen, "On Why Is It that Mao Zedong Made the Most Outstanding Contribution to the Formation of China's Revolutionary Road," *Teaching and Research in CPC History*, 1997 (2).

Jinggang Mountains. During the period of establishing revolutionary bases in the Jinggang Mountains, Mao Zedong wrote some essays such as "Why Is It That Red Political Power Can Exist in China?" and "The Struggle in the Chingkang Mountains" to explain the reasons and conditions for the emergence and survival of Red political power in China and to elaborated his idea of establishing independent regimes of the workers and the peasants by armed force.

However, some researchers have pointed out in their papers that Mao's independent regimes understanding were different from that of the CPC Central Committee. First, rural independent regimes the Central Committee wanted to establish were just temporary measures it should take to get prepared for seizing provincial/urban political power; while the independent regime Mao Zedong wanted to establish should be durable and long-term. Second, the Central Committee had ignored the important role of the revolutionary army in creating an independent regime, believing that uprisings of the masses were enough; while Mao Zedong had emphasized the importance of armed force in an independent regime, saying: "Therefore, even when the masses of workers and peasants are active, it is definitely impossible to create an independent regime, let alone an independent regime which is durable and grows daily, unless we have regular forces with adequate strength."[1]

Some researchers have also advanced in their papers that the idea of establishing independent regimes of the workers and the peasants by armed force was different from the theory of the revolutionary road with Chinese characteristics.[2] They were both related and differentiated. They were related because that idea was the prerequisite and basis for the theory and the theory was the goal and destination of the idea. They were differentiated because of three reasons. One, in content, the idea had explained the reasons and

---

[1] *Selected Works of Mao Tse-tung*, Eng. ed., FLP, Peking, 1965, Vol. I, p. 66.
[2] Guo Zhimin and Xue Lixin, "Mao Zedong Created the Revolutionary Road with Chinese Characteristics," *Research of Mao Zedong Thought*, 1993 (3).

conditions for the emergence and development of Red political power but had not defined a line guiding the armed struggle, or the Agrarian Revolution and also the establishment of revolutionary bases; the theory had solved problems about the ultimate goal of the Chinese revolution and the focus of armed struggle. Two, in practice, the idea had aimed to expedite uprisings in Hunan, Hubei, Jiangxi and Guangdong provinces, while the established theory was designed to seize state power. Three, according to directives from the Communist International and the CPC Central Committee, the idea was regarded as a measure only to cooperate actions to seize key cities; the theory, no matter how the Communist International and the CPC Central Committee thought about it, was designed to seize state power by encircling the cities from the countryside. To sum up, the three reasons can be embodied in one sentence—the idea had put the centre of the CPC's work on the cities while the established theory, on the countryside. In January 1930 Mao Zedong, on the basis of his review of experience of revolutionary bases in Jinggang Mountains and in other areas, had written "A Single Spark Can Start a Prairie Fire" to expound on his assertion that only a revolutionary road of encircling cities from the countryside could lead the Chinese revolution into a nationwide victory. He also had advanced in this essay the idea of shifting the focus of the CPC's work to the countryside.

Second, Mao Zedong had made great theoretical exploration on the revolutionary road.

In order to theoretically oppose dogmatism within the Party and the Red Army, Mao Zedong had written the essay "Oppose Book Worship (originally named 'Investigation and Research')" in May 1930, in which he advanced the ideological line of seeking truth from facts for the first time. He had pointed out that all Party members should study the theory of Marxism-Leninism because it was needed in the revolutionary struggle. He said, "When we say Marxism is correct, it is certainly not because Marx was a 'prophet' but because his theory has been proved correct in our practice and in our struggle.... We do need books but resolutely oppose book worship that is divorced from reality." "What can we do to correct book worship? We should investigate into the reality."[1] Therefore, this essay has been regarded by researchers as the philosophical basis for the revolutionary road with Chinese characteristics. The leadership of Mao Zedong in the Party and in the Red Army was established at the Zunyi Meeting in 1935. Thereafter, the theory of encircling the cities from the countryside was implemented. Mao Zedong had not stopped theoretical exploration during the period of the War of Resistance against Japan. He had written a number of essays such as "Problems of Strategy in China's Revolutionary War," "Problems of War and Strategy," "On the New Stage" and "The Chinese Revolution and the Chinese Communist Party" from December 1936 to December 1939 to give a systematic elaboration on the theory of encircling the cities from the countryside.

History has proved that the theory of the revolutionary road of encircling the cities from the countryside produced by Chinese Communists represented by Mao Zedong had always been developing and progressing along with the accumulation of practice and experience in the Chinese revolution. It embodied the unique law of the Chinese revolution and represented great development of Marxism-Leninism. Therefore, some papers have advanced the opinion that "the revolutionary road of encircling the cities from the countryside marks the initial formation of Mao Zedong Thought."[2]

4.2.1.1.3 The theory of China's revolutionary road is a crystallization of the collective wisdom of the entire Party

Mao Zedong had not created the revolutionary road of encircling the cities from the countryside by himself although he indeed made the most outstanding contribution to its formation. This road represents the collective wisdom of all Chinese Communists and was a scientific review of their experience. The Central Committee had begun to explore it before the Sixth National Congress from the following aspects:

The first was about armed struggle in mountains. After the August 7th

---

[1] *Selected Works of Mao Zedong*, Chin. ed., Vol. I, pp. 111-112.

[2] Du Weihua, "On the Revolutionary Road of Encircling the Cities from the Countryside—the Formation of Mao Zedong Thought," *Marxism Study*, 1987 (1).

Meeting held in 1927, the CPC Central Committee has declared that "the Chinese revolution had entered a new period—the period for the Agrarian Revolution," that "we should integrate the Agrarian Revolution with the struggle for political power," and that "revolutionary armed force should be mobilized to guarantee the success of rural political power and the Agrarian Revolution." These ideas have laid a foundation for the formation of the idea of establishing independent regimes of the workers and the peasants by armed force.

The second was about building rural base areas. After drawing lessons from failures to seize big cities such as Changsha and Guangzhou and reviewing experience of establishing revolutionary bases in rural areas, the CPC Central Committee had instructed that independent regimes should be set up by establishing revolutionary bases in uprising areas. Although the focus of its work was still in cities, it had noticed the meaning of establishing rural bases. As a result, the struggle to establish rural base areas had spread to many parts of the country.

The third was about the strategy of encircling cities by establishing independent regimes in surrounding rural areas to achieve victory in one or more provinces. Some localities, based on review of experience in the Autumn Harvest Uprising and other armed insurrections, had begun to make plans for encircling cities by initiating uprisings in surrounding rural areas. The CPC Central Committee had timely reviewed such practices and experiences and had considered rural independent regimes to be the prerequisite for taking actions to seize political power in a provincial center. After the failure of Guangzhou Uprising in 1927, the Central Committee had clearly set forth the principle that in order to seize the capital city of a province "we should first form independent regimes in some key areas to encircle the key area of the province."[1] Although the Central Committee still put the center of its work in cities at that time, it had changed its original manner of initiating uprisings first in cities and later in rural areas. These had laid the initial foundation for the formation of the theory of encircling the

---

[1] Shi Zhongquan (ed.), *A Review of Study on Mao Zedong*, p. 140.

cities from the countryside.

In addition, quite a few papers also have discussed how revolutionary bases scattered around the country have helped exploring the road for the Chinese revolution. Among these papers were "The Path of Revolutionary Bases in Jinggang Mountains Is a Typical Integration of Theory with Practice," "Fang Zhimin's Idea of Independent Regimes of the Workers and the Peasants," "The Formation of Independent Regimes of the Workers and the Peasants in West Anhui Province," "Independent Regimes of the Workers and the Peasants in Zuojiang-Youjiang Area," "Revolutionary Bases in Haifeng-Lufeng Area—Beginning of Independent Regimes of the Workers and the Peasants," "Discussion on Independent Regimes of the Workers and the Peasants in Hubei, Henan and Anhui Provinces," "Revolutionary Practice in West Fujian Province and the Formation of China's Revolutionary Road" and "Thinking on China's Revolutionary Road by Party Organizations in Hubei Province." There were also papers introducing how other Party leaders, such as Qu Qiubai, Cai Hesen, Zhu De and Fang Zhimin, had contributed to the revolutionary road of encircling the cities from the countryside both in practice and in theory.

4.2.1.2 The Second Period (After the 1990s)

Research results in this period have focused on the following aspects.

4.2.1.2.1 How Zhou Enlai and other major Party leaders had contributed to the theory of the revolutionary road of encircling the cities from the countryside

Many papers have pointed out, "Zhou Enlai and Zhu De, as the capable aides of Mao Zedong, had made extraordinary contributions to the exploration of China's revolutionary road."[1]

Zhou Enlai's contributions were as follows.

First, he had been the earliest Chinese communist to lead armed insurrections and build revolutionary armies after the failure of the Great

---

[1] Yu Boliu, "Zhou Enlai and the Revolutionary Road of Encircling the Cities from the Countryside," *Jiangxi Social Science*, 1998 (3).

Revolution in 1927. It was him who had initiated the practice of establishing independent regimes of the workers and the peasants by armed force, which laid a solid foundation for the CPC's later practice of building rural revolutionary bases and encircling cities from the countryside. After the failure of the Great Revolution, he was the first to recommend a punitive eastern expedition against Chiang Kai-shek and initiating an uprising in Hunan Province. He had successfully led the Nanchang Uprising on August 1, 1927, which was the earliest armed insurrection initiated by the CPC and represented its start to independently lead revolutionary armed force and build revolutionary armies.

Second, he had been the actual leader in the CPC Central Committee in making decisions on the work of rural revolutionary bases, which laid the strategic basis for the revolutionary road of encircling the cities from the countryside. He had guided the practice of the Red Army groups led by Zhu De and Mao Zedong in establishing independent regimes and introduced the experience of armed struggle in the Jinggang Mountains to other base areas. The "Letter from the Central Committee to the General Frontline Committee of the Fourth Army Group of the Red Army" drafted according to his dictation had laid the ideological foundation for the opening of Gutian Meeting in 1929. He had advanced the idea of "establishing Central Soviet Political Power" and put forward a set of supporting measures.

Third, he was one of the major leaders in the Central Revolutionary Base Area guiding the revolutionary struggle of the CPC and the Red Army and making decisions on strategic retreat. He was in charge of the work of leading the CPC and the Red Army in the Central Soviet Area and had greatly expanded and developed the Central Revolutionary Base Area. He had led the fourth counter-campaign against the KMT's "encirclement and suppression" in the Central Soviet Area into glorious victory. He, in the hard times of the fifth counter-campaign, did lots of work to support the decision of strategic transfer in order to reduce the losses of the Red Army to the minimum.

Fourth, he was a firm supporter in the leading group of the Central Committee of Mao Zedong's idea as encircling cities from the countryside.

From the Seventh Party Assembly of the Fourth Army Group of the Red Army in 1929 to the Ningdu Meeting in 1932, he had strongly supported Mao Zedong no matter what difficult situation they faced. After thoroughly reviewing the Party's historical experience and lessons, he had firmly affirmed Mao Zedong's idea of putting the center of Party's work in the rural areas and encircling the cities from the countryside. In short, Zhou Enlai was one of the main founders of the theory of the revolutionary road of encircling the cities from the countryside, and Mao Zedong was their representative.

4.2.1.2.2 How the theory of the revolutionary road of encircling the cities from the countryside was established as the guideline of the Party and what marked its establishment

First, it should be understood that the formation of the theory and its establishment as the guideline of the Party are two different concepts. It is believed that "the main reason that researchers disagree with each other on the time and symbols of the formation of the theory over many years is that they confused its formation with its establishment as the Party's guideline."[1] The two concepts have two differences. First, they are different in nature. A theory is formed when it has developed all its content, but it should first be accepted by the Party as a guiding principle before being established as the guideline. Second, they are different in time. The theory was first formed and then needed a period of time to be established as the guideline.

Second, the criteria for the theory to be established as the guideline of the Party. Some researchers believe there are three criteria. One, it should contain a complete system of mature theories, which is the prerequisite. Two, it should be accepted by the Party, who applies it to guide its work, and what matters here is where the focus of Party's work was—cities or the countryside. Three, the entire Party should clearly realize that the idea of

---

[1] Wang Fuxuan, "How the Theory of 'Encircling the Cities from the Countryside' Was Established as the Line of Guidance for the Party," *Teaching and Research in CPC History*, 1992 (3).

"focusing the work of the Party on cities" is wrong.

Third, the historical process for the theory to be established as the Party's guideline. Some researchers believe that Mao Zedong's "A Single Spark Can Start a Prairie Fire" in January 1930 marks the basic formation of the theory because the essay had put forward the idea of focusing on armed struggle in rural areas and discussed all the basic content of the theory—one focus (struggle in rural areas) and three basic points (armed struggle, the Agrarian Revolution and establishment of revolutionary bases). However, the theory was not immediately accepted by the Party because Mao Zedong was not the chief leader in the CPC Central Committee at that time, and because the theory was just beginning to take shape, needed to develop and tested and checked by practice, and was not fully understood by the entire Party. The Party finally applied the theory to guide its work and action as it gradually realized that the idea of encircling the cities from the countryside could bring victory to the Chinese revolution while the idea of focusing on cities would only bring defeats. But it took three periods for the Party to realize that. During the first period—from the second half of 1930 to the eve of Zunyi Meeting in 1935—some Party members began to realize the importance of shifting the focus of the Party's work to rural areas. During second period—from the Zunyi Meeting in January 1935 to the Sixth Plenary Session of the Sixth CPC Central Committee in 1938—the theory was further developed and improved and was organizationally named as the Party's guiding principle. During the third period—from the Sixth Plenary Session of the Sixth CPC Central Committee to the Seventh Plenary Session of the Sixth Central Committee in 1945, at which the Resolution on Certain Questions in the History of the Communist Party of China was passed—the theory was formally established as the Party's guideline. We can see that the period from the 1930s when it began to take shape, to the year 1945 when it was finally established as the Party's guiding line, was in fact a period, during which it was enriched and developed, and in this time period the dispute between the idea of focusing on cities and the idea of focusing on the rural areas was settled, and the CPC had gradually developed a better understanding on the laws of China's revolutionary road.

4.2.1.2.3 The relationship between the revolutionary road of encircling the cities from the countryside and the path of building socialism with Chinese characteristics

Studies on the relationships between the road of encircling the cities from the countryside and the path of building socialism with Chinese characteristics has become a hot issue in recent years. Some researchers have pointed out that the road of encircling cities from the countryside and the path of socialism with Chinese characteristics are both the inevitability of historical development. The former was a unique road for seizing state power—"victory in the Chinese new-democratic revolution was indeed a success of the path of revolutionary bases in Jinggang Mountains;"[1] the latter is a path for socialist modernization created by Deng Xiaoping after review of historical experiences and lessons in China's socialist construction. They both represent the inevitable historical development and embody the creative spirit of Mao Zedong and Deng Xiaoping. They are both the result of emancipating minds, seeking truth from facts and applying the theory of Marxism-Leninism to the Chinese conditions. In addition, the former has inspired the latter in the following aspects: one, to proceed from realities and break the shackles of dogmatism; two, to emancipate minds and think and explore boldly; three, to attach great importance to the work on peasants; four, to strengthen and improve the Party's leadership.

Besides, there are several papers discussing the influence of the theory of encircling the cities from the countryside on China's present political and economic restructuring. Among these papers are "Village Self-Governance: A New Practice of Encircling the Cities from the Countryside," "The Inner Relationship between the Theory of Encircling the Cities from the Countryside and Seizing State Power by Armed Force and the Theory of the Socialist Market Economy," "The Idea of Cultivating Famous Brands

---

[1] Cui Shuhai, "The Path of Revolutionary Bases in Jinggang Mountains and the Path of Building Socialism with Chinese Characteristics," *Research of Mao Zedong Thought*, 1996 (1).

in Township Enterprises: To Encircle the Cities from the Countryside," "On the Theory of Encircling the Cities from the Countryside and the Practice of Integrating Development of Rural and Urban Areas," "On the Reapplication of the Theory of Encircling the Cities from the Countryside in Establishing a Market System," "A New Practice of Encircling the Cities from the Countryside: Road for China's Economic Restructuring," "Deng Xiaoping's Economic Reform and the Developing Road of Encircling Cities from the Countryside" and "From Jinggangshan to Shenzhen: On Jinggangshan Spirit and Shenzhen Spirit."

4.2.2 Disputed Issues Among Researchers

The study on the theory of encircling the cities from the countryside in recent years has focused on the following issues: elaboration on the idea of China's revolutionary road; relationships among ideas of establishing independent regimes of the workers and the peasants by armed force, setting up Red political power and encircling the cities from the countryside; and the time and symbol of formation of Mao Zedong's theory of encircling the cities from the countryside. After a long time of discussion and argument, some disputes have been solved, but some, still not.

4.2.2.1 When Mao Zedong's Theory of the Revolutionary Road of Encircling the Cities from the Countryside Was Formed and What Marks Its Formation

After the founding of the People's Republic, scholars studying the history of the CPC believed that Mao Zedong's letter to Lin Biao on January 5, 1930 [referring to the essay "A Single Spark Can Start a Prairie Fire"—*Tr.*] had embodied the idea of shifting the focus of the Party's work to the countryside. There was no argument on this opinion at that time. However, after the Third Plenary Session of the Eleventh Central Committee of the CPC, many researchers have begun to discuss and argue on this issue. Below is a brief introduction to some views.

First view: Mao Zedong's "A Single Spark Can Start a Prairie Fire" in January 1930, in which the idea of establishing independent regimes of the workers and the peasants by armed force was further developed, had explained the necessity for the Party to shift its focus from cities to the countryside, and had formed a theory about the new revolutionary road of first carrying out a guerilla war and the Agrarian Revolution and establishing Red political power in rural areas and then seizing state power when conditions became mature.[1]

Second view: The revolutionary road was shaped during the period from the Luofang Meeting in October 1930, at which the principle of "luring the enemy in deep" was put forward, to early 1931 when the Red Army had defeated the enemy's first "encirclement and suppression attack". This view is based on the following argument. Although Mao Zedong in his essay "A Single Spark Can Start a Prairie Fire" had challenged the fetters imposed by the idea of focusing the Party's work on cities, he had not established a firm belief that the focus of the Party's work should be shifted to rural areas. When the essay was published, the Party regarded the revolutionary base in rural areas as an important revolutionary force as well as "an important factor in accelerating the revolutionary high tide throughout the country"— but regarded it not a decisive policy. Later, when the essay was collected and edited into *Selected Works of Mao Zedong*, the wording "an important factor" was changed into "the most important factor," which makes a great difference. Besides, the essay had indeed manifested a better understanding of the Chinese realities and characters of the Chinese revolution, but it had still overlooked to some extent the reality that the enemy was strong and the revolutionary forces were weak, was a little bit overly optimistic about the situation, and as a result supported the plan to take Nanchang, Jiujiang and all other cities in Jiangxi Province in a short time. That was why the Party had decided to attack Changsha for the second time in June 1930. After retreat from Changsha, Mao Zedong had reviewed experience and lessons, both positive and negative, gained since the Autumn Harvest Uprising and better understood the situation and the necessity of shifting the focus of the

---

[1] *History of the Communist Party of China*, Vol. I, compiled by the Party History Research Center, Beijing, People's Publishing House, 1991.

Party's work from cities to rural areas. The principle of "luring the enemy in deep" put forward at the Luofang Meeting in October 1930 marked the start of the Party to shift its focus of work to the countryside. At that time, the revolutionary road of encircling the cities from the countryside and seizing state power by armed force was formed on the basis of integration of theory with practice.[1]

Third view: Mao Zedong had completed the shift from "focusing the Party's work on cities" to "focusing the Party's work on the countryside" from 1930 to the second half of 1931. Researchers holding this view have argued that Mao Zedong in his essay "A Single Spark Can Start a Prairie Fire" had not yet freed himself from the idea of focusing on cities. It took the Party a long period of time—from 1930 to the second half of 1931—to solve the argument in the Party over the focus of its work, oppose Li Lisan's idea of focusing on cities, review the practice in the Chinese revolution, and eventually shift the focus of its work from cities to the countryside. They believe that Zhou Zijing's letter published in Volume 104, the journal *Hongqi* in May 1930 had clearly advanced the idea of focusing the Party's work on the countryside, encircling cities from countryside and eventually winning nationwide victory. In the letter, Zhou Zijing had pointed out that under the condition that "the peasant movement was developing faster than the workers' movement," the Party should "abandon cities temporarily" and mobilize most or even "all its strengths to develop revolutionary forces in the countryside" so that "the Party could mobilize and organize strong revolutionary forces in rural areas to encircle and take cities." As Li Lisan's erroneous practice of initiating armed insurrections in key cities and concentrating the Red Army units to attach big cities was criticized and corrected, the Party gradually established the idea of focusing its work on the countryside. In August 1931, the Presidium of the Executive Committee of the Communist International had instructed the CPC that all its organizations should concentrate their attention on "continuing to expand Soviet areas" and

[1] Du Weihua, "On the Revolutionary Road of Encircling the Cities from the Countryside— the Formation of Mao Zedong Thought," *Marxism Study*, 1987 (1).

the party work in non-Soviet areas "should be centered on mobilizing the broad masses to protect and help Soviet areas." An editorial published in the weekly journal *Hongqi* in September the same year had argued that the CPC's central task was to "support the Soviet areas and the Red Army." Not until then did the Party establish the idea of focusing its work on the countryside. Thereafter, the idea of focusing on cities was no longer adopted by the Party as a guiding idea again. Therefore, some researchers have argued that the conclusion that the essay "A Single Spark Can Start a Prairie Fire" marked the formation of the theory of encircling the cities from the countryside "cannot stand" because the thinking put forward in the essay "applied only to some localities and had not been applied by the Party as a guiding idea."[1]

Fourth view: Mao Zedong's essay "Problems of Strategy in China's Revolutionary War" in December 1936 marks the basic formation of the theory of the revolutionary road of encircling the cities from the countryside.[2] This view is based on the following argument. First, this essay had clearly explained the necessity of reviewing the experience in China's revolutionary war, understanding the specific laws of China's revolutionary war and finding a road for China's revolution. Second, it had discussed all the basis for the road of encircling the cities from the countryside. Third, it had explicitly pointed out to the protracted character of the Chinese revolution. Fourth, it had criticized the erroneous "Left" practice of leading the Red Army to take big cities when it was still weak and the dogmatic copy of experience in the Soviet Union and in the First Revolutionary Civil War (1924-1927) in China. Fifth, Mao Zedong had pointed out in this essay that "encirclement and suppressions" and counter-campaigns against them were the main pattern of China's civil war, and "that pattern would remain the same till the day the enemy becomes the weaker contestant and the Red Army the stronger one."

---

[1] Lu Zhenxiang, "Discussion on the Formation of the Theory of the Revolutionary Road of Encircling the Cities from the Countryside," *Study of the History of the Communist Party of China*, 1990 (6).

[2] Jia Weichang, "The Time of Formation of the Theory of the Road of Encircling the Cities from the Countryside," *Study of the History of the Communist Party of China*, 1981 (3).

In addition, there are also researchers believing that Mao Zedong's "Problems of War and Strategy," "The Chinese Revolution and the Chinese Communist Party" or certain other essays from 1938 to 1939 marks the formation of the theory.

4.2.2.2 The Relationship between the Communist International and China's Revolutionary Road of Encircling the Cities from the Countryside

How did the Communist International react to and influence the CPC's efforts to explore and find the revolutionary road of encircling the cities from the countryside? Researchers have given some answers to this question in recent years.

Some researchers have argued that in general the influence of the Communist International on the road of China's revolution after the failure of the Great Revolution had been negative, although it did give China some help at some time. Prevalent in the International Communist Movement from late 1920s to early 1930s was an erroneous tendency understanding Marxism dogmatically, which has guided China's revolution by copying Russia's October Revolution without considering China's realities or the characters and objective laws of the Chinese revolution. Such a tendency could in no way find a correct path for China's revolution, and could only lead the Chinese revolution into failure.

Many researchers have pointed out that an erroneous tendency to understand Marxism dogmatically and deify experience in Russia's October Revolution was prevalent in the International Communist Movement and in the CPC from late 1920s to early 1930s. As a result, when the rural revolutionary bases were developing rapidly, the Communist International had instructed the CPC in October 1929 to "mobilize all its strengths to organize political strikes and make plans for staging a general political strike" and urged CPC to continue focusing its work on cities. Although it admitted in October 1930 that the peasant movement was developing faster than the workers' movement in China, it still urged the CPC to "initiate armed insurrections in big cities and large industrial centers," establish Soviet government and focus its work on cities.

However, there is another different view arguing that the Communist International did not stick to the idea of focusing on armed struggle in cities all along; on the contrary, it had realized the importance of seeking a specific road for the Chinese revolution even earlier than the CPC did. Just like the process it had changed its attitude towards China's road for revolution—from underestimating and doubting and then to support and encourage, it had also through a process in guiding China's revolution—from advocating armed insurrections in cities, and then to attaching equal importance to armed struggle in cities and in rural areas, and eventually to shifting focus of work to the countryside. From accepting and then to abandoning the idea of focusing on cities, the CPC was influenced by the Communist International all along. Some researchers believe that at the Eleventh Plenum the Executive Committee held in March 1931, the Communist International had realized that the CPC should shift the focus of its work from cities to rural areas. They had several reasons for this opinion. One, it definitely demanded that the CPC should give top priority to establishing and consolidating rural revolutionary bases. Two, it laid immense emphasis on the work of Soviet areas. Three, it had explicitly declared that work in cities should be subordinate to work in the countryside and praised Mao Zedong's historical achievement in finding revolutionary road suited to Chinese conditions.[1]

4.2.3 Issues Requiring Further Research and Discussion

4.2.3.1 About the Time and Symbols of the Formation of the Theory of the Revolutionary Road of Encircling the Cities from the Countryside

We are convinced with the opinion put forward in the first volume of the *History of the Communist Party of China* compiled by the Party

---

[1] Yuan Nansheng, "Did the Communist International Stick to the Idea of Focusing on Armed Struggle in Cities after the Failure of the Great Revolution," *Social Science Front*, 1989 (4).

History Research Center under the CPC Central Committee which seems more reasonable and scientific. According to that opinion, Mao Zedong's essay "A Single Spark Can Start a Prairie Fire" in 1930 should be a symbol that his thinking on the revolutionary road of encircling the cities from the countryside has basically taken shape. After the failure of the Great Revolution, the entire Party had made desperate efforts to explore ways to bring about a revolutionary high tide. The Central Committee had favored the idea of seizing state power by focusing on armed struggle and workers' movement in cities; and supported Mao Zedong, putting the focus of the Party's work in rural areas, and emphasized on the ways to bring about a nationwide revolutionary high tide by consolidating and expanding rural revolutionary bases. The Central Committee had, by developing armed forces for seizing state power, wanted to learn from the experience of Russia's October Revolution, which placed little emphasis on the Red Army units in rural areas; Mao Zedong had advocated that experience in Russia's October Revolution did not suit the conditions of the Chinese revolution and China should create a Red Army of peasants and workers that could establish and consolidate rural revolutionary bases and "this would become the chief weapon for the great revolution of the future." So, Mao Zedong had made it clear in his essay that China should take a revolutionary road suited to the Chinese revolution, which was the road of encircling the cities from countryside, and shifting the focus of the Party's work to rural areas and to establish rural revolutionary bases were vital to seizing state power.

More study efforts are needed to further discuss how the Communist International had reacted to China's revolutionary road of encircling the cities from the countryside, especially how it had instructed the CPC after 1930.

4.2.3.2 On the Relationship between the Theory of the Revolutionary Road of Encircling the Cities from the Countryside and the Idea on Establishing Revolutionary Bases

One of the most important components of the theory of the

revolutionary road of encircling the cities from the countryside was the thinking on establishing independent regimes of the workers and the peasants by armed force, which includes theories about armed struggle, the Agrarian Revolution and the establishment of revolutionary bases. That's why many researchers study the thinking on establishing revolutionary bases as a part of the thinking on establishing independent regimes of the workers and the peasants.

We believe that Mao Zedong's thinking on establishing revolutionary bases is an important component of the theory of encircling the cities from the countryside. However, their relationship should not be understood too simply. The theory of encircling the cities from the countryside had its own laws governing its development. It should answer two questions—could the Party gain a footing in rural areas? And why China should take the revolutionary road of encircling the cities from the countryside? Solution to the two questions can mark its formation. After it had taken shape and continued to develop, the thinking on establishing revolutionary bases was of greater importance. When studying Mao Zedong's thinking on establishing revolutionary bases, we should not consider it merely as a component of the thinking on establishing independent regimes of the workers and the peasants, but should study it under the broader context of the theory of China's revolutionary road in order to better understand its strategic role in the theory of encircling cities from the countryside. By doing so, we can fully understand the significance of Mao Zedong's thinking on establishing revolutionary bases and deepen the study on the theory of encircling cities from the countryside.

4.3 Theory of People's Revolutionary War

The CPC, leading an extensive as well as protracted class war and national war in semi-colonial and semi-feudal China, had achieved a great victory rarely seen before in the world history, despite of huge numerical disparity between the enemy and revolutionary forces. Mao Zedong's military thinking is a system of military science formed on the basis of a review of experience in China's protracted revolutionary war which includes summing up the laws of those wars, and its core is the thinking on the people's revolutionary war.

4.3.1 Introduction to Study Efforts

The thinking on the people's revolutionary war had emerged and taken shape during the revolutionary war. The studies on it had begun after founding of the People's Republic. In the early 1960s, a number of high-ranking officers in the People's Liberation Army, based on their experience of applying the thinking on the people's revolutionary war and in directing military operations, had written dozens of valuable writings to discuss and elaborate on some basic principles of the thinking such as active defense, the strategic role of guerilla war, strategies and tactics for the people's war and on the ten major principles of operation. Among these writings were "Great Decision War" by Ye Jianying, "Mao Zedong Thought and the Victory in Beiping-Tianjin Campaign" by Liu Yalou, and "Boldly Struggle to Win Victory" by Chen Geng. They reflect the level of theoretical research on the thinking on people's revolutionary war before the "cultural revolution."

After the Third Plenary Session of the Eleventh CPC Central Committee, there was an upsurge in study of Mao Zedong's military thinking, and the study on the thinking on people's revolutionary war has vigorously flourished. The work of the People's Liberation Army to compile *Encyclopedia of China (Volume of Military)* and *Encyclopedia of the China Military* since 1980 and the many symposiums on Mao Zedong's military thinking held in and after 1983 have greatly promoted the study on the thinking. During that period, a large number of books such as *A Preliminary Study of Mao Zedong's Military Thinking* by Song Shilun and *The History of Development of Mao Zedong's Military Thinking* by Liao Guoliang and Li Shishun, as well as thousands of academic papers were published to study the strategies and tactics for the people's war. These books and papers have discussed every aspect of the CPC's view of war and methodology, enabling the people to better understand Mao Zedong's thinking on people's revolutionary war.

4.3.2 The Theory of Building the People's Army

After failure of the national revolution in 1927, the CPC was confronted with the fresh task of independently leading the Chinese revolution and building a people's army. It is generally believed that the CPC's theory of building the people's army includes the following ideas.

4.3.2.1 The Sole Purpose of the People's Army Is to Serve the People Wholeheartedly

This purpose has always been clear. However, according to some researchers, this purpose should develop somewhat under the new historical conditions. They have argued that after the founding of the People's Republic, to serve the people wholeheartedly has become the purpose of not only the people's army but also the CPC or even all industries and sectors of society, so the purpose of the people's army should move further forward and become more concrete—to safeguard national security and interests. But most researchers have suggested that to serve the people wholeheartedly should forever be the purpose of the people's army because this is what makes this army different from the army of the exploiting classes. Army is a tool of class struggle, and it belongs to and serves the interests of a certain class. So, which class does it serve is a fundamental problem. Mao Zedong said, "Our Communist Party and the army led by our Party are battalions of the revolution. These battalions of ours are wholly dedicated to the liberation of the people and work entirely for the people's interests. The sole purpose of this army is to stand firmly with the Chinese people and to serve them wholeheartedly." In fierce revolutionary struggles and brutal wars, the people's army fought heroically for the liberation of the people, fearing neither hardship nor death. In peacetime, the people's army, stationed at places with the most difficult conditions and worked at the most needed positions, always protected the interests of the people. The development of the people's army for over eighty years has proved that this purpose is exactly why it is always invincible.

4.3.2.2 The People's Army Should Be under the Absolute Leadership of the Party

The Party's absolute leadership over the army is crucial to preserving the proletarian character of the army and to the survival and development of the Party. The issue under argument is that is it still necessary for the Party to strengthen its absolute leadership over the army after having seized state power. But this issue is often overlooked by some researchers.

(1) The Party should establish absolute leadership over the army. This idea was first put forward by Mao Zedong in the Resolution of the Gutian Meeting. Later in his "Problems of War and Strategy," he said, "Our principle is that the Party commands the gun, and the gun should never be allowed to command the Party." Thereafter, the Party maintaining absolute leadership over the army had become a principle for army building.

(2) The Party leads the army mainly by political leadership. First of all, the Party needs to educate soldiers in Marxism, the Party's line, principles and policies and the army's fundamental purpose. Second, the Party needs to establish its organizations through all levels in army units, such as Party branches at the company level, and create a system of Party representatives and a system of political commissars. Third, Party members should to set an example to other soldiers.

(3) The question of military power has a direct bearing on the standing of the Party in China and on the success of the revolution. Mao Zedong believed that the Party should command military power, which was determined by the special characteristics of the Chinese revolution. Without military power, the Party cannot get political power, let alone transform the Chinese society. The Party's absolute leadership over the army is crucial not only to preserving the proletarian character of the army but also to the standing of the Party and the people in China and the prospect of the

revolution. Mao Zedong had said that Chinese Communists should not fight for personal military power, but they should fight for military power for the Party, for military power for the people and for military power for the nation. So, the principle of the Party's absolute leadership over the army should be understood from the above two aspects.

(4) The Party should continue to preserve the proletarian character of the army after having seized power, which is generally affirmed by most scholars and researchers. However, there are people advocating nationalization, de-partification or de-politicization of the army. They argue that the army no longer needs to preserve its proletarian character because classes have been eliminated in China, and that the Party no longer needs to maintain absolute leadership over the army because the army has become an instrument of governance. This wrong idea is heavily criticized by most researchers, who advocate that the Party should never waver on the principle of maintaining absolute leadership over the army and waver on preserving its proletarian character. The practice of leading the army by two military commissions—the Party's Central Military Commission and the Central Military Commission of the People's Republic of China—is an embodiment of this principle in the new current situation. Some researchers have quoted what Deng Xiaoping said when he was to retire from his position as Chairman of the Central Military Commission: "I am convinced that our army will be able to steadfastly maintain its own character, that is, that it will continue to belong to the Party, the people and our socialist country. In this respect our army is different from the armies of other countries."[1]

4.3.2.3 Political Work Is the Lifeline of Army Building

The fundamental principle for building and running the army is strengthening it politically. Soon after the Gutian Meeting, Mao Zedong had discussed the dialectical relationship between political work in the army and all other work and put forward the idea that political work is the lifeblood of army building. To strengthen the army politically is to ensure it is under the

---

[1] *Selected Works of Deng Xiaoping*, Eng. ed., FLP, Beijing, 1994, Vol. III, p. 323.

absolute leadership of the Party and takes serving the people wholehearted as its fundamental purpose. Mao Zedong had advanced a series of principles for political work in the army such as the principles of the unity between officers and men, the unity between army and people and the disintegration of the enemy forces, the Three Main Rules of Discipline and Eight Points for Attention[1], and the principle of democracy in military, political and economic affairs under centralized guidance. The document "On the Political Work in the Army" drafted by Mao Zedong in 1944 had formulated a general principle for political work in the army: uniting our own ranks and defeating the enemy to liberate the people; and giving top priority to ideological work in the army. That was an important document in the history of the people's army after the Gutian Meeting and had greatly guided its future political work.

4.3.2.4 The Army and the People Are the Foundation of Victory in the Revolutionary War

(1) In fighting revolutionary wars, the Party should rely on revolutionary bases and on the people's army, so it was very necessary for it to establish solid bases during its protracted struggle against the enemy. All researchers have written books or papers to expound on this strategic necessity, but some of them have overlooked how Mao Zedong thought about revolutionary bases in a dialectical way. On the one hand, revolutionary bases, which the revolutionary forces had relied on in fighting the war, should not be abandoned if not left with another choice. On the other hand, to defend bases recklessly without considering the enemy's forces could only lead to failure in the war. According to Mao Zedong, the loss of a Red Army unit or a revolutionary base did not mean a total failure for the Red Army, neither

---

[1] The Three Main Rules of Discipline are as follows: (1) Obey orders in all your actions. (2) Don't take a single needle or piece of thread from the masses. (3) Turn in everything captured. The Eight Points for Attention include: (1) Speak politely. (2) Pay fairly for what you buy. (3) Return everything you borrow. (4) Pay for anything you damage. (5) Don't hit or swear at people. (6) Don't damage crops. (7) Don't take liberties with women. (8) Don't ill-treat captives.

could the victory in one or more counter-campaigns or the establishment or development of one or more bases meant its final victory. The Red Army could suffer a total failure only when all its forces and bases were annihilated. But, that would not happen in China, whose extremely uneven political and economic development and extensive territory could give the Red Army enough room to maneuver. Therefore, although it had failed in its resistance to the fifth encirclement and suppression campaign and had to set out on the arduous Long March, the Red Army could not be defeated in the whole revolutionary war—it just moved to new base areas. So, it became a strategic thinking: We should not take desperate and reckless actions by fear of losing a piece of ground because it could only result in loss of both the ground and our forces; on the contrary, we should have the courage to leave the base but preserve our forces so that we have the opportunity to recover the lost ground. In fighting against encirclement and suppression campaigns, the number one concern for the people' army was to grow stronger, not weaker, so it should not conquer a city or a piece of ground when the position was obviously and definitely unfavorable. The people's army was the core force in China's revolutionary war. Only after having a people' army, could the Party establish and develop base areas, utilize manpower and material resources in base areas, and march toward victory by taking the road of encircling the cities from the countryside and seizing state power by armed forces.

(2) The revolutionary war was a war of the masses; all the masses should be mobilized. The people's army was the core force in the revolutionary war, but the masses needed be fully mobilized to provide it with a solid foundation. According to Mao Zedong, the richest source of power to wage war laid in the masses of the people; they were a true bastion of iron which no force could smash; relying on millions upon millions of people who genuinely and sincerely supported the revolution and expansion of the revolutionary war, the Party winning the rule in the whole of China. China's revolutionary forces were divided into three parts—the main forces, the regional forces (field armies and local troops) and militia. In warfare,

they fought battles and combats separately or in cooperation to bring their strengths into full play. They made the most of the advantages of the people's war and fully embodied the saying that the army and the people are the foundation of victory in the revolutionary war. Workers, peasants, women, young people and even children did their best to strive for victory in the revolutionary war. The unarmed masses of people supported the war by supplying manpower and material and financial resources and sharing various kinds of political, economic, cultural and health work. The idea that the army and the people are the foundation of victory in the revolutionary war reflects the basic feature of the people's revolutionary war in China and was therefore the Party's basic line in directing the war.

4.3.3 Strategic and Tactical Principles for the People's War

Strategic and tactical principles for the people's war were embodied in some of Mao Zedong's works such as "Problems of Strategy in China's Revolutionary War," "Problems of Strategy in Guerilla War Against Japan," "On Protracted War" and "Problems of War and Strategy." His idea of despising the enemy strategically and taking full account of it tactically was the general principle for the people's war. Below is a brief introduction to strategies and tactics for the people's war.

4.3.3.1 Principle of Active Defense

According to the overall situation of the revolutionary war, the enemy was strong and was attacking and the revolutionary force was weak and was defending. Active defense was the only correct strategic principle that could be taken to allow the revolutionary force to change from weakness to strength and defeat the enemy during a protracted revolutionary war.

Active defense did not mean ceaseless retreat or flight-ism. The idea of "luring the enemy in deep and creating opportunities to wipe it out; but being cautious in the initial battle" was an application of active defense, in concrete—lure the enemy into the base areas, select or create conditions favorable to ourselves but unfavorable to the enemy so as to bring about a change in the balance of forces, then begin the counter-offensive. This strategy was the surest method often used by the people's army in defeating the enemy's encirclement and suppressions.

A correct understanding of active defense should be: conduct tactical offense within the strategic defense, realize campaigns and battles of quick decision within the strategically protracted war, and realize campaigns and battles on exterior lines (that is, out of the base area) within strategically interior lines (that is, in the base area). Its application includes retreat in order to advance, mounting attacks as a means of defense, bringing about a change in the balance of forces, "breaking up the whole into parts" (the dispersal of guerrilla units) and "assembling the parts into a whole" (concentration of forces).

4.3.3.2 The Strategic Role of Guerrilla Warfare

Guerrilla warfare is a method of operation that enables guerrilla units, which are usually composed of militia, guerrillas and regular troops and supported by the masses, to attack the enemy with much flexibility and mobility. Guerrilla warfare and mobile warfare of a guerrilla character are methods of operation, which the principle of active defense is best suitable. Unlike in regular warfare, guerrilla warfare does not have fixed positions and lines and can attack the enemy whenever the conditions are favorable. Guerrilla units led by the Party are often stationed in base areas, but they can also leave the base area to fight mobile warfare, which is an important way for them to defeat the enemy's encirclement and suppression, and they can establish new base areas from time to time. Therefore, their method of fighting is completely different from that of roving rebels.

As early as in May 1928, Mao Zedong in Jinggang Mountains had solved some basic principles of guerrilla warfare: "The enemy advances, we retreat; the enemy camps, we harass; the enemy tires, we attack; the enemy retreats, we pursue." Later during the period of the War of Resistance against Japan, a new principle "the enemy advances, we advance." was put forward. Mao Zedong had pointed out that during China's revolutionary war, especially during the War of Resistance against Japan, guerrilla warfare was not a tactic but a strategy, which made him the first military strategist in the world who realized the strategic role and importance of guerrilla warfare. His opinion was well reasoned. During the revolutionary war, the basic situation that the enemy was strong and the revolutionary force was weak— especially the great disparity in strength between China and Japan—could not be changed in short time. If China was a small country in which the role of guerrilla warfare was only to render direct support over short distances to the campaigns of the regular progressive army, there would, of course, be only tactical problems but no strategic ones. On the other hand, if China were a country as strong as the Soviet Union and the invading enemy could either be quickly expelled or occupy only small areas, then again guerrilla warfare would naturally involve only tactical but not strategic problems. However, in fact, China was both a large and a weak country, whose vast areas were occupied. The anti-Japanese guerrilla warfare would not be short or small-scale, but would be protracted and extensive. Therefore, guerrilla warfare was not a tactic but a strategy.

4.3.3.3 Adjusting Strategies Timely According to Change in the Balance of Forces and Development of the War

The ability of the Party to adjust its military strategies in a timely fashion by judging the hour and sizing up the situation was an important reason why it could win the Chinese revolutionary war. Mao Zedong had said, "All the laws for directing war develop as history develops and as war develops; nothing remains unchanged." Therefore, in directing China's revolutionary war, the Party should not allow itself to be limited to any particular form of warfare or be restrained by certain experience without a moment's flexibility. On the contrary, it should apply mobile, guerrilla and positional warfare flexibly and as needed, which was a feature of the revolutionary war in China. Throughout the complete period of the new-democratic revolution, there were three fundamental changes in strategies in China's revolutionary war: the first was the change between guerrilla warfare and regular warfare; the second was the change from mobile warfare of a guerrilla character to guerrilla warfare as the main form; and the third was the change during the War of Liberation from guerrillas and guerrilla warfare prevailing during the War of Resistance against Japan to regular army and regular warfare (mainly massive mobile and positional warfare).

4.3.3.4 Principle of Gathering Superior Forces and Destroying the Enemy Forces One by One

China's revolutionary war was protracted, and the enemy was strong. A battle in which the enemy was routed could not basically change the enemy's strength against our weakness and consequently did not have much meaning. "Injuring all of a man's ten fingers is not as effective as chopping off one." Therefore the people's army should concentrate its forces to form absolute superiority against the enemy on a certain battlefield and battle in order to annihilate the enemy's effective strength one by one. This principle was compatible with the principle of active defense. Later during the period of the War of Liberation, Mao Zedong, on the basis of reviewing experiences gained in the revolutionary war, had advanced the ten major principles of operation, the core idea of which was concentrating a superior force to wipe out the enemy's effective strength. Of course, the ten major principles of operation dealt with more than those problems related to active defense. Military theorists in China and other countries commonly believe that, as the further development of Mao Zedong's military thinking, there is also a doctrine of strategic offensive focusing on concentrating a superior force to wipe out the enemy's effective strength. Dealing with a full set of major strategic and tactical problems in the people's revolutionary war, these thoughts had provided the people's army with systematic ideas for fighting the war. They were results achieved by the tempering of the People's Liberation Army in long years of fighting against domestic and foreign enemies and they were completely suited to the then existing situation in China.

In conclusion, correct strategies and tactics for the people's war should be: oppose adventurism when on the offensive, oppose conservatism when on the defensive, and oppose flight-ism when shifting from one place to another; oppose guerrilla-ism in the army, while recognizing the guerrilla character of its operations; uphold the strategy of protracted war and campaigns of quick decision; oppose fixed battle lines and oppose positional warfare; oppose fighting merely to rout the enemy, favor fluid battle lines and mobile warfare, and uphold fighting to annihilate the enemy; oppose the strategy of striking with two "fists" in two directions at the same time, and uphold the strategy of striking with one "fist" in one direction at one time.

4.3.4 Development of the Thinking on the People's Revolutionary War

The theory of strengthening peacetime national defense was a new development of Mao Zedong's thinking on the people's revolutionary war. Under the new historical conditions, the principle of active defense is still the basic tenet of Mao Zedong's military thinking. Added to the principle are a change in the focus of the army's military strategy from seizing power by armed force to building a powerful national defense system for New China, the unity of factors pertaining to people and weapons, and the integration of the main forces, the regional forces and militia. Mao Zedong had always upheld the basic principles of the thinking on people's revolutionary war created during China's democratic revolution. He stressed the need to keep the army under absolute leadership of the Party, educate the army in its fundamental purpose of serving the people wholeheartedly, and promote unity between the army and the people and between officers and soldiers. He had frequently emphasized that the principle of active defense should be upheld in fighting against foreign invasion in the future. According to changes in the domestic and international situations, he had also advanced the idea of building a people's army that is standardized and modern.

Researchers have argued that this military idea of Mao Zedong had begun to take shape during the revolutionary war. When stressing the importance of strengthening the army politically, he had also attached great attention to problems of military technology. As early as in the days in the

Jinggang Mountains, he had stressed that improvement in military technology was just as important as political work and that all Red Army soldiers should learn military technologies. During the period of the War of Resistance against Japan, Mao Zedong had pointed out that the people's army would develop from a low stage to a higher stage and from the Chinese type to the world type. After winning the War of Liberation in 1949, he had put forward that efforts should be made to make all field armies more standardized, develop technical arms, improve the sense of organization and discipline in the army, and quickly enact military laws and regulations.

After the liberation of the whole country, Mao Zedong had pointed out that the people's army, having won a nationwide victory in the people's revolution, should develop into a higher stage—a stage to grasp modern military technology. For that purpose, he definitely put forward the slogan "build a modern and standardized army to protect our country." He advanced that in addition to a powerful army, China also needed to build a powerful air force, a powerful navy and other technical arms, and develop modern defense technologies such as defense type nuclear weapons. In addition, he asked the whole army to "grasp the newest equipment and upcoming new tactics."

There are two different kinds of understanding on the targets for army building in the new period. Most researchers believe that the fundamental target is to build a strong army that is modern, revolutionary and standardized. To modernize it is the core, to standardize it is to guarantee that it is capable of fighting warfare of the future, and to revolutionize it is to make sure that it carries on its fine historical tradition.

Other researchers believe that Mao Zedong's idea of building a modern and standardized army includes lots of content such as new weapons and military equipment, logistics, sense of organization and discipline and military regulations. They argue that such content shows that the army is developing toward a world type army. However, they have also argued that under the new technological revolution, the army needs to develop toward a world type army in a step-by-step manner because it cannot catch up with every aspect of world military development all at once but has to first focus on key aspects of it.

As pointed out by military theorists, Mao Zedong in 1958 had discussed the problem of stages for the development of the army: the first was a stage for millet plus rifles; the second was a stage for rifles plus planes and artillery; and the third was a stage for conventional weapons plus special weapons. The division of the three stages also indicate the army's plan to develop from the Chinese type to the world type and to realize modernization of national defense.

4.3.5 Tendencies Deserving Much Attention and Problems for Further Discussion

As pointed out by scholars researching Mao Zedong's military thinking, there were few people before the Third Plenary Session of the Eleventh CPC Central Committee who thought differently on the above principles of Mao Zedong's thinking on people's revolutionary war. Along and after the debate over whether practice is the sole criterion for testing truth, a few researchers have put forward some extremely different opinions, and some tendencies among them deserve attention. They mainly misapprehend modern warfare and are confused about whether to continue upholding the basic principles of Mao Zedong's military thinking. In order to refute theses erroneous opinions, the basic issues below need to be further considered and studied.

4.3.5.1 Dialectical Relationship between People and Weapons and Their Roles in War

Mao Zedong had commented, "Weapons are an important factor in war, but not the decisive factor; it is people, not things, that are decisive. The contest of strength is not only a contest of military and economic power, but also a contest of human power and morale. Military and economic power is necessarily wielded by people." According to him, human power is material strength and morale is people's inner strength. He believed that people's inner strength—the conscious dynamic role they displayed in the war—was very important for winning the war.

It is universally believed by military theorists that Mao Zedong had elaborated on the relationship between people and weapons more incisively than any other Chinese and foreign strategists did. His above ideas are still important and can guide future warfare. However, there are also researchers holding an opposite view. They argue that modern warfare is about a contest of strength and high technology, human power and morale can no longer make a crucial difference, and people's dynamic role can do nothing if faced with highly-sophisticated weapons. In other words, they believe that Mao Zedong's ideas are outdated. But, most military theorists refute this erroneous view. It is the people who invent, produce and use weapons, and there is no such a modern high-tech weapon that could do everything and could be restricted by nothing-everything has its vanquisher. Future wars are still to be divided into just wars and unjust wars, as well as invasion wars and anti-invasion wars, so it is very wrong to assert that human power and morale can do nothing in a future war. Besides, in order to succeed modern weapons achieve the anticipated results, there should be people conducting reconnaissance to find out about the enemy's forces and the terrain and its features and analyzing climate and opportunities for combat. Therefore, factors pertaining to people will continue to play a decisive role in future war-even a still bigger role.

4.3.5.2 Does the People's War Apply to Future Warfare?

Some researchers believe that the answer is negative. Their argument is as follows. The strategies and tactics for the people's war apply only to warfare of millet plus rifles. In future war, the enemy can attack us by using precisely-guided missiles and intercontinental missiles without showing themselves, how should we apply the strategies and tactics for the people's war? Most military theorists agree that the era of millet plus rifles has gone. So, to carry on Mao Zedong's thinking on the people's war is not to copy its concrete ways of fighting but to carry forward its ideas, methods and basic principles. First of all, the war China might need to fight in the future should be a defense war against invasion because China will never invade any other country, so it will have the strong backing of the entire Chinese people. Second, principles for the people's war such as despising the enemy strategically and taking full account of it tactically, practicing active defense, fighting a protracted war, and concentrating a superior force to destroy the enemy forces one by one, as well as its methods of "know the enemy and know yourself, and you can fight a hundred battles with no danger of defeat" and "breaking up the whole into parts (the dispersal of guerrilla units) and assembling the parts into a whole (concentration of forces)" still apply in future war. So the people's war is still the key to defeating the enemy.

4.3.5.3 Problems about Carrying on and Developing Mao Zedong's Thinking on People's Revolutionary War

Originated during the revolutionary war, Mao Zedong's thinking on people's revolutionary war is inevitably restricted by historical conditions. How should we carry on and develop it? Most military theorists, opposing to taking it as dogma, argue that we should enrich it according to the new conditions while carrying forward its basic principles. Some of them advance that the people's army needs to apply the principle of active defense flexibly in future anti-invasion war—to practice strong defense at important directions or positions with field troops practicing offense by fighting battles of quick decision on the exterior line. Some also advance that in applying the principle of concentrating a superior force in a future war, the superiority over the enemy can be in number or in quality. In short, to carry on and develop the thinking under the new historical conditions is to apply and develop its basic principles. Of course, it cannot be developed by mere theoretical talk, but only by practice. Mao Zedong himself also said that military thinking should be developed according to actual conditions. At an enlarged meeting of the Central Military Commission in 1958, he had commented, "The ten major principles of operation, put forward when the people's army began to launch the countrywide counter-offensives on the basis of a review of experience in the period of the ten years' civil war, the period of the War of Resistance against Japan and the early period of the War of Liberation, are the result of integration of the basic tenets of Marxism-Leninism with the practice of the Chinese revolution. By applying them, we won the War of Liberation and the War to Resist US Aggression and Aid Korea—but the victory in the latter war was attributable to other reasons as well. They are still applicable to the present situation, and may be applicable in the future. However, Marxism-Leninism never ceases developing, so they will also develop and some of their content might even need to be corrected according to concrete realities in future war." In conclusion, researchers believe that Mao Zedong's military thinking is a scientific system and his thinking on the people's revolutionary war is the core of his military thinking, and that his theories about army building, people's war and strategies and tactics for a people's war are applicable as long as they meet the requirement of new realities.

Researchers have produced a large number of results in studying Mao Zedong's thinking on people's revolutionary war because they began to study it earlier and have studied it deeply. However, there are also problems needing to be addressed for future studies. For instance, theoreticians of the Party and military theorists should cooperate more closely in their studies so that both of them can get their range and fields of research broadened. In addition, researchers have not given a clear definition to the thought on people's revolutionary war, the thought on people's war, and the thought on armed struggle, which is one of the three talismans for the Chinese revolution.

4.4 Theory of the United Front

The united front was one of the three talismans for the Chinese revolution as well as an important component of Mao Zedong Thought. Researchers have thoroughly and systematically studied this theory and have achieved remarkable results.

4.4.1 How Mao Zedong's Theory of the United Front Has Enriched and Developed Marxist Theory of United Front

According to generalization and summarization by researchers, Mao Zedong has enriched and developed Marxist theory of united front in the following aspects.

(1) He introduced the fundamental idea guiding the work of the Communist Party on a united front basis—the proletariat cannot free itself before it has freed the entire human race.

(2) He had expounded that the united front is one of the three talismans for the Chinese revolution.

(3) He had scientifically explained the nature of the united front. According to some researchers, Mao Zedong held that the nature of a united front is to expand revolutionary forces and isolate the enemy to the maximum. There are also researches believing that the nature is the relationship between being firm in principle and the flexibility permitted and necessary for carrying out the principle, which is also the core of the united front thought.

(4) He had advanced a series of basic principles for adhering to and developing the united front such as the principle of "independence and initiative within the united front," the principle of treating different groups differently, making use of contradictions and winning over the many, and the principle of unity between principle and flexibility.

(5) He had elaborated on the importance for the CPC to lead the united front, which he believed to be the most fundamental feature of the united front, and he also pointed out the way for the CPC to achieve leadership over the united front.

(6) He had stressed that the worker-peasant alliance is the foundation of the united front.

(7) He divided the Chinese bourgeoisie into two groups and advanced the strategy of realizing unity with them through struggle. During the socialist construction, he advanced the theory of correctly handling contradictions

among the people.

(8) He had expounded the relations between the CPC and the democratic parties—as long-term coexistence and mutual oversight.

(9) He affirmed that the Chinese People's Political Consultative Conference (CPPCC) is an important organizational form for the people's democratic united front.

(10) He proposed that a broad international united front should be established on the basis of independence and self-reliance to promote development of revolution and construction in every nation. During the socialist construction period, he developed his idea of peaceful co-existence into the Five Principles of Peaceful Coexistence, which became a basic norm for international relations.

4.4.2 Mao Zedong's Theory of the United Front during the New-Democratic Revolution

4.4.2.1 Encapsulation of the Theory

There were two encapsulations before the Third Plenary Session of the Eleventh Central Committee of the CPC. The first one was made by Zhou Enlai in his report "On the United Front" to the CPC's Seventh Congress in 1945: "To establish a new-democratic united front, we should have a clear understanding of the enemy, secondly our own ranks and the question of 'the commanding officer'." The second one was made by Li Weihan in the early 1960s, who summarized the theory into seven aspects. Research into this theory thereafter has focused on the above two encapsulations. The dominant encapsulation at present is as follows: (1) the united front was a talisman for the Chinese revolution; (2) the united front includes two alliances, with the worker-peasant alliance being the foundation; (3) proletarian leadership in the united front should be upheld; (4) the Chinese bourgeoisie could be divided into two groups, with which the CPC needed to realize unity through struggle; and (5) unity between principle and flexibility should be upheld.

4.4.2.2 Theoretical Sources of Mao Zedong's Thinking on New-Democratic United Front and Its Formation and Development

There are two different views on the theoretical sources of Mao Zedong's thinking on new-democratic united front. One-source believers hold that the Marxist theory of united front was the sole theoretical source. Two-source believers hold that in addition to the Marxist theory of united front, Mao Zedong was also influenced by China's traditional culture. The latter view is more widespread at present. But, efforts are needed to study which was the primary source and which was the secondary one and how they interrelate with each other.

In recent years, researchers are beginning to focus on studying the history of Mao Zedong's thinking on the united front during the new-democratic revolution. There are three opinions on its stages of development. The first one is that its stages of development were the same as that of the CPC. The second one is that it could be divided into the thinking on revolutionary united front (1919-1935), the thinking on anti-Japanese national united front (1935-1945) and the thinking on the people's democratic united front (1946-1949). The third one is that it was in accord with the appearance, formation and development of Mao Zedong Thought. Generally, researchers agree that Mao Zedong's thinking on the united front became mature during the War of Resistance against Japan. In addition, most of them oppose that its development should not be simply divided according to stages in the history of the CPC and the history of united front. In short, deeper and more detailed analyses are needed on this issue.

4.4.3 The Theory of the Chinese Bourgeoisie

4.4.3.1 Content of the Theory of the Chinese Bourgeoisie

Researchers universally agree that the theory includes the following content: the Chinese bourgeoisie can be divided into big bourgeoisie and national bourgeoisie; the national bourgeoisie had a dual character; the alliance between the proletariat and the national bourgeoisie was an important part of the united front; the proletariat could form a united front with certain big bourgeois groups under special conditions; the proletariat should have the leadership; the proletariat should adhere to a strategy of realizing unity through struggle during its alliance with the bourgeoisie; the economic policy of confiscating bureaucrat-capital and protecting the industry and commerce of the national bourgeoisie.

4.4.3.2 The Time and Symbols of the Formation of the Theory of the Chinese Bourgeoisie

Some researchers believe that Mao Zedong's "Analysis of the Classes in Chinese Society" and the Third Plenary Session of the Fourth CPC Central Committee marks the basic formation of the theory of the Chinese bourgeoisie. Others believe that when the Third Plenary Session of the Fourth CPC Central Committee was held, the Central Committee's understanding of the dual character of the Chinese bourgeoisie was different from that of Mao Zedong, and that it was not until the Wayaobao Meeting and the publication of Mao Zedong's "On Tactics Against Japanese Imperialism" that the Central Committee had finally recognized Mao Zedong's correct understanding of the dual character of the Chinese bourgeoisie and consequently worked out some correct policies.

4.4.3.3 On the Principle of Realizing Unity through Struggle in the United Front

Researchers generally agree that the principle was put forward to deal with the dual character of the Chinese bourgeoisie with the aim of suppressing its negative effects and getting the alliance with it to supplement the worker-peasant alliance. But they disagree with each other on targets of the principle. Some of them believe that it was targeted only to the anti-Japanese sections of the big landlords and big bourgeoisie as well as the intermediate classes which were in the united front. Others believe that it was also targeted on some of the puppet troops, the traitors and the pro-Japanese elements.

Researchers are also studying if the principle applies to the united front in the new period in the current situation. Some believe that participants in a united front always need to strive for unity of opposites, so, as long as the united front exists, the principle of realizing unity through struggle is always applicable. Others believe that since the class relations and the nature of contradictions in the united front have changed, the principle for dealing with contradictions in the united front also need to change, so, the principle of realizing unity through struggle is not applicable to the united front in the new period. In fact, what they are arguing about is whether the principle is universally applicable.

4.4.4 The Thinking on Proletarian Leadership in the United Front

4.4.4.1 The Meaning of the Thinking on Proletarian Leadership and Its Initiators

There are two opinions on the meaning of the thinking on proletarian leadership. The first opinion believes that the thinking answered the sole question of who was to lead China's democratic revolution. The second opinion believes that the thinking, in addition to declaring that the Chinese proletariat should lead and was capable of leading the Chinese democratic revolution, had also worked out a set of strategies, principles and policies for realizing that idea. So, the thinking required that the proletariat should correctly understand its nature and strength and its place among the classes in Chinese society; correctly understand problems of the peasantry and the importance of worker-peasant alliance; and correctly understand the Chinese bourgeoisie and find out ways to contest for leadership over the alliance it has formed with the bourgeoisie.

Due to differences on the meaning of the thinking, researchers disagree with each other on who initiated the idea of contesting for leadership. Some believe that the Party's certain early leaders such as Qu Qiubai, Gao Junyu, Cai Hesen, Yun Daiying, Deng Zhongxia and Peng Shuzhi have initiated this idea in their writings. Others disagree. They argue that no one had written elaborating on ideas about leadership before the CPC's Fourth Congress, so it was the CPC as a collective body which had initiated the idea.

4.4.4.2 The Theoretical Source and Formation of the Thinking on Proletarian Leadership

Researchers all believe that the thinking generally came from Lenin and the Communist International, but disagree with each other on its direct source. Some hold that Peng Shuzhi had brought it to China from the Communist International and intermingled it with his idea of "natural leadership." Others think that the CPC had advanced the thinking at its Fourth Congress after reviewing its practice and experience in struggling for leadership in the Chinese revolution and consulting with the Communist International. As a result, researchers have different opinions on the question of whether the CPC's Fourth Congress marked the formation of the thinking.

One opinion believes that the CPC's Fourth Congress did mark the formation of the thinking because the CPC at the Congress not only put forward the question of proletarian leadership but also formulated a set of principles and policies on how the proletariat could achieve leadership and lead the revolution. For instance, it raised the issue of regarding the peasantry as the chief ally in the revolution, explained the significance of establishing worker-peasant alliance, and made a resolution on the peasant problem. It had stressed the need for the CPC to seek independence within the united front and criticized the "Left" and Right deviationist mistakes, with the latter being the main danger inside the Party. In addition, it formulated the CPC's principles concerning the work in the KMT-to help and expand the left-wing of KMT, criticize and unite the middle-wing and oppose the right-wing.

Another opinion believes that Mao Zedong's essay "Analysis of the Classes in Chinese Society" marked the formation of the thinking, because: (1) The essay had scientifically analyzed the proletariat, and the CPC's Fourth Congress did not. Although the essay did not directly put forward the idea of proletarian leadership, the terms "mainstay" and "the main force" it used had expressed the meaning of "leading force." (2) The essay divided the Chinese bourgeoisie into big bourgeoisie and middle bourgeoisie and formulated the basic principle on how to treat them differently, which laid an ideological foundation for proletarian leadership. (3) The essay had scientifically analyzed the petite bourgeoisie and the semi-proletariat, solved the peasant problem, and found reliable friends for the proletariat. (4) The essay had discussed the important role of the proletariat in the revolution.

Still another opinion believes that it was not until the August 7th Meeting in 1927 that the CPC Central Committee had basically solved the problem of leadership in the revolution because it had not formulated correct strategies and policies for realizing proletarian leadership before that, although it did put forward the problem of leadership at its Fourth Congress.

It is believed in this book that, the fact that the problem of proletarian leadership is raised does not necessarily mean it has been solved. The Party's Fourth Congress had definitely advanced the problem of proletarian leadership, stressed the importance of regarding the peasantry as the chief ally, and had formulated a set of policies and principles for realizing proletarian leadership. Mao Zedong's "Analysis of the Classes in Chinese Society" had scientifically analyzed all the classes in Chinese society and introduced some policies and principles for treating the bourgeoisie and the peasantry. All this shows that the CPC was deepening its understanding of the problem of proletarian leadership. However, the problem was still not solved. To solve the problem under the social and historical conditions at that time, the following two problems should first be solved: (1) the problem of armed struggle—the proletariat should command revolutionary armed force and find a correct road for armed struggle; and (2) the problem of the peasantry—to lead the peasantry in launching the Agrarian Revolution. The two problems were not solved until the CPC found the revolutionary road of encircling the cities from the countryside and put forward corresponding theories. Therefore, the problem of proletarian leadership was fully solved around 1930, when the theory of encircling the cities from the countryside took shape.

4.4.5 On the Theory of Anti-Japanese National United Front

4.4.5.1 The Theoretical Source of the Theory of Anti-Japanese National United Front

There are two different views in this regard. The first is that the theory was derived from principles of the Seventh Enlarged Plenum of the Executive Committee of the Communist International. The second is that the CPC had developed the theory according to the concrete realities in China. The two views both make some sense. In fact, the theory was produced by the CPC after its long-term practice and exploration but was also influenced by the international united front against Fascism formulated by the Communist International.

4.4.5.2 The Principle of "Independence and Initiative within Anti-Japanese United Front" and Its Relationship with Proletarian Leadership

Some researchers hold that the principle of "independence and initiative within the united front" was in essence proletarian leadership. Others believe that they were not the same. The principle was a measure to develop and expand the proletariat and gain leadership and also was a norm for handling party to party relations within the united front. It was introduced under complicated historical conditions to fight against Chiang Kai-shek's anti-Communist policy, crush Wang Ming's new capitulationism within the Party, and oppose the tendency within the Party to accept directives from the Communist International and the Soviet Union as dogmas. Therefore, one could say that the principle was aimed to gain leadership in the united front. However, the principle of "independence and initiative within the united front" did not stop developing and gradually became a core idea of Mao Zedong Thought and the proletariat's worldview and methodology. In conclusion, the principle was not the same as proletarian leadership although they were closely related to each other.

After the theoretical concept of "one country, two systems" was advanced for Taiwan and Hong Kong issues, some researchers put forward that the then co-existing anti-Japanese base areas and KMT-controlled areas in China was an initial form of "one country, two systems." Other researchers disagree because there was no coexistence of public and private ownership at that time-only some democratic reform measures had been carried out in liberated areas.

4.4.6 About the Thinking on KMT-CPC Cooperation

4.4.6.1 The Foundation for KMT-CPC Cooperation

Researchers of the mainland China generally believe that KMT-CPC cooperation had both class foundation-the national bourgeoisie and the proletariat both had the revolutionary need to fight against imperialism and feudalism, and also political and ideological foundation-the new Three People's Principles of Dr. Sun Yat-sen. Scholars in Taiwan hold that KMT-CPC cooperation was due to the then political situation and revolutionary environment. The fundamental difference between the mainland and Taiwan researchers is that the former think KMT-CPC cooperation was inexorable while the latter group thinks it was not.

4.4.6.2 The "Intra-Party Cooperation" during the Great Revolution

Some researchers consider that the idea of "intra-party cooperation," just like Chen Duxiu's idea of "second revolution," had overestimated the power of KMT and underestimated the CPC, had restrained the CPC from striving for leadership, and eventually led the Great Revolution (1924-1927) into failure. But, most researchers believe that the idea of "intra-party cooperation" was totally different from Chen Duxiu's idea of "second revolution" or the Right opportunism but had greatly promoted the Great Revolution.

4.4.6.3 The Nature of Relations Between the KMT and the CPC

Some researchers hold that the relation between the KMT and the CPC should be one in which they co-exist and complement and support each other in their common efforts to solve the contradictions in Chinese society and struggle for a bright future of the nation because they both shouldered the responsibility of making the country independent, democratic, prosperous and strong, although they seemed to be contradictory to each other because they represented the interests of different classes. But, some other researchers believe that the contradiction between them was a cultural one because the KMT and the CPC respectively represented the American and English bourgeois culture and CPC the Marxist culture.

In addition to the above discussions and arguments in the study of Mao Zedong's thinking on the united front during the new-democratic revolution, scholars also studied the theoretical contributions Zhou Enlai, Liu Shaoqi and other Party leaders have made to Mao Zedong's thinking on the united front, and researched the CPC's united front work concerning the working classes, the international united front, Party relations, intellectuals, and ethnic and religious groups and elements This book will not dwell on them in detail.

4.4.7 Development of Mao Zedong's Thinking on the United Front during the Socialist Period

Research in this area are relatively weak—not many fruits were produced and most of them are elaborations instead of arguments. They are focused on the following aspects.

(1) The importance of upholding the united front during the socialist period—the united front is still a talisman in the socialist period.

(2) Concrete policies on the socialist united front—upholding the principle of long-term coexistence and mutual oversight in the relations between the CPC and the democratic parties; strictly distinguishing between the two different types of contradictions, those between the people and the enemy and those among the people themselves, and handling them correctly; and focusing on correctly handling contradictions among the people in the country's political life.

(3) The CPPCC, as the highest organizational form of the people's democratic united front, has an irreplaceable role in the country's political life.

(4) Contributions to the Marxist theory on united front—the importance

of an international united front for peaceful coexistence, Mao Zedong's strategic idea of differentiating three worlds, and the Five Principles of Peaceful Coexistence.

4.4.8 The Practical Significance of Mao Zedong's Thinking on the United Front

Researchers generally focus their study on the following aspects although they have different emphases.

4.4.8.1 Upholding the CPC's Leadership in the United Front

As a unity of contradictions, the united front was comprised of different parties, classes, strata of society and groups. So, there should be a leading force in the united front to lead them in seeking common ground while preserving differences, forming a better and greater force, and achieving unity. Without such a leading force, they were sheep without a shepherd thus very easily, secondary contradictions hidden in the united front could aggravate, weakening or even eliminating the strength in solving the main contradictions in the country.

The proletariat is the representative of advanced productive forces, is the most farsighted, promising, disciplined, and militant revolutionary class in the history of mankind, and is most capable of interpreting the laws of historical development and making China independent, prosperous, strong and democratic. So the leading force in the united front should be a proletarian party—the CPC. If the CPC surrendered the leadership to any other parties or groups, China's revolution and construction could suffer severe setbacks. As pointed out by Mao Zedong, no revolutionary united front could lead to victory without the strong leadership of the CPC.

4.4.8.2 Adjust Principles for the United Front in Line with Different Historical Phases and Social and Political Changes to Recruit New Forces and Expand and Consolidate the United Front

The primary aim of the united front was to unite with all forces possible to together fight the chief enemy. However, in different historical phases and revolutionary situations, what forces could be firm allies in the united front, what forces could be united, and what forces should be fought against were different. Mao Zedong had always been adjusting the principles for the united front according to historical phases and revolutionary situations, which was an important reason that the Chinese revolution and construction was victorious.

4.4.8.3 Balance the Interests of Forces in the United Front to Stimulate Their Enthusiasm for the Revolution and Construction

The united front was a unity, in which relations were interwoven. Different parties, classes, strata of society, groups and individuals hailed from all corners of the country, represented their own interests and had their own worldview, pursuit, goals and characters. They had gathered in the united front conditionally and for a certain period of time because they shared a common purpose. Naturally, they had contradictions. Therefore, the leading force in the united front should find ways to solve and ease the contradictions, bring their initiative into full play and prevent them from fomenting conflicts.

4.4.8.4 Use Both Principles and Flexible Measures to Expand and Consolidate the United Front

Mao Zedong had made a thorough discussion about the problem of upholding principles in the united front. He had commented that CPC should not yield on matters of principle. At the same time, he also stressed the use of flexible strategies and methods to solve problems. He had commented that flexible measures and strategies should be used to address specific problems and solve concrete conflicts realistically, otherwise, the revolutionary united front could be destroyed. In doing united front work in the new period today, Mao Zedong's idea of both acting on principle and being flexible should be implemented.

4.4.8.5 Fully Understand the Protracted Character of United Front Work

The united front was a talisman the CPC used to achieve victory in the new-democratic revolution; it was also a talisman for China's socialist revolution and construction. The CPC was chosen by the Chinese people as the ruling party; the political system of multiparty cooperation under the leadership of the CPC is determined by the Chinese realities. Therefore, the CPC should work hard to ensure a long-term success of the united front work in order to arouse the enthusiasm of the democratic parties and patriots from all walks of life for participating in the deliberation and administration of state affairs and stimulate the enthusiasm of the people of all ethnic groups for building the country. If the CPC holds that it had become the ruling party, and gained absolute leadership, therefore could issue orders subjectively, it could soon get isolated. Mao Zedong had repeatedly warned the Chinese communists should not isolate themselves from the people.

4.4.8.6 Give a Full Play to the Role of the CPPCC and Mass Organizations in United Front Work

The united front is a political alliance with many participants. The key to fully implement the CPC's policies on united front work and uniting with all members of the democratic parties, persons without party affiliation and patriots from all walks of life is to carry out united front work through regular organizations and groups. The CPPCC is a national political organization, and mass organizations which is made up of representatives of various spheres and groups. Their role in united front work should be fully utilized.

4.4.8.7 Attach Great Importance to and Properly Settle Ethnic and Religious Issues

Ethnic and religious issues have a direct bearing not only on consolidating and expanding the domestic united front but also on establishing a broad international united front. For this reason, the CPC has always attached great importance to ethnic and religious issues, adhered to the principle of ethnic equality, unity and common prosperity, has perseveringly implemented the system of regional ethnic autonomy, and fully carried out the policy of freedom in religious belief. Its efforts have produced desirable results.

4.4.8.8 The Principle of Independence and Initiative in China's Opening Up Period

During China's opening up process, the principle of independence and initiative applies not only to issues in economic development, but also to issues of political principle—safeguarding national independence and state sovereignty, and adhering to Marxist principles, preserving the proletarian nature of the state power, and adhering to socialist orientation in reform and opening up stage. China can be more flexible in dealing with other countries and in developing economic and trade relations with them in the efforts to open wider to the outside world and promote socialist development, but should never waver from the basic principles. China should resolutely counter and oppose the attempt of any foreign bourgeoisie to encroach on its sovereignty, interfere in its internal affairs, or impair its socialist orientation and economic development, and should never barter away from principles. China should insist on analyzing and dealing with the bourgeoisie in other countries realistically, and follow the principle of realizing unity through struggle.

It should be noted that although the bourgeoisie in different countries share some common attributes, they can also be very different. For instance, the bourgeoisie in developed capitalist countries is very different from that in developing countries; the bourgeoisie in the United States is also different from that in Western European countries, although they are both developed countries. Furthermore, the bourgeoisie in the same country in its different stages or its different parts could treat China differently. Therefore, in dealing with the bourgeoisie in foreign countries, we should apply Mao Zedong's theory of the united front and learn from experience. We should always keep our heads clear, analyze them scientifically and realistically to better know them, and adopt corresponding policies and strategies according to actual conditions. By doing so, we can use a variety of methods to develop relations with various countries and groups of countries and achieve our purpose of winning friends, isolating the enemy and developing the country.

Nowadays, the principle of realizing unity through struggle still applies to relations with foreign bourgeoisie. The aim of realizing unity with them is to develop economic and trade relations and improve scientific and technological exchanges with developed capitalist countries and to serve country's socialist development. The struggle here includes not only struggles to strive for economic interests but also struggles to prevent peaceful evolution toward capitalism. Of course, it is necessary to have good skills in the struggle and struggle should be carried with reasonable, advantageous and restrained policies.

4.4.8.9 International United Front for Peaceful Coexistence

China's revolution was dependent on the revolutionary united front; and today China's development demands an international united front. Peace and development have become the main themes or trends in today's world. China's main objective is to develop, but it cannot develop in isolation from the rest of the world. To develop, China needs primarily a peaceful international environment and secondarily foreign assistance. Therefore, China should ensure success in two things: opposing hegemony politics and safeguarding world peace; making more friends around the world and constantly expanding and consolidating the international united front on the basis of the Five Principles of Peaceful Coexistence.

4.5 Theory of Party Building

As an important component of Mao Zedong Thought, Mao Zedong's thinking on Party building, also called as Mao Zedong's theory of Party building, deals with issues concerning Party building. Focusing on the clarification of the objective laws governing the founding, development and self-improvement of the CPC, it is an indispensable part of the scientific system of Mao Zedong Thought. It is the application and development of the party building theory of Marx, Engels and Lenin in the CPC's practice of self-improvement, and is the scientific and theoretical generalization of the CPC's experience in its self-improvement efforts. Like the other components of Mao Zedong Thought, it is the crystallization of the collective wisdom of the entire Party. Its detailed content is manifested in the works of Mao Zedong, Zhou Enlai, Liu Shaoqi, Zhu De and other revolutionaries of the older generation as well as in the documents produced by the Party's first generation of collective leadership.

Among revolutionaries of the older generation, Liu Shaoqi and Deng Xiaoping had comprehensively summarized and assessed Mao Zedong's thinking on Party building.

In his Report on the Revision of the Party Constitution to the Seventh National Congress of the CPC in May 1945, Liu Shaoqi had put forward the term "the theory of Party building enriched by Comrade Mao Zedong during the past three great revolutionary periods," and said that "Comrade Mao Zedong's correct line of Party building" should include ideas such as "first of all lay stress on ideological and political building without neglecting organizational building," "ideological education and leadership should come first when our Party exercises leadership," and "link the building of the Party closely with the Party's political line, and with our Party's relationship to the bourgeoisie and to armed struggle."[1] He was the first to put forward the terminology "Mao Zedong's theory of Party building" and "Mao Zedong's line of Party building," and he had also made an initial elaboration on this theoretical system.

Deng Xiaoping had also highly appraised Mao Zedong's thinking on Party building in his speech at the Third Plenary Session of the Tenth CPC Central Committee in July 1977. He had commented, "It was Comrade Mao Zedong who developed Lenin's theory of Party building most comprehensively. Even in the period of revolutionary struggle in the

---

[1] *Selected Works of Liu Shaoqi*, Eng. ed., FLP, Beijing, 1984, Vol. I, pp. 316, 328-329.

Jinggang Mountains, that is, just in the period of the formation of the Chinese Red Army, his ideas on Party building were already well defined.... His comprehensive theory on the subject took shape, on the basis of practice, in the Yan'an rectification movement. He developed an integral theory on the type of party to be built and its guiding ideology and style of work. By creating a comprehensive theory of Party building in the Yan'an rectification movement—and by educating the whole Party, army and people in this theory—he made it possible for us to build a fine party; that was why we were able to win complete victory in the War of Resistance Against Japan (1937-1945) and in the War of Liberation (1946-1949). After the founding of the People's Republic of China our Party continued to be vigorous and dynamic. Later, Comrade Mao Zedong's theory of Party building was developed further."[1] This statement was an incisive summary of the basic contents of Mao Zedong's thinking on Party building and its contribution, as well as the social conditions for its formation and the historical process of its development, and was consequently crucial to understanding and studying it.

The Resolution on Certain Questions in the History of Our Party Since the Founding of the People's Republic of China passed at the Sixth Plenary Session of the Eleventh CPC Central Committee in 1981 and the book Program for Studying Deng Xiaoping's Theory of Party Building compiled by the CPC Central Committee Policy Research Office, the CPC Central Committee Organization Department and the CPC Central Committee Party School in 1998 were the authoritative materials in expounding Mao Zedong's thinking on Party building. The above Resolution had encapsulated the thinking in a focused manner but had not thoroughly explain Mao Zedong's ideas of building the Party as a ruling party. This weakness was solved in the above book, which gave this thinking an objective, comprehensive, precise and scientific encapsulation. This indicates that after twenty years of reform and opening up, the CPC had developed a deeper and more comprehensive understanding of this thinking.

The CPC had started to study this thinking as early as during the period

---

[1] *Selected Works of Deng Xiaoping*, Eng. ed., FLP, Beijing, 1995, Vol. II, pp. 56-57.

of Yan'an rectification movement. A number of books such as *Communism and the Communist Party of China*, *On the Communist Party of China* and *Collection of Writings on Party Building* were published to study and publicize this thinking. As more and more people began to learn and study Mao Zedong Thought after the founding of New China, many study materials as well as writings and books were published to learn, study and publicize this thinking. But, only Party schools at that time had offered courses and conducted researches in this regard, while general colleges and universities seldom touched upon this subject. During the "cultural revolution," the learning and study of this thinking was severely interrupted by the erroneous "Left" ideas.

After the Third Plenary Session of the Eleventh Central Committee of the CPC, the study on this thinking has progressed greatly both in width and in depth. First, number of researchers have increased tremendously. In addition to teachers and scholars in Party schools, many teachers teaching political theory in colleges, personnel responsible for Party affairs and researchers from other sectors of the society all have begun to study this thinking. Second, both the number and quality of research results have improved noticeably, and a large number of important fruits have been produced. Among the most influential ones are two-volume *History of Mao Zedong's Theory of Party Building* written by Zhang Weiping and Zhang Liejun (Jiangxi People's Publishing House, 1987, 1990) and *Study on Mao Zedong's Thinking on Party Building* edited by Zhou Yi (The CPC Central Committee Party School Publishing House, 1989). Third, researchers have utilized some new research methods to study the thinking. They study both its history of development and its basic principles, both Mao Zedong's ideas of Party building and Party building ideas of Zhou Enlai, Liu Shaoqi and other Party leaders, and both the CPC's experience in self-improvement and the experience of foreign communist parties. In addition, they understand the importance of integrating theory with practice, which makes their research more comprehensive and systematic.

There are reasons for this huge progress in the study of this thinking.

On the one hand, the third and sixth plenary sessions of the Eleventh CPC Central Committee rectified the erroneous ideological and political lines in the CPC and scientifically and realistically described and assessed Mao Zedong Thought, which laid a healthy theoretical foundation for the study of this thinking. On the other hand, faced with the many new situations and problems arising in the course of reform, opening up and development of socialist market economy, the CPC needed a scientific theory to guide its action and turned to Mao Zedong's thinking on Party building for answers. In addition, the free and open academic atmosphere also facilitates researches. As a result, this thinking has always been a focus in the study of Mao Zedong Thought, the history of the Party and the Chinese revolution, and Party building in recent years.

The following is a summary of issues and achievements in the study of Mao Zedong's thinking on Party building.

4.5.1 The Historical Conditions under Which Mao Zedong's Thinking on Party Building Emerged

The thinking had emerged in the era of imperialism and proletarian revolution in semi-colonial and semi-feudal China with a backward economy and culture. Compared to communist parties in capitalist countries, the CPC had the following unique features.

First, the CPC was founded under the guidance and with the help of the Communist International according to the model of the Communist Party of Russia led by Lenin. It was not affected by the reformism and revisionism of the Second International. However, the Communist International had in several occasions given the CPC erroneous guidance because it was too far from China and did not know the conditions of the Chinese revolution, and the Communist Party of Russia had influenced the CPC both positively and negatively.

Second, founded in a country with only a comparatively small number of industrial workers but an extremely large number of peasants and petite bourgeoisie, the CPC had expanded its alliance with peasants and petite bourgeoisie, which brought many difficulties to its ideological and organizational improvement and made it harder to maintain its nature as a proletarian vanguard.

Third, the CPC had developed in unity with and struggle against the bourgeoisie, which made it a challenge for it to adhere to the correct political line and uphold proletarian leadership.

Fourth, the CPC had long been in an illegal position for a long period and expanded in protracted armed struggle, which made it very difficult for it to integrate its improvement with armed struggle and to maintain absolute leadership over the people's army.

Fifth, the CPC had developed in rural revolutionary base areas and was frequently cut apart or surrounded by the enemy, which also brought problems to its unity.

In conclusion, old China was a semi-colonial, semi-feudal, large Asian country, and the CPC had to face situations that were different from what European communist parties faced. The situations in China were very different from and more complicated than that in Western capitalist countries where Marx and Engels engaged in revolutionary activities in the nineteenth century and that in Russia where Lenin engaged in revolutionary activities and led the Russian October Revolution. As a result, the CPC met great difficulties in improving itself and shouldered more arduous tasks. Faced with these difficult situations and arduous tasks, the CPC's first generation of collective leadership with Mao Zedong at the core had creatively formulated the thinking on Party building by integrating Marxist-Leninist theory of party building with the CPC's realities and practice.

4.5.2 The Historical Course in Which Mao Zedong's Thinking on Party Building Took Shape and Developed

This thinking had undergone a long historical course in its formation and development. From a broad point of view, its development stages should accord with that of Mao Zedong Thought. At the same time, it had also some unique exclusive development stages because it had to deal with and solve some exclusive problems concerning Party building. Below, it will be divided into five stages.

The first stage was when the thinking emerged (1920-1927; from the preparation and founding of the CPC to the failure of the Great Revolution). The problem of what kind of Party to build was solved in this stage. The three letters on building the Party between Mao Zedong and Cai Hesen and Mao Zedong's essays "Analysis of the Classes in Chinese Society" and "Report on an Investigation of the Peasant Movement in Hunan," which had discussed some basic issues concerning building the Party such as its class foundation and nature, were the symbols that the thinking emerged.

The second stage was when the thinking had taken initial shape (1927-1935; from the failure of the Great Revolution to the Zunyi Meeting). Problems of ideological leadership and ideological improvement were solved during this stage. Mao Zedong's essays "The Struggle in the Chingkang Mountains," "The Resolution of the Gutian Meeting" and "Oppose Book Worship," and the "Letter from the Central Committee to the General Frontline Committee of the Fourth Army Group of the Red Army" (the September letter of the Central Committee) drafted by Chen Yi according to Zhou Enlai's dictation had raised the problem of correcting and opposing various non-proletarian ideas in the Party and advanced the principle of building the Party ideologically. They should be the symbols that the thinking had taken initial shape. More accurately, "The Resolution of the Gutian Meeting" marked the initial formation of the thinking.

The third stage was when the thinking had become mature and complete (1935-1945; from the Zunyi Meeting to the CPC's Seventh Congress). As the CPC grew mature, the thinking developed greatly during the Yan' an period and gradually became a complete system of theories. During this stage, Mao Zedong had written "On Contradiction," "On Practice," "Combat Liberalism," "The Role of the Chinese Communist Party in the National War," "Introducing *The Communist*," "Reform Our Study," "Rectify the Party's Style of Work," "Oppose Stereotyped Party Writing," "Some Questions Concerning Methods of Leadership," "Our Study and the Current

Situation" and "On Coalition Government" and Liu Shaoqi wrote "How to Be a Good Communist," "On Inner-Party Struggle" and "On the Party." These writings had defined the three talismans for the Chinese revolution, declared that Party building was a great undertaking, put forward the ideas of linking the building of the Party closely with the Party's political line, first of all laying stress on building the Party ideologically and correctly carrying out inner-Party struggles, and advanced the theories about how should Party members cultivate and temper themselves and how should the Party improve its three main work styles [integrating theory with practice, maintaining close ties with the masses and engaging in self-criticism—Tr.]. All this indicated that the thinking had developed into a comparatively complete system of theories. Researchers generally hold that Liu Shaoqi's article "On the Party" was the symbol that the thinking had become mature and fully developed.

The fourth stage was when the thinking had further developed (1945-1949; from the CPC's Seventh Congress to the Second Plenary Session of the Seventh CPC Central Committee). During this stage, Mao Zedong had written "On Setting Up a System of Reports," "On Some Important Problems of the Party's Present Policy," "A Circular on the Situation," "On Strengthening the Party Committee System" and "Methods of Work of Party Committees" to stress the importance of strengthening Party committees and adhering to correct policies and principles. Thus he had further developed the thinking.

The fifth stage was when Mao Zedong's theory of building the Party as a ruling party had taken shape and developed in twists and turns (1949-1976; from the Second Plenary Session of the Seventh CPC Central Committee to the end of the "cultural revolution"). As early as in the 1930s when the CPC was exercising power in the Soviet areas, Mao Zedong and Liu Shaoqi had thought about the problems that the Party might encounter after becoming a ruling party, arguing that Party members and cadres should guard against the tendency to become self-complacent or degenerate. This could be the symbol that Mao Zedong's thinking of building the Party as a ruling party had begun to take shape. Around the founding of New China, Mao Zedong and other revolutionaries of the older generation have discussed, both in theory and in practice, the new problems the CPC should face after it became the ruling party, such as how to shift the focus of its work, how to improve the quality of its members, how to prevent its members from becoming degenerate, how to maintain close ties with the masses as always, and how to further improve its democratic centralism and strengthen its solidarity and unity. Both Mao Zedong in his "Report to the Second Plenary Session of the Seventh Central Committee of the Communist Party of China" and "Combat Bureaucracy, Commandism and Violations of the Law and of Discipline" and Liu Shaoqi in his "Eight Requirements for Communist Party Membership" and "Try to Measure Up to More Rigorous Requirements of Party Membership" have thoroughly discussed these problems. All this indicated that Mao Zedong's thinking on building the Party as a ruling party had taken shape, and his thinking on Party building formed during the democratic revolution had registered new development. After the Party's Eighth National Congress in 1956, the erroneous "Left" ideas have started to prevail in the Party, and Mao Zedong has deviated from the correct direction and made some mistakes in building the Party. However, he had still advanced some correct, foresighted ideas, such as preventing peaceful evolution toward capitalism and training millions upon millions of successors to carry forward the revolutionary cause of the proletariat.

4.5.3 Main Content of Mao Zedong's Thinking on Party Building

With regard to the system of theories about Mao Zedong's thinking on Party building, researchers have different opinions. The book *Communism and the Communist Party of China* compiled by the CPC Central Committee during the Yan'an period had made the earliest summarization of these theories. Liu Shaoqi's "On the Party" had systematically expounded this scientific system of theories from the aspects of the Party's nature, its ideological, political and organizational building, and improvement in its work style. The textbook *Mao Zedong's Theory of Party Building* (for restricted circulation) compiled by the Party Building Research Office in the CPC Central Committee Party School in 1960 divided the theory into 13 parts. The book *Excerpts From Works of Mao Zedong* (for restricted circulation) compiled by the People's Publishing House in 1964 had also reviewed this system of theories. In recent years, researchers have attempted to encapsulate Mao Zedong's thinking on Party building by finding out the relations between its basic components or by focusing on its basic theories and key ideas. They have produced many different opinions.

The Resolution on Certain Questions in the History of Our Party Since the Founding of the People's Republic of China passed at the Sixth Plenary Session of the Eleventh CPC Central Committee in 1981 had encapsulated the thinking as follows. Mao Zedong had laid special stress on strengthening the Party ideologically, demanding that Party members should truly become Party members both organizationally and ideologically and constantly use proletarian ideas to transform and overcome non-proletarian ideas. He had stressed that the work style of integrating theory with practice, maintaining close ties with the masses and engaging in self-criticism is what clearly differentiated the CPC from all other political parties. When opposing the erroneous "Left" idea that resorted to the method of "ruthless struggle and merciless blows" in inner-Party struggle, he had put forward the correct principle of "learning from past mistakes to avoid future ones and curing the sickness to save the patient," and emphasized that the aim of inner-Party struggle was to achieve the twofold objective of clarity in ideology and unity among comrades. He had created the rectification method of educating all Party members in Marxism-Leninism through criticism and self-criticism. As the CPC became the ruling party after the founding of New China, he had repeatedly warned all Party members to carry on the tradition of being modest and prudent and working hard while avoiding arrogance and impetuosity, resist the corrosive influence of capitalist ideas, and oppose the bureaucratic practice of divorcing from the masses.

The book *Program for Studying Deng Xiaoping's Theory of Party Building* published by Party Building Readings Publishing House in 1998 summarized Mao Zedong's thinking on Party building in eight sentences: the Party's leadership over the Chinese revolution should be upheld; the Party should first of all be strengthened ideologically, and all its members should not only be committed to the ideal of communism but should also have the determination to work hard to accomplish the Party's present tasks; the principle of democratic-centralism should be upheld to create a political situation in which there are both centralism and democracy, both discipline and freedom, and both unity of will and personal ease of mind and liveliness; contradictions within the Party should be resolved correctly, and the aim of inner-Party struggle is to achieve the twofold objective of clarity in ideology and unity among comrades; every effort is needed to be made to establish Party branches at the company level and get primary Party organizations to play their role as bastions; cadres should be tempered and tested through practice, and millions upon millions of successors need to be cultivated and trained to carry forward the socialist cause; the Party's fine work style of integrating theory with practice, maintaining close ties with the masses and engaging in self-criticism should be upheld and carried on; all Party members should carry on the tradition of being modest and prudent and working hard while avoiding arrogance and impetuosity, and resist the corrosive influence of capitalist ideas. This summarization is more comprehensive.

According to published writings and books in this regard, the following ideas in Mao Zedong's thinking on Party building have overall significance for the building of the Party.

4.5.3.1 First of All, Strengthen the Party Ideologically

It was determined by the specific realities in China—the number of industrial workers was too small—that the CPC should take the revolutionary road of carrying out armed struggle and encircling the cities from the countryside. The CPC had to put the focus of its work in rural areas for a long period of time and expand its forces mainly by recruiting revolutionary peasants and petite bourgeoisie. As a result, it had too many members who were once peasants and petite bourgeoisie, and it was all along surrounded by ideas of the peasantry and petite bourgeoisie. Under such conditions, the Chinese Communists should find answers to the question of how to preserve the nature of the Party as the vanguard of the working class and how to build a genuine Marxist Party. Neither works of Marx and Lenin nor experience in other countries could answer that question. In its early years the CPC had not understood that question clearly and had once erroneously believed that it should ensure workers make a majority in its membership to preserve its nature as the vanguard of the working class, which was harmful to some extent.

After the failure of the Great Revolution, the Party and the Red Army was transferred to the countryside. The Party, surrounded by petite bourgeois ideas, was not theoretically well prepared for the new conditions and could not educate its members in theory and ideology sufficiently. As a result, various non-proletarian ideas had developed in the Party and greatly weakened its militancy. Revolutionaries of the older generation such as Mao Zedong, Liu Shaoqi and Zhou Enlai had noticed the problem almost simultaneously. They had realized that the Party should first of all be improved ideologically in order to preserve its nature as the vanguard of the working class. In fact, Mao Zedong had clearly stressed the importance of proletarian ideological leadership when the Red Army was just beginning to establish revolutionary bases in rural areas. In his essay "The Struggle in the Chingkang Mountains" in November 1928, he said, "In our opinion the question of proletarian ideological leadership is very important. The Party organizations in the border area counties, which are composed almost exclusively of peasants, will go astray without the ideological leadership of the proletariat."[1] That was the first time Mao Zedong had talked about the importance of building the Party ideologically. In the resolution drawn up by him for the Ninth Party Congress of the Fourth Army of the Red Army in December 1929, he had particularly discussed the problem of correcting mistaken ideas in the Party. In the resolution, he had pointed out the manifestations of various non-proletarian ideas in the Party organization

---

[1] *Selected Works of Mao Tse-tung*, Eng. ed., FLP, Peking, 1965, Vol. I, p. 97.

in the Fourth Army, their sources, and the methods of correcting them, and stressed the importance of ideological improvement in the Party. The "Resolution at the Ninth Party Congress of the Fourth Army of the Red Army," namely "the Resolution of the Gutian Meeting," indicated that the principle of first of all laying stress on building the Party ideologically had basically taken shape and Mao Zedong's thinking on Party building had also begun to take shape. In his essay "Oppose Book Worship" in May 1930, Mao Zedong had put forward the term "ideological line" and the idea of always proceeding from reality. The rectification movement in Yan'an from 1942 to 1945 was a great effort made by the Party to strengthen itself ideologically. A review of experience in the rectification movement had facilitated the development of the principle of building the Party ideologically. In the Report on the Revision of the Party Constitution to the Seventh National Congress of the CPC in May 1945, Liu Shaoqi had made a systematic, theoretical review of this principle and regarded it as a major component of Mao Zedong's thinking on Party building. Thereafter, first of all laying stress on building the Party ideologically became an important principle for the CPC in its self-improvement.

The principle of first of all laying stress on building the Party ideologically includes three major ideas. First, utilize the guiding role of revolutionary theories, educate Party members in Marxist theory, and arm the whole Party with scientific theories. Both Mao Zedong, in his essay "Reform our Study" and in the part "Study" of his essay "The Role of the Chinese Communist Party in the National War," and Liu Shaoqi, in his "Reply to Comrade Song Liang," "On the Party" and "Speech Delivered to the First Class of Students of the Institute of Marxism-Leninism," had reviewed historical experience and thoroughly analyzed why the theoretical level of the Party was low. They had stressed the importance of studying the Marxist theory and discussed how to establish correct style of study, how to grasp correct method of study and how to guide revolutionary practice with correct theories.

Second, uphold correct ideological line, always proceed from reality, and integrate the universal truth of Marxism with the concrete realities in China. Mao Zedong had made a deep discussion in this regard in his "Oppose Book Worship" and "On Practice."

Third, Party members should cultivate and temper themselves, truly become Party members both organizationally and ideologically, and constantly use proletarian ideas to transform and overcome non-proletarian ideas. Liu Shaoqi in his "How to Be a Good Communist," Zhou Enlai in his "Guidelines for Myself," and Chen Yun in his "How to Become a Communist Party Member" all had systematically explained the reasons why Communists should undertake self-cultivation and the ways and methods for them to cultivate themselves.

It should be said that the principle of first of all laying stress on building the Party ideologically is the most fundamental component of Mao Zedong's thinking on Party building and is the CPC's most effective experience in its self-improvement.

4.5.3.2 Link the Building of the Party Closely with the Party's Political Line

After reviewing the Party's experience and lessons, both positive and negative, gained in the struggle against the mistaken Right opportunism of Chen Duxiu and the erroneous "Left" ideas of Qu Qiubai, Li Lisan and Wang Ming, Mao Zedong had realized that to formulate and implement a correct political line had a direct bearing on the Party's future. He had pointed out in his "Problems of Strategy in China's Revolutionary War" in December 1936 that the Party needed a correct Marxist political line. In his "Introducing *The Communist*" in October 1939, he had reviewed the Party's experience of growth and struggle and put forward the idea of linking the building of the Party closely with the Party's political line. Thereafter, he had emphasized in many of his works that the Party should target formulating and implementing a correct political line as its central task, and should educate its members in the political line to ensure they maintain a high degree of political unity with the Party.

4.5.3.3 Strengthen the Party in Line with the Principle of Democratic-Centralism

Democratic centralism is a basic principle in the Marxist theory of party building and is a fundamental organizational principle for proletarian parties. Marx and Engels had outlined its basic philosophy, and Lenin had defined it scientifically and developed a system of theories out of it. Always taking democratic-centralism as its fundamental organizational principle, the CPC was organized and had carried out activities in accordance with that principle from the very beginning. The principle was embodied in the Party's platform at its First National Congress, in its Constitution at its second through fourth National Congresses, and in its rules that regulate how should the Party establish its organizations and carry out activities. The Third Final Amended Constitution of the Communist Party of China passed at a meeting of the Political Bureau of the CPC Central Committee in June 1927 had clearly stipulated for the first time that "work of Party headquarters should be guided by the principle of democratic centralism." Compared to communist parties in capitalist countries, the CPC was confronted with situations far more complicated when implementing the principle of democratic centralism. Democratic tradition in the Party was quite weak, and the feudal patriarchal system and the petite bourgeoisie's individualistic aversion to discipline still had strong influences. The Party's organizations were frequently cut apart or surrounded by the enemy and some of them were far away from the Central Committee, which made it difficult for the Central Committee to communicate with them and guide their work and easily gave rise to de-centralism and the "mountain-stronghold" mentality. In order to solve these problems, Mao Zedong and other revolutionaries of the older generation had further enriched and developed the principle of democratic centralism.

First, democratic centralism is a dialectical unity of democracy and centralism. During the War of the Agrarian Revolution, Mao Zedong had stressed the importance of "ensuring democracy under centralized guidance." During the period of the War of Resistance against Japan, he had discussed "the relationship between democracy and centralism." In the

Report on the Revision of the Party Constitution to the Seventh National Congress of the CPC, Liu Shaoqi had stressed, "As laid down in the Party Constitution, democratic centralism means centralized guidance on the basis of democracy and democracy under central guidance. It is both democratic and centralized."[1] The dialectical relationship between democracy and centralism was thoroughly discussed.

Second, democratic centralism has a number of basic principles. What does democratic centralism require from the Party? What should be done to implement democratic centralism? Marx, Engels and Lenin had not answered the two questions. In order to answer them, the CPC had implemented some measures that have proved practicable and gained some valuable experience in doing so. Then the Party had developed some theories from the experience and incorporated them into its Constitution so that all its members implemented them accordingly. The Party's Constitution passed at its Sixth Congress had defined three basic principles for democratic centralism, and the Constitution passed at the Seventh Congress had stipulated four principles. After times of additions and amendments, the current Constitution of the Party defines the following six basic principles for democratic centralism. (1) Individual Party members are subordinate to the Party organization, the minority is subordinate to the majority, the lower Party organizations are subordinate to the higher Party organizations, and all the constituent organizations and members of the Party are subordinate to the National Congress and the Central Committee of the Party. (2) The Party's leading bodies at all levels are elected except for the representative organs dispatched by them and the leading Party members' groups in non-Party organizations. (3) The highest leading body of the Party is the National Congress and the Central Committee elected by it. The leading bodies of local Party organizations are the Party congresses at their respective levels and the Party committees elected by them. Party committees are responsible, and should report their work, to the Party congresses at their respective levels. (4) Lower Party organizations should report on their work to, and

---

[1] *Selected Works of Liu Shaoqi*, Eng. ed., FLP, Beijing, 1984, Vol. I, p. 353.

request instructions from, higher Party organizations. Higher and lower Party organizations should exchange information and support and oversee each other. (5) Party committees at all levels function on the principle of combining collective leadership with individual responsibility based on division of work. All major issues should be decided by the Party committees after discussion. (6) The Party forbids all forms of personality cult. Well targeted and perfectly feasible, the six principles represent the CPC's long efforts to develop the theory of democratic centralism.

Third, the aim of implementing democratic centralism is to stimulate the whole Party's enthusiasm and strengthen its solidarity and unity. In his essay "Win the Masses in Their Millions for the Anti-Japanese National United Front" in May 1937, Mao Zedong said, "If we are to make the Party strong, we should practice democratic centralism to stimulate the initiative of the whole membership.... Let us apply democracy, and so give scope to initiative throughout the Party. Let us give scope to the initiative of the whole Party membership and so train new cadres in great numbers, eliminate the remnants of sectarianism, and unite the whole Party as solidly as steel."[1] Liu Shaoqi had written the essay "How to Be a Good Communist Both Organizationally and in Discipline" in November 1941 criticizing the statement that "democracy is only a means to realize centralism." He said, "The fundamental aim of building the Party is to strengthen its unity and increase its militancy, and democratic centralism is exactly the path to achieve this aim."

Fourth, the correct way for implementing democratic centralism is to enhance intra-Party democracy and rigorously enforce Party discipline. According to Mao Zedong, China was a country in which small-scale production and the patriarchal system prevailed, and taking the country as a whole there was as yet no democracy under the reactionary rule. That state of affairs were reflected in the Party by insufficient democracy in Party life. In addition, the ideas of the peasantry and petite bourgeoisie easily led to decentralism and anarchism. Faced with that difficult situation of

---

[1] *Selected Works of Mao Tse-tung*, Eng. ed., FLP, Peking, 1965, Vol. I, p. 292.

both insufficient democracy and inadequate centralism, Mao Zedong had pointed out that the Party should first of all enhance intra-Party democracy and promote democracy in Party life, and at the same time strictly enforce Party discipline. He had also said that two erroneous tendencies should be prevented: one was centralism without democracy such as bureaucracy, autocracy, patriarchal system and "rule by the voice of one man alone;" and the other one was democracy without centralism such as ultra-democracy, decentralism, liberalism and anarchism. Liu Shaoqi had thoroughly discussed the relationship between democratic centralism and Party discipline, advancing that Party discipline was an important guarantee for the implementation of democratic centralism.

4.5.3.4 Strengthen the Party by Preserving and Developing Its Fine Work Style

Among all the proletarian parties in the world, the CPC was the first to elevate its understanding and solution of problems concerning its work style to the height of world-view and Party spirit and worked hard to improve its work style. That was an important creation of the Party in its self-improvement efforts, and is a unique component of Mao Zedong's thinking on Party building. In his essay "Rectify the Party's Style of Work" in February 1942, Mao Zedong for the first time had defined the concept of "Party's work style." In his report "On Coalition Government" in April 1945, he had summarized the CPC's fine traditions and work styles formed in its long revolutionary struggles as three main work styles—integrating theory with practice, maintaining close ties with the masses, and engaging in self-criticism, and had said that they were what clearly differentiated the CPC from all other political parties. He had repeatedly stressed that without fine work style the Party could not improve itself effectively or win support from the masses because its work style could greatly influence the people and general social conduct.

At Mao Zedong's suggestion, the CPC had formulated a full set of effective principles and measures to improve its work style. The Party had defined the class basis and ideological reasons for both fine and bad work styles, and stressed that work styles should be constantly improved because they were closely related to the Party's world-view and spirit. CPC has incorporated conduct norms into its Constitution and resolutions to lead its members what is advocated and what is opposed so that they can conduct accordingly. It stressed that in addition to ideological education, organizational and disciplinary measures should also be taken as a requirement to correct bad work styles and the entire Party should work concerted in taking these measures, and that the Party's efforts to improve its work styles should be subject to effective oversight by non-party people. It emphasized that the Party's leading cadres should lead by being example. It asked its members to cultivate themselves by studying China's fine tradition and culture so that they can consciously develop fine work styles and correct bad ones.

4.5.3.5 Correct Lines and Policies Regarding Party Cadres

The organizational line is the line to ensure the implementation of ideological and political lines. In this sense, training a large number of cadres and using them correctly is the key to Party building. Mao Zedong had stressed the essential role of cadres in carrying out the Party's lines. He said, "A great revolution requires a great party and many first-rate cadres to guide it."[1] He had also said, "Cadres are a decisive factor, once the political line is determined."[2]

Mao Zedong had put forward the principle of training cadres who combined ability with political integrity. They should be cadres and leaders versed in Marxism-Leninism, politically far-sighted, competent in work, full of the spirit of self-sacrifice, capable of tackling problems on their own, steadfast in the midst of difficulties, and loyal and devoted in serving the nation, the class and the Party. He had advanced the cadre line of "appointing people on their merit," and stressed that Party members came

---

[1] *Selected Works of Mao Tse-tung*, Eng. ed., FLP, Peking, 1965, Vol. I, p. 291.
[2] *Ibid.*, Vol. II, p. 202.

together from every corner of the country and sectarianism or "mountain-stronghold mentality" should not be allowed in the Party. He had directed the formulation of a series of correct cadre policies, which included the following points: do not confine judgment to a short period or a single incident in a cadre's life, but consider his life and work as a whole; unite and take good care of them and allow them a free hand in their work so that they have the courage to assume responsibility and, at the same time, give them timely instructions; raise their level by giving them the opportunity to study; check up on their work, and help them sum up their experience, carry forward their achievements and correct their mistakes; use the method of persuasion and education with cadres who have made mistakes and do not lightly wage struggles against them; and help them overcome difficulties and solve practical problems. He had especially stressed the need to strengthen education and cultivation of cadres to raise their ideological and political levels and improve their professional skills and to temper and test them in revolutionary practice.

4.5.3.6 Correctly Carry Out Inner-Party Struggle

Contradiction and struggle in a proletarian party is an objective reality, independent of man's will. Marx, Engels and Lenin all brilliantly have expounded on this issue. Mao Zedong had pointed out, "Opposition and struggle between ideas of different kinds constantly occur within the Party; this is a reflection within the Party of contradictions between classes and between the new and the old in society. If there were no contradictions in the Party and no ideological struggles to resolve them, the Party's life would come to an end."[1] Therefore, he stood for using active ideological struggle to ensure unity within the Party and the revolutionary organizations. Opposing the erroneous "Left" idea that resorted to the method of "ruthless struggle and merciless blows" in inner-Party struggle, he had put forward the correct principle of "learning from past mistakes to avoid future ones and curing the sickness to save the patient," and emphasized that the aim of inner-Party

---

[1] *Selected Works of Mao Tse-tung*, Eng. ed., FLP, Peking, 1965, Vol. I, p. 317.

struggle was to achieve the twofold objective of clarity in ideology and unity among comrades. In addition, he had created the rectification method of educating all Party members in Marxism-Leninism through criticism and self-criticism.

It should be noted that the problem of inner-Party struggle was also clarified in many works of Liu Shaoqi, such as his "Eliminate Closed-Door-ism and Adventurism," "Overcome Unhealthy Tendencies in Our Party," "Eliminate Menshevist Ideology Within the Party," and "Several Problems on Building Our Party." His writing "On Inner-Party Struggle" was well-known for its penetrating analyses on the problem of inner-Party struggle. The writing was originally a speech he had made at the Party school of Central China Bureau of the Central Committee in July 1941, and was later telegraphed to Yan'an and published in the *Liberation Daily* in October 1942. He had thoroughly and systematically discussed the objectivity and necessity of inner-Party struggle, its source, nature and manifestations, deviations in previous inner-Party struggles and lessons there from, and the principles and methods for correctly launching inner-Party struggles. This article was written when the entire Party was preparing to launch a rectification movement to correct the erroneous "Left" or Right ideas about inner-Party struggle that had harmed the Party severely, so it was of great significance. At that time, the problem of the Party's ideological line had not been completely solved, and the Party had not been able to learn from its past experience in inner-Party struggles. The writing represented a great development in Marxist-Leninist theory on inner-party struggles. For that reason, Mao Zedong wrote a preface for that essay, when it was published in the *Liberation Daily*, hailing the writing as an "essay that every comrade should read because it has solved the problem of inner-Party struggle both in theory and in practice."

In addition to the above introductions, Mao Zedong's thinking on Party building also includes numerous other contents such as the idea of establishing Party branches at the company level and letting primary Party organizations play their role as bastions, the principle that the Party commands the gun, and the idea that the Party should maintain absolute leadership over the army. All this is scientific and theoretical generalization of the Party's experience in building itself and represents great development of the Marxist-Leninist theory on party building. It was under the guidance of Mao Zedong's thinking on Party building that the Party had successfully developed itself into a new proletarian party that has strict discipline, maintains close ties with the masses, and is united and ever-victorious.

4.5.3.7 The Thinking on Building the Party as a Ruling Party

After the founding of New China, Mao Zedong had upheld and further developed the thinking on Party building formed during the democratic revolution period in the course of socialist revolution and construction. In that course, he had gradually formulated the thinking on building the Party as a ruling party. In fact, the thinking could be traced back to far earlier times. It had emerged when the Party was ruling revolutionary base areas, was introduced at the Second Plenary Session of the Seventh CPC Central Committee, was formally formulated at the CPC's Eighth National Congress, and developed in twists and turns thereafter. It was the correct application and fresh development of Mao Zedong's thinking on Party building formed during the democratic revolution in the new period when the Party had become the ruling party. It is a set of correct theories and ideas that the first generation of collective leadership with Mao Zedong at the core, faced with the many new situations and problems that have arisen after it became the ruling party, had developed to answer the questions of how to improve itself in the new historical circumstances and how to lead the socialist cause, and a summary of experience therein. It had also developed Lenin's thinking on building a ruling party. It should be said that Mao Zedong's thinking on Party building is a complete system that includes theories both of the democratic revolution period and of the socialist period. In the past, some researchers have not discussed and studied Mao Zedong's thinking on Party building completely and consequently had reached the conclusion that it applied only to the democratic revolution and revolutionary war period. That was not objective and was totally incorrect. In recent years and they have reviewed these mistaken tendencies.

According to published papers and books in this regard, Mao Zedong's thinking on building the Party as a ruling party includes the following ideas.

4.5.3.7.1 The ruling party should increase its awareness of governance and strengthen its governing position

According to Marxism, the proletariat and its party can accomplish its historical mission only by seizing and utilizing state power. Lenin had also discussed much on how should a communist party exercise leadership after it became the ruling party. Mao Zedong held that at the core of proletarian party's leadership is wielding political power. He stressed, "The force at the core leading our cause forward is the Chinese Communist Party. Without it, the cause of socialism cannot be victorious." In his essay "On the Correct Handling of the Contradictions Among the People," he had said that the most important criterion for telling right from wrong in the country's political activities was that the right trend should help to strengthen, and not shake off or weaken, the leadership of the Communist Party. He refuted the wrong viewpoints that negated the Party's position in power on many occasions and greatly increased the Party's awareness of governance.

4.5.3.7.2 The ruling party should take economic construction as its central task

According to Mao Zedong, the leadership role of the Party should be manifested in its effectiveness in promoting the development of the productive forces. In his report "On Coalition Government," he had written, "In the last analysis, the impact, good or bad, great or small, of the policy and the practice of any Chinese political party upon the people depends on whether and how much it helps to develop their productive forces, and on whether it fetters or liberates these forces." "When the political system of New Democracy is won, the Chinese people and their government will have to adopt practical measures in order to build heavy and light industry step by step over a number of years and transform China from an agricultural into an industrial country."[1] All this indicates that the fundamental task of the Party is to liberate and develop the productive forces.

After the basic completion of the socialist transformation in 1956, Mao Zedong had conducted thorough investigations and studies and written the essay "On the Ten Major Relationships," in which he advocated the idea of "path of socialist modernization suited to the Chinese conditions". Later, the CPC at its Eighth National Congress in 1956 had defined the correct line of concentrating resources on developing the productive forces to industrialize the country and meet the material and cultural needs of the people. Thereafter, Mao Zedong had stressed on many occasions that the Party should provide effective leadership not only in political, military, cultural and diplomatic affairs but also in economic development, and that the Party should improve the membership composition of its leading bodies in terms of intellectual background and set up a "a central science committee" to make its leadership even more effective. Liu Shaoqi in many of his writings such as "Industrialization of the Country and Improvement of the People's Living Standard" and "The Future Historical Tasks of the Communist Party of China" also had pointed out that the central task of the Party was economic construction and discussed the problem of how to develop productive forces and promote economic development. Regretfully, although Mao Zedong and other revolutionaries of the older generation had realized the importance of economic construction and had advanced some correct principles, the Party still could not focus on economic construction due to various obstructions.

4.5.3.7.3 The ruling party should resolutely prevent and oppose corruption

The biggest danger for the ruling party is becoming self-complacent or degenerate and estranged from the people. From the later period of the War of Resistance against Japan, Mao Zedong had begun to think about the problem of how to prevent the Party, after it led the Chinese revolution into victory, from becoming self-complacent or degenerate and from repeating

---

[1] *Selected Works of Mao Tse-tung*, Eng. ed., FLP, Peking, 1965, Vol. III, pp. 301, 303.

the mistakes that the feudal dynasties and peasant uprising leaders in the Chinese history had made. Greatly impressed by Guo Moruo's essay "The Tercentenary of the 1644 Uprising"[1] published in the *Xinhua Daily* in Chongqing in 1944, he called on the Party ranks to study the essay and learn lessons from the failure of Li Zicheng's peasant uprising. After he arrived at Xibaipo Village, Pingshan County, Hebei Province in 1948, he mentioned Li Zicheng's lessons many times and called on Party members to see the opera "Li Zicheng's Army Entering Beijing." He said, "New China is soon to be founded, and we the Chinese Communists are to be recorded in history. We should not enter Beijing like Li Zicheng; we should have rules." He said at the Second Plenary Session of the Seventh CPC Central Committee in 1949 that it was difficult to blaze a new path, but it would even be more difficult to keep it. He tirelessly warned the entire Party: The Chinese revolution is great, but the road after the revolution will be longer, the work greater and more arduous. All Party members should remain modest, prudent and free from arrogance and rashness in their style of work and preserve the style of plain living and hard struggle.

After the founding of New China, Mao Zedong had put into practice the principles for preventing corruption and degeneration. He had led the entire Party in starting the movement against the "three evils" [corruption, waste and bureaucracy—*Tr.*] and launching rectification movements to improve the Party's work style. He stressed that the Party should strengthen ideological education of its members and cadres to improve their sense of preventing corruption and degeneration and make them fully understand the social, historical, moral and ideological causes of corruption and its harm to the Party's undertakings, so that they should bear in mind the Party's fundamental purpose of serving the people wholeheartedly and share joys and sorrows with the people. According to him, the Party should be strict with

---

[1] "The Tercentenary of the 1644 Uprising" commemorates a peasant uprising 300 years before that toppled the Ming Dynasty. The essay shows that after the peasant army led by Li Zicheng entered Beijing and overthrew the Ming Dynasty in 1644, a number of leaders became complacent as a result of their victory, and factional strife arose. As a result, Li Zicheng's forces were finally defeated in 1645.

its members in the fight against corruption, resolutely conquering corruption in the Party and eliminating the small number of corrupt, degenerate Party members. He believed that rectification movement was an effective measure to conquer corruption and government bodies should also take rectification measures when needed, and that efforts to improve Party conduct and to clean up the government could be combined to produce better results. All this is the application and development of Mao Zedong's rectification theory in the new period when the Party had become the ruling party. He also advanced that special campaigns could be launched to tackle serious corruption in a certain period of time—the movement against the "three evils" led by him was a typical one. He emphasized that the Party should begin with punishing corrupt high-ranking cadres. He personally investigated and handled the first serious corruption case in New China and sentenced Liu Qingshan and Zhang Zishan to death. He demanded that high-ranking cadres should set an example of self-discipline. He opposed high salary and privilege of cadres and advocated to prevent them from being politically corrupted by luxurious living. He stressed that the struggle against corruption needed not only democracy and people's support but also strict adherence to policies and laws. He also stressed that the Party should be subject to both intra-Party oversight and oversight by the masses, the democratic parties and the media. In conclusion, Mao Zedong had developed a series of ideas about fighting against corruption.

Other Party leaders had also developed valuable ideas about fighting against corruption. Liu Shaoqi had said that the power of leaders should be restricted and the pursuit of personal privileges by cadres should be resolutely prevented, and that some systems in capitalist countries could be utilized in fighting against corruption. When serving as Secretary of the Central Commission for Discipline Inspection, Zhu De had specifically discussed the issue of how to uphold Party discipline and strengthen discipline inspection work in the Party. Zhou Enlai had put forward that leading cadres should meet the test in five domains—ideology, politics, social relations, family relations and daily life.

The theory and practice of the Party's first generation of collective leadership in fighting against corruption had greatly enriched and developed Mao Zedong's theory of improving Party conduct, effectively curbed the tendencies of corruption beginning to emerge after the Party was in power, and played an important role in building a clean Party and government in the early years of New China.

4.5.3.7.4 The ruling party should enable its members to reach more rigorous requirements

At the First National Conference on Organizational Work in Beijing in 1951, Liu Shaoqi has talked about the "Eight Requirements for Communist Party Membership" and made the summary report "Try to Measure Up to More Rigorous Requirements of Party Membership." He had thoroughly discussed the problem of upholding the standards for Party members and improving their quality after the Party was in power. He believed that improvement in the quality of Party members was of vital importance to build the Party as a ruling party, and the entire Party should fully understand the importance and urgency of this work from the new position of the Party as a ruling party and the new historical tasks it shouldered. He said that the key to improving the quality of Party members was to uphold the membership requirements, which should not be reduced casually, and people unqualified should not be admitted into the Party. After joining the Party, members should continue to be educated and tempered. He had proposed that the Party should effectively strengthen its organizations in order to ensure its purity and improve the quality of its members, and that proper measures should be taken to deal with unqualified Party members. Besides, he called on the entire Party to continue to work hard to maintain high standards for Party membership and improve its membership.

4.5.3.7.5 The ruling party should uphold and improve democratic centralism and strengthen its solidarity and unity

After the founding of New China, Mao Zedong had deepened his understanding of democratic centralism, dialectically discussed the relationship between democracy and centralism, and had defined the goals for improving democratic centralism. In his essay "On the Correct Handling of the Contradictions Among the People" in February 1957, he said, "Within the ranks of the people, democracy is correlative with centralism and freedom with discipline. They are the two opposites of a single entity, contradictory as well as united, and we should not one-sidedly emphasize one to the exclusion of the other. Within the ranks of the people, we cannot do without freedom, nor can we do without discipline; we cannot do without democracy, nor can we do without centralism. This unity of democracy and centralism, of freedom and discipline, constitutes our democratic centralism."[1] In an essay he had written in July the same year, he said, "Our aim is to create a political situation in which we have both centralism and democracy, both discipline and freedom, both unity of will and personal ease of mind and liveliness." All this represented Mao Zedong's great development of Marxist principle of democratic centralism and embodied the higher requirements for the Party after it had become the ruling party.

Mao Zedong had attached great importance to preventing two erroneous tendencies in the course of implementing democratic centralism. Before the Fourth Plenary Session of the Seventh CPC Central Committee, in order to solve the problem of growing decentralism, Mao Zedong had repeatedly stressed the importance of the Party's unity with the emphasis on combating decentralism. He had particularly stressed that the unity of high-ranking cadres was of great significance to the Party's cause and improvement, and had properly put an end to the anti-Party case of Gao Gang and Rao Shushi. During a period of time followed, the problem of undue emphasis on centralization became conspicuous, such as the tendency to make decisions arbitrarily and the practice for one individual to monopolize the conduct of affairs and decide on important issues. Mao Zedong had talked more about intra-Party democracy, demanding that all high-ranking cadres should correctly understand the relationship between one individual and the masses, between one individual and the Party, and between one individual

---

[1] *Selected Works of Mao Tse-tung*, Eng. ed., FLP, Peking, 1977, Vol. V, p. 389.

and the Party's collective leadership. The Party stressed at its Eighth National Congress in 1956 that it should enhance intra-Party democracy, strengthen intra-Party oversight and greatly improve democracy in Party life. According to Mao Zedong, the most fundamental way to prevent the two erroneous tendencies was to educate the entire Party in the principle of democratic centralism to make its members and cadres more conscious in implementing the principle. He had also talked about this issue on many occasions in the hope that all Party members would pay greater attention to it. Objectively speaking, Mao Zedong himself was quite cautious around the time of the founding of New China, and it was a tragedy for him and a profound lesson to the Party that he later showed dual attitude towards the problem of personality cult and even went to the opposite direction.

4.5.3.7.6 The ruling party should train millions upon millions of successors to carry forward the revolutionary cause of the proletariat

In order to meet the needs of large-scale economic construction in the 1950s, Mao Zedong had demanded that all cadres should enhance study and strive to be proficient in technical and professional work and should become both red and expert. After imperialist powers had launched a new strategy of "peaceful evolution toward capitalism" in 1960s. Mao Zedong exerted great efforts in preventing it. At a number of important meetings in the early 1960s, he had asserted that concerted efforts should be made to fight against revisionism and prevent peaceful evolution toward capitalism. He said that the Party should educate its members in Marxism, criticize revisionism, and cultivate and train millions upon millions of successors to carry forward the revolutionary cause of the proletariat. Although Mao Zedong had not fully understood correctly the concept "revisionism," especially the problem of who were the revisionists, and even went to a "Left" error, he was very farsighted to link the strategy of "peaceful evolution toward capitalism" of imperialist powers with the risk of revisionism in a socialist country and focus on improving the ruling party of the socialist country in preventing peaceful evolution toward capitalism. The demise of the Soviet Union and the drastic changes in Eastern Europe had proved the correctness of his ideas. He believed that the problem of cultivating a large number of successors to carry forward the revolutionary cause of the proletariat had a direct bearing on the survival of the Party and the country and was therefore a fundamental policy of the proletariat for many years to come. He stressed that the Party should temper and test cadres through the long practice of mass struggle, and select successors from them. He emphasized that the efforts to strengthen the Party's members and cadres should be linked with the efforts to cultivate and train millions upon millions of successors to carry forward the revolutionary cause of the proletariat, and clarified five criteria for the successors. Although these criteria were inevitably engraved with the then "Left" ideology and were incomplete because they stressed only political standards while neglecting professional standards, their basic ideas are correct and some are still applicable today.

Because the Party had just been in power for a short period of time and lacked governing experience, Mao Zedong's thinking on building the Party as a ruling party was elementary and incomplete, and he had not formulated ideas about the Party's institutional improvement. Just like Mao Zedong Thought does not include his mistakes in his later years, Mao Zedong's thinking on building the Party as a ruling party should similarly exclude his some erroneous ideas about Party building in his later years. In short, we should not negate his thinking on building the Party as a ruling party because of his later wrong ideas about Party building.

4.5.4 The Historical Position of Mao Zedong's Thinking on Party Building

Mao Zedong's thinking on Party building, which was formed from the 1920s to the 1960s as a party building theory of the proletariat, presents an important position in the history of Marxist thinking on party building, in the history of development of the Communist Party of China as well as in the history of international communist movement.

4.5.4.1 Mao Zedong's Thinking on Party Building and the Marxist Theory of Party Building

The Marxist theory of party building took shape and developed with the founding and development of proletarian parties, which was a long historical process. Marx and Engels had scientifically solved a series of basic problems concerning establishing a proletarian party and had directly guided the founding and building of the world's first wave of proletarian parties. The theoretical framework they had established laid a solid foundation for the development of the Marxist theory of party building. Lenin, in his practice of leading the Russian proletarians in struggling to seize power and build socialism, had solved a series of problems concerning establishing and consolidating new proletarian parties, answered the question of building a proletarian ruling party in a backward capitalist or socialist country, and developed the Marxist theory of party building into a complete, scientific system of theories.

The CPC's first generation of collective leadership with Mao Zedong at the core had creatively solved a series of unique and complex problems in the building of the Party and formulated Mao Zedong's thinking on Party building by integrating the Marxist-Leninist theory of party building with China's realities. Mao Zedong had made penetrating analyses of problems about how to strengthen the Party ideologically, politically and organizationally and improve its work style, and therefore had greatly enriched and developed the Marxist-Leninist theory of party building. Deng Xiaoping once pointed out, "And it was Comrade Mao Zedong who developed Lenin's theory of Party building most comprehensively."[1] Mao Zedong did not develop it in one or more aspects, but developed it "most comprehensively." By developing the Marxist theory of party building, he had formulated a unique, complete system of theories. The Chinese Communists represented by Mao Zedong had made great theoretical contributions to the development of the Marxist theory of party building.

---

[1] *Selected Works of Deng Xiaoping*, Eng. ed., FLP, Beijing, 1995, Vol. II, p. 56.

4.5.4.2 Mao Zedong's Thinking on Party Building Guided the Party through Its First Great Undertaking of Party Building

Due to the complex situations in China, the CPC, in its self-improvement efforts, had to solve many specific problems that communist parties in other countries did not have to face. Mao Zedong's thinking on Party building had successfully solved a series of unique and complex problems in the building of the Party, and answered the historical question of what the Chinese Communists should do to build a Marxist proletarian party of the broad masses in semi-colonial and semi-feudal, economically and culturally backward China where the proletariat was small in number but strong in militancy and the peasantry and petite bourgeoisie were in the majority, when they were struggling in rural base areas which were frequently cut apart by the enemy. The thinking had achieved and presented the first great undertaking of Party building in China.

4.5.4.3 Mao Zedong's Thinking on Party Building Is a Guide for Party Building in the New Period

Although Mao Zedong's thinking on Party building was formulated to guide the Party's building in the revolutionary war years and under the conditions of planned economy, some of its basic principles still apply to Party building in the new environment of reform and opening up and a socialist market economy, and even some ideas that were not implemented before can provide today with profound inspiration. For example, when the Party today focuses on arming the entire Party with Deng Xiaoping Theory and other scientific theories to improve problems concerning ideals, beliefs, worldview, outlook on life and sense of values among its members, Mao Zedong's principle of first of all laying stress on building the Party ideologically is still applicable and correct. When the problem of combating corruption has become a problem having a direct bearing on the survival of the Party, Mao Zedong's ideas about fighting against corruption can still be used as a powerful ideological tool for combating corruption. His idea of training millions upon millions of successors to carry forward the revolutionary cause of the proletariat can still guide the Party's efforts to train a large number of highly qualified cadres who can assume leadership roles in the twenty-first century. Despite the changes in historical conditions and the Party's position, Mao Zedong's thinking on Party building will forever be a powerful ideological tool for strengthening the Party and will be further upheld and applied in future practice.

References

Sha Jiansun, *Introduction to the Chinese New-Democratic Revolution*, Shandong People's Publishing House, Ji'nan, 1993.

Dong Shiming, *A Comparative Study of the Theory of the New-Democratic Revolution and the Three People's Principles*, Northeast Normal University Press, Changchun, 1995.

Song Ruxiang, "On the Process of Formation of the Basic Thinking on the Chinese New-Democratic Revolution," *Qilu Journal*, 1986 (3).

Wang Zhanyang, "The Historical Development of Mao Zedong's Two Theories on the Chinese Bourgeoisie," *Changbai Journal*, 1996 (1).

Dongfang Su, "The Communist International and the Formation of the Basic Thinking on the New-Democratic Revolution," *Qilu Journal*, 1996 (3).

Zhang Yong, "The Theory of New Democracy and Controversy over China's Modernization in the 1930s and 1940s," *Study of the History of the Communist Party of China*, 2000 (2).

Zheng Derong and Liu Guoqing, "A Brief Introduction to Mao Zedong's Thinking on Capitalism in New Democracy," *Party Literature*, 2000 (1).

Hu Kai, "A Comparison between the Basic Program for the New-Democratic Revolution and the Basic Program for the Primary Stage of Socialism," *Study of the History of the Communist Party of China*, 1999 (5).

Huang Shaoqun and Zhang Peilin, *A Unique Invention of Mao Zedong: Theory and Practice of the Road of Encircling the Cities from the Countryside*, Hebei People's Publishing House, Shijiazhuang, 1991.

The Party History Research Center, *History of the Communist Party of China*, People's Publishing House, Beijing, 1991, Vol. I.

Hu Sheng (ed.), *The Practice of the Communist Party of China in Seven Decades*, Chinese Communist Party History Publishing House, Beijing, 1991.

Yuan Jinghua, *Study on Mao Zedong Thought*, Shandong University Press, Ji'nan, 2000.

Jia Weichang, "The Time of Formation of the Theory of the Road of Encircling the Cities from the Countryside," *Study of the History of the Communist Party of China*, 1981 (3).

Li Hongwen, "China's Revolutionary Road of Encircling the Cities from the Countryside," *Journal of Northeast Normal University*, 1982 (6).

Gai Jun, "The Theory of Encircling the Cities from the Countryside Formed and Developed in the Struggle Against Dogmatism," *Study of the History of the Communist Party of China*, 1983 (6).

Wu Dianxiao, "Main Features of the Theory of Encircling the Cities from the Countryside," *Journal of University of International Relations*, 1983 (1).

Peng Hongzhi, "On the Formation of Mao Zedong's Theory of Encircling the Cities from the Countryside and Seizing State Power by Armed Force," *Journal of Guiyang Normal University* (Social Sciences), 1984 (1).

Wang Chaomei, "Development of the Theory of Encircling the Cities from the Countryside during the War of Resistance against Japan," *Journal of Beijing Normal University*, 1985 (4).

Du Weihua, "On the Revolutionary Road of Encircling the Cities from the Countryside—the Formation of Mao Zedong Thought," *Marxism Study*, 1987 (1).

Yuan Nansheng, "Did the Communist International Stick to the Idea of Focusing on Armed Struggle in Cities after the Failure of the Great Revolution," *Social Science Front*, 1989 (4).

Lu Zhenxiang, "Discussion on the Formation of the Theory of the

Revolutionary Road of Encircling the Cities from the Countryside," *Study of the History of the Communist Party of China*, 1990 (6).

Sun Qiming, "The Communist International and China's Revolutionary Road of Encircling the Cities from the Countryside," *Collection of Outstanding Writings on Study of the History of the Communist Party of China*, Chinese Communist Party History Publishing House, Beijing, 1992.

Wang Fuxuan, "How the Theory of 'Encircling the Cities from the Countryside' Was Established As the Line of Guidance for the Party," *Teaching and Research in CPC History*, 1992 (3).

Zhao Quanjun, "On the Difference between the Communist International's City-Centered Idea and Mao Zedong's Idea of Encircling the Cities from the Countryside," *Research of the Communist International*, 1993 (3).

Jia Weichang, "Rediscussion about the Formation of Mao Zedong's Theory of Encircling the Cities from the Countryside," *Journal of Shandong University*, 1995 (4).

Cui Shuhai, "The Path of Revolutionary Bases in Jinggang Mountains and the Path of Building Socialism with Chinese Characteristics," *Research of Mao Zedong Thought*, 1996 (1).

Yu Boliu, "Zhou Enlai and the Revolutionary Road of Encircling the Cities from the Countryside," *Journal Jiangxi Social Science*, 1998 (3).

Xie Huijun, "The Inner Relationship between the Theory of Encircling the Cities from the Countryside and Seizing State Power by Armed Force and the Theory of the Socialist Market Economy," *Theory Horizon*, 1998 (6).

Yan Chengliang, "Road to Victory in the Chinese Revolution: Zhou Enlai's Theory and Practice on the Theory of Encircling the Cities from the Countryside," *Over the Party History*, 1999 (2).

Xin Qiushui, "Village Self-Governance: A New Practice of Encircling Cities from the Countryside," *China's Politics,* 1999 (2).

PLA Academy of Military Sciences (ed.), *Collection of Mao Zedong's Military Writings*, the PLA Headquarters of the General Staff Publishing House, Beijing, 1961.

Zhang Jiayu, Institute of Mao Zedong's Military Thinking in PLA Academy of Military Sciences (ed.), *Chronicle of Mao Zedong's Military Life (1927-1958)*, the People's Liberation Army Press, Beijing, 1994.

Liao Guoliang and Li Shishun (eds.), *The History of Development of Mao Zedong's Military Thinking*, the People's Liberation Army Press, Beijing, 1991.

Hu Yongfeng and Liu Weiguo (eds.), *Mao Zedong's Military Operation Art*, Military Science Publishing House, Beijing, 1996.

Zhang Shude, *Study on Mao Zedong's Military Thinking in Other Countries*, Military Science Publishing House, Beijing, 1998.

Jiang Siyi, "Outline of Mao Zedong's Military Thinking," *Study of the History of the Communist Party of China*, 1994 (1).

Xie Yi, "Mao Zedong and the Theory of People's Revolutionary with Chinese Features," *Study of the History of the Communist Party of China*, 1993 (3).

Wang Zhen, "Mao Zedong's Idea of Modernizing the Army through Science and Technology," *Study of the History of the Communist Party of China*, 1994 (2).

Chang Qiaozhang, "Zhu De's Contributions to Mao Zedong's Military Thinking," *Research of Mao Zedong Thought*, 1994 (1).

Li Weihan, *Memory and Research*, Chinese Communist Party History Publishing House, Beijing, 1986.

Yan Zhimin (ed.), *Introduction to Marxist Theory of the United Front*, China Literature and History Publishing House, Beijing, 1990.

Li Zhisheng, "Mao Zedong's Idea that the United Front Should Serve Economic Construction," *Forum on Study of Mao Zedong Thought*, 1994 (2).

Chen Bingqiang, "The Practical Meaning of Mao Zedong's Thinking on the United Front," *Forum on Study of Mao Zedong Thought*, 1997 (4).

Yuan Yu, "The Formation, Development and Features of Mao Zedong's Thinking on the United Front during the New-Democratic Revolution," *Research of Mao Zedong Thought*, 2000 (2).

Zhang Weiping and Zhang Liejun, *History of Mao Zedong's Theory of Party Building*, (in two volumes), Jiangxi People's Publishing House, Nanchang, 1987, 1990.

Zhou Yi (ed.), *Study on Mao Zedong's Thinking on Party Building*, CPC Central Committee Party School Publishing House, Beijing, 1989.

Song Jingming et al., *History of Development of Mao Zedong's Theory of Party Building*, Wuhan University Press, Wuhan, 1998.

The CPC Central Committee Organization Department Party Building Institute (ed.), *On Upholding and Developing Mao Zedong's Thinking on Party Building*, Party Building Readings Publishing House, Beijing, 1993.

Zhang Liejun et al., "The Symbol of Formation of Mao Zedong's Theory of Party Building and Its Historical Features," *Study of the History of the Communist Party of China*, 1986 (5).

Wang Zhengping, "Mao Zedong's Great Contributions to the Theory of Party Building," *Collection of Writings on Mao Zedong Thought*, Shanghai People's Publishing House, Shanghai, 1984.

Ye Wuxi, "Formation of Mao Zedong's Complete Theory of Party Building during the War of Resistance against Japan," *Party History Materials and Research*, 1991 (1).

Chapter 5

The Theory of New Democracy (Second Part)

5.1 Theory of a New-Democratic Society

Over a long period of time in the past, the theory of New-Democracy and the theory of the new-democratic revolution were generally mistakenly considered the same. It was at the Symposium on Study of Liu Shaoqi in 1988 that some researchers have formally put forward the two terms "the theory of the new-democratic revolution" and "the theory of a new-democratic society," arguing that the two should together constitute the theory of New Democracy. Researchers have generally accepted this opinion in recent years. The theory of the new-democratic revolution focused on the problem of how to overthrow the rule of imperialism, feudalism and bureaucrat-capitalism in China and how to move from a semi-colonial, semi-feudal society to a new-democratic society. The theory of a new-democratic society was centered on the problem of how to build a new-democratic society and how to realize the transition from New Democracy to socialist revolution and construction after seizing state power. Although the two theories are closely related to each other, they have different tasks and theoretical priorities and should therefore be considered differently. In addition, some researchers hold that from the perspective of transition of the revolution, the theory of a new-democratic society "is even more important" because it "defined a concrete way for the transition of the revolution and formulated a theory of the transition," so it is "a great theoretical creation and an important supplement to the Marxist theory of scientific socialism."[1] What also makes it important is that it had "basically answered the question about how should an economically backward country that has achieved victory in its democratic revolution build itself and prepare for a transformation to socialism" and supplemented the Marxist-Leninist theory that a backward country after revolution could enter socialism bypassing the stage of capitalist development with "a scientific plan for implementation."[2]

Since the 1990s, a large number of researchers have began to reconsider and re-study the theory of a new-democratic society as the discussion relating the theory and practice of building socialism with Chinese characteristics progressed widely. After entering the new century, researchers have reviewed the country's experience in its reform and opening up process for two decades and therefore developed a better understanding of the theory and practice in the Chinese revolution. A review of experience over the past eight decades, both positive and negative, demonstrated the ideological importance of the

[1] Shi Zhongquan, *The Hard Exploration by Mao Zedong*, Chinese Communist Party History Publishing House, Beijing, 1990, pp. 111-112. Wang Lirong, "The Theory of a New-Democratic Society Is a Great Creation of the Communist Party of China," *Teaching and Research in CPC History*, 1992 (5).

[2] Lu Zhenxiang, "Important Development of the Theory of New Democracy during the War of Liberation," *Literature, History and Philosophy*, 1991 (4); "Application and Development of the Theory of Bypassing the Stage of Capitalist Development," *Study of the History of the Communist Party of China*, 1991 (3); Chen Tong, "A Brief Discussion of the Theory and Practice for New-Democratic Society," *Historical Review*, 1992 (1).

theory of a new-democratic society and has attracted researchers to study it deeply.

Efforts to study the theory of a new-democratic society since the late 1980s have focused on four major aspects as follows.

5.1.1 The Formation and Development of the Theory of a New-Democratic Society

This theory had gone through a course of emergence, formation, development, and being discarded. There are not many writings published to discuss its emergence, formation and development, and there is not much argument in this regard. It is believed in this book that Li Dazhao and some other earliest Chinese Marxists had noticed the need for every communist to apply the Marxist theory in a country "in accordance with his own actual conditions" during the May 4th Movement period. An essay published in the journal *New Youth* (No. 3, Volume 8) in early 1920 stated, "It will take a long period of time from the start of revolution to make private property become public and still a longer period of time to eliminate private property institutionally (as conduct) and ideologically. There will be a fairly long transition time." That term "transition time," here of course, was not the same as the idea "transition period" formed later. However, it reflected the backwardness of China at that time and should therefore be regarded as the initial emergence of the theory.

The CPC had formed a basic idea of a new-democratic revolution at its Second National Congress in 1922, at which it defined its minimum program and maximum program and differentiated between democratic revolution and socialist revolution. That laid the ideological foundation for the formation of the theory. In the Resolution on the Chinese Question issued at the Seventh Enlarged Plenum of the Executive Committee of the Communist International in 1926, the problem of "non-capitalist path" for the Chinese revolution was raised. According to the Resolution, the CPC had declared that after victory in the national revolution private capital should not be allowed to engage in big industries that have an important bearing on the overall national economy, but its operation in businesses that could not influence the overall national economy will be protected. The objective of doing so was to reduce the exploitation by the private capitalism and progressively transform to socialism via the transitional stage of non-capitalism. The CPC had also stated that a fundamental guarantee for the "non-capitalist path" was the leadership of the proletariat. All this indicated that the CPC had drawn a sketch for China's path of transformation into socialism, which represented an important step toward the formation of the theory of a new-democratic society.

Before the Chinese people's all-out War of Resistance against Japan broke out, the CPC had encouraged development of private industry and commerce and allowed the commercial and industrial capitalists their due political rights in the Shaanxi-Gansu-Ningxia Border Region, which facilitated the formation of the theory. Thereafter, under the domestic environment that the KMT and the CPC achieved cooperation and the international environment that the Communist International changed its policy toward China and proposed the establishment of an international united front against Fascism, the Chinese Communists made a great leap in integrating Marxism with Chinese practice from 1937 to early 1940—their basic theory of a new-democratic society had eventually taken shape, which could be proved by the publication of a series of works in this regard such as Mao Zedong's "The Chinese Revolution and the Chinese Communist Party" and "On New Democracy." In these works, Mao Zedong had pointed out, "The first stage in the Chinese revolution will result in the establishment of a new-democratic society under the joint dictatorship of all the revolutionary classes of China headed by the Chinese proletariat. The revolution will then be carried forward to the second stage, in which a socialist society will be established in China." This new-democratic society, namely this new-democratic republic, will be different from the old European-American form of capitalist republic under bourgeois dictatorship and on the other hand, it will also be different from the socialist republic of the Soviet type under the dictatorship of the proletariat. It will be a third form of state. Mao Zedong also discussed the basic program for a new-democratic society in terms of politics, economy and culture.

Other Party leaders such as Liu Shaoqi had not only totally agreed with the above ideas but also elaborated them additionally. With regard to the question of when and how to move from new democracy to socialism, Liu Shaoqi had said, "...only when China's economy has developed to its full extent in a new-democratic country, only when many necessary preparatory steps have been taken and, finally, only when the Chinese people feel the need and desire for it, can a socialist and communist system be set up in China."[1] This statement explained the necessary material base, which is of course very important, and the psychological base in society, which is often overlooked.

During the period from the early 1940s to the early years of New China, the theory was further enriched and developed. The CPC's Seventh Congress, which approved Liu Shaoqi's Report on the Revision of the Party Constitution, played an important role in this regard. The Congress established Mao Zedong Thought as the Party's guiding ideology, incorporated the "theories and policies with regard to New Democracy" into Mao Zedong Thought as one of its major components, and defined one of the Party's major tasks at that stage as "striving for new democracy in China." All this showed that the Party had regarded the theory of a new-democratic society as its guide in future construction. During the Congress, Mao Zedong repeatedly stressed the importance of a "stage of New Democracy" and the necessary existence and development of a non-socialist economic sector. He said, "...indeed, we have too little of capitalism." "We Communists clearly understand that under the state system of New Democracy in China it will be necessary in the interests of social progress to facilitate the development of the private capitalist sector of the economy (provided it does not dominate the livelihood of the people) besides the development of the state sector and of the individual and co-operative sectors run by the laboring people."[2]

---

[1] *Selected Works of Liu Shaoqi*, Eng. ed., FLP, Beijing, 1984, Vol. I, p. 336.

[2] *Selected Works of Mao Tse-tung*, Eng. ed., FLP, Peking, 1965, Vol. III, p. 283.

To some extent, it could be said that it was by using the theory of a new-democratic society that Mao Zedong and other Party leaders unified the whole Party's understanding.

At the Second Plenary Session of the Seventh CPC Central Committee in 1949 when the situation had changed greatly and the Party was to shift the focus of its work, the theory was still affirmed. In June of the same year Liu Shaoqi delivered the report "Guiding Principles for New China's Economic Development" to systematically discuss the strategy for economic development in the new-democratic society. This important report and Mao Zedong's "On the People's Democratic Dictatorship" respectively provided economic and political guidance for China's development in a pre-socialist period, namely the period of a new-democratic society, and therefore greatly enriched the theory of a new-democratic society.

The Common Program (New China's first interim Constitution) passed at the First Plenary Session of the Chinese People's Political Consultative Conference in September 1949 had proclaimed, "The People's Republic of China is a new-democratic state governed by a people's democratic dictatorship, in which all sectors of the economy will function satisfactorily with a due division of labor under the leadership of the socialist state sector." After being incorporated into the Common Program, which was an interim Constitution in the early years of New China, the theory of a new-democratic society had become the fundamental compass for all the Chinese people. In the early years of New China, a series of "new-democratic reforms" (Mao Zedong's words) were implemented, and the social structure gave a central manifestation of the features of a new-democratic society.[1]

Although researchers commonly agree on the general course of formation and development of the theory, they disagree to varying degrees with each other on how other Party leaders contributed to the theory in different historical periods. Their opinions, however, too dispersed, will not be discussed here. The unique contributions by Liu Shaoqi and Zhou Enlai

---

[1] Wang Zhi and Wen Hongyu, "How the Theory of a New-Democratic Society Was Created and Discarded," *Party Literature*, 2000(1).

on this theory during the early years of New China will be discussed later.

5.1.2 The Nature and Feature of a New-Democratic Society

Although researchers do not have much argument over the formation and development of the theory, they have hotly argued over the nature and feature of a new-democratic society. In recent ten years researchers have discovered and discussed the nature and feature according to words and talks of Mao Zedong and other Party leaders. Definitions given by some researchers were unclear and even inconsistent. Arguments arise there from. Some researchers have argued that the nature and basic feature of a new-democratic society lies in a transition from New Democracy to socialism—it was "a transitional society featuring a combination of democracy and socialism, namely a half-democracy and half-socialism society." Some others persist in the ideas stated in the "general line of Party" for the transition period, and argue that it belongs to the system and concept of socialism. Still others believe that it was "a historical stage the Chinese society cannot skip in its development," and it is "an independent social form different from both capitalism and socialism, which has its own law of development and historical stages," and is a "special social form, which replaced capitalism, that the Chinese society should go through to realize socialism."[1]

Then, which one of the above opinions is correct? Some scholars have pointed out that new-democratic society should be understood not only logically but also historically. There is no doubt that it was transitional. However, Party leaders represented by Mao Zedong had understood its nature of being transitional differently in different historical periods. As some researchers have pointed out, before 1952, especially before the founding of New China, Mao Zedong and other Party leaders had stated that China should go through a transition period to realize socialism because that is the way and trend things develop. A new-democratic society was the outcome of China's new-democratic revolution and at the same time, an independent social form that embodied politics, economy and culture of New Democracy. Politically,

---

[1] Shi Zhongquan (ed.), *A Review of Study on Mao Zedong*, p. 208.

it aimed to build a united new-democratic state power. Economically, it aimed to revitalize the country's economy by developing the state's socialist sector, the private capitalist sector and the co-operative sector of the new-democratic economy. Culturally, it aimed to liberate and develop the individuality of the Chinese people by developing a national, democratic, scientific, and mass culture.

When the People's Republic was founded, Mao Zedong and other Party members, after taking into consideration the new conditions, had clarified the nature and basic feature of a new-democratic society again: it is a social form the country should go through to realize socialism; its principal problem was the contradiction between the working class and the bourgeoisie; the crucial question for the Party was "how to rehabilitate and develop China's economy" and its urgent task was to develop the productive forces to improve the national economy; the five sectors in the national economy— the state-owned sector, the co-operative sector, the state-capitalist sector, the private capitalist sector, and the small commodity sector—should be allowed to coexist and develop; it would be governed by a people's democratic dictatorship, the form of which is a people's democratic united front led by the working class, based on worker-peasant alliance, and participated by the working class, the peasantry, the petite bourgeoisie, the national bourgeoisie and other patriotic democrats. Compared to the definition during the War of Resistance against Japan, the basic content did not change except statement on the principal problem in that society.

After 1952, however, Mao Zedong's understanding of new-democratic society had changed fundamentally. He began to believe that the founding date of New China marked the beginning of transition from New Democracy to socialism and that the new-democratic society was itself just the process of transition to socialism. He no longer regarded it as an independent stage of development and did not talk about it anymore. Liu Shaoqi, Zhou Enlai and other Party leaders retained their understanding of the new-democratic society and upheld the original definition of its basic feature without violating or challenging Mao Zedong's general principles. They had greatly enriched and developed the theory of a new-democracy society. But, Liu Shaoqi's idea of "consolidating new democracy" and Zhou Enlai's idea of "firmly establishing the new-democratic social order" were both severely criticized by Mao Zedong and were consequently given up.

Many researchers hold that Liu Shaoqi's idea of "consolidating new democracy" should be fully affirmed and judged highly. His idea had clearly embodied how the Chinese Communists thought about China's reconstruction and development in their years of practice. And "Consolidating new democracy" was a strategic task for the Party in the first historical period after victory in the revolution; it did not mean that the country was to stay in a new-democratic society forever. Besides, this idea had played a positive role in the early years of New China.

Some researchers have pointed out that Mao Zedong and Zhou Enlai had understood the transition from New Democracy to socialism differently. Mao Zedong discussed mainly the goal of the transition but did not have a clear idea about when the transition began and what process the transition should go through to be completed. Zhou Enlai held that the transition period "is a period the country should go through to move from new democracy to socialism," that the transition should be based on construction and reform, and that the general line for the transition period of gradually accomplishing industrialization of the country and socialist transformation of agriculture, handicrafts, and capitalist industry and commerce should be upheld. Mao Zedong had focused solely on the three socialist transformations (agriculture, handicrafts, and capitalist industry and commerce), which was in fact a transition to socialism in the relations of production. Zhou Enlai had believed that the Party should act in line with the principle in the Common Program, firmly establish the new-democratic social order, and strengthen new democracy during the transition period. But Mao Zedong had criticized the idea of "firmly establishing the new-democratic social order" without mentioning names.

According to research in recent years, Mao Zedong's understanding of the nature of new-democratic society had again showed noticeable change after the Second Plenary Session of the Seventh CPC Central Committee in 1949. Before that date, he generally regarded New Democracy as a new capitalism despite some little changes in his understanding of the nature of new-democratic society. According to the Second Plenary Session of the Seventh Central Committee, a new-democratic society to be established after victory in the Chinese revolution wiould be neither a new-capitalist or bourgeois republic nor a republic in a third form, but will be a republic under the people's democratic dictatorship or under the dictatorship of the proletariat. The politics and economy of this republic would be similar to that of Lenin's dictatorship of the proletariat. All this indicated that Mao Zedong had deviated to a certain extent from his original idea about the new-democratic society. As a result, he generally did not use the term "new-democratic society" any more after the founding of the People's Republic. After the agrarian reform was completed, he immediately put forward the task of moving to socialism and criticized Party leaders "who wanted to continue New Democracy for failing to realize the change in nature of the revolution and making the Right mistakes". After then, he had considered new democracy the same as capitalism, which he believed posed a real threat to China's future. In order to urge the entire Party to drop the illusion of building new democracy, he had even called the transition period from New Democracy to socialism "the period of transition from capitalism to socialism" and totally discarded the theory and practice of new-democratic society.

5.1.3 The Reason the CPC Discarded the Theory of a New-Democratic Society and the Consequences

A lot of researchers in recent years make great efforts to study when and why Mao Zedong and the CPC had abandoned the theory of a new-democratic society. They generally believe that the CPC began to give up the theory in 1952, formally abandoned it in 1953 when the "general line for the transition period" was put forward, and put an end to it in autumn of 1955. As pointed out by some researchers, Mao Zedong, when reading a document drafted by the United Front Work Department under the CPC Central Committee on June 6, 1952, commented, "With the overthrow of the landlord class and the bureaucrat-capitalist class, the contradiction between the working class and the national bourgeoisie has become the principal problem in China." That had marked the beginning of the CPC to solve this "principle contradiction" by eliminating the bourgeoisie and to stop the development of a new-democratic society. At an Enlarged Meeting of the Central Committee's Political Bureau in June 1953, Mao Zedong had severely criticized the idea of "consolidating new democracy" and criticized Liu Shaoqi and others without mentioning their names. He said, "They have remained where they were after the victory of the democratic revolution. They fail to realize there is a change in the nature of the revolution and they go on pushing their 'New Democracy' instead of socialist transformation. This will lead to Right deviationist mistakes." It was also at that meeting that he put forward a general line for the transition period, which was very popular among the people, and transformed it into the will of the Party's central leadership. After the *Outline for Study and Publicity of the Party's General Line for the Transition Period* revised by Mao Zedong was published in December of the same year, to eliminate the private capitalist sector and the small commodity sector and remold capitalists, big and small, became the central work of the Party and the government. By then, the Party's Central Committee had formally abandoned the theory of a new-democratic society. In the "Report on the Draft Constitution of the People's Republic of China" in September 1954, Liu Shaoqi had to personally criticize the idea of "consolidation of the new-democratic order," which indicated that he no longer opposed the Party's decision to end the new-democratic society.

The formulation and implementation of the general line for the transition period undoubtedly played a crucial role in the CPC's decision to abandon the theory of a new-democratic society. Surprisingly, researchers have argued much over the relationship between the theory and the general line. Some researchers hold that the general line had deviated from the theory, while others believe that it was a continuation and development of the theory. Some researchers have even reached inconsistent conclusions. On the one hand, they believe that the theory is a great contribution Chinese Communists represented by Mao Zedong made to the theory of scientific socialism. On the other hand, they strive to prove the correctness of "the general line", which had obviously deviated to some extent from the theory. So, what then is the relationship between the theory and the general line?

Li Anzeng had thoroughly discussed the issue in his paper "The General Line for the Transition Period and the Theory of a New-Democratic Society" published in the journal *Teaching and Research in CPC History* (No. 6, 1999). According to him, the theory and the general line were generally identical in the objective, task and employing the method of the peaceful transition, but were different in the strategy for moving toward socialism— the theory stresses first developing the country and then moving to socialism. The "general line" stresses simultaneously realizing industrialization of the country and completing socialist transformation of private ownership of the means of production. In concrete, the new democratic society theory stresses a future sudden and complete transition while "the general line" stresses an immediate, gradual transition; the theory allows proper development of private capitalist economy while the general line eliminates it completely; the theory allows co-operatives of individual farming and handicrafts based on private ownership while the general line allows only co-operatives based on public ownership; the theory puts the emphasis of the Party on economic development while "the general line", puts the emphasis on the contradiction between the working class and the bourgeoisie. And, he does not think that the formulation and implementation of "the general line" meant the final end to the theory. When Mao Zedong used Marx's and Lenin's words to define the transition period as a period of "transition from capitalism to socialism" in September 1955, he was not only putting an end to the development stage of new-democratic society but also publicly denying that the republic founded after victory of the democratic revolution was a new-democratic republic. Mao Zedong's above definition of the transition period was soon incorporated into the political report of the Party's Eighth Congress in 1956, which put the final end to the theory. Although a number of researchers do not agree with Li Anzeng's discussion over the relationship between the general line and the theory, most researchers have accepted his opinion that the theory finally came to an end in 1955.

There are many reasons behind Mao Zedong's decision to discard the theory. And many researchers have discussed this issue. According to some researchers, the fundamental reason is that "Mao Zedong thought the theory is immature and naturally rejected the bourgeoisie," and another important reason is that "he compared China's transition period from new-democratic to socialist society with Lenin's theory of transition period before 1921." Besides, New China's foreign policy of "leaning to one side" (the side of the camp headed by the Soviet Union) around its founding and the influence of the Soviet Union and the Eastern Europe were also important reasons that can not be ignored. At that time, the Soviet Union hoped that China moved to socialism as soon as possible, and Eastern European countries were practicing their transformation according to Lenin's theory of transition period.[1] Other researchers stressed that Mao Zedong's arbitrary thinking at that time led him and the Party's Central Committee to wrongly judge the principal problem in Chinese society to be the contradiction between the proletariat and the bourgeoisie, which in fact should be how to meet the ever-growing material and cultural needs of the people under backward social production circumstances.

Some researchers have studied numerous literature and documents and taken into consideration the influence of Lenin's "Two Tactics of Social-Democracy in the Democratic Revolution" and influence of Russia's revolutionary experience on the CPC's theory of New Democracy and tactics of struggle. They have argued that the reason CPC developed the theory of New Democracy is that it needed to find a non-capitalist path. The CPC's statement that "China needs a great development of capitalism" was also made under the specific condition of an anti-Japanese national

---

[1] Cui Xiaolin, "A Discussion of Reasons for Mao Zedong's Decision to Abandon the Theory of a New-Democratic Society," *Academic Forum*, 1999 (3).

united front. After consulting Lenin's "Two Tactics of Social-Democracy in the Democratic Revolution" and taking into consideration the comparison of political strength between the KMT and the CPC, the CPC had made that statement in the hope to win majority support from both international strength (mainly the United States) and domestic strength (the national bourgeoisie) in the coalition government to be established after victory of the War of Resistance against Japan. So, the statement was the CPC's tactic to win political superiority and leadership. That is the reason Mao Zedong and other Party leaders had later never theoretically explained why China "needs a great development of capitalism." Therefore, some researchers have argued that it should not be surprising that Mao Zedong had abandoned the statement later.[1]

Now, we can also say that the theory of a new-democratic society has some flaws that became the fundamental reason behind Mao Zedong's decision to abandon it. So, what are these flaws? Shi Zhongquan in his book *The Hard Exploration by Mao Zedong* has summarized them into four aspects. First, it did not clearly define the connection between the two revolutionary stages—the socialist revolution should be started right after the end of the democratic revolution or should be started after a certain period of new-democratic society. Even the report of the Second Plenary Session of the Seventh Party Central Committee still had not answered this question—until it was later answered wrongly. Second, on the one hand it had clarified that the Party's central task and work after the founding of New China was economic development and on the other, it defined the principal problem in Chinese society as the contradiction between the working class and the bourgeoisie, which was self-contradictory. Third, the Party did not have a clear and unanimous understanding of the nature of a new-democratic society (this one has been discussed earlier and will not be continued here). Fourth, it did not define the transition period as a necessary long period. This summarization, accurate or not, will no doubt inspire further researches.

---

[1] Yang Kuisong, "The Reason Mao Zedong Abandoned New Democracy—the Influence of Russian Model," *Modern Chinese History Studies*, 1997 (4).

In fact, it was necessary and inevitable for China, which had just put an end to a semi-colonial, semi-feudal society, to practice a new-democratic social system for a fairly long period of time so that it could have the time to develop and create all the necessary conditions for moving to socialism. As pointed out by researchers, a new-democratic society "was a necessary, practical and correct choice for China with backward economy and culture and underdeveloped commodity economy to leap over the capitalist stage, get rid of poverty, put socialized mass production to the leading position in the economy, and eventually realize socialism." It was regret that the CPC had abandoned the theory and practice of the new-democratic society too early. As a result, "China hastily stopped developing commodity economy and assimilating progressive capitalist achievements and missed the rare, perfect opportunity offered by the new-democratic society to get well prepared for socialist construction. The socialist system with a high degree of centralization established by copying the Soviet model was obviously inappropriate for China's stage of development and was later eventually replaced by the socialism with Chinese characteristics."[1]

5.1.4 Similarities and Differences between the Theory of a New-Democratic Society on the One Hand and the New Economic Policy of Russia and the Theory of the Primary Stage of Socialism on the Other

In recent years, a large number of researchers have conducted comparative study of the theory of a new-democratic society and the theory of the primary stage of socialism and have produced many results. "From the perspective of methodology, Mao Zedong's theory of a new-democratic society is a prelude or a theoretical source of the theory of socialism with Chinese characteristics." Mao Zedong's strategic ideas on a new-democratic society can be understood in two modes and assessed by two yardsticks—the productive forces and ideology (understanding of

---

[1] Wang Zhi and Wen Hongyu, "How the Theory of a New-Democratic Society Was Created and Abandoned," *Party Literature*, 2000 (1).

communism). The yardstick of the productive forces requires that the country targets developing the productive forces as its central task and fully utilizes all possible methods, including the capitalist operation and management methods, to liberate and develop the productive forces. That is exactly the essence of the theory of a new-democratic society. The theory of the primary stage of socialism has absorbed and assimilated this essence.[1] At the same time, the two theories are also very different. If it could be said it was somewhat a tactic for the CPC advocating to support full development of capitalism under the theory of a new-democratic society under certain historical conditions. But it should be said that it was a long-term strategy to allow co-existence of various economic sectors and business methods and assimilate the finest achievements of other countries under the theory of the primary stage of socialism. Unlike the theory of a new-democratic society that was immature, imperfect and suddenly abandoned, the theory of the primary stage of socialism, which was formulated when the country had been placed back on the right track and the policy of reform and opening up had been implemented, was a result of long-term exploration by the entire Party including theoreticians and has been readily accepted by people both within and without the Party. It includes a system of theories about the Party's platform and basic line, economic restructuring, economic development strategy, political restructuring, improvement of democracy and the legal system, and cultural development all through the primary stage of socialism. In addition, the CPC has declared that it will uphold the theory of the primary stage of socialism for many years to come, so it can guide practice for a long time to come.

Because of the above noticeable differences, development of the theory on the primary stage of socialism, today can be in no way a "reversion or regress" to the construction in new-democratic society, although some researchers feel happily to believe that it can be such a "regress". In this regard, Hu Sheng's paper "Reassessment of Mao Zedong's New Democracy"

---

[1] Gu Hongliang, "On Mao Zedong's Ideas of a New-Democratic Society and Methodology Therein," *Research of Mao Zedong Thought*, 1998 (4).

(originally a speech he delivered on December 26, 1998 at the "Symposium on Mao Zedong, Deng Xiaoping and Application of Marxism in China" jointly hosted by the Party Literature Research Center under the CPC Central Committee and Hunan Provincial Committee of the CPC) published in the quarterly journal *Social Sciences in China* (No. 3, 1999) deserves much attention. He had said in that 22, 000 character paper that the CPC, no matter in the revolutionary era or during the construction period, was always faced with the same problem: should it use Populism or Marxism to understand and deal the relationship between capitalism and socialism. When this problem was well solved, revolution and construction had progressed smoothly; otherwise, setbacks had occurred. Mao Zedong's New Democracy found a path of moving from a semi-colonial, semi-feudal society to a socialist society—the path of the new-democratic revolution, which was totally different from Populism that had advocated a direct transition from peasant economy to socialism. A review of New China's experience and lessons in three decades after its founding indicates that any blind attempt to improve the socialist relations of production at the neglect of the level of productive forces could only block the development of the productive forces and progress of society. That is exactly the fundamental difference between Marxism and Populism. For that reason, Hu Sheng has stressed that re-studying Mao Zedong's theory of New Democracy "can help us fully understand the importance of the theory of the primary stage of socialism, the necessity and correctness of the policy of reform and opening up, and the historical and theoretical reason for the Party's decision to give high priority to develop the productive forces." Due to his high prestige in the circle of study of the history of the CPC, the paper was widely discussed and argued. Some critics have argued that he was advocating the old road of new democracy. In fact, he has clearly stated that China could no longer take the "road of new democracy" because conditions have changed completely after decades of socialist development, but can still draw lessons from it.

A paper has been recently published to compare the theory of a new-democratic society with the New Economic Policy of Russia in order to review historical experience and draw lessons therefrom. It deserves to be introduced here. The paper holds that the Russian Communist Party and the CPC shared some similar experiences in exploring a path of building socialism in an economically backward country, which was centrally manifested in Lenin's theory of New Economic Policy and Mao Zedong's theory of a new-democratic society. They both had showed a somewhat "deviation" from traditional socialism, believing that a backward country could not establish a "pure" socialist system neglecting assimilating progressive capitalist achievements. In fact, that is exactly why it was historically inevitable for the CPC to put forward the theory of a new-democratic society. The paper also discussed their differences, advancing that Lenin's New Economic Policy was not a prepared theoretical concept but was a set of ideas put forward to address urgent problems on the basis of a review of experiences in wartime communism, while China's theory of a new-democratic society had been defined before victory the democratic revolution. Therefore, it should be said that the CPC was more prepared and farsighted than the Russian Communist Party on the question of how to realize socialism, partially because the CPC underwent a longer period of revolutionary struggles and had gained practical experience in developing economy in the liberated areas. Regretfully, the CPC had not continued to make full use of this strength. In addition, Lenin and Mao Zedong had different understanding of commodity economy, market, individual economy and private capitalist economy. Lenin did not allow himself to be shackled by traditional notions and dogmas; he constantly transformed and upgraded backward traditional notions, explored boldly and bravely and advanced that commodity, market and currency as well as capitalism can all be utilized to build socialism. That was the most precious ideological legacy Lenin had left. On the contrary, Mao Zedong, deeply restricted by the notions of traditional socialism, believed that commodity and market categories belong to capitalism and always desired to eliminate them. All this shows that it is surely difficult to produce a creative theory, but it is even more difficult to implement it later. No matter how advanced and suitable theories we can produce, our great cause of socialism could not advance if we cannot implement them in practice due to failure to break the shackles of backward traditional notions.[1]

5.2 The Theory and Policy on the Peasant Problem and Agrarian Reform

The agrarian reform or revolution was the greatest movement in the twentieth century led by the CPC to raise productivity in agriculture and emancipate the peasants. Without this great movement that destroyed the feudal land system there would be no victory of China's new-democratic revolution, and thus no foundation for China's social progress and modernization. Its significance for China's democratic revolution and the contribution and benefits to the peasantry had made to the Chinese revolution deserve to be recorded in golden letters. Since the beginning of reform and opening up policy, many researchers have conducted studies in this respect, and dozens of papers were published in national authoritative journals. Books published are *China's History of Agrarian Reform* by Zhang Yongquan and Zhao Quanjun, *Development of the Land Policy of the Communist Party of China* by Kong Yongsong, *Agrarian Reform during the War of Liberation* by Dong Zhikai, *Chinese History of Agrarian Reform* by Zhao Xiaomin, *A Study on Peasant and Land Problem in Modern China* by Guo Dehong, *China's Agrarian Revolution* by Du Runsheng, and *Peasant Problem and Rural Society in Modern China* by Zhu Yuxiang. These papers and books, containing a large quantity of historical material, have analyzed China's history of agrarian reform from various perspectives, advanced many fresh ideas, and greatly broadened and deepened the research on the agrarian reform and peasant problem.

---

[1] Wang Lirong, "A Comparison of 'New Economic Policy' in Russia and China—Lenin's New Economic Policy and Mao Zedong's Theory of a New-Democratic Society," *Journal of Zhongnan University of Economics*, 2000 (6).

5.2.1 General Assessment of the Agrarian Reform

The assessment of the agrarian reform is focused on three aspects: the first is about its necessity and correctness; the second is about its role and historical significance; and the third is about the CPC's land policies in different historical periods. All research results have reached the same major conclusions that the agrarian reform had played an important role in the Chinese revolution and the CPC had correctly analyzed the peasant problem in China. In addition, some researchers have also discussed the different policies the Party had adopted to address problems concerning the peasants and land in different historical periods of the new-democratic revolution as well as the subjective and objective reasons for the change of policies, and explained how the CPC had improved its land policy.

To affirm the agrarian reform, researchers have first of all analyzed if it was necessary and reasonable. Du Runsheng's paper "On China's Agrarian Reform Movement" published in *Study of the History of the Communist Party of China* (No. 6, 1996) was a typical paper in this regard. Under the long feudal rule, the Chinese people were exploited by exorbitant taxes and miscellaneous levies, land rent and usury and led a life worse than beasts of burden. After the Opium War, reactionary governments in China collaborated with foreign forces of aggression. They oppressed the peasants by using the forces of the landlord class in rural areas and shackled them with feudal ethical code such as the three cardinal guides (ruler guides subject, father guides son, and husband guides wife) and five constant virtues (benevolence, righteousness, propriety, wisdom and fidelity) and clan mentality, and severely hindered development of the productive forces. All this is the fundamental reason why the CPC could lead the peasants to victory in the agrarian revolution. The agrarian revolution was a democratic reform happening in rural areas and was a severe class struggle, which was closely linked with the CPC's efforts to carry out armed struggle and establish and consolidate its political authority in rural base areas. With the support of that political authority, the revolutionary war and the agrarian revolution had progressed smoothly; otherwise, fruits in the agrarian reform were lost. Only by establishing and consolidating the political power of the peasantry through armed struggle, could the CPC protect achievements in the agrarian revolution and fully arouse the enthusiasm of all peasants for participating in the revolution and building their own political authority. For that reason, the CPC, in leading the agrarian revolution, always stressed the necessity of drawing a clear distinction between the people and the enemy, using class analysis method to analyze the various classes in the rural areas, studied their political attitudes, and formulating and implementing practicable policies after thoroughly analyzing social structure in rural areas. In addition, the agrarian reform required not only distribution of land but also transformation of political authority in rural areas so that the peasants could become the foundation for winning armed struggles and consolidating democratic political power. For this purpose, in addition to meeting the peasants' demand for land, the CPC should also educate them to improve their political consciousness and organizational ability and turn them from the oppressed to the masters of the new political power.

The CPC's land policy had changed a lot and sometimes even had different answers to the same problem. That was perhaps because the situation had changed or the Party had developed a better understanding of the problem. No matter what the reason was, its policy was getting more effective and complete.

5.2.2 Different Opinions on "Equal Distribution of Land"

The idea of "equal distribution of all land" reflected an incorrect demand for land of the peasantry. During the new-democratic revolution, this idea had influenced how the CPC formulated and implemented its land policy. It produced extensive harm during the Agrarian Revolutionary War. Economically, equal distribution of all land was not beneficial for capital accumulation and hindered capitalist development in China. Politically, it was detrimental to uniting the majority of the rural population. Therefore, most researchers hold a negative attitude toward it.

The CPC's land policy was comparatively more mature during the War of Liberation. During July to September 1947, the Working Committee of the CPC Central Committee called the National Land Conference and drew up the Outline Land Law of China, which was a complete program for China's agrarian revolution. The Outline Land Law had defined the principle of abolishing the land system of feudal and semi-feudal exploitation and putting into effect the system of land to the tillers, which was a way to destroy the feudal system completely and conformed to the demands of the peasants. Researchers, in general, affirm its constructive meaning. At the same time, some researchers have objectively pointed out that it still contained the idea of "equal distribution of all land." For example, it stipulated in Article 6 that, "All the land of the landlords and the public land in the villages is to be taken over by the local peasant associations and, together with all other land there, should be equally distributed among the entire rural population, regardless of sex or age." In actual implementation, the principle of equal distribution of land often encroached on the interests of the middle peasants and damaged industry and commerce. That caused some panic and complaints among the middle peasants, making it hard for the CPC to unite them and arouse their enthusiasm for production. Besides, the poor peasants and farm laborers had become afraid of "getting rich" or "getting conspicuous," and their contradiction with the middle peasants were further intensified. In short, the policy of equal distribution of all land with no doubt had weakened revolutionary forces. As pointed out by Dong Zhikai, "To equally distribute the land and property of the feudal class is revolutionary, while to equally distribute the land and property of classes other than the feudal class was backward, regress and reactionary and can be called absolute equalitarianism."[1] Kong Yongsong had commented, "Equal distribution of all land had gone too far beyond opposing feudal exploitation," and "did not accord with the purpose of the agrarian reform, which was to

---

[1] Dong Zhikai, *Agrarian Reform during the War of Liberation*, Peking University Press, Beijing, 1987, p. 164.

abolish the land system of feudal and semi-feudal exploitation."[1] Zhao Xiaomin et al. considered that the Outline Land Law "yielded to the idea of equalitarianism," and that "errors had inevitably occurred during actual implementation because it used a principle of equal distribution to replace of specific policies and did not explain how to equally distribute."[2]

However, there are also researchers who hold the opinion that Article 6 of the Outline Land Law should not be criticized too much. Du Jing have published the paper "A Number of Questions in the Research on China's Agrarian Reform" in the journal *Social Sciences in China* (No. 1, 1992) to prove this opinion. According to him, the CPC Central Committee had corrected the policy of equal distribution of land at the December meeting (a meeting of the CPC Central Committee held on December 25-28, 1947) held soon after the Outline Land Law was promulgated. In his report "The Present Situation and Our Task" to the meeting, Mao Zedong had declared that one of the two fundamental principles that should be observed in the agrarian reform is "uniting solidly with the middle peasants and never damaging their interests." He had also said, "Our policy is to rely on the poor peasants and unite solidly with the middle peasants to abolish the feudal and semi-feudal system of exploitation by the landlord class and by the old-type rich peasants." In its Directive on the Work of Agrarian Reform and of Party Consolidation in the Old and Semi-Old Areas issued on February 22, 1948, the CPC Central Committee specified that the excess land of middle peasants could only be taken when their average land was more than twice the average land of poor peasants and farm laborers and only if they consented, and added an important annotation to Article 6 of the Outline Land Law, which read: "in carrying out equal distribution of land, it is necessary to listen to the opinions of the middle peasants and make concessions to them if they object, and they should be allowed to keep more land than the average poor peasant." All this

---

[1] Kong Yongsong, *Development of the Land Policy of the Communist Party of China*, Jiangxi People's Publishing House, Nanchang, 1987, pp. 169, 171.

[2] Zhao Xiaomin (ed.), *Chinese History of Agrarian Reform*, People's Publishing House, Beijing, 1990, p. 354.

had, in fact, partly corrected the principle of "equal distribution of all land." Thereafter, the CPC Central Committee generally had no longer used the term "equal distribution of land" in its documents.

But, according to some researchers, "equal distribution of land" was after all the demand of revolutionary peasants, so the CPC had to manifest it in its policy in order to motivate all of them to participate in the agrarian reform. Although equal distribution of land inevitably brought about some negative impacts, it had indeed played an important role in the Chinese revolution. Zhang Yongquan made a thorough discussion in this regard in his paper "The Policy of 'Equal Distribution of Land' Should Be Basically Affirmed" published in *Study of the History of the Communist Party of China* (No. 6, 1994). According to him, the policy of "equal distribution of land" should be basically affirmed in both the theoretical and practical aspects. Theoretically, it completely negated the feudal land ownership system, met the demand for land for the majority of peasants, liberated rural productive forces, and was therefore revolutionary and progressive. In the practical aspect, it satisfied the demands of poor peasants and farm laborers with little or no land who accounted for seventy percent of the rural population, and also provided land for lower-middle peasants. That is to say, the majority of rural population (about seventy-five percent) had benefited from the policy, and another ten percent did not suffer any loss. Besides, the CPC Central Committee had never completely denied the policy, despite the fact that it did begin to add some limitations and make some corrections to the policy ever since the December meeting due to the consideration that it was still imperfect and easily led to absolute equalitarianism. For instance, in his "Speech at a Conference of Cadres in the Shanxi-Suiyuan Liberated Area" in April 1948, Mao Zedong had put forward a complete general line for the agrarian reform. He said, "We support the peasants' demand for equal distribution of land in order to help arouse the broad masses of peasants speedily to abolish the system of landownership by the feudal landlord class, but we do not advocate absolute equalitarianism." On the basis of the above analyses, Zhang Yongquan has reached his conclusion. The policy of "equal distribution of land" was aimed to abolish the land system of feudal exploitation; this is the primary aspect which should be affirmed. At the same time, the policy was imperfect and sometimes encroached on the interests of the middle and rich peasants, which is only the secondary aspect.

In assessing the policy of "equal distribution of land," Du Jing in his paper "A Number of Questions in the Research on China's Agrarian Reform" put forward a new issue that deserves attention. It was originally believed that in old China landlords and rich peasants accounted for no more than eight percent of peasant households and ten percent of rural population. That indicated that the total scope of attack in the agrarian reform would generally not exceed about eight percent of the rural households and about ten percent of the rural population (as also accepted by the CPC Central Committee). That is to say, the CPC could implement the reform assuredly because it could unite about ninety percent of the population in the villages without encroaching on the interests of the middle peasants. The realities, however, were not so simple. The above numbers were average figures across the country; and conditions in different parts of the country were largely different. When the total scope of attack was strictly controlled within the above numbers in place where landlords and rich peasants accounted for a larger percentage, the reform was not implemented thoroughly, some poor peasants could not get land, and feudal exploitation could not be abolished completely. On the contrary, in those places where landlords and rich peasants accounted for a smaller percentage, some middle peasants could also be deprived of land to make up the required numbers.

In conclusion, the agrarian reform was not designed to equally distribute all land; its scope of attack should be confined to the land system of feudal and semi-feudal exploitation, and any attack going beyond this scope was wrong. That is the common and fundamental criterion for judging the policies of "equally distributing land," "taking from those who had a excess and giving to those who had less" and "taking from those who had better and giving to those who had worse."

5.2.3 Arguments over Policies toward the Rich Peasants

The first argument is about which class the rich peasants belonged to. During the agrarian reform, they together with landlords were classified as the targets of the reform. However, according to the research results of some scholars, the rich peasants were fundamentally different from the landlord class who lived a parasitic life by exploiting the laboring people because they labored too. Only when their land had increased and they were not able to do all the farming work by themselves, would they hire labors or practice usury, but they had still worked. In fact, it was very difficult to define rich peasants by the proportion of their exploitation income in their total income. The CPC Central Committee had promulgated The Decision on Certain Questions Concerning the Agrarian Struggles in 1933 to prescribe that peasants with an income from exploitation should be classified as rich peasants if such income is more than fifteen percent of their total income. In 1948 the CPC Central Committee had prescribed that peasants with an income from exploitation accounting for more than twenty-five percent of their total income for consecutive three years should be classified as rich peasants. In fact, both of the above two criteria had recognized that the majority income of rich peasants came from labor and not exploitation. Some researchers have also analyzed statistical data. The rich peasants possessed more means of production than the middle and poor peasants did, but this was not too much. The average arable land owned by them was twice as much as that owned by middle peasants and about four to six times more than that owned by poor peasants. This fact did not change till the early days of liberation. Besides, according to statistics about average grain production in rural areas, the average grain production of rich peasants was twice as much as that of middle peasants and about five times more than that of poor peasants, which was in proportion to the arable land owned by them. All this indicates that the rich peasants were still relying on labor in farming and practicing a peasant economy, and did not have the ability to expand reproduction. In short, the rich peasants should belong to a stratum between landlords and general peasants—they were rich, but were still peasants, and it was reasonable to classify them as the peasantry.[1]

The second argument is about policies toward the rich peasants. Why was it that the CPC once implemented the policy of "allotting no land to the landlords and poor land to the rich peasants" during the agrarian reform? According to some researchers, that was partially because of the way the Communist International analyzed the class character of the rich peasants in China. Copying the experience and practice in Russia, it had asserted that the rich peasants in China were reactionary "semi-landlords" and should be excluded from the peasantry. It told the CPC not to worry that the rich peasants might withdraw from the revolution and not to "restrict the class struggles staged by farm laborers" or "yield to the rich peasants at the cost of its own initiative." It criticized the CPC for making severe mistakes of opportunism in dealing with the rich peasants and instructed the CPC in 1929 to "intensify struggle against the rich peasants." Its incorrect analyses of and attitude toward the Chinese rich peasants inevitably influenced the CPC's policies concerning them.[2] Of course, the CPC gradually recognized that the rich peasants in China were different from rich peasants in capitalist countries. As pointed out by some researchers, the rich peasants were classified as the peasantry in many of the CPC's historical documents. For instance, although the CPC had called the rich peasants "semi-landlords" as required by the Communist International in its Political Resolution passed at its Sixth National Congress, it had added, "it is not correct to intensify struggle against the rich peasants because that will make us deviate from the principal contradiction between the peasantry and the landlord class." In the Resolution on Land Problems passed at the same Congress, the CPC had stated that the peasantry included the rich, middle and petite peasants, which gave the rich peasants a different class character. In the Resolution of

---

[1] Xu Li, "On Our Party's Policies toward the Rich Peasants in the Land Struggle," *Historiography Research in Anhui*, 1988 (10).

[2] Lin Qiang, "Mao Zedong and the Chinese Peasant Problem," *Study of the History of the Communist Party of China*, 1993 (3).

the CPC Central Committee to Change Policies toward the Rich Peasants in December 1935, the CPC stated, "the strategy of intensifying struggle against the rich peasants will only push them to the counterrevolutionary side and strengthen the counterrevolutionary forces." In his essay "The Chinese Revolution and the Chinese Communist Party" in 1939, Mao Zedong had clearly classified the rich peasants under the peasantry and said, "We should not regard the rich peasants as belonging to the same class as the landlords and should not prematurely adopt a policy of liquidating the rich peasantry." All this indicates that the Chinese Communists had upheld the principle of integrating Marxism with Chinese realities in treating the rich peasants.

The third argument is about the nature of the rich peasant economy. Was their exploitation of the poverty-stricken peasants feudal or capitalist? According to the opinion of most researchers, no doubt it was a feudal exploitation that they earned money by renting out land but at the same time, it was a typical capitalist mode of production that they managed their land by hiring farm laborers. In other words, the farm laborers were the proletariat and the rich peasants were the bourgeoisie in rural areas. Mao Zedong had expressed a similar opinion in his essay "The Chinese Revolution and the Chinese Communist Party." Other researchers, however, have disagreed. They have argued that capitalist operation by hiring labor was very few in China's rural areas and was therefore not representative. Kong Yongsong analyzed, "The rich peasants in China, unlike rich peasants or rural capitalists in capitalist countries, neither utilized land to engage in capitalist production of rural products nor hired and exploited workers. In fact, they were just a little richer and engaged in a peasant economy, in which their exploitation on farm laborers was of a feudal and semi-feudal nature."[1]

The argument over the class character of the rich peasants and the nature of the rich peasant economy is in fact about one question—if the Chinese proletariat can strive to win over and unite the rich peasants as an ally in the new-democratic revolution or not? Isn't this question a better criterion for

---

[1] Kong Yongsong, *Development of the Land Policy of the Communist Party of China*, p. 160.

judging whether the CPC's policies toward the rich peasants conformed to the Chinese realities?

5.2.4 Issues Needing Further Study and Discussion

In the past, books studying problems of modern peasants had often focused on the land problem. However, many researchers have recently published some books and papers, in which they broadened their vision to rural commerce, banking, migration, associations, religious belief, education and customs. Besides, they have thoroughly discussed various problems in rural areas by integrating historical and sociological methods. As a result, they have produced many fresh and original opinions.

It was generally believed that landlords and rich peasants in old China owned over seventy percent of total arable land, which were clarified in works of Mao Zedong. This statement was never questioned before. In recent years, however, some researchers have pointed out that this number is inaccurate. First of all, the number "over seventy percent" came from the Agriculture and Commerce Statistics in the Seventh Year of the Chinese Republic (1918) published by the Ministry of Agriculture and Commerce of the Northern Warlords Government, which contained a lot of errors and was unreliable. Second, due to China's large territory, greatly differentiated natural conditions in different localities, and influence of social and historical conditions, the structure of ownership of land by various rural classes was different in different places, and the structure in the same place would also change. Therefore, the number "over seventy percent" could not apply to all rural areas. Third, the land owned by landlords and rich peasants should not be simply calculated as one. In order to calculate the accurate amount of land under feudal exploitation, the land the rich peasants farmed with their families should be excluded. In this way, the amount of land owned by landlords and rich peasants for feudal exploitation should not exceed fifty percent of total land. Of course, we should not deny the fact that the feudal land ownership system was dominant in old China. But we should also not exaggerate the concentration of land in order to prove the existence of feudal exploitation.[1]

In his paper "How Much Land Landlords and Rich Peasants Owned in Old China" published in the journal *Collected Papers of History Studies* (No. 1, 1998), Wu Tingyu reviewed land documents of 18,544 towns in 991 counties in twenty-four provinces in old China and reached a conclusion as follows. Landlords and rich peasants accounting for six to ten percent of total rural households owned twenty-eight to fifty percent of total land; the peasantry accounting for ninety to ninety-four percent of total rural households owned fifty to seventy-two percent of total land. The land owned by landlords and rich peasants in old China had never exceeded fifty percent of total. In short, the idea that landlords and rich peasants in old China owned over seventy percent of total arable land was unfounded.

Researchers have also discussed the role of the agrarian reform in the Chinese revolution. According to them, it is inaccurate to generally say that the agrarian reform was the main content and basic task of China's new-democratic revolution. The Chinese new-democratic revolution was to overthrow imperialism, feudalism and bureaucrat-capitalism; the agrarian reform was just a part of the efforts or task to fight against feudalism. From the perspective of direct effectiveness, armed struggle was more effective than agrarian reform. Therefore, the place of the land problem in the Chinese revolution should be understood properly. Most researchers, in general, fully affirm the role and importance of the agrarian reform in developing the productive forces. Some researchers have discussed and analyzed its role more concretely, advancing that it greatly raised productivity in agriculture, which should be fully affirmed, but at the same time, its some erroneous practices also produced bad or negative effect on the development of the productive forces, which should not be neglected as well. The CPC's policy of relying on the poor peasants in the revolution was correct, but it did not formulate systematic policies to correct their erroneous ideas and practices and had even supported or encouraged their "spontaneous" practices,

[1] Guo Dehong, *A Study on Peasant and Land Problem in Modern China*, Qingdao Publishing House, Qingdao, 1993, pp. 43-47.

which led to "Left" mistakes and confusions. The CPC should attach equal importance to uniting and educating them.

Researchers have also discussed the problem of polarization in rural areas. Researchers in the past generally held that the agrarian reform had polarized China's rural areas. Li Boyong refuted this idea in his paper "Changes of Classes in Rural Areas after the Agrarian Reform" published in the journal *Study of the History of the Communist Party of China* (No. 1, 1989). The thesis that the agrarian reform polarized China's rural areas did not conform to the actual conditions. After the reform, the rural population had enjoyed steady improvement in financial conditions. According to statistics, the proportion of middle peasants in total peasants in many localities had risen from twenty to eighty percent, while the proportion of poor peasants and farm labors had decreased from seventy to ten percent and was continuing to decrease. A survey of 14,344 rural households in twenty-one provinces in 1954 had also proved this fact. All this indicates that instead of polarization, the number of middle peasants had increased greatly. So, why is it that improvement in rural life was mistakenly evaluated as polarization? One reason is that the peasants' enthusiasm for individual production was confused with the spontaneous tendencies toward capitalism. The other reason was that some peasants prospering first were mistakenly regarded as a trend toward polarization. But it is incorrect to divide classes by differences in standard of living.

In general, the study on the agrarian reform and peasant problem in recent two decades has produced a large number of results. Researchers have thoroughly discussed and argued issues concerning land ownership systems, the policy of equal distribution of land, and structure of land ownership by different rural classes. Efforts still need to be made to discuss the relationship between land policies on the one hand and armed struggle, the united front and consolidation of political power on the other, the question of how to balance revolution and development of productivity in agriculture, the problem of how to define the nature of the rich peasant economy, and the issues concerning "polarization" in rural areas and tendencies toward capitalism. Finding clear answers to the above historical issues will help Marxists to better understand the rural economic reform since the Third Plenary Session of the Eleventh CPC Central Committee.

5.3 Theory of Building Revolutionary Bases

Mao Zedong's thinking on building revolutionary bases is composed of theories developed by Mao Zedong and other members of the CPC's first generation of collective leadership in their practice of establishing rural revolutionary bases during the War of the Agrarian Revolution, building anti-Japanese base areas behind the enemy lines during the War of Resistance against Japan, and developing political authority, economy, culture and education in liberated areas during the War of Liberation. It is an important component of Mao Zedong Thought, as well as an indispensable subject in the study of Mao Zedong Thought.

5.3.1 A Brief Review of Study on Mao Zedong's Thinking on Building Revolutionary Bases

The study on this thought had begun in the early 1940s. Over the past six decades, researchers, beginning with publicizing and repeating directives of Mao Zedong and the Party Central Committee, have begun to thoroughly discuss the Party's experience in establishing revolutionary areas and expound the essence of the thinking. They have studied both easy and difficult and both apparent and profound issues. Similar to study on other components of Mao Zedong Thought, all the major theoretical achievements in this regard were produced in the recent two decades.

Some Party leaders and theoreticians had begun to discuss Mao Zedong's ideas about establishing revolutionary bases in the 1940s. For instance, Liu Shaoqi, in the report to the Party's Seventh National Congress in 1945, strived to review and summarize Mao Zedong's ideas and policies concerning establishing revolutionary bases and had incorporated them into Mao Zedong Thought. Thereafter, Zhang Ruxin, Chen Boda and other theoreticians of the

Party had all discussed this thinking when clarifying Mao Zedong's theory of China's revolutionary road. However, they were just repeating or publicizing the thinking, and therefore did not thoroughly discuss and study it.

During the seventeenth years after the founding of the People's Republic, due to the influence of ideology and political climate at that time, researchers and scholars had still focused their study of this thought as publicizing and repeating it, but had produced far more books and papers than in the 1940s. During this period, with the publication of *Selected Works of Mao Zedong* (volumes 1-4), researchers and scholars wrote a large number of papers to express what they have learned from studying Mao Zedong's thinking on building revolutionary bases. All these papers were of the same pattern—first introducing the historical background in which Mao Zedong wrote an essay, and then repeating the main content of the essay, and finally proving the undoubted correctness of Mao Zedong's idea in the essay. According to incomplete statistics, during this period about fifty-six papers were published to study "On New Democracy," twelve papers to study "Get Organized," eight papers to study "We Should Learn to Do Economic Work," seven papers to study "Economic and Financial Problems in the Anti-Japanese War," five papers to study "A Most Important Policy," four papers to study "The Struggle in the Chingkang Mountains," three papers to study "On Policy," and one paper to study "Pay Attention to Economic Work." Also published during this period were booklets on understanding of the thought. Authors of the above papers, focusing on expressing what they have learned from Mao Zedong's works, did not thoroughly discuss or analyze any ideas in the thought. In addition, some textbooks on the history of the Chinese revolution were published during this period such as *History of China's Modern Revolution* edited by He Ganzhi and *General History of China's New-Democratic Revolution* edited by Li Xin et al., which had introduced the establishment of revolutionary bases by the Chinese Communists in various historical periods. Still, these textbooks did not penetrate deep into the thought.

During the ten years of "cultural revolution," the study on the thinking did not progress; rather it ran into twists and turns and even suffered setbacks. Due to the extreme personality cult of Mao Zedong and the distortion by the Gang of Four, the study on the thinking went astray into praising and extolling the thought—no valuable results were produced in the ten years. It should be noted that Zhou Enlai, Deng Xiaoping and other revolutionaries of the older generation, faced with the difficult and dangerous situation, carried out an unrelenting struggle against the Gang of Four, who distorted the Party's history, to safeguard the true history of the Party. In 1975 when Deng Xiaoping was in charge of the work of the Party Central Committee, the Political Research Center under the State Council had compiled a paper titled "A Review of the Work of the Party and State" to discuss Mao Zedong's ideas about economic development in base areas in his "Pay Attention to Economic Work" and "Economic and Financial Problems in the Anti-Japanese War," advancing that the Party should correctly grasp the dialectical relationship between politics and economy and between revolution and production and constantly pay close attention to economic development work.

After the erroneous ideological and political ideas were rectified in the late 1970s and early 1980s, the study on the CPC's history and Mao Zedong Thought began to flourish in the new historical period. The study on Mao Zedong's thinking on building revolutionary bases also began to develop from simple publicity and repeat to comprehensive discussion and elaboration, deeper and broader than in the previous four decades. This can be proved by many facts.

First, many books published in the new historical period to narrate the history of the Chinese revolution and study Mao Zedong Thought have all introduced and discussed the thought. Volume one of the *History of the Communist Party of China* compiled by the Party History Research Center under the CPC Central Committee contained chapters exclusively expounding on the thought such as the chapters of "Consolidation and Expansion of Rural Revolutionary Base Areas" and "Policies and Measures for Consolidating Anti-Japanese Base Areas." Besides, many other books also elaborated the thinking, such as *The Practice of the Communist Party of China in Seven Decades* edited by Hu Sheng, *Lectures on the History of the Chinese Revolution* edited by Hu Hua, *History of Mao Zedong Thought (Revised)* and *Lectures on the History of Development of Mao Zedong Thought (The New-Democratic Revolution Period)* edited by Zheng Derong et al., *Historical Development of Mao Zedong Thought* edited by Miao Chuhuang, *History of Mao Zedong Thought* edited by Yang Chao and Bi Jianheng, *Ideological History of the Communist Party of China* edited by Zhang Jingru, *Complete Collection of Studies of Mao Zedong Thought* edited by Chao Feng and Li Junru, *History of Development of Mao Zedong Thought* edited by Jin Chunming, *Study on Mao Zedong's Economic Thinking* edited by Xiao Gongda, *Study on Mao Zedong's Economic Thinking* written by Guo Shiping and Guo Jianning, and *Study on Mao Zedong's Thinking on Political Authority* written by Wang Chaobin.

Second, the CPC Central Committee Party History Research Center and local Party history research centers at various levels, working together, have published some historical documents on revolutionary base areas, which included many of Mao Zedong's letters and telegraphs about building base areas and a large quantity of other historical records concerning base areas. Their concerted efforts have provided reliable and detailed historical material for the study of the history of revolutionary base areas. On the basis of the historical material, some researchers compiled books on the complete history of base areas, which has introduced the history of development of the thought and revolutionary base areas in detail and laid a good foundation for thoroughly studying the thinking and reviewing experience of building base areas. The book *Complete History of the Central Revolutionary Base Areas* edited by Dai Xiangqing et al. is a typical example.

Third, autobiographies and memoirs written by revolutionaries of the older generation who were at leading positions in base areas contained lots of valuable historical material on building of base areas and introduced the thought in different aspects. The important ones are *Biography of Lin Boqu*, *Memoirs of Nie Rongzhen*, Li Weihan's *Memory and Research* and Xu Xiangqian's *A Review of History*.

Fourth, party history researchers and other scholars wrote a large number of books and nearly one hundred papers in this regard to introduce the thinking in detail and thoroughly discuss and study its each and every component.

5.3.2 Major Theoretical Achievements in the Study on Mao Zedong's Thought on Building Revolutionary Bases

The study on the thought is focused on the following aspects.

5.3.2.1 Mao Zedong's Ideas about Government Building in Base Areas

The above mentioned books of Zhang Jingru, Jin Chunming, Yang Chao and others all have introduced Mao Zedong's ideas about government building in base areas. Yang Chao's introduction is more comprehensive and detailed. He believes that the development of Mao Zedong's ideas about government building in base areas can be divided into three historical periods—the period of the War of the Agrarian Revolution, the period of the War of Resistance against Japan, and the period of the War of Liberation.

Mao Zedong's ideas about government building in base areas during the period of the War of the Agrarian Revolution include the following. First, he had advanced the idea of the Chinese Soviet Republic during the early period of the War of the Agrarian Revolution. It is a workers' and peasants' democratic republic based on the alliance of the workers, the peasants and the petite bourgeoisie. It adopts a system of the workers' and peasants' representatives, is governed by people's democratic dictatorship with both legislative and executive powers, and implements the system of democratic centralism. Its political program was as follows. Politically, ensure the laboring people are masters of the country. Economically, expropriate the capital of imperialist powers in China and distribute the land of the feudal landlord class to farm laborers and poor and middle peasants; the workers should supervise capitalist production. Culturally, ensure the rights of the working people for education. In ethnic relations, implement the principle of national self-determination and equality. In foreign relations, renounce the unequal treaties with foreign countries and sign new, equal treaties with them.

Second, he had advanced the idea and policies of the People's Republic during the later period of the War of the Agrarian Revolution (1929-1934). It is based on the workers and peasants and plus participated by all other classes willing to fight against imperialism and feudalism. Economically, it protects and encourages the development of industrial and commercial enterprises of the national bourgeoisie. This policy indicates that Mao Zedong had shackled off the Soviet model and begun to develop theories for building a people's democratic state in line with China's conditions.

Third, he had put forward the idea and policies of a "united democratic republic" in cooperation with the KMT during the final period of the War of the Agrarian Revolution. In the matter of the political system, the one-party dictatorship by the KMT should be changed into a democratic government based on the cooperation of all parties and all classes. The workers' and peasants' democratic republic should inevitably develop into a united democratic republic, which is a bourgeois-democratic state based on the alliance of the working class, the peasantry, the petite bourgeoisie, and the bourgeoisie. It could move toward both capitalism and socialism, and the CPC should struggle hard for the latter prospect. It should advocate freedom of speech, assembly and association for the people, release political prisoners, and remove the ban on political parties. The CPC should exercise political leadership over the democratic republic. After the united democratic republic is founded, the revolutionary base areas would become a part of the republic, and the Red Army will be re-organized into the National Revolutionary Army.

Later, Mao Zedong had developed the theory of a new-democratic state during the period of the War of Resistance against Japan between 1935-1944. It is a new-democratic state under the joint dictatorship of all the revolutionary classes of China, in which the Chinese proletariat takes the lead, the peasants and the urban petite bourgeoisie take an important position, and the national bourgeoisie participate as an ally. It adopts a system of people's congresses and implements the organizational principle of democratic-centralism. It upholds the system of multiparty cooperation on the basis of the CPC's absolute leadership over the state. Its prospect is socialism. Besides, Mao Zedong had also advanced some important ideas about the building of anti-Japanese democratic political power during this period, such as the principle of "three thirds system," under which Communists have only one-third of the places in the organs of political power, and the policy of better troops and realizing simpler administration.

Mao Zedong developed the theory of the people's democratic dictatorship during the period of the War of Liberation between 1946 to 1949.

The book *History of Mao Zedong Thought* edited by Zheng Derong et al. summarizes Mao Zedong's ideas about government building in base areas in two aspects. First, strengthen democratic centralism and expand people's democracy. In the base areas, enormous efforts should be made to improve election, give a full play to the role of the people's congresses and their members, and ensure the people's rights for democracy and self-determination. Second, strengthen dictatorship over the reactionary classes by allowing them no rights for democracy and freedom, and use revolutionary forces and revolutionary tribunals to put down counterrevolutionary activities.

In his paper "Mao Zedong and the Building of the Central Soviet Area," Yang Qing has discussed Mao Zedong's ideas about how should the Red political power in the Soviet area practice the broadest democracy for workers, peasants and soldiers. According to Mao Zedong, the Red political power should give all the people who had been exploited and oppressed the right to elect and to be elected; councils of workers, peasants and soldiers of towns and cities under Red political power should keep close ties with local residents to hear their opinions; the Red political power should give all revolutionary people complete freedom of assembly, association, speech and publication and to go on strike; the Red political power should abolish the old, bureaucratic division of administrative area in order to get closer to the people.

5.3.2.2 Mao Zedong's Ideas about Economic Development in Base Areas

Volume one of the *History of the Communist Party of China* has made a penetrating analysis of and comprehensive elaboration on Mao Zedong's ideas about economic development in base areas. Below is a brief introduction to the analyses and elaborations in the book.

Mao Zedong's ideas about economic development in base areas during the period of the War of the Agrarian Revolution include the following points. The principle for economic development in base areas is to vigorously develop economy to support war efforts and improve the life of the people, consolidate the worker-peasant alliance in the economic field, and strive to secure leadership by the state sector of the economy over the private sector, thus creating the prerequisites for the country's future advance to socialism. The focus of economic development is to increase agricultural and industrial production, develop the cooperatives, and expand trade with the outside. Agricultural production should be given the top priority. The economy in base areas is made up of three sectors—state enterprises, cooperative enterprises and private enterprises. The private sector of the economy should be promoted and encouraged. The cooperative and the state enterprises should develop in a coordinated way and should gradually prevail and assume leadership over the private sector. The financial policy in base areas is to increase revenue by developing the economy and practice thrift in government expenditure. The principle for trade in the base areas is first to supply needs in the base areas and second to trade with the outside. The government should handle certain essential commodities directly. All government personnel should concern themselves with the well-being of the masses and avoid the bureaucratic work style as divorcing from them.

Mao Zedong's ideas about economic development in base areas during the period of the War of Resistance against Japan include the following content. The general principle for economic development is to "develop the economy and ensure supplies." All-round development of agriculture, industry and commerce should be promoted with high priority given to agriculture. With regard to the relation between public and private interests, the principle is "giving consideration to both public and private interests and to both troops and civilians." The policy of "unified leadership and decentralized management" should be upheld in the relationship between higher and lower levels. The principle of "working hard for production and practicing economy" should be carried out in dealing with the relationship between production and consumption. Collective operation of agriculture based on the individual economy should be encouraged on a voluntary and mutual benefit basis.

In his book *Study on Mao Zedong's Economic Thinking*, Xiao Gongda summarized Mao Zedong's ideas about economic development in base areas during the complete new-democratic period into the following sentences: economic development should revolve around the central task of revolutionary war; the purpose of developing economy is to support war effort and improve the life of the people; the focus of economic development is to increase agricultural and industrial production, expand trade with the outside, and develop the cooperatives; the economy in base areas is made up of three sectors—state enterprise, cooperative enterprise and private enterprise; the economy should be developed according to plan; principles for developing economy include "developing the economy and ensuring supplies," "unified leadership and decentralized management," "giving consideration to both public and private interests and to both troops and civilians," and "working hard at production and practicing economy;" the base areas should primarily rely on their own efforts, while not ignoring any possibility of securing help from abroad.

Among the above-mentioned books, *Study on Mao Zedong's Economic Thinking* written by Guo Shiping and Guo Jianning gave the most detailed and all-round elaboration on Mao Zedong's ideas about economic development in base areas. Chapter Four "Theory of Economic Management in Base Areas" in the book has summarized Mao Zedong's ideas about economic management in base areas into five aspects: uphold the principle of "unified leadership and decentralized management" in economic and financial management; adhere to an economic management principle of "practicing economy and fighting waste;" implement an independent economic accounting principle; promote production to meet needs; concern with the well-being of the masses and stimulate their enthusiasm for revolution and production.

5.3.2.3 Mao Zedong's Ideas about Cultural and Educational Development in Base Areas

The book *History of Educational Development in Revolutionary Base Areas* edited by Dong Chuncai comprehensively and systematically expounded Mao Zedong's ideas about cultural and educational development in base areas. The before-mentioned books by Yang Chao, Zhang Jingru and others have also discussed these ideas.

According to *History of Mao Zedong Thought* edited by Zheng Derong et al., Mao Zedong developed the following basic principles for cultural and educational development in base areas: educate the toiling masses in the spirit of communism; vigorously develop culture and education to serve the needs of revolutionary war and class struggle; and combine education and labor to transform the broad masses into a new generation of civilized and happy people. The central task for cultural and educational development in base areas is to provide compulsory education and develop social education; strive to wipe out illiteracy; cultivate a large number of personnel who are capable of leading the revolution and development; and get the intellectuals to serve the Chinese revolution and development of culture and education.

During the period of the War of Resistance against Japan, Mao Zedong had advanced the following ideas for cultural and educational development in base areas: cultural work should play an important role in China's revolution and construction; the CPC's basic principle for cultural and educational work is to develop a national, scientific and mass culture, make the past serve the present and foreign products serve domestic needs, and get literature and art to serve the needs of the workers, peasants and soldiers; the intellectuals should play an important role in China's revolution and development, and the CPC's basic policy toward them is to unite, criticize, educate and transform them.

According to the book *Complete History of Mao Zedong Thought* edited by Yan Hongyuan et al., Mao Zedong's ideas about cultural development in anti-Japanese base areas should include the following content. First, he corrected the erroneous tendency to belittle the intellectuals and cultural work and resolutely affirmed their important place and role in the Chinese revolution. Second, he proposed to develop a national, scientific and mass type new-democratic culture. Third, he put forward that literature and art should serve the needs of the workers, peasants and soldiers.

Besides, the "National Symposium on Mao Zedong's Thinking on Education" held in Xiangtan in mid-December 1989 has thoroughly discussed Mao Zedong's ideas about cultural and educational development in base areas during the new-democratic revolution period, and some academic papers were published.

5.3.3 Suggestions for the Study on Mao Zedong's Thought on Building Revolutionary Bases

With regard to the study on Mao Zedong's thinking on building revolutionary base areas, researchers have formed a research system and produced a large number of results. However, they generally still focus their studies on introduction and summarization; not many of them have made great efforts to penetrate into and argued over some specific subjects. All this indicates that the study on the thinking needs to be strengthened and improved. First, more efforts need to be made to study how the thought had progressed and developed. As base areas were established, developed and expanded in different historical periods, the thinking also underwent a historical course to emerge, develop and become mature. To discover the law governing this historical course and review the logical development of the thinking is no doubt very important for deepening study on it. Second, the overall understanding and study of the thinking should be strengthened. The thinking is a complete system of scientific theories. Researchers, however, usually focus on describing and generalizing Mao Zedong's ideas about government building, economic development or cultural and educational development in base areas. In order to completely and correctly understand and grasp the thinking as a whole, they should study it as an integrated body and discover the logical relations between its components. Finally, it is necesarry to devote greater attention to study the relationship between the thinking and Mao Zedong's theory of China's revolutionary road. They should not simply regard the thinking as a part of the theory of establishing independent regimes of the workers and the peasants by armed forces, but should study it in the broader context of the theory of China's revolutionary road. That is to say, they should study how Mao Zedong thought about the strategic role of base areas in the revolutionary road of encircling the cities from the countryside. Doing so will enable them to better understand the great importance of the thinking and deepen study on the theory of China's revolutionary road.

5.4 Theory of the People's Democratic Dictatorship

The people's democratic dictatorship is the principal experience and main program for the Chinese revolution as well as an important component of Mao Zedong Thought. The study on the theory of the people's democratic dictatorship has produced the following achievements.

5.4.1 The Formation and Development of the Theory of the People's Democratic Dictatorship

The first opinion holds that the theory underwent a historical course to develop from the democratic dictatorship of workers and peasants to the people's democratic dictatorship. In the winter of 1925, Mao Zedong had said, "The revolution in the colonial and semi-colonial country of the present period is a revolution to be carried out by the petite bourgeoisie, the semi-proletariat and the proletariat in cooperation," "the purpose of the revolution is to build a country under joint governance by the revolutionary people."[1] This statement, which had embodied Mao Zedong's initial idea of building a new-democratic republic and provided some basic factors for his theory of the people's democratic dictatorship, marked the beginning of the theory. In 1928 at its Sixth National Congress in Moscow, the CPC had reviewed its experience after the failure of the national revolution and decided to "establish democratic political power of the workers and peasants" in revolutionary base areas. The provisional central government of the Chinese Soviet Republic founded in November 1931 was in fact a state of the workers' and peasants' democratic dictatorship. The CPC had changed its slogan from the "workers' and peasants' republic" into a "people's republic" at the meeting in Wayaobao in December 1935. It used a "democratic republic" to replace the "people's republic" on August 25, 1936. Mao Zedong had put forward the idea of building a new-democratic republic in his essay "On New Democracy" in January 1940. He said, "The state system, a joint dictatorship of all the revolutionary classes and the system of government, democratic centralism—these constitute the politics of New Democracy, the republic of New Democracy, the republic of the anti-Japanese united front."[2] In June 1949 Mao Zedong published the "On the People's Democratic Dictatorship" to give a full exposition of the theory of the people's democratic dictatorship, which marked the complete formation of the theory.

The second opinion agrees that the essay "On the People's Democratic Dictatorship" marked the formation of the theory, but argues a different view about its emergence. In his paper "The Ideas about the People's Democratic Dictatorship in the 'Report on an Investigation of the Peasant Movement in Hunan'," Zhang Xipo has argued that Mao Zedong made the earliest discussion of the theory in his essay "Report on an Investigation of the Peasant Movement In Hunan" in 1927, which "laid the theoretical foundation

---

[1] *Collected Works of Mao Zedong*, Chin. ed., People's Publishing House, Beijing, 1993, Vol. I, p. 25.

[2] *Selected Works of Mao Tse-tung*, Eng. ed., FLP, Peking, 1965, Vol. II, p. 352.

for the theory of the people's democratic dictatorship." In the book *History of Mao Zedong Thought*, Zheng Derong and other authors hold that the political power in base areas during the War of the Agrarian Revolution was a democratic dictatorship of workers and peasants and a joint dictatorship of workers, peasants and the urban petite bourgeoisie headed by the CPC, and that it developed into a people's democratic dictatorship when the anti-Japanese national united front was established and the CPC had changed its slogan from the "workers' and peasants' republic" into a "people's republic."

According to the *Annotations to Resolution on Certain Questions in the History of Our Party Since the Founding of the People's Republic of China*, the democratic dictatorship of workers and peasants developed into a people's democratic dictatorship when Mao Zedong had advanced the establishment of "a people's democratic republic" and "a people's democracy" in his essay "The Orientation of the Youth Movement" in 1939.

In paper "Understanding after Studying Mao Zedong's Works about Anti-Japanese National United Front Political Power," Xiao Yongqing has put forward that between the democratic dictatorship of workers and peasants and the people's democratic dictatorship was an anti-Japanese national united front political power, which was a dictatorship of the revolutionary classes led by the proletariat over traitors and reactionaries and later developed into a people's democratic dictatorship during the War of Liberation between 1946 to 1949.

The third opinion believes that the essay "On the People's Democratic Dictatorship" did give a systematic exposition of the theory of the people's democratic dictatorship. However, the theory was further developed later. Mao Zedong wrote an essay "On the Correct Handling of the Contradictions among the People" in 1957 to emphasize that the CPC should strictly distinguish between and handle correctly the two different types of contradictions in socialist society, those between the people and the enemy and those among the people themselves. This idea should be regarded as a part of the theory of the people's democratic dictatorship. Besides, the development of the theory after the Third Plenary Session of the Eleventh

CPC Central Committee in 1978 should also be studied. However, study in this regard is still weak.

5.4.2 The System and Main Content of the Theory of the People's Democratic Dictatorship

In this regard, researchers are divided into two groups: one group considers it a theory of the new-democratic state and a theory of political power for the transition period from new democracy to socialism; the other group regards it as a theory of the state applicable to both a new-democratic society and a socialist society.

As a theory of the new-democratic state and a theory of political power, the theory of the people's democratic dictatorship includes the following ideas: (1) the people's democratic dictatorship, flexible and suited to the revolution, wields state power in a new-democratic state; (2) it should be led by the working class (via the CPC) and based on worker-peasant alliance; (3) democracy for the people and dictatorship over the reactionaries should be coordinated; (4) the national bourgeoisie falls into the category of people and is therefore not a target of dictatorship; (5) it implements the system of multiparty cooperation and political consultation under the leadership of the CPC; (6) it adopts a system of people's congresses and implements the organizational principle of democratic centralism; and (7) it should unite with international revolutionary forces.

The book *Socialist Politics* (People's Publishing House, 1995) edited by Wang Yunguang considers the people's democratic dictatorship aa a state system spanning during both new-democratic and socialist society. The book has summarized it as follows: (1) it wields state power under the leadership of the working class, the core of which is the CPC, and takes Marxism-Leninism and Mao Zedong Thought as the guiding ideology; (2) it is based on an alliance of workers and peasants; (3) it is a dialectical unity of democracy and dictatorship; (4) it shoulders two historic tasks, the task of democratic revolution and the task of socialist revolution and later establishment of socialism; and (5) it should unite with international revolutionary forces by upholding and implementing the principle of uniting the proletariat and oppressed nations and people of the whole world.

5.4.3 The Nature of the People's Democratic Dictatorship in Different Historical Phases

Researchers all agree that the people's democratic dictatorship in China underwent two historical phases, the new-democratic revolution and the socialist revolution, but they disagree with each other on its nature in different historical periods in these two phases.

5.4.3.1 The Nature of the Political Power in Base Areas before the Founding of the People's Republic of China

Some researchers believe that the political power in base areas was in essence a democratic dictatorship of workers and peasants throughout the democratic revolution period. Other researchers disagree. According to them, it was a democratic dictatorship of workers and peasants during the War of the Agrarian Revolution, an anti-Japanese national united front political power during the War of Resistance against Japan, and a people's democratic dictatorship against imperialism, feudalism and bureaucrat-capitalism during the War of Liberation.

Researchers have also pointed out that the people's democratic dictatorship, which shouldered the dual historical task of democratic and socialist revolution, had showed features of the dictatorship of the proletariat or socialism during the democratic revolution period, because: first, it was led by the working class and its party (the CPC); second, it resolutely strived to eradicate bureaucrat-capitalism and expropriate its property; third, it was moving towards socialism and the dictatorship of the proletariat; and fourth, it belonged to the socialist camp headed by the Soviet Union.

5.4.3.2 The Nature of the People's Democratic Dictatorship after the Founding of the People's Republic of China

Researchers generally believe that it was in essence the dictatorship of the proletariat. There was a period of time when researchers even did not use the term "people's democratic dictatorship." According to some researchers, it was a new-democratic joint dictatorship of several classes during the early days of New China when the country was striving to revitalize its economy and complete the unfinished new-democratic tasks, and developed into the dictatorship of the proletariat in 1953 when the massive socialist transformation was launched to abolish classes in the country and establish new socialist order.

5.4.4 The Historical Position and Role of the People's Democratic Dictatorship

The people's democratic dictatorship has undergone the historical phases of new-democratic revolution, socialist revolution and socialist construction. It shouldered different historic tasks in different historical phases. The book *Historical Development of Mao Zedong Thought* (Hongqi Publishing House, 1987) edited by Miao Chuhuang described the historical position and role of the people's democratic dictatorship as follows: it "was created by the CPC on the basis of a review of experience in revolution, both victories and defeats, to wield state power in a new-democratic state; as the country moved from new democracy toward socialism, it changed to a dictatorship of the proletariat; it had linked the CPC's minimum program with maximum program."

5.4.5 The Theory of the People's Democratic Dictatorship Is a Continuation of the Marxist Theory of Dictatorship of the Proletariat

Many researchers hold that Mao Zedong's people's democratic dictatorship was in essence the dictatorship of the proletariat. Their argument is based on the following reasons. First, judging from the leading force, the leading force in the people's democratic dictatorship advanced by Mao Zedong is the working class, while the proletariat is also the leading force in the dictatorship of the proletariat advocated by Marx and Engels—they are basically the same. Second, from the perspective of worker-peasant alliance,

Mao Zedong's idea that the people's democratic dictatorship must be based on the alliance of workers and peasants in China, where the peasantry makes the majority of its population, is identical with the idea of Marx and Engels that an alliance of workers and peasants needs to be established to guarantee the leadership of the proletariat. Third, judging from the unity of democracy and dictatorship, the dictatorship of the proletariat advocated by Marx and Engels features democracy for the proletariat and dictatorship over the enemy, which constitute a complementary and indispensable unity, while Mao Zedong stressed that a broad people's democracy should be cultivated to consolidate proletarian dictatorship, stabilize political power, and prevent the reactionaries from staging a come-back. Therefore, the people's democratic dictatorship and the proletarian dictatorship are essentially the same. Fourth, both the people's democratic dictatorship and the proletarian dictatorship shoulder the same historical mission and task to safeguard the proletarian political power, develop the productive forces, abolish classes, and eventually realize communism.

5.4.6 The Theory of the People's Democratic Dictatorship Is a Development of the Marxist Theory of Dictatorship of the Proletariat

When striving to prove that the theory of the people's democratic dictatorship is a continuation of the Marxist theory of dictatorship of the proletariat, researchers have also discussed how it had developed the latter.

According to some researchers, the theory of the people's democratic dictatorship has developed the Marxist theory of dictatorship of the proletariat in the following aspects: it considers the national bourgeoisie a part of the people, but not a target of dictatorship; it implements the system of multiparty cooperation and political consultation under the leadership of the CPC; it adopts a system of people's congresses and implements the organizational principle of democratic centralism.

In the paper "Mao Zedong's Theory of the People's Democratic Dictatorship Has Greatly Enriched the Theory of Proletarian Dictatorship" published in *Nankai Journal (Philosophy, Literature and Social Science)* (No. 6, 1983), Wang Shizheng compared the theory of the people's democratic dictatorship with the theory of proletarian dictatorship and advanced that the former has developed the latter in the following aspects: (1) it has creatively formulated concrete policies for treating the national bourgeoisie while adhering to the Marxist universal principle of exercising dictatorship over all forces antagonistic to socialism; (2) it has creatively implemented the new system of multiparty cooperation under the leadership of the CPC while upholding the Marxist universal principle that leadership of proletarian party is the soul of proletarian dictatorship; and (3) it has creatively advanced the theory of strictly distinguishing between and correctly dealing with two different types of contradictions and the idea of people's democratic dictatorship, making the Marxist theory of proletarian dictatorship more complete.

Fu Hesheng, however, wrote the paper "How Mao Zedong Applied and Developed the Theory of the Democratic Dictatorship of Workers and Peasants" to study how Mao Zedong had developed Lenin's theory of the democratic dictatorship of workers and peasants. According to him, Mao Zedong's creative development is principally manifested in the following aspects: he had advanced the theory of encircling the cities from the countryside and seizing state power by armed force; integrated the efforts to build political power with those who carried out armed struggle and the Agrarian Revolution and established rural base areas; he had held that the workers' and peasants' political power could be participated by workers, peasants and the urban petite bourgeoisie, plus by the national bourgeoisie, and even by some sections of the comprador class to a certain extent, for a certain period and under particular situations.

Due to the fact that the theory of the people's democratic dictatorship concerns New China's system of state and government, researchers generally focus on describing and narrating it. Their ways of expression are different, but do not make fundamental difference, and their study of the theory is more about publicity than academic research.

References

Shi Zhongquan, *The Hard Exploration by Mao Zedong*, Chinese Communist Party History Publishing House, Beijing, 1990.

Bo Yibo, *A Review of Major Decisions and Issues*, Vol. I, the CPC Central Committee Party School Publishing House, Beijing, 1991.

Lu Zhenxiang, "Application and Development of the Theory of Bypassing the Stage of Capitalist Development," *Study of the History of the Communist Party of China*, 1991 (3).

Yang Kuisong, "The Reason Mao Zedong Abandoned New Democracy—the Influence of Russian Model," *Modern Chinese History Studies*, 1997 (4).

Pang Song, "Zhou Enlai's Ideas about Transition to Socialism," *Study of the History of the Communist Party of China*, 1998 (1).

Gu Hongliang, "On Mao Zedong's Ideas of a New-Democratic Society and Methodology Therein," *Research of Mao Zedong Thought*, 1998 (4).

Hu Sheng, "Reassessment of Mao Zedong's New Democracy," *Social Sciences in China*, 1999 (3).

Li Anzeng, "The General Line for the Transition Period and the Theory of a New-Democratic Society," *Teaching and Research in CPC History*, 1999 (6).

Wang Zhi and Wen Hongyu, "How the Theory of a New-Democratic Society Was Created and Abandoned," *Party Literature*, 2000 (1).

Kong Yongsong, *Development of the Land Policy of the Communist Party of China*, Jiangxi People's Publishing House, Nanchang, 1987.

Zhao Xiaomin (ed.), *Chinese History of Agrarian Reform*, People's Publishing House, Beijing, 1990.

Guo Dehong, *A Study on Peasant and Land Problem in Modern China*, Qingdao Publishing House, Qingdao, 1993.

Du Runsheng, "On China's Agrarian Reform Movement," *Study of the History of the Communist Party of China*, 1996 (6).

Du Jing, "A Number of Questions in the Research on China's Agrarian

Reform," *Social Sciences in China,* 1992 (1).

Xu Li, "On Our Party's Policies toward the Rich Peasants in the Land Struggle," *Historiography Research in Anhui*, 1988 (10).

Lin Qiang, "Mao Zedong and the Chinese Peasant Problem," *Study of the History of the Communist Party of China*, 1993(3).

Wang Jing, "Historical Inspiration for the Peasant Problem," *The World of Survey and Research*, 1998 (4).

Zheng Zhiting, "Exploration into the Historical Role of the Agrarian Reform during the War of Liberation," *Guizhou Social Sciences*, 1998 (3).

The Party History Research Center, *History of the Communist Party of China*, Chinese Communist Party History Publishing House, Beijing, 1991.

Wang Chaobin, *Study on Mao Zedong's Thinking on Political Power*, Chinese Communist Party History Publishing House, Beijing, 1997.

Guo Shiping and Guo Jianning, *Study on Mao Zedong's Economic Thinking*, Qinghai People's Publishing House, Xining, 1991.

Yang Chao and Bi Jianheng (eds.), *History of Mao Zedong Thought*, Sichuan People's Publishing House, Chengdu, Vol. I, 1991.

Zheng Derong and Huang Jingfang, *History of Mao Zedong Thought (Revised)*, Gansu People's Publishing House, Lanzhou, 1990.

Shi Zhongquan (ed.), *A Review of Study on Mao Zedong*, the Central Party Literature Press, Beijing, 1992.

Zheng Yiling, *Study on Mao Zedong's Theory about the Peasant Problem*, Xiamen University Press, Xiamen, 1999.

Wang Tianwen, Wang Demu, and Li Yifan, *Introduction to Mao Zedong Thought*, Henan University Press, Kaifeng, 1994.

Yang Qing, "Mao Zedong and the Building of the Central Soviet Area," see Liu Jingyu and Wang Xiuxin (eds.), *Mao Zedong and the Democratic Revolution with Chinese Characteristics*, Chinese Communist Party History Publishing House, Beijing, 1993.

Chao Feng and Li Junru, *Complete Collection of Studies of Mao Zedong Thought*, Shanghai People's Publishing House, Shanghai, 1993.

Zheng Derong and Bai Fulin (eds.), *History of Development of Mao*

Zedong Thought, Jilin University Press, Changchun, 1990.

Wang Yunguang, *Socialist Politics*, People's Publishing House, Beijing, 1995.

Wang Shizheng, "Mao Zedong's Theory of the People's Democratic Dictatorship Has Greatly Enriched the Theory of Proletarian Dictatorship," *Nankai Journal (Philosophy, Literature and Social Science)*, 1983 (6).

Fu Hesheng, "How Mao Zedong Applied and Developed the Theory of the Democratic Dictatorship of Workers and Peasants," *Study of the History of the Communist Party of China*, 1984 (3).

Chapter 6

The Theory of Socialist Revolution

As China's socialist reform and opening up progressed rapidly since the 1980s, a large number of researchers and scholars began to study the CPC's theory and practice of socialist revolution. They have published a large quantity of books and papers and advanced many fresh opinions. In general, their study have focused on the following issues: the theory of transition from new democracy to socialism; assessment of the CPC's general line for the transition period; assessment of socialist transformation; and the relationship between socialist transformation and socialist reform.

6.1 The Theory of Transition from New Democracy to Socialism

China completed a peaceful transition from a new-democratic society to the socialist society in the period from October 1949 to the end of 1956. Researchers have made some remarkable achievements in their efforts to study the historical phases in this transition, Liu Shaoqi's idea of establishing new democracy, and Mao Zedong's changeable attitude on new-democratic society.

6.1.1 Historical Phases in the Transition from the New-Democratic Society to Socialist Society

It is believed by some researchers that China has undergone four phases to complete its transition from the new-democratic to the socialist society.

The first phase was from the Second Plenary Session of the Seventh CPC Central Committee in March 1949 to the founding of New China in October 1949, which was the stage of preparation for the transition. First, the CPC made it clear for the first time in that Session the to move from new democracy to socialism and the country should be transformed from an agricultural into an industrial country and from a new-democratic state to the socialist one. Second, the Party got a better understanding of the conditions in China in that Session. Mao Zedong had brilliantly expounded on the economic strategy of fully utilizing the private capitalist sector in the new-democratic society. After the Session, Liu Shaoqi, entrusted by the Party Central Committee, had made a special trip to Tianjin where industry and commerce were concentrated and publicized the Party's principle of fully utilizing the private capitalist economy, among Party members and representatives from all sectors of society in Tianjin. All this indicated that the CPC had established the idea of building socialism by utilizing capitalism. Third, the CPC had stated at the Session that the new-democratic state should be based on the people's democratic dictatorship, which was the political guarantee for future transition from new democracy to socialism.

The second phase was from the founding of New China in October 1949 to the Third Plenary Session of the Seventh Party Central Committee in 1950, in which the transition began. First, the CPC became the party in power, which was a prerequisite for the transition to begin and key to China's socialist road. Second, some factors and contents of socialist revolution had appeared.

The third phase was from June 1950 to the end of 1952, in which the transition progressed. At the Third Plenary Session of its Seventh Central Committee, the CPC clarified its guiding principles for the first three years of New China. First, it advanced the strategic principle of "Don't Hit Out in All Directions," which had eased the worries of the national bourgeoisie. Second, it defined its central task as revitalizing and developing the productive forces and realized that it should strive hard to bring about a fundamental turn for the better in the country's financial and economic situation. Third, it clearly declared that it should give high priority to complete remaining new-democratic tasks and develop the country, and prepare for socialist revolution and construction. Guided by these principles, social reforms progressed had smoothly. At the end of this period the general line of the Party for the transition period was introduced.

The fourth stage is from the introduction of the general line for the transition period in 1953 to the completion of socialist transformation of agriculture, handicrafts, and capitalist industry and commerce at the end of 1956, in which the transition was accomplished.

6.1.2 Liu Shaoqi's Idea of Consolidating New Democracy

On the basis of Mao Zedong's theory of New Democracy, Liu Shaoqi had developed some ideas about building a new-democratic society. His ideas included the following. First, the new-democratic society is a stage for transition to the socialist society. In this stage, which will take about ten to twenty years, the CPC should work hard to consolidate new democracy. Second, the central task in the new-democratic society is to develop the productive forces and industrialize the country. He stressed, "As long as a third world war does not break out, we should focus on economic development. It looks unlikely that a war will break out in twenty or thirty years, so we should strive hard to develop the economy and industrialize the country." Besides, he had clearly stated the idea of "setting economic development as the central task." Third, the new-democratic society should implement an ownership structure under which the state-owned sector is dominant and the state-capitalist sector, the cooperative sector, the private capitalist sector and the small commodity sector co-exist and develop side-by-side. Fourth, the new-democratic society should not struggle against the national bourgeoisie, but should unite with it. Fifth, the new-democratic society should not rush to "weaken or negate the private ownership" too early but should allow its proper development because it plays a positive role in promoting development of the productive forces. Sixth, the future of the new-democratic society is socialism and communism, which, however, still needs a long way to go. The actual requirements of China's economic and social development and the demands of the overwhelming majority of the people should determine when China moves to socialism. The country's transition to socialism should also be based on developed industry and agriculture, dominant state-owned sector, a large number of cadres capable of economic management, and a consolidated alliance of workers and peasants. Generally, researchers have affirmed the above ideas.

At the same time, they have pointed out that Liu Shaoqi had some improper ideas as well, such as "it's good to exploit" and "exploit as much as you can."

6.1.3 The Reason Mao Zedong Changed from Favoring New Democracy to Criticizing It

Researchers believe the reasons are as follows. First, he had evaluated the objective situation one-sidedly. After three years of hard work, the face of New China's political, economic and social life had changed greatly. On the one hand, a series of reforms had laid certain political, material and organizational foundation for socialist transformation. On the other hand, the selfish nature of capitalists, polarization in rural areas, and the intensified conflict between the camps of socialism and capitalism in international politics had all urged Mao Zedong to speed up the pace of socialist transformation. This indicates that his change was due to objective realities, not pure preconception. However, he had also not fully realized the positive role of capitalist industry and commerce, and the peasants' individual ownership, and the urban and rural bourgeoisie in a people's democratic state. This was an important reason behind his decision to accelerate socialist transformation.

Second, he misunderstood socialism. He overlooked or did not realize the fact that the Chinese revolution had developed and won the victory in an economically backward country, whose fundamental task was to develop the economy. To develop its economy, China should arouse a development enthusiasm of both the public sector and the private sector, both the working class and the bourgeoisie, and both poor peasants and rich peasants. This was the only way China could promote economic development in urban and rural areas at that time. Mao Zedong's rush to socialist transformation was in fact due to a "Left" idea and a misunderstanding on socialism.

Third, he was influenced by utopian socialism in his early years. He even practiced some ideas of utopian socialism such as Atarashiki Mura (New Village) in Changsha and other areas, which had influenced him to some extent.

Fourth, he was influenced by Stalin and the Soviet model. In the early days of New China, the CPC had copied the Soviet model in every instance due to the special international environment. As a result, Mao Zedong had gradually accepted Stalin's ideas on socialist construction and abandoned his original idea of building new democracy.

Researchers have also argued over the starting point of the transition period, that is, to move from where to socialism. A generally accepted opinion believes that the transition is from a new-democratic society to a socialist society. According to researchers holding this opinion, Mao Zedong had advanced this idea in his essay "The May 4th Movement" in 1939. Thereafter, at the Second Plenary Session of the Seventh CPC Central Committee, the CPC had formally stated that China "will transform from a new-democratic state to a socialist state" after the victory of the Chinese revolution. The founding of the People's Republic of China marks the beginning of the transition because this time point embodies both the nature of the old society and the historical course of China's revolution. This opinion is accepted by most Party history researchers and has been adopted by college textbooks of Introduction to Mao Zedong Thought.

However, there are different opinions as well. The first one is that the transition was from a capitalist society to a socialist society. This opinion is based on the following facts. In his essay "Prefaces to *Socialist Upsurge in China's Countryside*" in September 1955, Mao Zedong had changed the term "transition from new democracy to socialism" to "transition from capitalism to socialism." This new term was adopted in the political report of the CPC's Eighth National Congress and was used until the Third Plenary Session of the Eleventh CPC Central Committee. The second one argues that the transition was from a semi-colonial, semi-feudal society to a socialist society. According to researchers holding this opinion, it fully embodies China's then conditions that capitalism was not fully developed. The third one argues that the transition was from a semi-colonial, semi-feudal society to the primary stage of socialism via a new-democratic society. Researchers holding this opinion assert that semi-colonial, semi-feudal society is the origination, a new-democratic society is the avenue, and the primary stage of socialism is the destination.

6.2 The General Line for the Transition Period

Suggested by Mao Zedong, the CPC Central Committee deliberated and introduced in 1952 the general line for the transition period which defined gradually accomplishing industrialization of the country and socialist transformation of agriculture, handicrafts, and capitalist industry and commerce over a fairly long period of time. As a general strategy and policy for the country's socialist transformation, the general line was a macro guiding principle. Therefore, when studying on socialist transformation, researchers often start their investigations on the general line.

6.2.1 Theoretical Foundation of the General Line

In his opening speech at the National Conference of the CPC in

March 1955, Mao Zedong had stated that the Party Central Committee put forward the Party's general line for the transition period on the basis of Lenin's thoughts on the transition period. Researchers have two entirely different opinions about how Mao Zedong understood Lenin's thoughts on the transition period and New Economic Policy. One opinion holds that Mao Zedong's general line for the transition period was based on Lenin's theories in the transition period before 1921 and also Stalin's theories on the transition period, and not on Lenin's New Economic Policy. This opinion has offered some facts to support that. According to the Outline for Study and Publicity of the Party's General Line for the Transition Period drafted by the Publicity Department under the CPC Central Committee, what the CPC had learned from Lenin's thoughts on the transition period was principally those produced in the period of "war communism" in Soviet Union, and they were later developed by Stalin. Those ideas had focused on transforming private ownership of the means of production. CPC had not studied and learned from Lenin's ideas on the New Economic Policy, which he had developed in his later years. The other opinion holds that Mao Zedong had borrowed ideas from Lenin's teachings on the New Economic Policy, especially from his theory on state capitalism and commodity production and exchange based on currency in a socialist society.

6.2.2 The Historical Circumstances of the General Line

Researchers have three expressions on this issue, all of which, however, make no fundamental difference. First, there were three circumstances: unified management of national revenues; basic completion of the agrarian reform; and recovery of the post-war national economy was completed successfully. Second, there were four circumstances: a strong and rapidly developing socialist state sector; rich experiences on utilizing and limiting private industry and commerce sectors; completion of the agrarian reform and substantial experiences on mutual aid and peasants' cooperation activities in rural areas; and the international environment. Third, group argues that, there were six circumstances: recovery of the national economy and completion of unfinished tasks of democratic revolution; a strong and rapidly developing socialist state sector; a considerable proportion of capitalist sector operating in the national economy; experiences of mutual aid and cooperation between peasants and handicraftsmen; and the CPC's prestige rising among the people; and the international environment.

6.2.3 The Relationship between the General Line for the Transition Period and the Theory of New-Democratic Society Raised in the Second Plenary Session of the Seventh CPC Central Committee

Researchers have argued much over this issue. Generally, there are four different opinions.

According to the first opinion, the general line for the transition period and the theory of a new-democratic society were basically the same—they were different only in expression and form. In some sense, it could be said that the general line was a development of that theory. The general line had not deviated from the resolution passed in the Second Plenary Session of the Seventh Central Committee. The resolution had clarified the two tasks of transformation in the country "from an agricultural into an industrial society" and "from a new-democratic to a socialist state," and the general line had developed the theory on new-democratic society by integrating those two tasks into one line. In conclusion, this opinion believes that the general line was basically the same or had developed the theory.

The second opinion holds that the introduction of the general line indicated a "Left" tendency in the Party's guiding ideology, so the general line had negated the theory of a new-democratic society. The general line was the result of the Party's incorrect understanding on the principal contradiction in the country and represented a shift in the Party's strategy, and its objective was to eliminate the private ownership of the means of production. Therefore, the basic idea and guiding ideology in the general line were fundamentally different from the resolution of the Second Plenary Session of the Seventh Central Committee. Besides, Mao Zedong had actually negated the theory of a new-democratic society, which was created by him and had developed greatly over the years, and he had started to criticize the idea of "firmly establishing the new-democratic social order." Therefore, the introduction of the general line should be the symbol that the CPC had formally abandoned the theory of a new-democratic society. In conclusion, this opinion believes that the general line had opposed or negated the theory.

The third opinion believes that the general line and the theory were both similar and different. They were similar because they had both served the peaceful transition to socialism, had the same objectives and tasks, and needed equal length of time. They were different because their understanding on the principal contradiction and major tasks were different, their attitudes and policies toward those sectors under non-socialist forms of ownership were different, and their ideas about when the transition began and how to complete the transition were different.

The fourth opinion holds that the introduction of the general line had both positive and negative effects.

6.2.4 General Assessment of the General Line for the Transition Period

Researchers argue much over how to generally assess the general line. There are three different opinions arguing that, it was correct; had flaws; and it was premature.

6.2.4.1 Arguments Affirming the General Line

This opinion holds that the introduction of the general line reflected the inevitability of historical development and was the objective requirement for the development of the new-democratic social order.

Politically, after the movements against the "three evils" [corruption, waste and bureaucracy—Tr.] and the "five evils" [bribery, tax evasion, theft of state property, cheating on government contracts and stealing of economic information—Tr.], the class relations in China had changed fundamentally, the national bourgeoisie had clearly expressed its willingness to accept the leadership of the CPC, and the tendency toward socialism had become obvious. The alliance of peasants and workers was developing positively, the leadership of the working classes was basically established, and after the agrarian reform the peasantry had become even more enthusiastic to support the CPC. All those had laid necessary class and social foundation for a great social change. At the same time, some new situations and problems had arisen in both cities and countryside. In countryside, some peasants naturally became inclined to strive for getting rich, and the gap between the rich and poor peasants was widening. In cities, restriction versus opposition to restriction between the working class and the state sector of the economy on the one hand and the bourgeoisie on the other was still existent. Some bourgeoisie were opposing the country's objective of industrialization, which intensified conflicts with the proletariat. As a result, the conflict between the proletariat and the bourgeoisie and between socialism and capitalism had become the principal problem in Chinese society. Under such conditions, the CPC had to reconsider the orientation of social development. As a result, to accelerate cooperative transformation of agriculture and carry out socialist transformation of capitalist industry and commerce was raised to a higher level on the Party's agenda.

Economically, after three years of hard work since the founding of New China, the national economy had witnessed recovery and initial development, and the gross output value for both industrial and agricultural production had exceeded those levels before the founding of the People's Republic. After confiscation of bureaucrat-capital and initial transformation of the industry and commerce of the national bourgeoisie, the state sector had begun to take a dominant position in the national economy. All this had laid necessary economic and material foundation for the country to carry out industrialization according to plans. It should be noticed that after the objective of industrialization was set, the low productivity in the scattered, backward peasant economy and urban private enterprises was unable to meet the needs of industrialization. In addition, China had a weak economic foundation and limited financial resources. As a result, conflicts were bound to occur between the state sector and non-public sectors because they were contesting for funds, raw materials and market share. The most simple and feasible way to use the limited resources more efficiently was to take administrative measures to manage all the resources in a unified, planned manner, which required abolishment of the non-public sector of the economy. Under the historical conditions at that time, a fundamental change in social system and the relations of production was required to further liberate and develop the productive forces and promote rapid development of both industry and agriculture. In this sense, the general line, which recognized, reviewed and affirmed the Party's three-year practice after the founding of New China, was in fact an indispensable part of the theory of a new-democratic society. It put forward the task of industrialization, advanced the idea of step-by-step transition, and defined a path for socialist transformation suited to Chinese circumstances.

6.2.4.2 Arguments Refuting the General Line

If it could be said that the above opinion affirmed the general line, it should be said that this opinion refuted it. This opinion is based on the following reasons.

(1) The general line was heavily influenced by Stalin's Soviet model. It cannot be denied that Mao Zedong and the Party had learned from Lenin's thoughts on the transition period and New Economic Policy when formulating the general line, but they were most influenced by Stalin. As early as during the democratic revolution, the CPC and Mao Zedong had regarded socialism as the future of China's social development, and to realize socialism as early as possible had become the common ideal tirelessly pursued by the Chinese Communists represented by Mao Zedong. At that time, Stalin's socialist model was believed to be the sole correct model for socialism. As a result, when China was to build socialism, it naturally copied the Soviet experience, which required to build a pure socialism. The idea that to accomplish socialist industrialization could take roughly eighteen years was also copied from the Soviet model.

(2) A comparison of the general line and the resolution of the Second Plenary Session of the Seventh CPC Central Committee clearly indicates that the general line had deviated from the latter by changing the latter's strategic priorities. First, it had placed new democracy and transition to socialism in opposition to each other. Second, it rushed to abolish capitalism and all non-public sectors of the economy without considering China's concrete realities. Third, it did not shift the focus of the Party's work to developing the productive forces as required by the Session; on the contrary, it continued to take class struggle as the key link.

(3) The general line had exaggerated some facts when judging and analyzing the principal problem in Chinese society. For example, it exaggerated the severity of the struggle between the proletariat and the national bourgeoisie, denied the previous effective practices, and repudiated many theories and policies that were formulated through long-term theoretical exploration which had been proved correct in practices. By doing so, it had intensified the conflict between the proletariat and bourgeoisie and undermined the central task of economic development. In short, the introduction of the general line started fundamental changes in the country's overall strategy: it had changed the central task from realizing industrialization of the country and developing the productive forces to transform the relations of production and realizing socialist public ownership, and its policy toward the non-public sectors was shifted from utilizing, restricting and transforming to transforming and abolishing them.

6.2.4.3 Arguments Evaluating It as Premature

According to this opinion, the general line was meant to produce good results, was reasonable theoretically, and generally accorded with the theory of a new-democratic society in overall objectives and development orientation. However, it had changed the original strategy of first developing the country and then moving to socialism and established a new strategy of simultaneously developing the country and completing socialist transformation. And it had rushed to implement those measures that could be suitable only in the future. As a result, it not only deviated from the basic concept of Marxism but also outstripped the concrete realities in Chinese society. According to historical materialism, socialism is the product of a highly developed capitalism. China's overall level of economic development at that time could not meet the requirements for building the economic base for socialism. So, the economically and culturally backward China needed a fairly long new-democratic period of development, during which the private capitalist sector should be allowed to exist and help improving the national economy and people's lives. It would be more desirable if the general line was introduced and implemented when China's economy had developed to a certain level.

6.3 Assessment on Socialist Transformation

After the Resolution on Certain Questions in the History of Our Party Since the Founding of the People's Republic of China was deliberated and passed at the Sixth Plenary Session of the Eleventh CPC Central Committee in 1981, researchers have attached great importance to evaluate the socialist transformation. They have three different opinions: it should be fully affirmed; it should be basically denied; and it should be half affirmed half denied.

6.3.1 It Should Be Fully Affirmed

Researchers holding this opinion believe that the socialist transformation was a path with Chinese characteristics created by the Chinese Communists represented by Mao Zedong to move from new-democratic society to socialist society. When answering the question of how to move from capitalist democratic revolution to socialist revolution in semi-colonial and semi-feudal China, a backward large agricultural country, the Chinese Communists did not accept Marxism-Leninism as dogma or blindly imitate the Soviet model. On the basis of a thorough analysis of realities in China, they have creatively developed the idea of using new-democratic society to link the two steps in the Chinese revolution.

They formulated the line, principles and policies for socialist transformation in line with China's conditions and did not copy the Soviet model. First, China had carried out the socialist transformation first in the countryside and then in cities and realized collectivization before mechanization in rural socialist transformation. In addition, the Party had achieved smooth socialist transformation of the capitalist industry and commerce by adopting the policy of peaceful redemption which was suggested by Engels and also considered by Lenin but was not put into practice. Second, China did not strive to complete the socialist transformation in a short period of time, but did it in a step-by-step manner. Third, compared to the Soviet Union, China's socialist transformation caused little social tension and produced more positive but less negative effects.

According to this opinion, it does not accord with historical facts to think that socialist transformation was a "sudden idea" raised by Mao Zedong, and that he ordered it to be implemented. First of all, to effect socialist transformation was a group decision of the entire Party. Before the transformation Mao Zedong had repeatedly stressed that no change should be made without support from the overwhelming majority of the people. Second, it was true that peasants and handicraftsmen had enthusiasm for both individual and collective economy and it can be said that during the later period their enthusiasm for socialist transformation was overestimated. But it was a doubtless fact that overwhelming part of the people were willing to take the road of socialism under the leadership of the CPC. All democratic parties and people from all walks of life had given a warm support for the general line after it was declared to public for open discussion. Its incorporation into the country's Constitution has showed that the people had welcomed it. It will not be fair to argue that the socialist transformation, which had been accepted and supported by hundreds of millions of people and achieved success; was caused by the will of a leader or a party. In addition, the problems in socialist transformation should be realistically analyzed and reviewed. The Resolution on Certain Questions in the History of Our Party Since the Founding of the People's Republic of China had offered an objective judgment on socialist transformation: "After the summer of 1955, the work on cooperative transformation of agriculture and socialist transformation of handicrafts, and capitalist industry and commerce was a little too hurried while sufficient preparations were not made. Besides, the work methods were simple and inefficient. As a result, some problems arose and remained unsolved." This opinion is accepted by most researchers.

6.3.2 It Should Be Basically Denied

According to this opinion, New China began to make mistakes after the beginning of socialist transformation, which was the origin of the "Left" mistakes in the later two decades. Even if we assume that the goal of realizing pure public ownership was planned to be completed in fifteen or twenty years, problems would still arise. In some sense, the quick success in socialist transformation was exactly the seed of later mistakes and setbacks. The reasons are as follows.

(1) It had simply re-defined the transition period as a period of "transition from capitalism to socialism," which connotes a direct transition. The original ideas and definition of "transition from new democracy to socialism" formulated after the founding of New China had made a clear statement that "the country was still a new-democratic state, in which diverse economic sectors should co-exist and develop. The socialist public sector should develop rapidly to take the dominant position in the national economy and win superiority over the capitalist sector; non-socialist sectors should not be immediately eliminated". However, Mao Zedong had changed this formulation to "transition from capitalism to socialism" in the summer of 1955 and afterwards. Due to this change, numerous various economic sectors in the society were simply categorized into two as: sectors of capitalist private ownership and socialist public ownership, and all sectors other than state and collective sectors were classified under capitalist private ownership. Under the slogan of eliminating capitalism and realizing socialism, the state-capitalist sector, the private sector, and even small farm land allotted for

personal needs were regarded as capitalist operation and were eliminated. As a result, the relations of production and the productive forces were artificially placed in opposition to each other.

(2) It had one-sidedly shifted the focus of the country's work to transform the ownership of the means of production. As a result, the country's industrialization, which was the main body of the general line, was outpaced by the two wings of the general line, namely, socialist transformation of agriculture and handicraft industry on the one hand and socialist transformation of private capitalist industry and commerce on the other. After the founding of New China, the Party and government had always focused on production and development in the first place, and regarding country's transformation from an agricultural into an industrial country as a prerequisite for moving to socialism. Just from the very beginning, the general line had required that efforts should be made to promote industrialization and carry out socialist transformation simultaneously. In this course, normally socialist transformation should be subordinated to and serve industrialization, with higher priority. This was no doubt correct because the Party needed to transform not only non-socialist sectors into socialist sectors but also non-socialist modes of production to socialist modes of production. However, Mao Zedong had gradually deviated from this correct idea during the implementation of the general line. He began to one-sidedly stress the importance and meaning of transforming the ownership of the means of production and asserted that the objective of the general line was to solve mainly the problem of ownership and reach socialist public ownership as the sole economic base. Consequently, the transformation of the relations of production had outpaced the development of the productive forces, and "the main body" had lagged far behind "the two wings." Figuratively speaking, when the body of a bird had just started to fly, its two wings had reached the destination.

(3) It had rushed things in a hurriedly manner and blindly strived for pure socialism. The socialist transformation should be carried out progressively. For this reason, the Party had soberly and cautiously

formulated the general line of gradually accomplishing industrialization and socialist transformation of agriculture, handicrafts, and capitalist industry and commerce "over a fairly long period of time." Mao Zedong, however, had suddenly changed his mind in the second half of 1955 and severely criticized some Party leaders who believed that the country's socialist transformation was going too fast, saying that they were making Rightist mistake of conservatism. Consequently, the socialist transformation, originally designed to be completed progressively in at least fifteen years, was completed rashly in less than four years under the drive of the mass movement in the second half of 1955. As a result, only the state and collective sectors of the economy had survived; economic activities were solely regulated by concentrated administrative orders; the market was abandoned, the state had monopolized the purchase and marketing of important agricultural products such as grain, cotton and oil; in the income distribution the policy of limiting social consumption while allocating much for the state and investments was implemented, and income distribution had become similar to the ration system tainted by equalitarianism. All those that had divorced from China's conditions, was principally due to the influences of Stalin's Soviet model.

6.3.3 It Should Be Half Affirmed Half Denied

According to this opinion, the socialist transformation had followed the correct path of socialism and defined correct steps for gradual transition, all of which should be fully affirmed. But at the same time, the mistakes and errors that occurred during its implementation should not be overlooked and deserve thorough reflection.

(1) It had allowed only the socialist public sector in the country's economy neglecting the requirement that public ownership should be dominant and diverse economic sectors should develop side by side in the primary stage of socialism.

(2) The understanding on how to realize public ownership was too narrow. First, it defined the collective ownership and state ownership as the only forms of public ownership and further believed that the collective

ownership could only be realized by organizing higher-stage type cooperatives and the state ownership could only realized by state-owned enterprises. Second, it was believed that the state ownership was a higher stage than collective ownership. The above approaches indicate that it took the degree of socialization, not the "three favorable(s)"[1] as the criterion for judging right or wrong and success or failure in the socialist transformation.

(3) The socialist transformation had proceeded too fast, and methods for this work were simple and inefficient. All this was because the country had failed to integrate its industrialization with the socialist transformation of agriculture, handicrafts, and capitalist industry and commerce and did not timely adjust the relations of production to keep them synchronized with the development of the productive forces. For instance, if the country had spent a certain period of time for consolidating its achievements in lower-stage type cooperatives, even mistakes or errors occurred, they could be corrected in practice after a reconsideration.

(4) It was necessary to begin socialist transformation of peasants' individual production and capital held by individuals, but it had largely outstripped the primary stage of socialism targeting at eliminating them.

6.4 The Relationship between Socialist Transformation and Socialist Reforms in the Primary Stage of Socialism

At present, it is generally agreed that China is still in the primary stage of socialism and its tasks at the present stage is to promote reform and opening up and build socialism with Chinese characteristics. As a result, researchers, when studying the success and failure of socialist transformation,

---

[1] The "three favorable(s)" are criteria put forward by Deng Xiaoping for judging right or wrong and success or failure in all of our economic reform work by whether it is favorable to developing the productive forces in a socialist society, favorable to increase the overall national strength of the socialist state, and favorable to raising the living standards of the people.

naturally compare it with recent socialist reforms in the primary stage of socialism. They have three different opinions: they are not linked; they are closely linked; socialist reforms are further development of those made in socialist transformation.

6.4.1 They Are Not Linked

According to this opinion, the criterion of the "three favorable(s)" should be applied in judging the relationship between socialist transformation and socialist reforms. In fact, socialist reform has denied and corrected the ideas or approaches in socialist transformation, so they are not necessarily linked with each other. Capitalist economy in the transition period, which was different from the capitalist economy before the founding of New China, should be allowed to develop. And today's privately owned enterprises are also different from the capitalist economy during the transition period, therefore it should surely be allowed to develop. However, neither the socialist transformation nor the socialist reforms should be affirmed so simply, because allowing economic entities with diverse ownership forms to develop side by side is an essential requirement for socialism. The biggest mistakes in socialist transformation were its objective and measures—it had mechanically copied the Soviet socialist model and rashly eliminated non-public sectors of the economy. Besides, its methods had often focused on simply achieving quick results, and its concentrated management system based on plan mechanisms had greatly weakened the vitality of the country's socialist economic development. In this sense, the socialist reform approach has denied and sublated socialist transformation by correcting its many major mistakes and errors.

This opinion is partly one-sided because it overlooks the essential connection between socialist transformation and socialist reforms and sharply separates New China's five decades of economic development into parts.

6.4.2 They Are Closely Linked

According to this opinion, socialist transformation and socialist reforms are closely linked and consistent with each other. It could be said that without the socialist transformation in the 1950s, the socialist reforms would not happen in the 1980s. They have the same fundamental objective and purpose.

(1) In terms of nature of Chinese society, the socialist reforms are carried out in a socialist society, which is in the primary stage of socialism and is the historical achievement of socialist transformation. Consequently, if the socialist transformation and its historical achievements are denied, socialist reforms could not be carried out because it would have no foundation—like water without a source or a tree without roots.

(2) In terms of social development objectives, the objectives of socialist reforms are to accomplish industrialization of the country and build a modern, market-oriented economy, which in essence accords with the direction of socialist transformation. In fact, socialist transformation had also targeted accomplishing industrialization of the country as its objective and put top priority on it. History has demonstrated that China cannot achieve industrialization and modernization without socialist transformation or following the path of socialism. The fundamental orientation to socialism should be upheld unswervingly in China's socialist reforms, social development and modernization.

6.4.3 Socialist Reform Is a Development of Socialist Transformation

Similar with the above opinion, this opinion believes as follows. The historical course in which the Chinese proletariat—in its first attempt—carried out socialist transformation after seizing state power does not accord with the law of historical development. But on the other hand, both socialist transformation and socialist reforms were designed to liberate and develop the productive forces, and the latter was implemented because the former had failed to develop into the stage of commodity economy. It took a long period of time for the Party to better grasp the country's conditions and understand the true characteristics of socialism. It is unrealistic to expect that people at that time could have today's understanding, so it is incorrect to fully deny socialist transformation efforts.

Socialist reform approach has developed socialist transformation in the following aspects.

(1) In terms of objectives and pattern of social and economic development, the objective of socialist transformation was to achieve sole public ownership, while today's principle is keeping public ownership in the dominant position and allowing other economic entities with diverse ownership forms to develop side by side.

(2) In terms of how to realize public ownership, socialist transformation had defined that the highest form of public ownership in industrial enterprises was state-owned enterprises, and in agriculture was higher-stage type agricultural producers' co-operatives, which later developed into people's communes. In addition, it divided public ownership into collective ownership and state ownership according to degree of socialization, stating that public ownership should develop from lower to higher stages—from collective ownership to partly state ownership and to complete state ownership. All this was partly due to the influence of the Soviet model and partly due to some one-sided conception on socialism. Today, the Chinese people have deepened their understanding on socialism and recognized that public ownership can be realized in many forms such as joint ventures, joint stock companies, joint stock partnerships, and enterprise operations under contract or leasing systems.

(3) In terms of economic operating mechanisms, socialist transformation aimed to establish a socialist planned economy and stated that a market economy was unique to capitalism, while a planned economy was the fundamental feature of socialism. Today in the primary stage of socialism, China's economy is a socialist market economy. A planned or a market economy is no longer understood as the fundamental difference between socialism and capitalism—planning and market forces can be both effective means of regulating economic activities.

References

Shi Zhongquan (ed.), *A Review of Study on Mao Zedong*, the Central Party Literature Press, Beijing, 1992.

Gong Yuzhi, *A New Study of Mao Zedong Thought*, People's Publishing House, Beijing, 1991.

Wang Haiguang, "Introduction to the Symposium in Commemoration of the 40th Anniversary of the Completion of Socialist Transformation," *Theory Front*, 1997 (1).

Li Jie, "The Primary Stage of Socialism and Socialist Transformation of Agriculture, Handicrafts, and Capitalist Industry and Commerce," *Theoretical Front in Higher Education*, 1999 (9).

Chen Junjing, "Soviet Experience and China's Theory and Practice of the Transition Period," *Journal of Ningbo Normal College*, 1996 (5).

Wang Shiyi, "The Transition from New Democracy to Socialism in the Early Years of New China," *Journal of Qingdao Administrative Science College*, 1999 (2).

Xiao Dong, "Introduction to Study on the General Line for the Transition Period in Recent Two Decades," *Teaching and Research*, 2000 (10).

Liu Baosan, "Some Opinions on the Returned Argument over 'Consolidating New Democracy'," *Journal of Zhongnan University of Economics*, 1998 (5).

Chapter 7

The Theory of Socialist Construction

Theory of Socialist Construction is an important component of Mao Zedong Thought as well as a major starting point of Deng Xiaoping Theory. Recent studies on the theories of the socialist construction created by the first generation of collective leadership of the CPC focus on how Deng Xiaoping Theory has carried forward and developed Mao Zedong Thought in this respect. In recent years, researches in this area have increasingly enhanced and attracts more and more researchers and scholars. They generally focus on studying theories and policies on the path of industrialization suited to China's conditions, the socialist commodity economy and the role of the law of value, correct handling of two types of contradictions differing in nature, cultural development, approaches to intellectuals, and differentiation of the three worlds.

7.1 Research Achievements

Before the Third Plenary Session of the Eleventh CPC Central

Committee, theoretical and academic studies on Mao Zedong's theory of socialist construction had focused only on some separate ideas from the perspective of political economy and were far from systematic.

The Resolution on Certain Questions in the History of Our Party Since the Founding of the People's Republic of China passed by the CPC at the Sixth Plenary Session of its Eleventh Central Committee in 1981 has summarized Mao Zedong's theory on socialist construction in four basic principles: one, to recognize the basic contradictions in a socialist society and to correctly handle two types of contradictions differing in nature; two, to learn from the lesson of the Soviet Union and to take a path of industrialization suited to China's conditions; three, to implement the principle of cadres' participation in productive labor and workers' participation in management, reforming irrational and outdated rules and regulations and realizing close cooperation among cadres, workers, and technicians; four, mobilizing all positive factors to build a socialist country.

In the following two decades, this theory is studied as an important component of Mao Zedong Thought by researchers who deepen their research as more and more progress is achieved in the country's modernization and reform and opening up process. In addition, researchers studying on the history of the CPC have also paid close attention to this theory.

In the 1980s, theoretical studies on this theory has centered on its four basic principles summarized in the above Resolution.

With regard to studies on the first basic principle, there were more papers elaborating on the principle of "unity—criticism—unity" and the principle of "long-term co-existence and mutual oversight". Articles were produced on the importance of these two principles and lessons to be learned by their practice. But less articles were written, which discussed the principle of letting a hundred flowers bloom and a hundred schools of thought contend. Besides, many papers were published to discuss the importance of making overall arrangements in economic work and on the idea of coordinating or considering the interests of the state, collectives and individuals. But most of these papers have focused on drawing lessons from the experiences after the founding of New China and reached similar conclusions which argue that recent economic reforms were necessary and important.

In terms of the second basic principle, a large number of penetrating articles were published. Numerous articles have recounted and discussed Mao Zedong's ideas in his "On the Ten Major Relations" and some related talks: "China should proceed from its own realities in learning from other countries and avoid blindly copying their practice and experience; China should correctly handle the relationship between heavy industry on the one hand and light industry and agriculture on the other in its course of industrialization; China needs to arrange the development of its national economy in line with the priority order of agriculture, light industry and heavy industry." Some articles have pointed out that China had often failed to maintain overall balance in economic development because it wrongly targeted unpractical high speed of economic development and taken the production of steel and grain as the key link, which both had violated the principle of seeking truth from facts and hindered the normal and orderly development in economy. All these show that although China has found or discovered the path of development it should take, it had experienced great difficulties during its journey on this path.

With regard to the third basic principle, many articles have discussed the principle of factory directors assuming overall responsibility, the practice of delegating more powers to enterprises, and other economic reform measures. But, few papers were published to conduct academic and theoretical study on the "Charter of the Anshan Iron and Steel Company." In addition, researchers have paid little attention to the role of reforms in the enterprise management system during socialist construction period.

In terms of the fourth basic principle, published articles have generally agreed that the idea of mobilizing all positive factors to build a socialist country was a major strategy of Mao Zedong. This idea has laid the fundamental principle for socialist construction because it was an important working method and way of thinking and also embodies the Party's mass line principle. Some articles have also discussed the importance of this idea for developing socialist economy, improving socialist democracy and the socialist legal system, and safeguarding social stability.

According to rough statistics, papers studying Mao Zedong's theory of socialist construction in the 1980s had totaled over 400, but books in this regard were only few. Most of the papers published have debated in line with the Resolution on Certain Questions in the History of Our Party Since the Founding of the People's Republic of China. They have explained the basic theoretical principles of this theory, elaborate the original meanings of these principles and their content, and analyze the international and domestic situations in which these principles had emerged. Most research results could not exceed the ideas stated Resolution's summarization. There were only few arguments over specific issues because the researches were not so deep. In particular, few researchers have linked their study with China's experiences in reform and opening up.

In the 1990s, namely, more than a decade after the Resolution on Certain Questions in the History of Our Party Since the Founding of the People's Republic of China was passed, the studies on Mao Zedong's theory of socialist construction have started to progress much deeper. The theory of building socialism with Chinese characteristics was systematically summarized for the first time in 1990 at the Seventh Plenary Session of the Thirteenth CPC Central Committee and was summarized again in 1992 at the Fourteenth National Congress of the CPC. In 1997, the CPC had formally classified this theory under Deng Xiaoping Theory at its Fifteenth National Congress. In last recent decade, the study on Mao Zedong's theory of socialist construction was greatly deepened as more and more theoretical researchers affirm that Deng Xiaoping Theory is a continuation and development of Mao Zedong Thought. They have started to explore the source of Deng Xiaoping Theory by combining theoretical studies with practical issues. There were so many research papers published in this decade that their number is hard to compute precisely, and research efforts on special topics have produced a great deal of valuable fruits. For example, books such as *A Review of Some Major Decisions and Events* by Bo Yibo, *On Twenty Issues of Socialism with*

Chinese Characteristics by Gong Yuzhi and *The Hard Exploration by Mao Zedong* by Shi Zhongquan have produced plenty of research results. Besides, many books about history of the country and the CPC have also discussed many issues concerning Mao Zedong's theories on socialist construction. In conclusion, research achievements in the 1990s, which covered many aspects of this theory, have far exceeded those in the 1980s, both in quantity and in quality.

7.2 The Theory of Contradictions in Socialist Society

Mao Zedong's theory on contradictions in socialist society is the first basic principle of his thinking on socialist construction. Studies on this theory have always been an important part of study of Mao Zedong Thought and are often linked with studies on the theory of building socialism with Chinese characteristics.

Studies on this theory can be generally divided into three periods: the first period is from the official publication of Mao Zedong's "On the Correct Handling of Contradictions among the People" in June 1957 to the eve of the "cultural revolution;" the second is during the "cultural revolution" when Mao Zedong's ideas on contradictions in socialist society were falsely taken as the theoretical basis for "continuing revolution under dictatorship of the proletariat;" and the third is from the Third Plenary Session of the Eleventh CPC Central Committee to present when this theory was studied more comprehensively.

7.2.1 Assessment of Studies in the First and Second Periods

Quite a few papers had been published to discuss Mao Zedong's ideas on contradictions in socialist society before the "cultural revolution." The influential ones were "'On the Correct Handling of Contradictions among the People' Is a Great Contribution to Marxism-Leninism" by Xu Liqun et al., "The Contradictions between the Relations of Production and the Productive

Forces and Contradictions among the People" by Ai Siqi, and "Contradictions Are the Forces Driving Development of Socialist Society" by Wu Zhifu. These papers had studied those several issues contained in Mao Zedong's essay "On the Correct Handling of Contradictions among the People," such as the basic contradictions in socialist society and their features, the two types of contradictions differing in nature, cooperative transformation of agriculture, and also the path of industrialization. Although these papers could not fully reveal the deep meaning of this important theory, they reflect the way theoretical researchers and publicity workers understood these major issues at that time. As the scope of the anti-Rightist struggle was broadened and the Great Leap Forward[1] was launched, study on Mao Zedong's theory of contradictions in socialist society went astray due to the social and political climate at that time. Therefore many researchers had affirmed the erroneous ideas of taking class struggle as the principal problem in Chinese society and simply targeting achieving quick results in economic development.

Soon after the "cultural revolution" was started, Mao Zedong's essay "On the Correct Handling of Contradictions among the People" was taken as the theoretical basis for continuing revolution under dictatorship of the proletariat, and the study on contradictions in socialist society went totally astray. For instance, a paper named "The Theoretical Weapon for Continuing Revolution under Dictatorship of the Proletariat—In Commemoration of the Tenth Anniversary of the Publication of 'On the Correct Handling of Contradictions among the People'" published in No. 10 of the Journal *Hongqi* in 1967 had rigidly linked the correct ideas in the essay to the erroneous theories advocating the "cultural revolution." In his report to the CPC's Ninth National Congress in 1969, Lin Biao had asserted that, in this essay Mao Zedong, had comprehensively set forth the existence of contradictions, classes and class struggle under the conditions of the dictatorship of the proletariat, set forth the great theory of continuing the revolution under the dictatorship of the proletariat, and laid the theoretical foundation for the

---

[1] A movement that was started in 1958 disrupted normal economic development by exaggerating achievements and striving for unpractical goals in the production of iron and steel.

Great Proletarian Cultural Revolution. Without referring and evaluating the international and domestic situations under which Mao Zedong had written the essay and the true meaning of Mao Zedong's ideas, Lin Biao had severely distorted Mao Zedong's theory on contradictions in the socialist society. As a result, many researchers had solely focused on Mao Zedong's statement pointing to the existence of contradiction between the enemy and the people and on class struggles in the ideological field. Mao Zedong's theory on contradictions in socialist society was completely fragmented and distorted.

7.2.2 Assessment of Studies after the Third Plenary Session of the Eleventh CPC Central Committee

During a fairly long period of time after the Resolution on Certain Questions in the History of Our Party Since the Founding of the People's Republic of China was promulgated in 1981, researchers focused their study on the question of correctly handling contradictions among the people. A large number of valuable essays were published in 1982 and 1987 to commemorate the twenty-fifth and thirtieth anniversary of the publication of "On the Correct Handling of Contradictions among the People." In order to correct the mistakes of the "cultural revolution" and the "Left" mistakes before that period, many researchers proposed that great efforts should be made to fully understand that class struggle is no longer the principal problem in Chinese society and correct handling of contradictions among the people has become the main theme in the country's political life. Research results published during this period not only rectified some wrong ideas but also learned lessons from history.

7.2.2.1 Reinterpretation on the Meaning of Mao Zedong's Theory of Contradictions in Socialist Society

According to some researchers, the historical background in which Mao Zedong had advanced his theory of contradictions in socialist society should not be neglected. As the country moved from new democracy to the primary stage of socialism, profound changes had emerged in every field of Chinese society. Domestically, since the socialist transformation had been completed in 1956, the principal problem in Chinese society was how to meet the ever-growing material and cultural needs of the people under the conditions of backward social production, and the central task of the Party and government was to develop the productive forces. The principal task in the Party's political work was no longer to wage turbulent class struggles against the enemy, but to properly handle the increasingly conspicuous contradictions among the people. Internationally, the Communist Party of the Soviet Union had criticized Stalin's mistakes at its Twentieth Congress, disturbances had occurred in Poland and Hungary, and the western capitalist camp waged an anti-communist, anti-socialist campaign. All this had influenced China's revolution and construction in different degrees. Faced with the new trends in the international communist movement and the disturbances in some places in China, the CPC Central Committee began to think about the question of how to understand and handle the various types of contradictions differing in nature in the spring of 1956. Consequently, Mao Zedong had advanced his theory of contradictions in socialist society.

According to some researchers, Mao Zedong had first commented on the contradictions in socialist society in the essay "On the Historical Experience of the Dictatorship of the Proletariat" published in the *People's Daily* in April 1956; initially differentiated the two types of contradictions differing in nature in his essay "On the Ten Major Relationships;" had clearly stated that there were two types of contradictions differing in nature in socialist society in that essay titled "A Further Review of the Historical Experience of the Dictatorship of the Proletariat;" and formally formulated a complete theory of contradictions in socialist society and correct handling of contradictions among the people in his essay "On the Correct Handling of Contradictions among the People" in February 1957.

The content of this theory should not be distorted. Mao Zedong had clearly explained the reasons behind this theory. He said, "Many do not recognize that contradictions still exist in socialist society, which results that they become irresolute and passive when confronted with social contradictions; they do not understand that socialist society grows more united and consolidated through the ceaseless process of correctly handling and resolving contradictions. For this reason, we need to explain things to our people, and to our cadres in the first place, in order to help them understand the contradictions in socialist society and learn to use correct methods for handling them." He also explained the reason why he had focused on discussing how to correctly handle contradictions among the people. He said, "Today, matters stand as follows. The large-scale, turbulent class struggles with mass characteristic of those times in the revolution period have in the main come to an end, but class struggle is by no means entirely over.... In other words, time is needed for our socialist system to be established and consolidated, for the masses to become accustomed to the new system, and for government personnel to learn and acquire experience. It is therefore imperative for us at this juncture to raise the question of distinguishing contradictions among the people from those between ourselves and the enemy, as well as the question of the correct handling of contradictions among the people, in order to unite the people of all nationalities in our country for the new battle, the battle against nature, develop our economy and culture, help the whole nation to traverse this period of transition relatively smoothly, consolidate our new system and build up our new state."[1]

Mao Zedong's above statement has demonstrated that his theory should not be necessarily linked to the erroneous theory of continuing revolution under the dictatorship of the proletariat.

7.2.2.2 The Reason Why the Theory of Contradictions in Socialist Society Was Linked with the Theory of Continuing Revolution under the Dictatorship of the Proletariat

Why is it that the theory of contradictions in socialist society was linked to the theory of continuing revolution under the dictatorship of the proletariat during the "cultural revolution"? Researchers have three different answers to this question: the theory of contradictions in socialist society was distorted; it

---

[1] *Selected Works of Mao Tse-tung*, Eng. ed., FLP, Peking, 1977, Vol. V, pp. 393, 395-396.

had failures; it was misunderstood.

According to researchers who argue that the theory of contradictions in socialist society was completely distorted during the "cultural revolution"; Mao Zedong had stated that the class struggle in the ideological field is protracted and tortuous and at certain times becomes even very sharp and revisionism was then even more dangerous than dogmatism, but he had not meant that class struggle was still the principal problem in Chinese society. His theory was very foresighted, and many of its ideas are still correct and practical today. However, truth can also become falsehood if it is treated wrongly. During the "cultural revolution," this theory was understood in absolutes, its ideas about class struggle were exaggerated, and it was wrongly linked to the theory of continuing revolution under the dictatorship of the proletariat. The theory had become false because it was distorted.

As pointed out by researchers who believe that this theory had defects, there should be a reason that all the editorials and papers published during the "cultural revolution" had asserted that the essay "On the Correct Handling of Contradictions among the People" was the first article to propose the theory of continuing revolution under the dictatorship of the proletariat. When formulating his ideas of two types of contradictions, Mao Zedong had focused too much on the political field, which made it possible for the class struggle to be broadened. In other words, this theory itself had failings. Although Mao Zedong had put forward quite a few correct principles in his "On the Correct Handling of Contradictions among the People" and had implemented them, he still gradually move to the wrong direction. During the "cultural revolution," this theory had actually become a theory about how to "correctly handle the two types of contradictions" under those circumstances when class struggle was expanded. In essence, this opinion argues that the theory of contradictions in socialist society was in some way inevitably to be linked with the theory of continuing revolution under the dictatorship of the proletariat.

According to those researchers who believe that the theory of contradictions in socialist society was misunderstood, the reason why this theory and the theory of continuing revolution under the dictatorship of the proletariat, which were two completely different theories, were linked to each other during the "cultural revolution" was that people had misunderstood the basic ideas about class struggle in this theory. They had confused Mao Zedong's different approaches on the principal problem in Chinese society before and after this essay was published.

7.2.2.3 The Significance of the Theory on Contradictions in Socialist Society

7.2.2.3.1 This theory was a great achievement in applying Marxism in China

According to Bo Yibo in his book *A Review of Some Major Decisions and Events*, Mao Zedong's essay "On the Correct Handling of Contradictions among the People" had made the following theoretical contributions. First, a systematic, complete theory of contradictions in socialist society was created for the first time in the history of Marxism. As pointed out by Bo Yibo, although Lenin had first admitted and affirmed that contradictions still exist in socialist society, he failed to make a full elaboration on this issue due to his limited practice of socialism. It was Mao Zedong who had first created a systematic theory on contradictions in socialist society. Second, the contradiction between the working class and the national bourgeoisie was categorized as a contradiction among the people for the first time in the history of world socialist movement. This principle, never discussed in Marxist works, was a great creation of Mao Zedong and the CPC and attracted worldwide attention soon after it was introduced. Guided by this principle, China had accomplished the peaceful transformation of the national capitalist industry and commerce and smoothly eliminated the Chinese national bourgeoisie as a class.[1]

Mao Zedong's analyses on contradictions in socialist society had comprehensively defined the class relations in Chinese society after

---

[1] Bo Yibo, *A Review of Major Decisions and Issues*, Vol. II, the CPC Central Committee Party School Publishing House, Beijing, 1993, pp. 596-599.

completion of socialist transformation and discussed the problem of class struggle in socialist society. These analyses, together with his essay "On the Ten Major Relationships" constitutes Mao Zedong's theory on contradictions in China's socialist construction period. He had defined the basic contradictions in socialist society, discussed the problem of correctly handling contradictions among the people, and advanced a series of new principles and policies on cooperative transformation of agriculture, transformation of industry and commerce, and on the issue of ethnic minorities. Theory of contradictions in socialist society had guided the work of the Party and government at that time, but it can still guide today's efforts to build socialism with Chinese characteristics. Discussion on contradictions in socialist society should be based on the essence of this theory; otherwise, the discussion will go astray.

7.2.2.3.2 Mao Zedong's propositions on class struggle in the ideological spheres has great practical significance

When discussing contradictions in socialist society, Mao Zedong said, "The class struggle between the proletariat and the bourgeoisie in the ideological sphere will still be protracted and tortuous and at times can even become very sharp." "It will take a fairly long period of time to decide on the winner in the ideological struggle between socialism and capitalism in our country." "In present circumstances, revisionism is more pernicious than dogmatism. It is an important task for us to unfold criticism of revisionism on the ideological front now."

According to some researchers, Mao Zedong's above ideas were exactly the theoretical origin of the theory of continuing revolution under the dictatorship of the proletariat. Other researchers, however, have argued that these ideas should be assessed in a comprehensive, fair and objective manner. After China had gone through the political disturbances in 1989 and observed the drastic changes in the Soviet Union and some Eastern European socialist countries, a re-study on Mao Zedong's above penetrating statements, especially his incisive remarks on revisionism, explicitly demonstrate how foresighted they were and how important they are for preventing peaceful evolution toward capitalism, also opposing and checking ideas of revisionism, and preventing Party cadres from degenerating.

7.2.2.3.3 The theory on contradictions in socialist society is the theoretical basis for today's reforms

Many researchers have discussed this theory by focusing practical problems and conclude that it laid the philosophical foundation for socialist reforms. Some of them even believe that the theory "is the theoretical basis for socialist reforms." As China's socialist reform and development proceed, contradictions among the people attain new characteristics, and various measures need to be taken to solve them, such as those to adjust interests, reform systems, strengthen policies, and improve democracy and the legal system. Correct handling of these contradictions can directly promote the development of socialism. Mao Zedong's general principles in this regard should be researched and developed in the light of the new realities to guide today's concrete practice. So, still more efforts should be made to further discuss this theory.

According to some researchers, Deng Xiaoping had drawn correct ideas from this theory and realistically estimated how contradictions have changed in the new period. This can be embodied in the following four aspects. First, his ideas that China should take economic development as its central task and the fundamental characteristic of socialism is to liberate and develop the productive forces and achieve common prosperity have become the fundamental guiding ideology for understanding and solving basic contradictions in socialist society. Second, he has fully affirmed the correspondence between the relations of production and the productive forces and between the superstructure and the economic base, stressed the importance of upholding the Four Cardinal Principles[1] through

---

[1] Four Cardinal Principles was proposed by Deng Xiaoping when socialist reform policy was started; the CPC, when leading the reforms should not lose the main direction and adhere to these principles: Keep the socialist road, adhere to Marxism-Leninizm and Mao Zedong Thought, uphold to people's democratic dictatorship (proletarian dictatorship), uphold the leadership of CPC in socialism building.

socialist reforms, and defined the prerequisite and ideological and political guarantee for solving basic contradictions in socialist society. Third, he has scientifically analyzed the contradictions between the relations of production and the productive forces and between the superstructure and the economic base, defined reform as a way to liberate the productive forces, and clarified detailed tasks and practical methods for adjusting basic contradictions in socialist society. Fourth, he pointed to the development of productive forces as the fundamental criterion for judging how the basic contradictions in socialist society should be solved.

Some researchers have also discussed how China's third generation of collective leadership has applied and developed this theory. According to them, Jiang Zemin, core leader in this group has applied this theory when he defined twelve major relationships that should be correctly handled in the country's socialist modernization drive at the Fifth Plenary Session of the Fourteenth CPC Central Committee. Jiang Zemin, has also elaborated on them when he analyzed the principal problem in the primary stage of socialism in his report to the CPC's Fifteenth National Congress. We can say that the theory of properly balancing reform, development and stability was the a guiding idea of the third generation of collective leadership for adjusting basic contradictions in society and handling contradictions among the people.

7.2.3 Limitations of the Theory of Contradictions in Socialists Society

7.2.3.1 Mao Zedong's Analyses of Social Contradictions Had Failings

Mao Zedong had emphasized that there was correspondence as well as contradiction between the relations of production and the productive forces and between the superstructure and the economic base. He had asserted that the relationship between conformity and contradiction was one in which the former was the primary and fundamental aspect and the latter was subordinate to it. He had stressed the superiority of the socialist system and advanced that the fundamental task of the country was to protect and develop the productive forces under the socialist relations of production. These ideas were basically correct and accorded with the social circumstances at that time. But it was improper to believe that the productive forces would develop so rapid and immediately after the socialist system was established.

As pointed out by some researchers, later studies on Marxist dialectics and investigations on the actual state of China's socialist construction in those days both indicate that the relationship between conformity and contradiction could change. Mao Zedong had also noticed that. But he had still believed, this change was unlikely to occur in a short period of time after the socialist system was established. In a talk in November 1956, he had commented that "currently the socialist relations of production are conformity with the productive forces and the socialist superstructure and economic base are also basically compatible, but an antagonistic contradiction between the relations of production and the productive forces might occur in 200 or 2,000 years, and their solution should be a revolution". That clearly indicates that Mao Zedong had believed that conformity was the fundamental aspect. As a result, he overlooked the need to further liberate the productive forces under the socialist system and did not have a clear understanding on the necessity of reforms.[1]

There are also researchers suggesting that Mao Zedong's analyses on contradictions among the people were inadequate. When discussing the root of contradictions, Mao Zedong had rather focused on the political and ideological field while overlooked economic reasons. He had believed that most contradictions could be solved by drawing a clear distinction between right and wrong and applying the principle of "unity—criticism—unity." However, contradictions caused by disputes over economic interests do not involve right or wrong and can only be adjusted through economic means. Mao Zedong neither discussed such economic contradictions nor analyzed how to handle them. So, that was a clear limitation in his understanding.

---

[1] Yan .Shuqun, "A Comparison of Mao Zedong's and Deng Xiaoping's Theories of Basic Contradictions in Socialist Society," *Humanities*, 2000 (1).

According to some researchers, although Mao Zedong had stressed that the democratic method should be the primary choice to solve contradictions among the people, he had improperly believed that the mass movement was the principal form of democracy and did not realize the importance of institutionalization and establishing democracy on a legal basis. As a result, in his opinion, problems such as bureaucracy that could and should be solved by improving laws and systems, could only be solved by raising people's ideological standards. When these problems worsened, class struggle was erroneously regarded as the principal problem in society and mistaken struggle methods were used to solve them. As a result, the contradictions among the people were confused with those between the people and the enemy. In addition, in regard to identity and struggle of the aspects of a contradiction, Mao Zedong focused on the struggle aspect and stressed that the opposites of a contradiction can transform to each other only through struggle. This kind of "struggle theory" certainly cannot correctly handle the two types of contradictions.

7.2.3.2 Did Mao Zedong Clearly Define the Principal Problem in Chinese Society or Not

This has been a hot issue for discussion. According to some researchers, Mao Zedong had clearly defined class struggle as the principal problem in Chinese society after the Third Plenary Session of the Eighth CPC Central Committee in September 1957, although he had stated in his essay "On the Correct Handling of Contradictions among the People" that the Party's task was to "unite the people of all nationalities in our country for the new battle, the battle against nature" and all along regarded economic construction as the Party's major task till early 1960s. In fact, he did not totally agree, in the first place, with the Party's resolution, which had regarded the principal problem as the contradiction between the advanced socialist system and the backward social productive forces, passed at its Eighth Congress in 1956. But he did not argue on it because he had not studied it throughly. He still made no mention of this question in his above essay, which made it possible for him to change his ideas about the principal problem and central task later.[1]

According to other researchers who think differently, Mao Zedong had regarded contradictions among the people as the principal problem in 1957, although he had not declared that so definitely. He had generally agreed with the Party's judgment at its Eighth Congress that class struggle was no longer the principal problem in Chinese society, but had said that the term "contradiction between the advanced socialist system and the backward social productive forces is theoretically unreasonable." The basic contradictions in socialist society are not antagonistic ones between rival classes, but are non-antagonistic ones within the ranks of the people. The socialist society is made up of ranks of people such as workers, peasants, and intellectuals, and the fundamental task of socialism is to develop the productive forces and develop economy. That is to say, the basic contradictions in socialist society are closely related with the true nature of socialism. So, Mao Zedong's statements of uniting the people of all ethnic groups for the new battle against nature, protecting and developing the productive forces, and building a socialist country had defined what the principal problem was. However, because he had not totally agreed with the Party's resolution on the principal problem passed at its Eighth Congress, he had not used the term "principal problem" in his essay "On the Correct Handling of Contradictions among the People," although he had actually discussed about it in the essay.[2]

The past two decades have witnessed sound achievements in the study of Mao Zedong's theory of contradictions in socialist society. This theory, important and at the same time imperfect, has caused much confusion among researchers. It is not enough just to distinguish the correct ideas of this theory from the incorrect ones; but an answer should be found to the question—what makes this correct theory imperfect? First, the simple formula "basic contradictions determine the principal problem; the principal

[1] Zhou Cheng'en et al., *Mao Zedong's Exploration into China's Path of Socialist Construction*, Zhejiang People's Publishing House, Hangzhou, 1993, p. 50.

[2] Shi Zhaoyu, "How Mao Zedong Thought about the Principal Problem in 1957," *Study of the History of the Communist Party of China*, 1991 (2).

problem determines the major task" is not enough to clarify Mao Zedong's understanding on the relationships among the three: basic contradictions, the principal problem, and the major task. Second, quotations from Mao Zedong's works should not be taken as the sole evidence for discussing how Mao Zedong understood the relationships among the above three terms. On the contrary, this theory should be studied by taking into consideration the historical conditions under which it took shape, as well as finding out Mao Zedong's consistent line of ideas, relevant historical material, and works of other Party leaders in this regard. More available historical material is very important for the studies. With regard to the study on the practical significance of this theory, it is enough to evaluate that it had provided the theoretical basis for today's socialist reforms; it will be an exaggeration to rigidly link ideas of Deng Xiaoping Theory to it. Mao Zedong Thought and Deng Xiaoping Theory took shape under different historical conditions; their difference should not be overlooked. All the above problems need to be further investigated in future studies.

7.3 The Theory of Socialist Economic Development

7.3.1 Introduction to the Studies on the Theory of Socialist Economic Development

As stated earlier, during the several years after the Resolution on Certain Questions in the History of Our Party Since the Founding of the People's Republic of China was promulgated in 1981, most research results on the theory of socialist construction had not exceeded the Resolution's summarization. But, some researchers did not restrict themselves by the ideas in the Resolution. Study on Mao Zedong's theory of socialist economic development was deepened in the late 1980s. Some researchers have produced a number of papers with high academic value after thoroughly studying the guiding ideology, fundamental principle and strategy of socialist construction and reviewing the experience therein. Shi Zhongquan in his paper "The Hard Exploration" divided the course in which Mao Zedong developed his theory of socialist construction before the "cultural revolution" into five periods. Besides, the paper has discussed some of Mao Zedong's ideas about socialist construction that were not mentioned in the Resolution.

Some researchers have produced valuable results in attempting to find out the ideological reasons behind the mistakes in socialist construction. For instance, some of them put forward that these mistakes were due to two reasons: impetuosity and rashness in economic development and expanding class struggle in political work. According to some other researchers, Mao Zedong and the Party had once believed that socialist construction was easy and the socialist system would soon be replaced by communist system. That was exactly what led to the hurried transformation of the relations of production and impetuosity and rashness in production and construction.

Some researchers have pointed out that utopian ideas had once prevailed in China's socialist construction. According to Wang Lulin in his paper "A Study on Mao Zedong's 'Notes on the Report of Further Improving the Army's Agricultural Work by the Rear Service Department of the Military Commission',," the Great Leap Forward and the "cultural revolution" demonstrated that Mao Zedong had always nurtured an utopian socialist model, which had caused the "Left" mistakes in socialist construction. Zhou Cheng'en in his paper titled "People's Communes and Utopian Ideas in Socialist Construction" has stated that the existence of those utopian ideas was due to three reasons: dogmatic understanding of Marxist theory of socialism; the influence of Western European utopian ideas of 19th century; and the influence of notions of agrarian socialism in the Chinese history.

Liang Xiufeng has pointed out in the paper "Historical Review and Reflections of China's Economic Construction" that the strategic goal of "surpassing England and overtaking America" should be analyzed comprehensively. On the one hand, it represented a period of setbacks in the course of China's industrialization because it entailed overly development in the heavy industry. On the other hand, it had indeed played a noticeable role in accelerating China's industrialization.

In the article "An Investigation into Reasons behind Establishment of the 'Left' Theory of Class Struggle at the Tenth Plenary Session of the Eighth CPC Central Committee," Cong Jin has pointed out that the fundamental reason that the CPC accepted Mao Zedong's theory of class struggle in socialist society at the Tenth Plenary Session of its Eighth Central Committee in 1962 was that it did not have a clear understanding on the law governing development of socialist society and understood Marxist principles as dogmas, although there were other international and domestic reasons as well. Some researchers have further pointed out that Mao Zedong's mistakes in class struggle had begun with his understanding on the intellectuals.

The above opinions were novel in the 1980s and showed high academic value although some of them need further discussion.

In the 1990s, the CPC has clarified the theory of building socialism with Chinese characteristics in nine aspects at its Fourteenth Congress; later defined and affirmed its historical position of the Deng Xiaoping Theory at its Fifteenth Congress. Since then researchers and scholars have started to take a deep interest in the relationship between Mao Zedong Thought and Deng Xiaoping Theory and consequently broadened their study on Mao Zedong's theory on socialist construction. Most researchers have renewed their description of this theory, compared it with Deng Xiaoping Theory, and argued that Deng Xiaoping Theory has carried on, corrected and developed it. Study on Mao Zedong's ideas on socialist construction in the recent decade has far exceeded the summarization in the Resolution on Certain Questions in the History of Our Party Since the Founding of the People's Republic of China. Below issues were argued by researchers.

7.3.2 China's Experience and Principles for Socialist Economic Development

Around the fortieth anniversary of the founding of New China, many researchers have focused their study in reviewing China's course of socialist construction. This work still attracts much attention from researchers today. As pointed out by some researchers, China's exploration into the theory of socialist construction had begun with the problem of industrialization, and Mao Zedong had developed a complex system of ideas about the path of industrialization.

7.3.2.1 Main Content and Features of the Path of Industrialization

7.3.2.1.1 Breaking with the Soviet Model

The CPC's first generation of collective leadership led by Mao Zedong had developed a path of industrialization, which contained a variety of ideas. Their major ideas about economic development include the following. The principle of opposing both rash advance and conservatism and progressing steadily by maintaining overall balance should be upheld. The overly centralized economic management system should be reformed, power should be rationally divided between the central and local governments, and planning should play leading role in economic management, supplemented by regulation through market forces. At the Party's Eighth Congress, Chen Yun had said that the overly unified methods in production, operation, purchase, sale and planning that were originally adopted during the socialist transformation could no longer meet the needs of long-term economic development and therefore should be corrected. To solve these problems, he advanced the well-known idea of "three mainstays and three supplements."[1] In a talk in late 1956, Mao Zedong had said, "Now that capitalism has been eliminated, we can operate some capitalist economy." "Illegal private factories can be transformed into legal ones, and they will not be confiscated for a long period of time to come only if they do not violate laws." Liu Shaoqi had also stated that in China the socialist sector, which accounted for more than ninety percent of the national economy, should not be afraid to be

---

[1] In the management of industry and commerce, the mainstay will be state and collective management, to be supplemented to a minor degree by individual management. For industry and agriculture, planned production will be the mainstay, to be supplemented by unregulated production within the scope prescribed in the state plan and in accordance with market fluctuation. In the unified socialist market, the state market is the mainstay, to be supplemented by a free market under the guidance of the state.

supplemented by capitalist sector, which accounted for only several percents. All this indicates that the CPC's understanding on socialism had far exceeded the traditional socialism.

The above breakthroughs in understanding on socialism had occurred because the CPC was striving to find a path of development suitable to China's conditions. As pointed out by researchers, when New China was considering the problem of industrialization, the Soviet Union and Eastern European countries had also begun to reform the traditional socialist model in different degrees. That is to say, the Soviet model entailing priority on development of heavy industry that New China had learned from the Soviet Union needed to be reformed in the first place, and the CPC had noticed that from the very beginning of China's industrialization. Consequently, the Party had purposefully strived to find a path of industrialization suitable to China's realities.

7.3.2.1.2 Focusing Heavily on Agricultural Development Is a Prominent Feature of Mao Zedong's Theory on Industrialization

Mao Zedong had always given high priority to agricultural development, which was also embodied in his theory on industrialization. He was fully aware of the importance of cementing the position of agriculture as the foundation of the economy. In China, industry could not develop without the support of agriculture; top priority should be given to agricultural development. Agriculture was of vital importance for feeding the country's hundreds of millions of people, supplying raw materials for light industry, and building up foreign exchange reserves and financial resources. In some sense, it could be said that how agriculture is developed would determine how industry could be developed. Mao Zedong had therefore stressed that China should not copy the Soviet model of focusing on developing heavy industry while neglecting the development of agriculture and light industry like it did in the First Five-Year Plan (1953-1957).

Mao Zedong had argued that the problem of China's path of industrialization was in essence about how to handle the relationship among heavy industry, light industry and agriculture. According to him, investment in agriculture should be increased, which would help to build a solid foundation for the development of heavy industry. After learning lessons from the mistakes of the Great Leap Forward and the movement to establish people's communes, Mao Zedong had stressed that China should arrange the development of its national economy in line with the priority order of agriculture, light industry and heavy industry. At a working conference of the Party Central Committee in 1964, Mao Zedong had pointed out, "In the past, the method of planning was essentially learned from the Soviet Union. First you determine how much steel is needed, then on this basis estimate how much coal, electricity, transport facility, and so on are needed. This kind of method is impractical and therefore should be changed." "Our policy is to take agriculture as the foundation and industry as the leading factor. It should first be ascertained what quantity of food grains can be produced and then how much industry can be planned on this foundation." The aim of the Party to correctly handle the relationship among agriculture, light industry and heavy industry was to find a path for China to develop faster and better than capitalist countries, and the Soviet Union, and Eastern European countries and better serve the people's needs. Thus, the CPC had broken with the Soviet model and given an important place to agriculture.

The path of socialist transformation and the general line for the transition period had also stressed the importance of agriculture because a correct handling of the contradiction between industrial development and individual farming was required to realize industrialization. Later, the position of agriculture was further consolidated with the formulation of the idea to modernize the country's agriculture, national defense, industry, and science and technology. All those demonstrate that Mao Zedong's theory on socialist construction had all along given high priority to agricultural development.

The principle of giving equal emphasis to industry and agriculture was also a major feature of Mao Zedong's theory of industrialization. According to some researchers, this principle required giving equal emphasis not only to industry and agriculture but also to local industrial enterprises and those industrial enterprises under the central government, large industrial enterprises and small and medium-sized industrial enterprises, and industrial enterprises in rural areas and in urban areas, all of which together constituted Mao Zedong's theory on industrialization.

7.3.2.2 The Role of Economic Development

According to most researchers, Mao Zedong had defined the country's major task as developing the productive forces around the time when he had published his essay "On the Correct Handling of Contradictions among the People." They have offered facts supporting their opinion. Mao Zedong had clearly stated at the CPC's Eighth National Congress in September 1956 that China's major task after completion of socialist transformation was to protect the productive forces. In addition, Mao Zedong's such ideas "the large-scale class struggles mobilizing masses have come to an end" and "unite all the people for the new battle against nature and develop our economy and culture" are also convincing proofs.

Other researchers, however, have insisted that Mao Zedong's above statements cannot prove that he had taken developing the productive forces as the country's major task. After all, he had clearly stated at the Third Plenary Session of the Eighth Party Central Committee in October 1957 that class struggle was still the principal problem in Chinese society. At the Nanning Conference in January 1958, Mao Zedong had said, "From this year on, we should put emphasis on technological revolution on the basis of carrying on socialist revolution on the political and ideological fronts," which meant that the Party still had two "emphases" and therefore had not actually shifted the focus of its work.

As pointed out by some researchers, compared to Mao Zedong, Liu Shaoqi had remained clearheaded on this question all along. Before liberation, he had advanced the correct idea that the central task of New China was to develop the economy as long as there was no war. After the founding of New China, he had repeatedly stressed that the country should focus on economic development. After Mao Zedong had stressed class struggle again, Liu Shaoqi had still believed that the Party should focus on economic development, and not class struggle. He had seldom participated in political movements or criticisms in the ideological field; on the contrary, he had used every opportunity to stress the importance of economic development.

In conclusion, many researchers admit that Mao Zedong did attach great importance to economic development and wanted to shift the focus of the Party's work to economic development after the founding of New China. However, he had failed to do so. This is a question which needs further research, and draw lessons from that reality.

7.3.2.3 The Question of Socialist Commodity Economy

How the CPC understood the socialist commodity economy and market economy had a direct bearing on New China's overall economic development in fifty years and is the motif in the theories on socialist economic development. This is, in essence, a question about "what socialism is and how to build it." In recent years, researchers have produced a large number of profound results in studying how the CPC's first generation of collective leadership represented by Mao Zedong had explored to answer this question. To answer it, the CPC should better understand the theory of scientific socialism and future society as well as China's concrete realities. It should develop and enrich the existing theories in line with the new conditions and at the same time "should not forget our forefathers." It was therefore a real challenge for Mao Zedong and other members of the first generation of collective leadership who had just recognized socialism. They had registered achievements and at the same time made some obvious mistakes in this course.

The idea of "three mainstays and three supplements" advanced by Chen Yun in 1956 was actually talking about the planned economy playing the leading role, supplemented by regulation through market forces. Mao Zedong's statement "Now that capitalism has been eliminated, we can operate some capitalist economy" was also a new economic policy suitable to the Chinese conditions. After the Great Leap Forward and the movement to establish people's communes, Mao Zedong had talked on the issue of commodity economy at a conference in Zhengzhou; including the following ideas, some of which can even inspire us today.

First, China needs to go through a fairly long period of commodity production and it is against the laws of economy to abolish commodity. Mao Zedong had stated: development of a commodity economy is essential for improving the people's living standard; commodity production and exchange is the only desirable method to guide the peasants to expand production and follow the path of socialism; all communes should be encouraged to produce commodities, and there is nothing wrong with the word "commodity." He had also stressed that it is an incomplete and frivolous understanding of Marxism to refuse using commodity production and distribution and the law of value to serve socialism.

Second, the socialist production is a planned commodity economy, which requires vigorous development of socialist commodity production. According to Mao Zedong, commodity production accords with the laws of economy, the Party's line, principles and plans in the socialist society should conform to the demands of commodity production and the law of value, and commodity production and exchange (circulation) should be developed vigorously in a planned manner.

Third, the entire Party should learn to use the law of value to guide socialist economic development. Mao Zedong had said, "The law of value is an objective law that should not be violated." "This law is a great school and only by making use of it can we teach our several tens of millions of cadres and several hundred million people and build our socialism and communism."

Fourth, commodity production and capitalism should not be considered the same. Mao Zedong had pointed out: Commodity production should not be considered in isolation; there is capitalist commodity production under capitalism and socialist commodity production under socialism. The economic base for capitalism has been eliminated in our socialist society, so commodity production will not lead us to capitalism.

Mao Zedong's above statements about commodity economy were unquestionably very important. At the same time, it should also be noticed that his ideas about commodity economy had obvious limitations. In the privacy of his thoughts, he had till believed commodity economy belonged to capitalism and was inimical to socialism, but he could not deny it too rashly because it could still be utilized to help develop the country's backward economy. This led to an intractable conflict between theory and practice: theoretically, its necessary existence had to be admitted; but in practice, restrictions should be imposed on it to prevent it from developing freely and fully. In addition, Mao Zedong had one-sidedly concluded that co-existence of collective and state sectors inevitably led to commodity production, and it will become unnecessary and disappear when the state sector becomes the sole ownership in the economy and the central government controls all production. He had overlooked the diversified division of labor and material needs in society and, in particular, the fact that China should uphold the ownership structure under which socialist public ownership is dominant and diverse other economic sectors co-exist. Consequently, he had failed to realize that a fully developed commodity economy could be the basis for realizing common prosperity.

Because he had still evaluated commodity economy as a fundamental feature of capitalism, Mao Zedong had not transcended the traditional idea of socialism and during the "cultural revolution" he had advanced the erroneous "Left" idea that socialist commodity production and exchange makes no great difference from that in the old society and should therefore be restricted under dictatorship of the proletariat. Although the CPC's first generation of collective leadership had met great difficulties in exploring the commodity economy, those explorations above represent the first step of the Party to break with the planned economy—an indispensable step in its way to explore a socialist market economy.

7.3.2.4 Assessment of Mao Zedong's Ideas on Socialist Stages of Development and China's Economic Development Strategy

7.2.3.4.1 Assessment of Mao Zedong's ideas on stages of development in socialist course

According to Mao Zedong, socialism and communism are different stages in economic development and China should undergo a long and complicated course to move from socialism to communism. He had stated on many occasions that socialism could also be divided into various stages of development. For instance, when reading *Soviet Union's Political Economy, Textbook* in late 1959 and early 1960, Mao Zedong had said, "Socialism can be divided into two stages: the first one is an underdeveloped stage and the second one is a longer and developed stage. At the end of the latter stage when there is vast material and cultural wealth in society and the people are well prepared for communism, our country can move into a communist society." When meeting with Field Marshal Montgomery Pipe Band in 1961, Mao Zedong had talked of leading one hundred years or longer to carry out socialist modernization. He had talked about this again at the conference attended by 7,000 comrades in January 1962.

Researchers have argued much on how to assess Mao Zedong's above ideas. According to most researchers, Mao Zedong had realized that China should greatly develop its productive forces to move from socialism to communism. He had repeatedly stressed the need to promote socialist transformation of the relations of production in order to accelerate development of the productive forces and the country's industrialization. He had realized the importance of developed productive forces for socialism and recognized the essence of socialism. His ideas had later inspired Deng Xiaoping to formulate the theory of the primary stage of socialism.

Other researchers have argued that the conditions under which Mao Zedong had advanced these ideas should be considered—Mao Zedong had put them forward to correct the mistake of confusing collective sector with state sector and socialism with communism and rushing to enter communism. They did play a role in correcting the "Left" mistake of premature leap toward communism. However, his understanding of socialism and communism had not exceeded that of classical Marxist writers, and he had not given a clear statement that China was still in the underdeveloped stage of socialism. As a result, "Left" mistakes still kept occurring. In conclusion, his ideas on stages of development in socialist course had only played a limited positive role in guiding socialist construction.

7.2.3.4.2 Assessment of Mao Zedong's ideas about China's economic development strategy

Mao Zedong's ideas on China's economic development strategy have two major points: first, China has a large population, a weak foundation, and backward economy and culture and is still in the underdeveloped stage of socialism; second, China can build socialism in two steps. He had said that, China had entered in the socialist society but had not built socialism, and it would take China three five-year plan periods to complete building of socialism, and as long as several decades, maybe five decades, to build it into a strong, highly industrialized country.

On the basis of Mao Zedong's above ideas, Zhou Enlai had stated the task of four modernizations at the First Session of the Third National People's Congress in 1964. He had also formulated the two steps to achieve this objective: the first step was creating an independent and relatively complete industrial system and national economic system; the second step was achieving modernization of agriculture, industry, national defense, and science and technology and making China's economy rank among the world's leading countries. Thereafter, industrialization target was replaced by the task of four modernizations as the objective for China's economic and social development. However, the Third National People's Congress had not set a deadline for attaining those two-step goals. At the Fourth National People's Congress in January 1975, Zhou Enlai had restated the objective of four modernizations and set a clear deadline for the two steps: to build an independent and relatively complete industrial system and national economic system within fifteen years, that is, before 1980; and to completely achieve four modernizations before the end of the century (the twentieth century).

Researchers generally have argued two different opinions on the above strategic plan for economic development. Most researchers affirm it, believing the objective of four modernizations and the two-step strategy for achieving it were important both in theory and in practice and have inspired Deng Xiaoping to formulate the theory of the primary stage of socialism and the three-step economic development strategy.

Other researchers have suggested a different opinion, holding that Mao Zedong did not clearly and sufficiently understand the economic backwardness in China and the fact that to overcome this situation would be a long and difficult process. Mao Zedong had once said, "I made it a point to state at the conference attended by 7,000 comrades that it would take us fifty or one hundred years or even still longer to build socialism. The reason I said that is that I wanted all the people to keep in mind that the bourgeoisie and class struggle still exist."[1] According to him, it would be a long process to build socialism because there was the risk that the bourgeoisie and capitalism would make a comeback. So it could be said that he had stressed class struggle because he wanted to make the process of building socialism shorter. He had also mentioned that unlike democratic revolution that lasted twenty-eight years, economic development could be completed in a shorter period of time, like twenty or twenty-two years. Those ideas clearly indicate he had not fully understood the protracted character of economic development and consequently strived to achieve quick results.

---

[1] Gu Longsheng, *Chronicle of Mao Zedong's Economic Ideas*, the CPC Central Committee Party School Publishing House, Beijing, 1993, p. 568.

7.4 Deeper Studies on the Theory of Socialist Construction

7.4.1 Summarization of Mao Zedong's Theory of Socialist Construction

Apart from the theory on contradictions in socialist society, the idea of a path for economic development suited to the Chinese conditions, and the idea of giving top priority to economic development that have been discussed above, researchers and scholars have also studied the following five points.

First, China had moved from new democracy to socialism and established a socialist economic system based on public ownership. In line with the general line for the transition period formulated in 1953, the country had completed the socialist transformation of private ownership of the means of production, eradicated the system of exploitation, and entered into the primary stage of socialism. The establishment of the socialist economic system basically—in the main—had laid the necessary economic foundation for material progress, cultural and ethical progress, and improvement of the socialist democracy and the socialist legal system.

Second, the CPC's first generation of collective leadership represented by Mao Zedong had established a framework for the political system of the People's Republic of China and laid the necessary theoretical foundation for the creation of a political system with Chinese characteristics. The system of the people's democratic dictatorship and the system of people's congresses are the basic systems of government. The system of multiparty cooperation and political consultation under the leadership of the CPC and the system of regional ethnic autonomy are basic supporting political systems. These systems determine the class character and organizational form of state power as well as social systems, inter-party relations, and government structure. The establishment and improvement of political systems with Chinese characteristics is an effective guarantee for carrying out socialist construction.

Third, the CPC has formulated a set of principles to mobilize all positive factors to build a socialist country, such as the principle of long-term co-existence and mutual oversight concerning inter-party relations, the principle of letting a hundred flowers bloom and a hundred schools of thought contend regarding cultural development, the principle for ethnic relations, the principle of properly handling the relationship between the central and local authorities, the principle of taking the interests of the three: state, collectives and individuals into consideration, and the principles and policies for science and technology and intellectuals.

Fourth, China has formulated an independent foreign policy of peace. China was a big and poor country, and independence in foreign affairs should be based on independence in economy. Therefore, the principle of relying mainly on our own efforts with external assistance subsidiary and the policy of building up the country through diligence and thrift should be upheld in order to raise China's international standing. China has formulated many principles and policies concerning foreign relations such as the Five Principles of Peaceful Co-existence and the policies of actively developing friendly relations with all countries to create a good external environment, opposing hegemony, supporting the just struggles of oppressed nations and peoples, and safeguarding world peace.

Fifth, party building should be strengthened as the party had become the ruling party to improve its leadership. Mao Zedong, Liu Shaoqi and Deng Xiaoping had all attached close attention to Party building. Mao Zedong had stated, "The force at the core leading our cause forward is the Chinese Communist Party." In order to strengthen the Party's leadership, the principle of democratic-centralism should be improved because it is a fine tradition of the Party with a bearing on the fate of the Party and the country. Mao Zedong, Liu Shaoqi, Deng Xiaoping and other major Party leaders had all stressed that the Party should improve itself as a ruling party ideologically, organizationally, institutionally and in work style.

7.4.2 How Other Members of the Party's First Generation of Collective Leadership Contributed to the Theory of Socialist Construction

Study on this issue was not on the stage in the 1980s. However, in the 1990s, a large number of researchers have studied this issue and produced numerous works. They have discussed how Liu Shaoqi, Zhou Enlai, Chen Yun and other Party leaders had contributed to the theory on socialist construction which proves that this theory is also a crystallization of the Party's collective wisdom.

Liu Shaoqi had developed the following ideas about socialist construction: diverse economic sectors including the private sector should be allowed to co-exist and develop; transformation of ownership should be in accord with the level of productive forces, and the businesses of independent handicrafts and vendors should be allowed to meet the needs of people's life after the completion of socialist transformation in the ownership of the means of production; the socialist economy should allow diversity and flexibility; local governments, enterprises and individuals should be allowed certain appropriate freedom in economic activities. Liu Shaoqi's above novel ideas were in conformity with the Party's principles for economic development; some of them can still guide today's economic practice.

Chen Yun had the following economic ideas: socialist construction should proceed from China's realities; make the scale of development commensurate with the national strength; the expanded reproduction should be carried out on the basis of simple reproduction; the relationship between improvement of people's lives and economic development should be properly handled; and he had proposed the idea of "three mainstays and three supplements" which was also mentioned above.

Zhou Enlai had the following ideas about socialist construction: agriculture is the foundation; the relations of production should be suitable to conditions in China; properly handle the relationship between national development and improvement of people's lives; the economy should be developed in an orderly, gradual and steady manner on the basis of overall arrangements and concerted efforts made by various departments.

Zhang Wentian had many valuable ideas about socialist construction, which was studied by many researchers. First of all, researchers have discussed his theories on socialism. In order to correct the mistakes of the Great Leap Forward and the "cultural revolution," he had said, "Our country's productive forces are still underdeveloped, so we will stay in the present stage of socialism for a very long period of time. The length of the revolution period could be neglected if compared to the time needed to move from socialism to communism. Today's stage of socialism is still very far from communism; it is incorrect to consider socialism and communism the same or attempt to enter communism without going through the present stage." During the "cultural revolution," he had courageously pointed out that the fundamental task of socialism was to develop the productive forces.

Second, researchers have also introduced his economic ideas, which include: administer economic affairs on the basis of economic laws, production costs should be calculated, and integrate the administration of political and economic affairs; both industrial and agricultural programs should strive to make profits, otherwise neither simple reproduction nor non-production (service producing) agencies could survive; it is undoubtedly desirable that workers produce more surplus labor for the society, but at the same time the material benefits they deserve should be effectively protected, and it is stupid and harmful to avoid talking about the economic and material interests of the proletariat and the people; economic measures, not administrative measures, should be taken to administer economic affairs.

The above theories and ideas on socialist construction by the Party's first generation of collective leadership had greatly contributed to the formation and development of Mao Zedong's theory on socialist construction and laid a theoretical foundation for the formation of Deng Xiaoping Theory.

7.4.3 Approaching Mao Zedong's Theory on Socialist Construction from Different Viewpoints

Since the 1990s, researchers and scholars, under the guidance of Deng Xiaoping Theory, have conducted an all-round study on Mao Zedong's theory on socialist construction, focusing on the fundamental task of socialism, the motive forces, external conditions and political guarantees for socialist development, and the issue of the re-unification of the motherland. They have produced a large number of papers such as "The Party's Leadership and Socialist Cultural and Ethical Progress" by Xing Bensi, "The Party's Great Change in Its Diplomatic Strategies around 1969" by Zhang Baojun, "Some Questions of Understanding in the Change of China's Ownership Structure in the 1950s" by Pang Song, "Discussion on Mao Zedong's Ideas about Liberating and Developing the Productive Forces" by Ding Junping, "The Party Policies on the Intellectuals during 1956-1966" by Yang Fengcheng, and "Democracy, Legal System and Rule of Law—How Mao Zedong, Deng Xiaoping and Jiang Zemin, Chose, Innovated and Developed the Principles for Running the Country" by Zhang Liqiang. These papers have discussed the wide content of Mao Zedong's theory on socialist construction from different viewpoints.

7.5 Analysis of the Mistakes in Socialist Construction

When studying Mao Zedong's positive ideas on socialist construction, researchers and scholars also have discussed the mistakes he had made in exploring a path for socialist construction as well as reasons behind these mistakes. They have objectively pointed out that the degree of maturity of a political party, a leader or a collective leadership is relative, not absolute. It is unrealistic to hope that the Party has prepared well and thoroughly established theories for all the stages in the revolution or would greatly develop its understanding in a short period of time. This is also true for the leaders. Undoubtedly, the CPC's first generation of collective leadership represented by Mao Zedong had achieved great achievements in exploring a path for socialist construction. However, what they had achieved were only relatively general principles that had not been fully elaborated, thus some of which changed or developed later. For instance, Mao Zedong's analyses on basic contradictions in socialist society were correct, but he had not defined the correct way to solve them. He had correctly understood the issues of focus in Party's work and stages of development in socialist course, but he had not clarified them definitely. All this had left room for mistakes. In addition, the Party had unconsciously used the experiences and methods gained in the past revolutionary wars to guide socialist construction, which had also led to mistakes.

7.5.1 Major Mistakes in Theoretical Exploration

7.5.1.1 Utopian Ideas That Outstripped the Stage of Social Development

To overcome the backward and poverty-stricken state in China and reach the level of developed countries as soon as possible was not only the demand of the Chinese people but also the ambition of the Party's first generation of collective leadership. However, such a strong desire to overtake developed countries had inevitably led to blind pursuit of high speed in development. Mao Zedong had stated that China should neither follow the old, western path of industrialization nor slavishly copy the Soviet model; rather, it should take a path of development suited to the Chinese conditions. An important reason behind this statement was to find a path of faster development. Theoretically, Mao Zedong had admitted that the country's economic development would be a long and arduous task; but in practice, he had believed that the course of economic development could be shortened by high speed in growth. According to some researchers, Mao Zedong had overlooked or knew very less about the objective laws governing economic development, and exaggerated or overestimated the role of people's dynamism in developing the productive forces. He had wrongly believed that the people could produce any miracle under the leadership of the Party if they have the enthusiasm, just like in the revolutionary wars of the past. Even one day of development in China could match development for twenty years in western countries. As a result, the country began to blindly pursue unrealistic high speed of development without considering the actual level of productive forces, which had led to imbalances in the national economy and hindered development of the productive forces. The reason behind theses mistakes was that the crucial role of the productive forces in social development was overlooked. The Great Leap Forward and the movement to establish people's communes had reflected utopian ideas from the very beginning, these movements had spread the "Left" mistakes around the country, and severely damaged socialist construction. Both, the "cultural revolution" and the theory that overemphasized development of forces of production were also utopian ideas that outstripped the stage of social development at that time.

7.5.1.2 The Principal Problem in Chinese Society and Expanding the Class Struggle

In regard to why Mao Zedong changed the Party's assessment of the principal problem at its Eighth Congress, researchers have different opinions. Most of them have argued that Mao Zedong had wrongly assessed the political situation. Since the anti-Rightist struggle in 1957, Mao Zedong had wrongly analyzed the situation in class struggle, denied the correct assessment made at the Party's Eighth Congress, and re-defined class struggle as the principal problem in Chinese society. The two types of contradictions differing in nature were increasingly confused, and the scope of class struggle was greatly broadened. Furthermore, Mao Zedong had incorrectly linked the so-called revisionism within the CPC with the intensified anti-China and anti-communist campaigns in the international political arena in the 1960s and 1970s and also the problems existing in the socialist camp. He had envisaged that mass movement methods should be utilized to completely solve these problems.

According to other researchers, the political situation was not the only reason behind Mao Zedong's changing his definition on the principal problem in Chinese society. The CPC's exploration of a path for socialist construction was also a major reason. Mao Zedong had suspected that all those who disagreed with him on the speed and objective of socialist construction were Rightists, anti-Party elements and anti-socialist elements or capitalist roaders in power in the Party and should be overthrown by applying dictatorship. During the "cultural revolution," a theory of continuing revolution under dictatorship of the proletariat had emerged on the basis of the slogan: "taking class struggle as the key link"; thus the class struggle was intensified to an unprecedented degree. According to Mao Zedong, class struggle was the key link while economic development was a subordinate aspect; socialist construction could proceed smoothly only after all enemies without guns were eliminated. These demonstrate that the mistake of expanding class struggle was due to mistakes in the exploration of a path for socialist construction.

7.5.1.3 Cognition on the Fundamental Nature of Socialism

To progress on the path of socialism, China should first of all solve the issue of what socialism is and how to build it. Mao Zedong had made mistakes in his later years because he had wrongly understood this issue.

First of all, "establishing large people's communes and building pure socialist economy" was wrongly regarded as the unquestionable nature of socialism. Mao Zedong was certainly aware of the backwardness prevalent in China's economy, and had once reasonably stated that certain capitalist sectors should be kept to help developing the economy. But that was contrary to communist party's overall objective of eliminating exploitation in any form. Eventually, he had denied the positive role of all kind of non-public sectors due to his dogmatic understanding on fundamental characteristics of socialism. Although it is definitely correct to abolish all exploiting classes and uphold the public ownership, some researchers have pointed out that the question whether private ownership could be completely eliminated in the stage of socialism still needs to be further discussed and answered by practice. Due to lack of a full understanding on unique features of socialist road in China, Mao Zedong had eventually denied the reasonable existence of any economic sector other than the public sector and advocated sole state sector; denied the system of distribution according to work, and necessary, rational income differences in the stage of socialism thus he had advocated equal distribution; rushed to move from socialism to communism.

Some researchers have also pointed out that a socialist economy should naturally include various other ownership forms. In the past, however, the relationship between the public sector and non-public sector was wrongly considered a struggle for survival. Before the policy of reform and opening up was introduced, the country had tried its best to eliminate private ownership, and the economic sectors that could invigorate the economy and satisfy people's needs was regarded as capitalism. Even, some operational and managerial methods which could suit to China's conditions were criticized and objected by classifying them as capitalism. As a result, neither were the productive forces developed, nor the socialist relations of production could be improved; on the contrary, "poverty and backwardness" became the nature of socialism, and the socialist system in the country could not demonstrate its innate superiority.

Second, too much focus was put on stressing the planned economy and differentiating or classifying what belongs to socialism and what belongs to capitalism in the economic sphere. It was long believed that a planned economy was the fundamental feature of socialism, while a market economy was peculiar to capitalism. Consequently, the planned economy was stressed, while market factors were rejected. Furthermore, the system of distribution according to work, commodity production, exchange based on currency and other economic forms which were in conformity with socialist nature were also categorized as capitalism and were rejected or restrained.

Third, overcautious attitude toward opening up had prevented China from drawing on the strong aspects of capitalism and utilizing them to serve socialist construction. As pointed out by some researchers, China had already begun to import equipment and technology from western countries before reform and opening up, but the country was often overcautious in doing so. In international economic exchanges, China had often stayed away or rejected things it thought belong to capitalism. When meeting with a group of guests from a western country in August 1970, Mao Zedong had said, "Our country is a socialist country. That means we should not run joint venture with you. This is clear." This statement indicates Mao Zedong thought that socialist China should neither use capitalist funds or technologies to develop its national economy nor allow foreign businesses to establish enterprises in China as joint or sole ownership basis. Undoubtedly, this idea of isolation from the rest of the world had adversely affected China's socialist construction.

In conclusion, when the Party had not correctly answered the fundamental question of what socialism is and how to build it; and not fully understood China's conditions in the primary stage of socialism, it could not be expected that the Party could formulate and lead a correct political line and stay away from mistakes on the questions of nature, fundamental task and central link of socialism.

7.5.2 Two Trends in the Exploration of Socialism

During the twenty-two years from 1956 to 1978, two trends, interrelated and contradictory, had emerged in the Party's exploration of a path for socialist construction. One trend had carried on and developed Mao Zedong's correct ideas in his "On the Ten Major Relationships" and "On the Correct Handling of Contradictions among the People" and the valuable theories of other members of the Party's first generation of collective leadership about socialist construction around the Party's Eighth Congress, while the other trend had deviated from and negated them. Many researchers have pointed out that achievements had co-existed with mistakes in the exploration process. The paper "On the Hard Exploration by the CPC's First Generation of Collective Leadership for a Path of Socialist Construction" by Huang Shaoqun et al. has divided the exploration course into a period of correct development and a period of development in twists and turns and evaluated the correct and wrong trends. The book *A Review of Study on Mao Zedong* edited by Shi Zhongquan has also discussed the two trends. However, only a few papers were published focusing on the study of the two trends. Among them, the paper "Investigation into the Two Trends in the CPC's Exploration for a Path of Socialist Construction" by Zeng Xiankai and Zhao Quanjun published in *Study of the History of the Communist Party of China* (No. 4, 1996) has introduced and discussed the two trends and produced some valuable ideas in detail, which includes the following:

First, both the two trends underwent two historical periods. They had co-existed during the first period, from the Party's Eighth National Congress to the eve of the "cultural revolution." During the second period, from the beginning of the "cultural revolution" to the Third Plenary Session of the Eleventh Party Central Committee, the wrong trend had developed into a wrong line and become dominant, but the correct trend had survived, though it was suppressed. This Session has made a turnaround by correcting the wrong trend.

Second, the two trends were guided by different ideologies, had advocated different theories, ideas, policies and principles, and had different understanding and analyses on the country's conditions in the primary stage of socialism, the principal problem in Chinese society, the Party's major task, principles for economic development and path of construction. In this course, the Party had not only acted more or less correctly under the guidance of generally correct theories and principles, but also acted incorrectly led by wrong theories, ideas and principles.

Third, the two trends have manifested two remarkable features. First, they have co-existed and were interwoven with each other. They have co-existed not only in the exploration and cognition of the entire Party but also in the mind of an individual. Some theoretical viewpoints were basically correct, but still imperfect; some were basically correct, but later went too far and became incorrect; some were basically incorrect but contained correct points. Second, the relationship between theory and practice in the existence of these trends were interestingly varied. On the one hand, correct theory could led to a correct practice, and incorrect theory had produced wrong practices. On the other hand, correct theory could not lead to correct practice if it was not fully implemented. A typical example—for the latter—throughout the two decades was the implementation of the principle of letting a hundred flowers bloom and a hundred schools of thought contend.

Fourth, the two trends have developed in opposite directions. The wrong trend eventually was ended through a worsening process. The correct trend has constantly overcome mistakes and eventually developed into correct line, policies and principles. After the Third Plenary Session of the Eleventh Party Central Committee in 1978, the Party's theories, line, principles and policies concerning the path for socialist development has progressed rapidly.

In conclusion, in the recent two decades, the studies on the theory of socialist construction developed by Mao Zedong and other members of the Party's first generation of collective leadership was has been deepened and broadened substantially. Theoreticians and researchers studying the history of the CPC have also studied a wide variety of issues in this regard and produced a numerous good works. But we can still raise a question: should Mao Zedong's theory of socialist construction be specifically defined? In other words, what should the contents of this theory include? Till today, researchers and scholars still have not given a definite answer to this question. It will be a too broad definition when we include the thoughts on building the Party as a ruling party and the Five Principles of Peaceful Coexistence in it. In terms of overall arrangements for socialist construction, many aspects and issues could be all related with socialist construction. Today as economic development has long been defined as the central task, study on this theory should focus on its ideas about economic development such as the Party's guiding ideology in economic work, development strategies and principles, and handling well the economic sectors possessing diverse forms of ownership. In short, today Mao Zedong's theory on socialist construction is still a focus among researchers and scholars, who generally believe that it has inspired the formation of the Chinese path for socialist modernization and the road of building socialism with Chinese characteristics.

References

Bo Yibo, *A Review of Major Decisions and Issues*, Vol. II, the CPC Central Committee Party School Publishing House, Beijing, 1993.

Gong Yuzhi, *On Twenty Issues of Socialism with Chinese Characteristics*, the CPC Central Committee Party School Publishing House, Beijing, 1995.

Zhou Cheng'en et al., *Mao Zedong's Exploration into China's Path of Socialist Construction*, Zhejiang People's Publishing House, Hangzhou, 1993.

Gu Longsheng (ed.), *Chronicle of Mao Zedong's Economic Ideas*, the CPC Central Committee Party School Publishing House, Beijing, 1993.

Zhu Yang and Guo Yongjun (eds.), *Mao Zedong's Theory of Socialism*, People's Publishing House, Beijing, 1994.

Lin Yunhui, "The Theory of Correct Handling of Contradictions among the People and Review of International Communist Movement," *Study of the History of the Communist Party of China*, 1997 (5).

Chen Lixu, "How Mao Zedong Understood the Principal Problem in Chinese Society around the Party's Eighth National Congress," *Journal of Shanxi Normal University*, 1997 (1).

Chen Xuewei, "Experience and Lessons in Modern China's Economic Construction," *Study of the History of the Communist Party of China*, 1994 (2).

Chen Xuewei, "Reflections on the Exploration and Establishment of a Path of Socialism with Chinese Characteristics," *Study of the History of the Communist Party of China*, 1995 (1).

Huang Rujun, "Mao Zedong's Exploration into China's Path of Socialist Construction during 1956-1966," *Study of the History of the Communist Party of China*, 1995 (2).

Huang Shaoqun and Wang Zhitang, "On the Hard Exploration by the

CPC's First Generation of Collective Leadership for a Path of Socialist Construction," *Party Literature*, 1997 (4).

Tong Changping, "A General Review of China's Socialist Construction in One Decade," *Study of the History of the Communist Party of China*, 1999 (4).

Yan Shuqun, "A Comparison of Mao Zedong's and Deng Xiaoping's Theories of Basic Contradictions in Socialist Society," *Humanities*, 2000 (1).

Zeng Xiankai and Zhao Quanjun, "Investigation into the Two Trends in the CPC's Exploration for a Path of Socialist Construction," *Study of the History of the Communist Party of China*, 1996 (4).

Chapter 8

Studies on the Living Soul of Mao Zedong Thought

The Resolution on Certain Questions in the History of Our Party Since the Founding of the People's Republic of China passed at the Sixth Plenary Session of the Eleventh CPC Central Committee in 1981 has clearly defined the living soul of Mao Zedong Thought: it is the stand, viewpoint and method that permeate to all components of Mao Zedong Thought. This stand, viewpoint and method include three basic points: seeking truth from facts, the mass line, and self-reliance. Researchers and scholars have attached great importance studies in this regard, especially on seeking truth from facts. They have explained why seeking truth from facts, the mass line, and self-reliance are the three basic points of the living soul, by investigating historical documents and conducting theoretical analysis from the perspective of philosophy, politics and Party building. They generally affirm that Mao Zedong had first introduced those three basic points in his essay "Oppose Book Worship" in May 1930.

The living soul is the most fundamental, crucial and vital aspect of a thing, and it permeates all other aspects. Seeking truth from facts, the mass line, and self-reliance are exactly the essence and core of Mao Zedong Thought. Representative research results in this regard are papers such as "Grasp the Living Soul of Mao Zedong Thought" by Jia Chunfeng, "Discussion on the Living Soul of Mao Zedong Thought" by Teng Wensheng and Jia Chunfeng, "On the Living Soul of Mao Zedong Thought" by the Marxism-Leninism Research Office in Guilin Army College, "Formation of the Three Basic Points in the Living Soul of Mao Zedong Thought and Their Relationships" by Huang Deyuan, "On the Living Soul of Mao Zedong Thought" by Sun Haigen, "Formulation of the Living Soul of Mao Zedong Thought and Its Three Basic Points" by Wang Shunsheng, and the book *On the Living Soul of Mao Zedong Thought* by Li Fengwu. These works have systematically studied the content of seeking truth from facts, the mass line, and self-reliance and their relationships and importance.

First, about the relationships among seeking truth from facts, the mass line, and self-reliance. It is generally agreed that seeking truth from facts, the mass line, and self-reliance are intimately interrelated and inseparably bound together and provide conditions for each other; together they comprise a dialectical unity of the stand, viewpoint and method of Mao Zedong Thought. First, they are all based on dialectical and historical materialism. Second, they all deal with the same fundamental problem as integrating the universal tenets of Marxism with the concrete realities of China's revolution. Seeking truth from facts answers the question of why Marxism should be integrated with the Chinese realities. The mass line answers the question of how to integrate Marxism with the Chinese realities by analyzing the forces for revolution and construction. Self-reliance defines the base and strategic principles for realizing the integration. Third, they are interdependent and complement each other. Seeking truth from facts is the fundamental point and at the core, while the mass line and self-reliance are its inevitable conclusions and fundamental guarantees. In other words, seeking truth from facts is a worldview and methodology and the essence of Mao Zedong Thought, the core point of the living soul, and the theoretical foundation for the mass line and self-reliance. The mass line and self-reliance are the fundamental requirement and essence of seeking truth from facts. In conclusion, they are a dialectical unity interdependence and restraining each other.

In order to seek truth from facts, we should proceed from the basic reality of people's lives and practice and integrate theories with people's activities. Therefore, respecting and relying on the masses is an inherent requirement of seeking truth from facts. At the same time, the mass line will become empty talk if the fundamental principle of seeking truth from facts is violated. Self-reliance means upholding the fundamental principle of seeking truth from facts, proceeding from China's realities and relying on the masses in the country's revolution and construction. The principle of seeking truth from facts cannot be realized in isolation neglecting mass line and self-reliance, which are its fundamental guarantees.

Second, the reason why seeking truth from facts, the mass line and self-reliance are the living soul of Mao Zedong Thought. Researchers have argued that there are three major reasons. First, they embody the basic tenets of Marxism and are the major results of applying Marxism in China. Consequently, they are the essence and core of Mao Zedong Thought. Second, they are the most fundamental stand, viewpoint and method developed by the Chinese Communists that permeate every component of the scientific system of Mao Zedong Thought. They are not ideas or methods designed to solve certain individual problems, but are the Party's fundamental ideologies, principles and methodologies for guiding China's revolution and construction. They are the stand, viewpoint and method, on which Mao Zedong Thought is based. Third, they are the fundamental guarantees for overcoming difficulties and leading the country's revolution and construction to success. In short, seeking truth from facts, the mass line, and self-reliance are the most fundamental and crucial ideas in Mao Zedong Thought. They have determined the course in which Mao Zedong Thought took shape and developed. They embody the unity in worldview and methodology between the essence of Mao Zedong Thought and the Party's line and its fine work style, and they are the powerful weapon that the Party and people can use to learn about and transform the world. In order to understand the essence of Mao Zedong Thought, first it is necessary understand well the three basic points.

Third, study on the three basic points. First, researchers generally agree that seeking truth from facts is not only an ideological line and method but also a work style. They have defined the dialectical unity between seeking truth from facts and emancipating the mind, thus they have critized the incorrect metaphysical idea which for a long time advocated that seeking truth from facts was antagonistic to emancipating the mind. Second, they have discussed the importance of investigations and studies on the mass line, and argued making investigations and studies are the basis to implement mass line. Finally, they have expounded the idea that independence and self-reliance, which means proceeding from China's realities, integrating the universal tenets of Marxism with the Chinese conditions, and relying on the broad masses, and finding a path for revolution and construction suited to Chinese conditions, are the inevitable conclusions derived from seeking truth from facts and the mass line.

Some researchers have also argued that the living soul of Mao Zedong Thought has four notable features: first, it is scientific; second, it is revolutionary; third, it is practical; fourth, it is suited to China.

Other researchers have suggested that in addition to the above three basic points, the living soul of Mao Zedong Thought should also include the spirit of innovation. And some have proposed that it should even include the idea of liberating and developing the productive forces.

8.1 Studies on the Principle of Seeking Truth from Facts

8.1.1 The Content and Essence of Seeking Truth from Facts

The following opinions were advanced in this regard.

(1) Seeking truth from facts is the result of understanding the basic problem of philosophy in China. Mao Zedong had not overemphasize the materialist principle that matter is primary and consciousness is secondary. On the contrary, he had rather focused on elaborating and discussing the most common relationship between subjective and objective, thus enriching the content of the basic problem of philosophy.

(2) Seeking truth from facts is a materialist idea. Mao Zedong had believed that "facts" are all the things that exist objectively and "seek truth" means to study their internal relations, that is, the laws governing them. In other words, he had emphasized the materialist principle that matter is primary and consciousness is secondary and the idea that everything could be known. This means the essence of seeking truth from facts is materialism.

(3) Seeking truth from facts is an epistemological idea. By creating this principle, Mao Zedong had greatly developed the Marxist theory of knowledge.

(4) Seeking truth from facts is a unity of materialism, dialectics and epistemology and embodies their principles.

(5) Seeking truth from facts is a unity of materialism, dialectics, epistemology and methodology, embodying basic principles of dialectical and historical materialism.

8.1.2 The Historical Development of Seeking Truth from Facts

The history of development of that principle as seeking truth from facts is also the history in which the CPC was founded, developed and expanded and the Chinese revolution occurred, developed and came to victory. It took shape and developed in the struggle against idealistic and metaphysic mistaken ideas. Historical facts have demonstrated that whenever the Party followed the ideological line of seeking truth from facts, China's revolution and construction has succeeded and developed; whenever the Party deviated from this line, the country's revolution and construction had regressed and suffered setbacks. The essence of seeking truth from facts and the law of its development should be understood on the basis of this historical fact.

8.1.3 The Reason for the Formation of the Principle of Seeking Truth from Facts

(1) Class foundation. The revolutionary tasks at that time have required the people to understand the relations between classes, tactics for struggle and the revolution's main motive forces and distinguishing friends from enemies, which necessiated through investigations and studies. Consequently, the principle of seeking truth from facts was created to help people better understand class relations, and it has inevitably embodied the interests, demand and future of revolutionary classes. This is its class foundation.

(2) Party spirit. Mao Zedong in his essay "Oppose Book Worship" had criticized the opposite of seeking truth from facts. He had said that it is disgraceful for a Communist to be opinionated and keep his eyes shut and talk irresponsibly; the ideas of rigidly worshiping books and following established methods were absolutely wrong and have nothing in common with the idea that Communists should create favorable new situations through struggle. In his essay "Reform our Study," Mao Zedong had defined the idea of seeking truth from facts. He said that seeking truth from facts is the manifestation of Party spirit, the Marxist-Leninist work style of uniting theory and practice, and an attitude that every Communist Party member should have in the minumum.

(3) Ideological source. Mao Zedong had read Chinese classical literature widely and paid close attention to ancient Chinese thought and culture. The realistic style of Liu De recorded in the *History of the Earlier Han Dynasty* by Ban Gu, a celebrated Chinese historian in the first century A.D., was fully manifested in Mao Zedong's "Oppose Book Worship" and was raised to the level of a philosophical issue in his article "Reform our Study," which had discussed it as an issue of dialectical materialism. This indicates that Mao Zedong's idea of seeking truth from facts had emerged from the soil of ancient Chinese thinking and culture.

(4) Understanding reason. Only by "seeking truth" from "facts", honestly and comprehensively understanding all objective things without any subjective impression or prejudice, can Mao Zedong and other Chinese

Communists really seek truth from facts. This is the understanding reason.

8.1.4 How to Seek Truth from Facts

The following opinions were advanced in this regard.

(1) There are four points. First, uphold the correct stand, viewpoint and method—the stand of the proletariat, the people and the Party and the viewpoint and method of dialectical and historical materialism. Second, opposing both "Left" and "Right" mistakes. Third, probe deep into reality, carry out investigations and studies, better understand the actual conditions, correctly analyze situations, and get to know the true character and nature of the situation in order to formulate correct tactics and methods for struggle. Fourth, uphold the principle that practice is the sole criterion for testing truth.

(2) There are four necessities. The first necessity is to uphold the principle of emancipating the mind in order to make thinking conform to reality and the subjective conform to the objective. The second is to uphold the Four Cardinal Principles. The third is to simultaneously oppose "Left" and "Right" mistakes. The fourth is to correctly handle the relationship between the interests of the part and those of the whole by subordinating the part to the whole.

(3) There are five necessities. The first necessity is to uphold the basic tenets of Marxism-Leninism and Mao Zedong Thought. The second is to adhere to correct political orientation and viewpoint. The third is to probe deep into reality and carry out investigations and studies. The fourth is to uphold Party spirit, putting facts before everything else and contributing to seeking truth. The fifth is to set up and implement good organizational systems.

8.1.5 Seeking Truth from Facts in Mao Zedong Thought and Deng Xiaoping Theory

8.1.5.1 It Is the Essence of Both Mao Zedong Thought and Deng Xiaoping Theory

Both Mao Zedong Thought and Deng Xiaoping Theory uphold the ideological line of seeking truth from facts. The idea of seeking truth from facts has become the ideological line of the Party immediately after it was formulated by Mao Zedong as an idea of dialectical materialism. It is the essence of Mao Zedong Thought, which permeates the complete theoretical system of Mao Zedong Thought, and is the fundamental basis and starting point for the Party's line, principles and policies. In his well-known essay "Oppose Book Worship" in May 1930, Mao Zedong had stressed, "Of course we should study Marxist books, but this study should be integrated with our country's actual conditions." Mao Zedong had never worshiped books; in stead, he had proceeded from reality in integrating the universal truth of Marxism with realities in the Chinese revolution. It is precisely for this reason that he had found a path to victory.

Deng Xiaoping upheld the ideological line of seeking truth from facts as well. He had stressed that this line requires not only proceeding from actual conditions and integrating theory with practice but also testing and developing truth in practice. This line is the essence of Deng Xiaoping Theory and permeates all its components. By adhering to this line, Deng Xiaoping had formulated a path for building socialism with Chinese characteristics.

8.1.5.2 Comparison of Mao Zedong's and Deng Xiaoping's Ideas of Seeking Truth from Facts

First, Mao Zedong's idea of seeking truth from facts stresses through investigations and studies. Mao Zedong had always attached great importance to investigations and studies throughout his revolutionary career. He had advanced a clear idea of knowing the Chinese society as early as in 1919 when he had published an essay in *Xiangjiang Review*. In 1920, he had further stated that the Chinese should conduct field investigations to better understand conditions in China. His essay "Analysis of the Classes in Chinese Society" published in 1925 was an influential investigation report. In 1927, he wrote the "Report on an Investigation of the Peasant Movement in Hunan," which was a programmatic document for guiding peasant movements, he had prepared this work on the basis of a first-hand investigation of conditions in five counties in Hunan Province. Thereafter, he had solved the problem of path for China's revolution on the basis of overall investigations and studies related political and economic situations in China. During that period, he had written his well-known essay "Oppose Book Worship," in which he had enunciated the famous proposition, "No investigation, no right to speak." He had stressed, "Of course we should study Marxist books, but this study should be integrated with our country's actual conditions." "Victory in China's revolutionary struggle will depend on the Chinese comrades' understanding of Chinese conditions." In order to overcome subjectivism and strenghten the ideological line of seeking truth from facts in the Party, Mao Zedong wrote the essay "Reform our Study," in which he had stressed that investigations and studies are the criterion for differentiating between subjectivism and Marxism-Leninism and defined the unity between seeking truth from facts and investigations and studies. Mao Zedong had also discussed the importance of conducting investigations and studies to make the subjective conform to the objective and theory conform to practice from the perspective of the Marxist theory of knowledge and dialectics. In addition, Mao Zedong had discussed the attitudes and methods in investigations and studies by stating that conclusions invariably come after investigation, and not before. This is very important for acquiring a correct understanding and seeking truth from facts.

Second, Deng Xiaoping's idea of seeking truth from facts stresses emancipating the mind. After the "cultural revolution," the ten-year disaster, China had moved from chaos to stability and construction, and the Party needed to find a socialist road fitting China's characteristics. Deng Xiaoping was confronted with two historical tasks: opposing the erroneous principle of the "two whatevers" and rectifying the erroneous ideological and political lines; emancipating the mind, overcoming the dogmatic understanding of Marxist principles, promoting reform and opening up, and building socialism with Chinese characteristics. To accomplish such great tasks, Deng Xiaoping has upheld the basic principle of emancipating the mind all along his efforts in restoring and implementing the Party's ideological line of seeking truth from facts. His idea of emancipating the mind was formulated to correct the mistake of "two whatevers" and break through prevalent rigid thinking. He had stressed that the "two whatevers" does not accord with Marxism, and that the Party should eliminate the harmful influences of Lin Biao and the Gang of Four, set things right and cast off mental shackles in order to really emancipate the mind. He had combined emancipating the mind with seeking truth from facts, holding that they are two indispensable aspects of one issue. Emancipating the mind means throwing off the shackles of the force of old habits and subjective prejudice by the guidance of Marxism, studying new situations and solving new problems, making thinking conform to reality and the subjective conform to the objective, and applying seeking truth from facts. He had said, "if we want to be practical and realistic in all our work, we should continue to emancipate our minds".

Some researchers have compared Mao Zedong's and Deng Xiaoping's ideas related to seeking truth from facts from several aspects such as: the role, target and content in their ideas.

In terms of their roles, Mao Zedong's idea of seeking truth from facts had long before become the ideological line of the Party, while Deng Xiaoping has restored this ideological line which was strongly abandoned for ten years.

In terms of their targets, Mao Zedong had put forward the idea of seeking truth from facts during the rectification movement in Yan'an to oppose subjectivism. Subjectivism could take the form of dogmatism, which worships Marxist works and scorns reality, or take the form of empiricism, which blindly restricts itself on particular experience and distains theory, with the former causing more harm at that time. The Yan'an rectification movement was indeed launched to oppose subjectivism, especially Wang Ming's dogmatic ideas. But when restoring and re-establishing the ideological line of seeking truth from facts, Deng Xiaoping had first aimed to correct the mistake of "two whatevers."

In terms of their content, Mao Zedong had integrated his idea of seeking truth from facts with making through investigations and studies, which are the basis for and require seeking truth from facts. Deng Xiaoping has integrated his idea of seeking truth from facts with emancipating the mind; emancipating the mind is a precondition for seeking truth from facts, and seeking truth from facts is the basis for emancipating the mind.

8.1.6 Comparing Mao Zedong's and Deng Xiaoping's Theories on Emancipating the Mind

Researchers have made some fresh progress in studying Mao Zedong's theory of emancipating the mind. Their opinions include the following points.

(1) There are four phases in the course of formation of Mao Zedong's theory of emancipating the mind. The first period was from the August 7th Meeting in 1927 to the Zunyi Meeting in 1935, during which Mao Zedong had initially introduced the idea of emancipating the mind. The second period was from the Zunyi Meeting in 1935 to the publication of Mao Zedong's "On Practice" and "On Contradiction," during which he had deepened this idea and advanced it into a theory. The third period, namely the period of rectification movement in Yan'an, had witnessed the systematic development of this theory. The fourth period was the period of socialist construction from the late 1950s to the early 1960s, during which he had formulated a complete theory of emancipating the mind by integrating theory with practice on the basis of reviewing the experience of international communist movement, and also the process of exploring the path of socialist construction suited to the country's conditions.

(2) Deng Xiaoping has carried forward and developed Mao Zedong's theory of emancipating the mind in the new period. At the same time, Deng Xiaoping has greatly elevated this theory. First, in order to bring order out of the chaos in the Party's ideological line and meet the needs of the new period, he has elevated emancipating the mind from a theory and task to a theory and political theme which marked the beginning of the new period in China. He has stressed the importance of emancipating the mind in solving new problems, creating new environments and building the Party and the country.

Second, Deng Xiaoping has elevated the idea of emancipating the mind from a component of seeking truth from facts to an important ideological line principle. He has stressed that emancipating the mind and seeking truth from facts are in accord with each other and are two aspects of one issue. According to him, emancipating the mind means making thinking conform to reality and the subjective conform to the objective and seeking truth from facts. He has upgraded the ideological line of seeking truth from facts advanced by Mao Zedong to an ideological line formulated as emancipating the mind and seeking truth from facts.

Third, he has re-defined the role of emancipating the mind from serving the rectification movements to employ it for improving systems in the Party and government. He has emphasized that the principle of democratic centralism should be upheld and improved in order to truly emancipate minds. If it could be said that Mao Zedong urged all Party members to emancipate their minds and work in a practical and realistic manner, it should be said that Deng Xiaoping, besides carrying forward Mao Zedong's ideas, has re-defined the ideological line of emancipating the mind and seeking truth from facts as an organizational system of the Party. For him, this line has fundamental and overall significance and needs to be implemented for a long time to come.

(3) There are both similarities and differences between Mao Zedong's and Deng Xiaoping's ideas on emancipating the mind.

First, they have both stressed the importance of emancipating the mind, both advocating that emancipating the mind involves proceeding from reality and working in a practical and realistic manner to create a new situation in the revolution and construction. Consequently, they have both advocated practice to emancipate people's minds. At the same time, there are differences as well. Mao Zedong had primarily regarded emancipating the mind as an issue or basic task in philosophical studies, and secondly as an important task for the Party. Whereas Deng Xiaoping has believed that it should pave the way for a new period and would have a direct bearing on the Party's and the country's success or failure.

Second, they have both opposed understanding Marxism dogmatically and deifying the experience in other countries. In detail, Mao Zedong had opposed book worship, which could be solved by correct ways of thinking. Deng Xiaoping has opposed not only book worship and personality cult but also blind faith in the traditional socialist model and mode of thinking, which were more difficult to overcome because they involved both theoretical education and adjustment of interest relationships among various strata in the society.

Third, they have both focused on thoroughly understanding the basic theoretical issue of what Marxism is and how to develop it and stressed the importance of distinguishing between true Marxism and false Marxism, between creative Marxism and dogmatic Marxism, and between the essence of Marxism and Marxist statements. However, Deng Xiaoping has believed that the solution on the problem of what socialism is and how to build it is crucial for correctly understanding and developing Marxism, and he has consequently focused on this question as the major task of emancipating the mind in the new period.

Fourth, they have both stressed the importance of studying Marxism and conducting investigations and studies. Mao Zedong had integrated emancipating the mind with improving the Party's work style through rectification movements. Deng Xiaoping, besides supporting rectification movements, integrated emancipating the mind with improving the systems of the Party and the government, believing that sound systems could be the fundamental guarantees for emancipating the mind.

Fifth, they have both believed that emancipating the mind means seeking truth from facts, integrating theory with practice and making the subjective conform to objective, and they have consequently both stressed that the effect of emancipating the mind should be tested by practice and development of the productive forces. However, Deng Xiaoping has further advanced a more mature criterion and defined it as "three favorables" in order to meet the needs of reform and opening up and modernization.

Sixth, they have both stressed that all Party members should use their heads and dare to think. In order to deepen reform and open wider to the outside world, Deng Xiaoping has further advanced that all Party members and the people should fundamentally change their way of thinking and change their values in order to meet the needs of transforming from a planned economy to a socialist market economy.

8.2 Studies on the Theory of the Mass Line

8.2.1 The Mass Line as a Unique Innovation Created by Chinese Communists

This issue has been argued over long years. The Resolution on Certain Questions in the History of Our Party Since the Founding of the People's Republic of China in 1981 had first stated that the mass line was a unique innovation by Chinese Communists and the result of practically applying in China the Marxist-Leninist theory which advocates it is the people who make history. The mass line is manifested in Mao Zedong's works and Party documents, permeates the entire revolutionary experience of Chinese Communists, and has greatly enriched and developed Marxism-Leninism.

8.2.2 The Content of the Mass Line

There are two different views in this regard. The first view holds that the mass line consists of the mass viewpoint and the mass line (leadership method). Liu Shaoqi, in the Report on the Revision of the Party Constitution at the CPC's Seventh Congress in 1945, was the first to clearly state that the Party's mass line is made up of two points: the mass viewpoint and the line's leadership principle as "from the masses, to the masses." Deng Xiaoping had repeated the above two points in his report to the CPC's Eighth Congress on the revision of its Constitution in 1956. Liu Shaoqi had given a second similar definition in his "Speech at an Enlarged Working Conference of the Central Committee of the Party" in 1962. In the Resolution on Certain Questions in the History of Our Party Since the Founding of the People's Republic of China passed in June 1981, the Party Central Committee had succinctly summarized the mass line as the principle of "doing everything for the masses and relying on the masses in everything; from the masses, to the masses."

The other view holds that the mass line includes not only the mass viewpoint and mass line but also mass work. The mass work is an important part of Party's leadership work. It means educating the mass in Marxism-Leninism and Mao Zedong Thought in order to organize and unite with them in the struggle to achieve their own interests; drawing upon the wisdom and experience of the masses and formulating lines, principles and policies to protect their fundamental interests; leading and supporting the people as masters of their country so that they can exercise their right to participate in the management of state and social affairs, give full play to their historical spirit of initiative, and help achieving the great historical task of the proletariat.

8.2.3 It Is the People Who Make History

That it is the people who make history is a basic theoretical idea in the mass line.

However, in 1984 some researchers have questioned this proposition by advancing three reasons. First, neither Marx and Engels nor Lenin had ever said so; it was an exagarated idea borrowed by Soviet philosophers from the book *History of the Communist Party of the Soviet Union (Bolsheviks)* and was therefore a misunderstanding of Marxism. Second, it was developed by a Chinese historian Fan Wenlan into the idea that the people are the masters of history, an idea that did not conform to reality and caused severe damage to society during the "cultural revolution." Third, Marx, Engels and other classical Marxist writers had always said that men make their own history, but in fact they cannot control their fate and make history before class differences are completely eradicated and before all men enjoy complete equality.

The above view is rejected by many researchers, who generally suggest the following two different opinions.

Most of them have argued that it is the people who make history is an issue of principal on which we should not vacillate. First, Marx, Engels, Lenin and other classical Marxist writers all have confirmed the role of ideological motive in creating history and stressed that only the people's motive or a motives driving them to act can really make history. This motive, subject of production development, people's economic interests and activities, provide the correct way to find out the law governing historical development. Consequently, that it is the people who make history is a fundamental principle of historical materialism and an indispensable scientific methodology for studying historical development. Second, as a historical concept, "people" could include some exploiting classes or some of their members in certain specific historical periods. Third, historical development should be considered as a dialectical unity of necessity and contingency; it is the people's production and activity and not the activity of emperors that shape the course of social and economic evolution. So, the principle that it is the people who make history is not a dogma that can explain all the particular occasions in history, but a general guide for finding out the law behind all these occasions.

Others, disagreeing with both the above two views, have argued that the correct formulation should be "the people are the driving force that creates history." First, mankind altogether, not the people alone, creates history. It makes sense to conclude that the people make history because everyone participates in this process, but it is incorrect to assert that only the people make history. Of course, the people are always the main force for making history. Mao Zedong had once said, "The people, and the people alone, are the motive force in the world history." Second, in the course of historical development, there are both forces pushing history forward and forces hindering historical progress, and the result of the struggle between those two types of forces is the creation of new history. In terms of the general course of social development, the positive forces always outweigh the negative forces, enabling the human society to move forward forever. This also manifests that the people are the main force for making history and developing the society.

8.2.4 The Mass Line and Mass Movements

In his investigative report "Report on an Investigation of the Peasant Movement in Hunan" in 1927, Mao Zedong had discussed the three alternatives in dealing with mass movements: To march at their head and lead them? To trail behind them, gesticulating and criticizing? Or to stand in their way and oppose them? In his report "On Coalition Government" in 1945, Mao Zedong had also opposed the two mistakes in dealing with mass movements: commandism that overstepped the level of political consciousness of the masses and tailism that fell below the level of their political consciousness. His above statements was proved correct by China's practice in the revolutionary war and socialist transformation.

However, during the period from 1958 to the end of the "cultural revolution," the mass line was almost replaced by the idea that "it is just and desirable to launch mass movements" as interpreted by "Left" ideas. The so-called "mass movement" was spread from the economic field to the political sphere and was expanded hugely, causing widespread damages to the people.

As erroneous ideological and political ideas were corrected after the Third Plenary Session of the Eleventh Party Central Committee, researchers have begun to re-explore the relationship between the mass line and mass movement. The *Annotations to Resolution on Certain Questions in the History of Our Party Since the Founding of the People's Republic of China* (revised edition) had pointed out as follows: "After the founding of the People's Republic, many movements launched in the form of mass movement had in fact contravened the wishes and interests of the masses, which was a major reason for the mistakes in the economic and political spheres. The heavy losses caused to the country's revolution by the 'cultural revolution' were fundamentally the result of the so-called 'mass movements' that had largely deviated from the mass line."

8.2.5 The Content of Mass Viewpoint

In the Report on the Revision of the Party Constitution at the CPC's Seventh Congress in 1945, Liu Shaoqi had defined viewpoints concerning the masses as follows: "It is the viewpoint of doing everything in the interests of the people and of serving them wholeheartedly; the viewpoint of being responsible to the people; the viewpoint of believing in the self-emancipation of the people; and the viewpoint of learning from the people." The above summarization is still accepted by most researchers today.

The Decision of the CPC Central Committee on "Strengthening the Party's Ties with the People" in 1990 had made another summarization: "the viewpoint that the people create history; the viewpoint of learning from the people; the viewpoint of serving the people wholeheartedly; the viewpoint that all power cadres possess is given to them by the people; the viewpoint that being responsible to the Party means being responsible to the people; and the viewpoint that the Party should rely on the people and educate and guide them in advancing forward".

In addition, some researchers have recently put forward a new opinion that Mao Zedong's theory concerning the masses can be summarized into five basic points: conserving manpower; improving the people's lives; promoting democracy; pooling the people's wisdom;and development should be for the people.

8.2.6 The Historical Periods in the Development of the Mass Line

Some researchers have argued that there are six periods in the development of the mass line: (1) 1921-1927, emerged; (2) 1927-1935, took shape; (3) 1935-1945, got mature; (4) 1945-1957, developed orderly; (5) 1957-1978, developed in twists and turns; (6) and since 1978, returned to the correct direction and continued to develop.

According to other researchers, the mass line had emerged first in the Party's Constitution passed at its Second National Congress in 1922; it was shaped as the Party had established close relations with the masses in the struggle against the white terror and in the counter-campaigns against the KMT's encirclement and suppressions after the failure of the Great Revolution in 1927; it was elevated to a scientific theory and had become mature during the War of Resistance against Japan.

Still other researchers have argued that the mass line had emerged and progressed during the period from 1921 to 1937, and was shaped completely and had become a systematic theory from 1937 to 1949.

With regard to when the mass line had emerged, there are three different opinions. One, it had emerged at the Party's Second Congress, by the resolution on Party's organizational constitution passed, which stated, "All Party members should go down and be among the masses in all their work." Two, it had emerged before the CPC was founded. When Mao Zedong had published his essay "The Great Union of the Popular Masses" in *Xiangjiang Review* in the summer of 1919, in which he had advanced the slogan that the "great union of the popular masses have the strongest power". Three, it had emerged before the founding of the Party when Communist groups across the country had established close ties with the workers in running evening schools for them, establishing workers' organizations and educating them in Marxism by periodicals.

8.2.7 The Symbols Indicating the Maturity of the Mass Line

There are three opinions in this regard. One, Mao Zedong's essay "Some Questions Concerning Methods of Leadership" in 1943 was the symbol that the mass line had become mature. Two, Mao Zedong's report "On Coalition Government" and Liu Shaoqi's Report on the Revision of the Party Constitution at the Party's Seventh Congress in 1945 were the signs, because in those two reports the methods of the mass line were integrated with the mass viewpoint. Three, Mao Zedong's essay "Be Concerned with the Well-Being of the Masses, Pay Attention to Methods of Work" in January 1934 was the sign. In this essay, Mao Zedong had purposefully integrated the methods of the mass line with the mass viewpoint. This last opinion accords with the idea of Mao Zedong himself. The mass line was given a standard formulation in 1943 and was elevated to a complete theory in 1945.

8.2.8 Mao Zedong's Theory Related to the People During the Socialist Period

For some time, researchers and scholars have believed that Mao Zedong had deviated from the correct mass line and mass viewpoint during the socialist period, which led to his incorrect idea on "great democracy" and the tragedy of the "cultural revolution." After entering the 1990s, however, researchers have started to reconsider and re-evaluate Mao Zedong's theory related to the people during the socialist period. They have argued that many ideas in that theory were correct and positive and should be analyzed in line with specific conditions. They have suggested the following opinions.

(1) After the founding of New China, Mao Zedong had incorporated the mass line into the state governance system and integrated it with efforts to build, consolidate and develop a socialist system. In particular, he had stressed the importance of defending and promoting people's enthusiasm for building socialism and defined the mass line as an effective method for correctly handling contradictions among the people.

(2) He had stressed that in order to implement the correct mass line, leaders at all levels should go to the people, live among them, work with them, and maintain close ties with them so that correct policies can be formulated.

(3) He had advocated the sovereignty of the people and their equal participation in political affairs. He had stressed that the Party and the people are of one mind, the people are always the main force making history, and the Party is the spearhead leading them to liberation. However, he did not handle this issue well, allowing it to lead to uncontrollable mass movements and dictatorship of the masses.

(4) He had stressed the role of the people in economic development and advocated equalitarianism. He believed that the people's equality in the economic field is the basis for their equality in political affairs, which is undoubtedly correct. However, his pursuit of equalitarianism was an utopian idea divorced from reality.

8.2.9 How Deng Xiaoping Enriched and Developed the Mass Line

Generally researchers agree that Deng Xiaoping has enriched and developed the mass line in the following four aspects.

First, he has defined the intrinsic relationship between the mass line and the principle of seeking truth from facts: "Implementing the mass line is the fundamental way of upholding the principle of seeking truth from facts, and upholding the principle of seeking truth from facts is the ideological guarantee for implementing the mass line. They are interdependent and they complement each other."

Second, he has defined the correct relationship between leaders and the people: "The role of leaders should be stressed, but should not be exaggerated; leaders should be respected, but should not be deified, and personality cult of leaders should be opposed. In short, both leaders and the people should be properly respected."

Third, he has integrated believing in and relying on the masses with educating and guiding them.

Fourth, he has confirmed the position of intellectuals and categorized them under the working class, advancing that the only difference between intellectuals and manual workers is that they do different work in society. Thus the definition of people was broadened.

8.3 Studies on the Theory of Self-Reliance

8.3.1 The Formation and Development of the Theory of Self-Reliance

According to some researchers, the Party's Fourth Congress and Mao Zedong's "Analysis of the Classes in Chinese Society" and "Report on an Investigation of the Peasant Movement in Hunan" had included the ideas about self-reliance. After the failure of the Great Revolution, the mistake of dogmatically understanding Marxism-Leninism and deifying the Communist International's instructions and Soviet experience, for which Wang Ming was the principal cause, had occurred in the Party concerning the path for the Chinese revolution. In the bitter struggle against this mistake, Mao Zedong had developed the theory of self-reliance. He had first clearly put forth this principle at the Luochuan meeting (a meeting of the Political Bureau of the Party Central Committee in August 1937). Thereafter, he had further discussed the content, purpose and significance of seeking independence and initiative in the anti-Japanese national united front in his essays such as "The Situation and Tasks in the Anti-Japanese War after the Fall of Shanghai and Taiyuan" and "The Question of Independence and Initiative within the United Front." Consequently, the theory of self-reliance gradually had become a systematic and scientific principle that the entire Party purposefully adhered to. Mao Zedong had further enriched and developed this theory by advancing the principle of relying mainly on our own efforts and taking external assistance as supplementary during the socialist construction period.

According to some researchers, Mao Zedong's theory of self-reliance had undergone three periods of development. The first period was from May 1930 to January 1935, during which the idea of making revolution independently was firstly put forward and applied. The second period, from January 1935 to October 1949, had witnessed the Party's efforts to apply and develop the principle of being independent and self-reliant. The third period was from October 1949 to present, during which the Party upheld the principle of being independent and self-reliant after becoming the ruling party and shifted its focus from seeking state power to developing the economy.

Other researchers have argued that the course in which Mao Zedong's theory of self-reliance took shape and developed can be divided into five periods. The first period was from the failure of the Great Revolution to the eve of the War of Resistance against Japan. During this period, Mao Zedong had stated, "oppose book worship," "no investigation, no right to speak," and "victory in China's revolutionary struggle will depend on the Chinese comrades' understanding of Chinese conditions." This was the first time that the CPC had developed a theory of being independent and self-reliant. It was under the guidance of this theory that the Chinese Communists represented by Mao Zedong had analyzed China's realities by Marxism and found the path of establishing revolutionary bases in rural areas and seizing state power by armed force.

The second period was throughout the War of Resistance against Japan. During this period, Mao Zedong had resisted the pressures from within the Party and the Communist International, and formulated a general line for the anti-Japanese war, upheld the principle of being independent and self-reliant in the anti-Japanese national united front, opposed the new-capitulationism of doing "everything through the united front" and blindly copying directives from the Communist International, and resisted to the Soviet national egoism. It was by doing so that the Party had effectively established and developed anti-Japanese democratic base areas behind the enemy lines, independently carried out guerrilla war against Japanese forces, and won the first great victory against foreign invasion since the Opium War.

The third period was during the War of Liberation. After the end of the anti-Japanese war, there was a tendency in the international communist movement that urged the Chinese revolutionary forces to yield to the compromise reached between international big powers in Yalta Conference. The CPC lead by Mao Zedong had resisted the international pressure, waged tit-for-tat struggles against Chiang Kai-shek and against the KMT supported by the United States, and finally achieved victory of the Chinese revolution.

The fourth period was from the founding of New China to the completion of the socialist transformation. After New China was founded and the national economy began to recover, the Party was faced with the new problem of moving from new democracy to socialism. Mao Zedong had solved this problem by adhering to the principle of independence and self-reliance. He had found the path of socialist transformation of private ownership of the means of production suited to China's conditions and successfully established socialist system in economically and culturally backward China.

The fifth period was after the completion of the socialist transformation. With regard to the issue of how to build socialism, Mao Zedong had advanced the principle of relying mainly on our own efforts with external assistance supplementary and stressed that China should proceed from its realities and take a path of industrialization with Chinese characteristics by relying on its own strength. In addition, New China has always adhered to an independent foreign policy in foreign relations.

Still other researchers have argued that the course in which the theory of self-reliance was developed can be divided into four periods according to the living soul of Mao Zedong Thought: it had emerged during 1921-1927; taken shape during 1927-1935; matured during 1935-1945; and continued to develop after 1945.

8.3.2 The Components and Significance of the Theory of Self-Reliance

Researchers and scholars have suggested the following opinions in this regard.

(1) The theory has a strategic significance. Being independent and self-reliant is of critical importance for a proletarian party in any country that strived to lead the country's revolution, because only by doing so can it proceed from the country's realities, integrate the universal tenets of Marxism-Leninism with the country's conditions and find a revolutionary road suited to the country.

(2) The theory is made up of two components. They are: in China's revolution and construction, relying on the country's own strength and independently following a path of revolution and construction suited to China's conditions; also in foreign relations, pursuing an independent foreign policy and at the same time respecting other countries' right of independence.

(3) The theory consists of three components. They are: first, seeking independence and initiative in the united front when dealing with inter-class relations; second, adhering to the integration of proletarian patriotism and internationalism in foreign relations, which also include state-to-state

and party-to-party relations; third, upholding the principle of relying mainly on our own efforts with external assistance supplementary in economic development.

(4) The theory possesses four components. In addition to the three components in the above paragraph (3), the fourth component added suggests independence in dealing with the relations between parties and between parties and international organizations in the international communist movement, and also dealing with military affairs.

(5) The theory is a methodology. According to many researchers, being independent and self-reliant is the stand, viewpoint and method of the Chinese Communists and their worldview and methodology. Anyone in doing anything should uphold that stand, viewpoint and method of being independent and self-reliant in order to correctly handle the relations between internal and external resources, between individual and group, and between domestic strength and external assistance.

8.3.3 The Philosophical Foundation the Theory of Self-Reliance

Researchers and scholars have generally suggested that the theoretical basis of self-reliance is the Marxist philosophy—the dialectical materialism and historical materialism. In detail, it includes: (1) the materialist principle that matter is primary and consciousness is secondary and the principle of the dialectical relationship between the universality and particularity aspect of contradiction; (2) the principle of the dialectical relationship between domestic and international factors; and (3) the principle that the people create history. By creatively applying the above principles in China's revolution and construction, Mao Zedong had formulated the theory of self-reliant characteristic of the Chinese Communists, which scientifically summarized the law governing the progress in China's revolution and construction and greatly enriched and developed Marxism-Leninism.

In general, today we can say that the study and publicity of the theory on self-reliance is weaker compared to the other two basic points of the living soul of Mao Zedong Thought, and this tendency has increasingly become clear as China's reform and opening up progresses. Therefore, it is necessary to increase study efforts, research and publicize Mao Zedong's theory on self-reliance. It is necessary to broaden and deepen study on this theory and integrate it with the present realities. At present, peace and development are the two main themes in the world, the monopoly capital is still dominant around the globe, and the socialist movement is at a low ebb. How can the CPC and the Chinese people continue to be independent and self-reliant ideologically, politically, economically and culturally? How to strengthen the Party in an independent and self-reliant way? How to apply and develop this theory so that it can better meet the needs of reform and opening up? What is the relationship between Mao Zedong's theory of independence and self-reliance and the traditional Chinese culture? All these questions need to be further discussed and answered.

References

Resolution on Certain Questions in the History of Our Party Since the Founding of the People's Republic of China, Chin. ed., People's Publishing House, Beijing, 1985.

Shi Zhongquan (ed.), *A Review of Study on Mao Zedong*, the Central Party Literature Press, Beijing, 1992.

Li Fengwu, *On the Living Soul of Mao Zedong Thought*, Shandong People's Publishing House, Ji'nan, 1991.

The Party Literature Research Center, *On the Mass Line of the Communist Party of China*, the CPC Central Committee Party School Publishing House, Beijing, 1991.

Shen Baoxiang (ed.), *New Discussion on the Mass Viewpoint and Mass Line*, the CPC Central Committee Party School Publishing House, Beijing, 1991.

Qi Weiping, "Mao Zedong Thought and the Spirit of Innovation,"

Research of Mao Zedong Thought, 2001 (1).

Li Shengzhang, "On the Philosophical Foundation of Mao Zedong's Principle of Seeking Truth from Facts," *Research of Mao Zedong Thought*, 2000 (4).

Wu Yuanhua, "No Investigation, No Right to Speak—Mao Zedong's and Deng Xiaoping's Ideas about Studies and Investigations," *Research of Mao Zedong Thought*, 2000(4).

He Xianglin, "Seeking Truth from Facts: the Essence of Opposing Book Worship—On Seeking Truth from Facts, Being Opinionated and Worshiping Books," *Social Sciences (Shanghai)*, 1998 (6).

Hou Yuji, "The Features of Mao Zedong's and Deng Xiaoping's Ideas on Seeking Truth from Facts," *Research of Mao Zedong Thought*, 1999 (6).

Guo Jianning, "On Mao Zedong's and Deng Xiaoping's Theories on Seeking Truth from Facts," *Forum on Study of Mao Zedong Thought*, 1994 (2).

Wu Jiahua, "Analyses on Mao Zedong's and Deng Xiaoping's Theories of Emancipating the Mind," *Forum on Study of Mao Zedong Thought*, 1997 (4).

Chen Guocan, "Mao Zedong's Theory Related to the People during the Socialist Period," *Forum on Study of Mao Zedong Thought*, 1993 (3).

Zheng Derong, "A Brief Discussion on Mao Zedong's Theory of Self-Reliance," *Forum on Study of Mao Zedong Thought*, 1995 (1).

Chapter 9

Studies on the Relationship between Mao Zedong Thought and Deng Xiaoping Theory

Both Mao Zedong Thought and Deng Xiaoping Theory are the fruits of the integration of the basic tenets of Marxism with China's concrete realities. Deng Xiaoping Theory is the continuation and development of Mao Zedong Thought; they together constitute a unified scientific system imbued with the same spirit. At the same time, they were formulated in different times and consequently dealt with different themes. The study on their relationship has always been an important issue in the research and teaching of Mao Zedong Thought and Deng Xiaoping Theory. In recent years, researchers and scholars have produced a lot of valuable results in this regard.

9.1 Two Tendencies Deserving Special Attention

There are generally two incorrect tendencies in the studies on the relationship between Mao Zedong Thought and Deng Xiaoping Theory. The first tendency is to deprecate or even fundamentally negate Mao Zedong Thought and especially his theory and practice of socialist construction. This tendency argues that Mao Zedong's understanding of socialism was complete utopianism; the rigid socialist system established in his era had hampered the development of the productive forces, prevented the socialist system from demonstrating its superiority, and severely harmed the development of the socialist cause; the socialism advocated by him had taken class struggle as the key link, strived to establish large people's communes and achieve pure public ownership of the means of production, and allowed only the unified planned economy with a high degree of concentration, advocated equalitarianism and poorness socialism, isolated the country from the rest of the world, and allowed no change in the socialist system. These ideas are obvious incorrect.

The other tendency is to incorrectly believe that all the content of Deng Xiaoping Theory had already been mentioned and elaborated in Mao Zedong Thought.

The above two tendencies are definitely incorrect which sever the relationship between Mao Zedong Thought and Deng Xiaoping Theory or even place them in opposition to each other.

9.2 How Did Deng Xiaoping Theory Inherit and Develop the Mao Zedong Thought

Almost all researchers agree that Deng Xiaoping Theory, which was defined in the political reports to the Party's fourteenth and fifteenth national congresses, is a continuation and development of Mao Zedong Thought. Studies in this regard have focused on the following aspects.

9.2.1 Deng Xiaoping Theory Has Carried Forward Mao Zedong Thought

9.2.1.1 They Share the Same Philosophical Foundation and Ideological System

Emancipating the mind and seeking truth from facts are the essence of both Mao Zedong Thought and Deng Xiaoping Theory; seeking truth from facts, proceeding from actual conditions, and integrating theory with practice and the basic tenets of Marxism with the Chinese realities are not only the living soul of Mao Zedong Thought but also a line permeating through Deng Xiaoping Theory. This is generally been agreed by most researchers. Some of them have further suggested that Mao Zedong Thought and Deng Xiaoping Theory are like two runners in a relay race—the former has facilitated the latter and the latter has carried forward the former. The correct theories about the path of socialist construction in Mao Zedong Thought has inspired Deng Xiaoping Theory, which in return has corrected the mistakes Mao Zedong made in his later years. Ideas about keeping to the path of socialism, seeking truth from facts, correctly handling the basic contradictions in socialist society, being independent and self-reliant in building up the country, taking agriculture as the foundation in economic work, serving the people wholeheartedly, and upholding the mass line in Mao Zedong Thought has provided important historical and theoretical conditions for the formation of Deng Xiaoping Theory. Consequently, many researchers assert that Mao Zedong Thought and Deng Xiaoping Theory are inseparable and Deng Xiaoping Theory could be impossible to take shape without Mao Zedong Thought. In short, Deng Xiaoping Theory is a continuation and development of Mao Zedong Thought.

9.2.1.2 Mao Zedong's Theory on New Democracy Is the Most Important Theoretical Source for Deng Xiaoping Theory

According to some researchers, the complete scientific system of Mao Zedong Thought, especially his ideas about building up the new-democratic country and building socialism with Chinese features, is the most direct and important theoretical source for Deng Xiaoping Theory. In terms of worldview and methodology, both Mao Zedong's theory of new democracy and Deng Xiaoping Theory are the product of the integration of Marxism with the Chinese conditions, opposing both "Left" and "Right" mistakes, but especially "Left" mistakes, and are the crystallization of the Party's collective wisdom. From the perspective of practice, the Party's practice under the guidance of the theory of new democracy has provided a prerequisite for Deng Xiaoping Theory, which in return enriched and developed the theory on new democracy.

Besides, some researchers have pointed out that Deng Xiaoping Theory has re-erected Mao Zedong's theory on new democracy, and Deng's ideas about economic structure in the primary stage of socialism has re-established Mao Zedong's model for the new-democratic economy. Consequently, they have argued that Mao Zedong Thought and Deng Xiaoping Theory should merge to form a "Mao Zedong and Deng Xiaoping Thought," which could be a unified ideology for the Chinese nation.

9.2.1.3 Mao Zedong's Exploration for a Path of Socialist Construction Inspired the Theoretical Development of Deng Xiaoping Theory

Some researchers have argued that Deng Xiaoping Theory has re-established and carried forward Mao Zedong's new economic policies which he introduced after the completion of socialist transformation of agriculture, handicrafts, and capitalist industry and commerce. The major theoretical viewpoints Mao Zedong had argued in the mid-1950s to solve the problem of how to develop socialism in an economically and culturally backward country like China has provided the crucial theoretical material for the formation of Deng Xiaoping Theory and become its main components. Mao Zedong's ideas concerning socialist construction, such as the path and principle, objectives and fundamental tasks of development, stages and steps in development, institutional reforms, external environment for development, and opening to the outside world, was all embodied in Deng Xiaoping Theory. Mao Zedong's idea about the path of industrialization has inspired Deng Xiaoping's theory for a Chinese path to modernization. The principle that keeps the state and collective sectors in the dominant position, supplemented by a private sector, and the planned production playing the leading role, supplemented by free production, passed at the Party's Eighth Congress has inspired the theory of keeping the public ownership in the dominant position and developing diverse economic sectors and a planned commodity economy. The analysis of the principal problem in Chinese society, the judgment that socialism can be divided into a underdeveloped stage and a developed stage, and the objective of building a strong socialist economy in fifty or one hundred years at this Congress has also inspired the theory of the primary stage of socialism.

According to other researchers, the assertion that Deng Xiaoping Theory is a continuation of Mao Zedong Thought is manifested in the similarities between them. They have analyzed this idea in the following four aspects.

(1) **Continuity in theoretical creators.** Both Mao Zedong Thought and Deng Xiaoping Theory are the crystallization of the collective wisdom of the CPC and are created by the first and second generations of collective leadership with Mao Zedong and Deng Xiaoping at the core respectively. There is also a continuity in the membership of the two generations of collective leadership. Deng Xiaoping and Chen Yun were important members of both the first and second generations. Other members in the second generation of collective leadership were leaders in the central agencies or chief leaders in certain localities or departments in the works of the first generation. They have shouldered the historical mission to build on past successes and carry forward the ideals of the Party. Their task after the Third Plenary Session of the Eleventh Party Central Committee was to accomplish the ideals that the Party's first generation of collective leadership had failed to complete. As pointed out by Deng Xiaoping, "We have been restoring the correct things advocated by Comrade Mao Zedong.... In many respects, we are doing things Comrade Mao suggested but failed to do himself, setting

right his erroneous opposition to certain things and accomplishing some things that he did not. All this we should continue to do for a fairly long time."

(2) **Continuity in theoretical line.** The theoretical line here does not mean concrete lines of doing things, but refers to the fundamental line that permeates both Mao Zedong Thought and Deng Xiaoping Theory. This line is the principle of integrating the basic tenets of Marxism-Leninism with realities in China's revolution and construction, which means seeking truth from facts and formulating the Party's line, principles and policies in line with the country's realities. Deng Xiaoping has repeatedly stressed that the principle of seeking truth from facts "is the essence of Mao Zedong Thought" and "is the point of departure, the fundamental point, in Mao Zedong Thought." And, Deng Xiaoping himself has always advocated seeking truth from facts.

(3) **Continuity in theoretical character.** There are both differences and similarities between the theoretical character of Mao Zedong Thought and Deng Xiaoping Theory. There are two prominent similarities. First, they have both focused on studying realities in China. Second, they have oth stressed the importance of developing Marxism on the basis of upholding it. Mao Zedong had repeatedly stressed that Marxism should necessarily advance; it should develop along with practice and cannot stand still. It would become lifeless if it were stagnant and stereotyped. Deng Xiaoping has also stressed that: "we should not expect Marx or Lenin to provide ready answers to questions that arise fifty, one hundred or even two hundred years after their death. The world changes every day, and modern science and technology in particular develop rapidly. A year today is the equivalent of several decades, a century or even a longer period in ancient times. Anyone who fails to carry Marxism forward with new thinking and a new viewpoint is not a true Marxist." This continuity in theoretical character is an important embodiment that Deng Xiaoping Theory is a continuation of Mao Zedong Thought.

(4) **Continuity in theoretical content**. It is undoubtedly true that Deng Xiaoping Theory is mainly a summarization of new experience in China's

modern reform and opening up and socialist modernization. However, several of its ideas has origins in Mao Zedong's exploration of a path for socialist construction. Mao Zedong's more or less correct theories and ideas in this regard has provided necessary foundation for the creation of Deng Xiaoping Theory. At the same time, it should be noted that the existence of continuity in theoretical content does no way mean that all of Deng Xiaoping's theoretical viewpoints had already been discussed before, or that all the ideas that has origins in Mao Zedong's theoretical exploration had already been analyzed before. After all, these ideas do not mean exactly the same thing any more because the historical conditions have changed. Deng Xiaoping Theory did draw many ideas from Mao Zedong Thought, but they have changed and upgraded under the new circumstances and developed into theoretical viewpoints of Deng Xiaoping Theory.

9.2.2 Deng Xiaoping Theory Has Developed Mao Zedong Thought

In addition to carrying forward Mao Zedong Thought, Deng Xiaoping Theory has also made giant leaps in developing it. This can be manifested in the following four aspects.

(1) Deng Xiaoping Theory brought about the transformation from a theoretical system focusing on political revolution to a theoretical system focusing on economic development. The theoretical system of Mao Zedong Thought was formulated in the democratic revolution to guide a political revolution to overthrow reactionary classes. After the founding of New China, Mao Zedong had realized the strategic importance of shifting the focus of the Party's work from revolution to construction, gained certain experience in exploring a path of socialist construction, and had introduced some theories about socialist construction. For various reasons, however, the Party's first generation of collective leadership with Mao Zedong at the core had failed to achieve this strategic shift and had long marched in the wrong direction. At the Third Plenary Session of the Eleventh Party Central Committee, the second generation of collective leadership with Deng Xiaoping at the core

has corrected the erroneous principle of taking class struggle as the key link, realized this strategic shift in the focus of the Party's work, and formulated a set of lines, principles and policies regarding economic development. Thereafter, a theory of building socialism with Chinese characteristics gradually took shape and was formulated. The formulation of this theory refutes the opinion that the CPC has only complete theories about leading revolution but has no complete theory about socialist development.

(2) Deng Xiaoping Theory has upgraded many theories about socialist construction, which the first generation of collective leadership with Mao Zedong at the core had introduced but had not thoroughly discussed and fully elaborated, to a set of systematic, fully expounded, complete theories. For instance, when reading *Soviet Union's Political Economy, Textbook* in late 1959 and early 1960, Mao Zedong had divided socialism into two stages: an underdeveloped stage and then a comparatively developed stage. Obviously, this idea is a theoretical source of Deng Xiaoping's theory of the primary stage of socialism. Mao Zedong's other ideas about socialism, such as those that capitalists could set up factories after giving up a fixed rate of interest, investment by overseas Chinese would not be confiscated for a long period of time, and some capitalist economy could be operated after capitalism had been eliminated, also demonstrate the openness in thinking and flexibility in policies at that time, although they were introduced to deal with particular, not general, issues. Mao Zedong did not pay close attention to these ideas or draw theory from them. However, Deng Xiaoping, after reviewing Mao Zedong's above ideas, has introduced the theory of upholding the ownership structure under which socialist public ownership is dominant and diverse economic sectors coexist. This represents a significant leap in theoretical understanding.

(3) Deng Xiaoping Theory has upgraded the theory of planned economy to a theory of socialist market economy.

(4) Deng Xiaoping Theory has broadened the traditional notions about socialism in Marxism-Leninism and Mao Zedong Thought, developed a theory about socialist construction that is more in accord with the country's

realities, and has achieved a giant leap in understanding socialism.

9.3 Deng Xiaoping Theory and Mao Zedong Thought Constitute a Unified Scientific System

Both Deng Xiaoping Theory and Mao Zedong Thought are scientific systems of theories. The issue of how Deng Xiaoping Theory has both carried forward and developed Mao Zedong Thought can be discussed in three levels.

9.3.1 The First Level Is the Basic Stand, Viewpoint and Method

Deng Xiaoping Theory has carried forward and developed the three basic points of the living soul of Mao Zedong Thought: seeking truth from facts, the mass line and self-reliance.

After the Third Plenary Session of the Eleventh Party Central Committee, Deng Xiaoping has not only restored the ideological line of seeking truth from facts but also developed it in the following aspects.

First, he stressed the importance and role of seeking truth from facts in Mao Zedong Thought, arguing that the principle of seeking truth from facts "is the point of departure, the fundamental point, in Mao Zedong Thought" and is the essence and living soul of Mao Zedong Thought.

Second, he defined the basic content of the ideological line of seeking truth from facts as "proceed from reality in all things, link theory with practice and advocate practice to be the touchstone of truth."

Third, he has integrated emancipating the mind with seeking truth from facts and regarded the former as a necessary condition for the latter. Emancipating the mind in essence means making thinking conform to reality and the subjective conform to the objective, and seeking truth from facts.

Fourth, he has created a path of building socialism with Chinese characteristics on the basis of seeking truth from facts.

Deng Xiaoping has enriched and developed the mass line, another basic point of the living soul of Mao Zedong Thought, both in theory and in practice.

First, he took the principle of serving the interests of the people as the starting point and the objective in all of the Party's activities. In formulating the Party's principles and policies, he has advocated the criteria of whether they correspond to the interests and needs of the overwhelming majority of the people and whether or not the people support them, endorse them, are satisfied with them and agree to them as the fundamental principle.

Second, he has defined the intrinsic relationship between the mass line and the principle of seeking truth from fact: "implementing the mass line is the fundamental means of upholding the principle of seeking truth from facts, and upholding the principle of seeking truth from facts is fundamental guarantee for implementing the mass line".

Third, he has introduced methods and measures for preventing Party members from becoming estranged from the masses, such as reforming the political system, improving socialist democracy and legal system, solving the problem of bureaucracy, and guaranteeing implementation of the mass line through institutional means. He has resolutely upheld the mass line and opposed carrying out too many mass movements.

Deng Xiaoping has carried forward and developed the theory of self-reliance in the following aspects.

First, he has elevated the principle of being independent and self-reliant to the living soul and a basic stand of Mao Zedong Thought, and incorporated it as a viewpoint and method of the Party.

Second, he has integrated being independent and self-reliant with opening to the outside world.

9.3.2 The Second Level—How Deng Xiaoping Theory Has Developed Mao Zedong's Theory of Basic Contradictions in Socialist Society

One of Mao Zedong's most important theoretical contributions to

China's socialist construction is that he had clearly stated that the basic contradictions in socialist society are still those between the relations of production and the productive forces and between the superstructure and the economic base, and that a socialist society progresses amid these contradictions. Deng Xiaoping has not only carried on this idea but also defined socialist reforms as the method of solving these contradictions. "Reform is the self-improvement and self-development of the socialist system, is China's second revolution, and is the only way China can achieve modernization." He has also put forward that reform is the crucial driving force for developing socialism.

9.3.3 The Third Level—How Deng Xiaoping Theory Has Developed Mao Zedong's Some Correct Ideas on Developing Socialism

In leading China's socialist construction, Mao Zedong tirelessly explored the path of socialist construction and had scored many valuable theoretical achievements, such as the idea of a path of industrialization suited to China's conditions. He had proposed the initial concept of economic re-structuring, the theory of correctly handling contradictions among the people, the idea of developing socialist democracy and strengthening the Party as a ruling party, and the principle of letting a hundred flowers bloom and a hundred schools of thought contend and making the past serve the present and foreign products serve domestic needs in scientific and cultural development. All the above ideas and principles are important theoretical sources of Deng Xiaoping Theory.

By developing and improving these ideas and principles in line with China's realities in the new period, Deng Xiaoping has developed a new theory of building socialism with Chinese characteristics.

Part Two

Studies on Mao Zedong
Thought in Foreign Countries

Chapter 1

General Introduction

Study on Mao Zedong Thought is an important aspect of Chinese studies, especially modern Chinese studies, in foreign countries. It has spanned over half a century: appeared around the 1930s; started to develop in the strict sense in the 1950s; developed rapidly and showed a surge in some sense in the 1960s and 1970s; declined in the 1980s but at the same time produced a large number of objective results with high academic value. This indicates that it has entered a higher level of study. It is undoubtedly important for Chinese researchers and scholars who study or teach Mao Zedong Thought to understand how foreign Mao scholars have studied Mao Zedong Thought and what viewpoints and methods they have adopted in studying it. It should be noted that foreign researchers have always considered Mao Zedong Thought as the thought of Mao Zedong himself, and not "the crystallized, collective wisdom of the Party" as in China.

1.1 The Period of Prelude or Preparations

This period has continued from around the 1930s to the late 1940s. The Soviet Union and the Communist International had begun to introduce Mao Zedong's works as early as in the late 1920s. According to existing records, the first time Mao Zedong's works were published in other countries was in June 1927 when his well-known investigative report "Report on an Investigation of the Peasant Movement in Hunan" was published in the Russian edition of *Communist International*, the official organ of the Communist International. Thereafter, the *Communist International* had published Mao Zedong's "Our Economic Policy" in November 1934 and his "Letter to the Spanish People," "The Tasks of the Chinese Communist Party in the Period of Resistance to Japan," "Interview with a Correspondent from the *New China News*," "Interview with Journalist from the Associated Press," "Talk with a Delegation from the International Student Association," "On the New Stage," and "Interview with a *New China Daily* Correspondent on the New International Situation" from 1937 to 1939. The Communist International's aim of publishing these works was not to study them, but to show how the Soviet Union and the Communist International thought about the CPC's revolutionary strategies and tactics and its principal leaders, and to introduce China's revolution to the international communist camp. But, the publication of the above works had provided material for the study of Mao Zedong Thought by researchers around the world.

In addition to the Soviet Union and the Communist International, many foreign journalists, most of whom were from the United States, also did a great job introducing the CPC and its revolutionary cause as well as Mao Zedong and his thought to the world. Sympathizing with the anti-invasion war of the Chinese people or having the curiosity to know the leaders of the Chinese revolution, they had reached the revolutionary base areas after getting through the KMT's blockades and overcoming numerous difficulties. They wrote a large number of articles and reports to objectively introduce and describe the activities and positions of the Chinese Communists led by Mao Zedong. Among them, the most well-known was American journalist Edgar Snow, an old friend of the Chinese people, who was the first Western journalist who arrived in the Northern Shaanxi Revolutionary Base Area after an arduous journey in July 1936. In the following three months there, he tirelessly carried out investigations and conducted long interviews with Mao Zedong and other Party leaders. Many news reports written by him attracted worldwide attention and were later collected into his book *Red Star over China*, which was published by London: Victor Gollancz in October 1937. Over 100,000 copies of this book were printed in weeks, and it was published five times within one month. It was printed and reprinted across the world in nearly 20 languages such as French, German, Russian, Italian, Spanish, Portuguese, Japanese and Chinese. It had become a world-famous classic. The book foiled the KMT's attempts to slander the CPC and the revolution it led, repudiated the slanderous words such as "red bandits" and "bandit chieftain" that the KMT had heaped on the CPC and its leaders, and gave the people of the world a true and objective description of the CPC and its leaders and the revolution it led. Therefore, it was of great significance politically. Furthermore, it was also important for the study of Mao Zedong Thought in foreign countries.[1] In his introduction to the 1968 revised edition of this book, John King Fairbank, an expert on Chinese studies in University of Harvard, said, "It is very much to the credit of Edgar Snow that this book has stood the test of time on both these counts—as a historical record and as an indication of a trend." Stuart Schram, a famous expert on study of Mao Zedong's thought and an American professor of politics in University of London, in his well-known book *Mao Tse-tung*, said: although *Red Star over China* had quite a number of mistakes in details, Mao Zedong's interview with Edgar Snow in the book was the only important material about his life. Although not completely accurate, the book is still interesting because it reflects how Mao Zedong himself thought about his past.[2] Jerome Ch'en, a well-known Canadian expert on study of Mao Zedong's thought, in his book *Mao and the Chinese Revolution* published in 1967, admitted that the book *Red Star over China* had greatly inspired him in his study on Mao Zedong

---

[1] The book's Part Four "Genesis of a Communist," which mainly introduced the life and revolutionary career of Mao Zedong, was compiled into a book *Biography of Mao Zedong* and printed in China in the late 1930s.

[2] Stuart Schram, *Mao Tse-tung*, Chin. ed., Hongqi Publishing House, Beijing, 1987, p. 1.

and the Chinese revolution. In fact, Edgar Snow's books are often quoted by foreign researchers in their study of Mao's thought.

Apart from *Red Star over China* by Edgar Snow, *Interviews with Mao Tse-tung* (1946) and *Mao Tse-tung* (1948) by Anna Louise Strong, *Interview with Mao Tse-tung* (1937), *This Is Mao Tse-tung: the Leader of the Chinese Communist Party* (1945) and *Mao Tse-tung in Chongqing* (1946) by Israel Epstein, *Interview with Mao Tse-tung and Zhu De* (1945) and *Interview with Mao Tse-tung* (1946) by Genther Steine, and *Interview with Mao Tse-tung* (1939) by Carman were also important materials for studying Mao Zedong and his revolutionary career. Although Edgar Snow and other Western journalists only honestly and objectively recorded and described Mao Zedong's life and revolutionary activities and did not conduct intensive research on his thought, their papers and books have been valuable records and documents for Mao studies in Western countries.

1.2 The Period in Which Studies in the Real Sense Began

This period has spanned over the 1950s.

The founding of the People's Republic of China in October 1949 and its achievements in national integration in the 1950s had attracted the world's attention. Naturally enough, the Communist Party of China, which founded New China and was to lead the country's construction and its leader Mao Zedong became the focus of researches across the world. Soon after New China was founded, his two philosophical essays "On Practice" and "On Contradiction" were published in the *People's Daily* respectively in 1950 and 1952, and Volumes I through III of *Selected Works of Mao Zedong* were published in 1951, 1952 and 1953. Mao Zedong had published his "On the Ten Major Relationships" and "On the Correct Handling of Contradictions among the People" in 1956 and 1957. All this was of great importance for the study of Mao Zedong Thought in foreign countries. During this period, the study on Mao Zedong Thought was mainly carried out in the Soviet Union, the United States, and Japan.

1.2.1 Studies in the Soviet Union

The Soviet Union was among the earliest countries to conduct studies on the thought of Mao Zedong. The magazine *Bolshevik*, No. 23, of the Communist Party of the Soviet Union (CPSU) published Mao Zedong's essay "On Practice" in December 1950, which was earlier than the essay was published in the *People's Daily* in China. On December 18, 1950, the *Pravda*, the official organ of the CPSU Central Committee had published an editorial entitled "On Mao Zedong's Essay 'On Practice'," which introduced and discussed the historical background against which Mao Zedong wrote the essay and its content, aim and features. The editorial had pointed out, "Mao Zedong's aim of writing the essay is to use Marxist epistemological standpoint to expose the mistake of empiricism and especially dogmatism; the essay clearly and figuratively has solved complicated philosophical problems by using Marxist methods; it has developed the basic tenets of Marxism-Leninism on epistemology, on the role of practice in the process of understanding, and on the significance of theory in revolutionary practice."

After being published in China, Mao Zedong's essay "On Contradiction" ran in the magazine *Bolshevik* No. 9 and 10 in 1952. V. Mikheev said, "The essay has studied the core issue of Marxist dialectics—how the law of contradiction drives development;" "it was aimed to oppose dogmatism and the narrow empiricism;" "it has conducted a creative, independent study on the interrelation between practice and theory." The 1953 Great Soviet Encyclopedia had also affirmed this essay when discussing dialectics. However, researchers in the Soviet Union had expressed reservations about or even objections to some ideas in the essay. When publishing the essay, the *Bolshevik* had changed the original wording "identity between war and peace" to "interrelation between war and peace," and "identity" in other sentences to "uniformity." The *Shorter Dictionary of Philosophy*, fourth edition, compiled by Mark M. Rozental and Pavel Judin had clearly stated that it is incorrect to apply the Marxist principle of identity to fundamentally opposite things, because doing so is an indiscriminate use of Hegel's words advocated by Menshevist idealists; there is no identity between war and peace, between the bourgeoisie and the proletariat and between life and death, because they are fundamental opposites repelling each other. This was, in fact, criticizing ideas in the "On Contradiction." Mao Zedong had refuted this criticism at a conference attended by Party committee secretaries of provinces, autonomous regions and municipalities directly under the central government in January 1957. It should be noted that although researchers in the Soviet Union had expressed certain objections to some ideas in the "On Contradiction," they had basically affirmed this essay.

Volumes I through IV of *Selected Works of Mao Zedong* in Russian (Volume II in Chinese was divided into two volumes in the Russian edition) were published during the period from 1952 to December 1953. Scholars in the Soviet Union such as Pavel Judin, V. Mikheev, and Aleksandr Danilovich Aleksandrov had all published papers in the *Pravda* and *The Communist* to introduce and assess Mao Zedong's these works. As they put it, "The Chinese Communist Party has successfully applied Marxism in line with China's conditions and greatly developed the Marxist theory because it understood and applied Marxism-Leninism not dogmatically, but creatively."[1] "These works provide a model of how to creatively understand Marxism and how to integrate the theory of Marxism-Leninism with the practice in the Chinese revolutionary war and with the practice of the Chinese Communist Party."[2] Mao Zedong had published his essay "On the Correct Handling of the Contradictions among the People" in 1957. Scholars in the Soviet Union fully had affirmed the essay and had a high opinion of Mao Zedong's idea about basic contradictions in socialist society.

There were three noticeable features in the study of Mao Zedong's thought by scholars in the Soviet Union during this period. First, they focused on Mao Zedong's philosophical thought, especially on his "On Practice" and "On Contradiction." Second, they had stressed the unity between Mao

---

[1] The *People's Daily*, 1952-09-10.
[2] *Ibid.*, 1953-10-31.

Zedong's thought and theories of the CPSU. "They had often focused on how the Soviet Union had influenced and helped the Chinese Communist Party, how Stalin had correctly predicted the development of the Chinese revolution, and how Mao Zedong had carried forward the thoughts of Lenin and Stalin."[1] Third, they integrated academic research with political needs and had made more effort to introduce and publicize Mao Zedong Thought than to discuss and study it. This was partially due to the friendly relation between China and the Soviet Union and the opposition between the socialist camp and the capitalist camp internationally.

Under the influence of social science scholars and researchers in the Soviet Union, theoreticians of communist parties in Eastern European socialist countries and other European countries had also introduced and assessed the thought of Mao Zedong. They focused mainly on Mao Zedong's "On Practice," "On Contradiction" and "On the Correct Handling of the Contradictions among the People."

1.2.2 Studies in the United States

The Americans were the earliest westerners to know Mao Zedong and his thoughts. As mentioned above, a number of American journalists including Edgar Snow had arrived in the Northern Shaanxi Revolutionary Base Area as early as in the 1930s to interview Mao Zedong and other leaders of the Communist Party of China. During the War of Resistance against Japan, the U.S. government took the CPC as an ally in the world anti-fascist war. Many American journalists, army officers and politicians consequently had more chances to communicate with Mao Zedong and the CPC to increase understanding between the two sides. After China's victory in the War of Resistance against Japan, the U.S. government had supported Chiang Kai-shek and the KMT in unifying China and at the same time strived to settle the dispute between the KMT and the CPC to avoid a civil war. After the all-out civil war broke out, the U.S. government was on the side of Chiang Kai-shek,

---

[1] Li Junru et al., *Study of Mao Zedong in Foreign Countries*, Henan People's Publishing House, Zhengzhou, 1993, p. 17.

and its relation with the CPC had worsened rapidly. The country-wide victory of the People's Liberation Army and the founding of the People's Republic of China in 1949 shook the United States and the whole world. In the same year, socialist Soviet Union successfully tested an atomic bomb, ending the American nuclear monopoly. As a result, fear of communism prevailed in Western countries and especially in the U.S. Far-right radicals represented by American Senator Joseph McCarthy launched fervent anti-Communist movements and persecuted a large number of communists and progressives in America. They declared that the U.S. State Department had been infiltrated by communists and accused the crypto-Communists in the State Department for "losing China." Many diplomats and China Hands, who had a high opinion of Mao Zedong and the CPC including John King Fairbank, suffered political prosecution. Under such horrible political atmosphere of McCarthyism, the study on Mao Zedong was negatively impacted.

Still and all, some books about the Chinese revolution and Mao Zedong Thought were published in the United States in the 1950s. The most influential two books were *Chinese Communism and the Rise of Mao* by Benjamin I. Schwartz and *A Documentary History of Chinese Communism* by John King Fairbank, Conrad Brandt and Benjamin Schwartz.

The book *Chinese Communism and the Rise of Mao* was first published in 1951 and had been reprinted seven times by 1968. This book marked the real beginning of study on Mao Zedong Thought in Western countries. In the book, the author had discussed the relationship between Mao Zedong Thought and Marxism and focused on Mao Zedong's idea about the peasant problem and on the difference between China's revolutionary road of encircling the cities from the countryside and the October revolution. As pointed out in the book, the general trend of Marxism in its Leninist form has been toward disintegration and not toward "enrichment" and "deepening." The Maoist heresy in action on the matter of the relations of party to class represents yet another major step in this process of disintegration. In spite of this movement toward disintegration, however, we would nevertheless maintain that other core elements of Marxism-Leninism still remain integral living elements in Chinese Communism.[1] It is desirable and objective for the author to highlight the creativity and Chinese features of Mao Zedong Thought by comparing the Chinese revolution with the October revolution and Maoism with Leninism and Marxism. However, this approach and perspective had focused too much on forms, and the conclusion that Mao Zedong Thought is a "heresy" of Marxism-Leninism is questionable. This book first used the term "Maoism" to refer to Mao Zedong Thought. This term has been universally accepted by western scholars.

The book *A Documentary History of Chinese Communism* edited by John King Fairbank, Conrad Brandt and Benjamin Schwartz in 1952 contained rich historical information and material. Many researchers quote from this book in studying Mao Zedong Thought.

In short, the books on Mao Zedong Thought published in the U.S. in the 1950s had produced profound influence. They had high academic value, advanced some novel opinions, and followed the principle of objectivism. Because both John King Fairbank and Benjamin Schwartz were professors in Harvard University, they and other scholars who shared similar opinions and standpoint with them were often called "Harvard school" or "liberal school" scholars, in order to be differentiated from the later left- and right-wing scholars.

It should be noted that many famous American universities such as Yale University, Columbia University, Harvard University and University of California had all established centers for oriental studies and Chinese studies. The Fairbank Center for East Asian Research established in Harvard University in 1956 is well-known for its effective East Asian and Chinese studies. As McCarthyism declined in the mid-1950s, the American government changed its attitude toward Chinese studies and passed an act of international education in 1958, which increased funds to teaching and research on Chinese studies. The Carnegie Foundation, the Rockefeller Foundation and Ford Foundation had all provided funds for Chinese

---

[1] Benjamin I. Schwartz, *Chinese Communism and the Rise of Mao*, Harvard University Press, 1951, p. 202.

studies. Study of Mao Zedong and his thought is no doubt an important part of Chinese studies. All this provided necessary foundation for the rapid development of Mao studies in the U.S. in the 1960s.

1.2.3 Studies in Japan

Japan is a close neighbor of China. During China's War of Resistance against Japan, some Japanese communists in China got a basic understanding of Mao Zedong's thought because they directly participated in or personally witnessed the activities of the Communist Party of China. However, it was not until in the 1950s that theoretical study of Mao Zedong's thought in the real sense began in Japan. Japanese scholars focused on analyzing and assessing Mao Zedong's philosophical thought, and their representative was Matsumura Kazuto.

In 1952, Matsumura Kazuto published three papers in Japanese journal *Thoughts* to analyze Mao Zedong's philosophical thought, making him the first to discuss the fundamental feature and core issue of Mao Zedong's philosophical thought. According to him, the fundamental feature of Mao Zedong's philosophical thought is that it is free from dogmatism. He pointed out that Mao Zedong always stressed the unity between theory and practice and between thought and action and his thought is suitable for the Chinese nation because it is the product of the integration of Marxism-Leninism with the Chinese revolution and is Marxism-Leninism applied in China. From the perspective of the relation between thought and action, Matsumura Kazuto has argued that Mao Zedong based himself on ancient Chinese philosophical ideas and integrated the Marxist philosophy with the wisdom of the Chinese nation. He published the paper "Development of Dialectics—Centered on Mao Zedong's 'On Contradiction'" in 1953, in which he pointed out that Mao Zedong's thought is the result of the integration of the universal tenets of Marxism-Leninism with the practice and experience in the Chinese revolution, and that Mao Zedong's philosophical ideas about contradiction greatly enriched and developed the philosophical theory of Marxism-Leninism. He had even stressed that one should first study Mao Zedong's philosophical thought before investigating on Marxist-Leninist philosophy, which has obviously gone too far.

In addition to Matsumura Kazuto, scholars such as Nosaga Sanzou, Michio Iwaki, Tadashi Ooi and Ken Yamazaki had also introduced and studied Mao Zedong's thought during this period, and some of them were Japanese communists who worked in the liberated areas during China's War of Resistance against Japan.

1.3 The Period of Rapid Development

This period has continued from the 1960s to the 1970s.

The 1960s and 1970s witnessed great progress in the study of Mao Zedong Thought in foreign countries, especially in the United States, European countries and Japan. A "Mao Zedong fever" even prevailed in the U.S. during this period. All this was closely connected to the then international situation, China's "cultural revolution" and changes in the academic trend on Chinese studies in Western countries.

With a thaw in US-Soviet relations in the late 1950s, the Sino-Soviet relations began to worsen. The relations between the CPC and the CPSU had ceased in 1966, and border conflicts between the two countries had occurred from time to time. At the same time, China's relations with the U.S. began to improve beginning after 1969. U.S. President Richard Nixon's visit to China in 1972 opened the door for the development of bilateral ties between the two countries. In September the same year, China and Japan signed a Joint Communique to establish diplomatic relations between the two countries. In short, China was reducing confrontation with the Western countries and attempting to establish and develop friendly relations and cooperation with them, which facilitated contemporary Chinese studies and studies on Mao Zedong's thought in the U.S., European countries and Japan.

China's "cultural revolution" in 1966 had shocked the world. What had happened in China? What was the CPC's leader Mao Zedong trying to do? These questions had attracted attention from more and more Western researchers, who kept a close eye on this shocking "change" in China and on Mao Zedong's acts. Their studies focused on the problems the "cultural revolution" posed and attempted to solve and on the new social model it strived to establish. The "cultural revolution" had seemingly rebelled against many problems such as bureaucracy, social status and privilege, democracy, reform of the educational system, income disparities between urban and rural areas and between mental and manual labor, morals and customs, and culture and traditions. Western scholars attached close attention to these problems because their countries were faced with these problems too. After the end of World War II, Western capitalist countries had enjoyed two decades of rapid economic development and social stability. However, they had social problems and conflicts as well. A social crisis was prevalent through the developed capitalist world in the late 1960s. The French May Storm Events staged by far-left intellectuals and students in 1968 had greatly shook the country's political and social system. Student protest movements in England, the Federal Republic of Germany, Italy, Holland, Sweden, Belgium and Spain had intensified. In the U.S., left radical movements prevailed in the country, the black people's fight against racial discrimination brought forth serious social conflicts, and college students have organized numerous anti-government pretests. Besides, the radicals demanded a change in the existing social system, juvenile crime rate had increased sharply, and sexual liberation was challenging the traditional code of behaviors. Under such conditions, Western scholars had become very interested in China's "cultural revolution," from which some left scholars believed they could find a way of solving social problems in Western countries, and they consequently had an impractical high opinion of the "cultural revolution" and Mao Zedong's thought in his later years. As a result, they were quite surprised when China negated the "cultural revolution."Another reason behind the rapid development of study on Mao Zedong and his thoughts in the 1960s in Western countries, especially in the U.S. is that American scholars in the 1960s had attempted to review and criticize the past Chinese studies. They have argued that researchers should free their academic studies from the influence of the Cold War and the U.S. government's domestic and foreign policies and upgrade their perspective on China by abandoning historical prejudice, racism and the colonialist values. In particular, Paul A. Cohen pointed out that American historians should move beyond the Western-centric paradigms of the past toward a more China-centered approach to Chinese history—an approach that should strive empathetically to reconstruct the Chinese past as the Chinese themselves experienced it rather than in terms of an imported sense of historical problem.[1] This guiding principle had urged Western scholars to study modern China and Mao Zedong's thought more objectively, comprehensively and thoroughly.

The book *A Review of Study on Mao Zedong in Foreign Countries* written by Bi Jianheng et al. and published by Zhejiang People's Publishing House in 1993 used ten pages (48-57) to enumerate nearly two hundred books on Mao Zedong studies that were published in foreign countries during 1960s and 1970s. These books have covered every aspect of study on Mao Zedong, and the majority of them were written by American and European authors, and next by Japanese authors. American scholar Robert A. Scalapino classified these books into four groups. The first group were biographies, represented by *Mao Tse-tung* by Stuart Schram and *Mao and the Chinese Revolution* by Jerome Ch'en. The second group discussed the history of development of Mao Zedong's thought, represented by *History and Will: Philosophical Perspectives of Mao Tse-tung's Thought* by Frederic E. Wakeman and *Prelude to Revolution: Mao, the Party and the Peasant Question, 1962-1966* by Richard Baum. The third group has assessed the values and position of Mao Zedong's thought, represented by *Mao's Way* by Edward E. Rice and *Mao Tse-Tung in the Scales of History* by Dick Wilson. The fourth group has focused on the psycho-cultural factors in Mao Zedong's thought, represented by *Mao's Revolution and the Chinese Political Culture* by Richard H. Solomon and *The Spirit of Chinese Politics: A Psychocultural*

---

[1] Paul A. Cohen, *Discovering History in China: American Historical Writing on the Recent Chinese Past*, Chin. ed., Zhonghua Book Company, Beijing, 1989, p. 7.

Study of the Authority Crisis in Political Development by Lucian W. Pye.[1]

The following is an introduction to studies of Mao Zedong Thought in foreign countries during this period.

1.3.1 The Two Heated Debates in American and British Studies of Mao Zedong Thought

As American and British scholars had intensified efforts to study modern China and Mao Zedong since the 1960s, they gradually formed three main schools of thought in this regard: the liberal school; the conservative rightists; and the leftists. The liberal school, also called the objectivists or Harvard school, included experts on Chinese studies in Harvard University such as John King Fairbank, Benjamin Schwartz, Stuart Schram and Maurice Meisner. The conservative rightists were represented by Karl A. Wittfogel. The leftists, or the "New Left," included mainly the younger scholars subject to the influence of China's "cultural revolution" and were represented by Richard M. Pfeffer and Andrew G. Walder. The two heated debates between the above three schools of thought in the 1960s and 1970s have produced great influence on later studies on Mao Zedong Thought in Western countries.

The first debate was between the conservative rightists led by Wittfogel and the liberal school led by Schwartz in the early 1960s. Wittfogel had published a long paper entitled "The Legend of 'Maoism'" in the inaugural issue of *China Quarterly* in 1960. In this paper, he had argued that Mao Zedong made no "original" contribution to Marxism-Leninism and the Chinese revolution was the result of an international plot manipulated by Moscow; that Mao's thought and movements since the 1930s were a restoration of Stalin's Orthodox Marxism; and that the so-called "Maoism" was only a legend. Wittfogel, born in Germany was a veteran expert on Chinese studies. He was a member of the Central Committee of the Communist Party of Germany and had later moved to the United States to escape from Nazi oppression. He was director of the Center for

---

[1] Bi Jianheng et al., *A Review of Study on Mao Zedong in Foreign Countries*, Zhejiang People's Publishing House, Hangzhou, 1993, p. 63.

Chinese studies in Columbia University and a professor at the University of Washington and was best known for his book *Oriental Despotism: A Comparative Study of Total Power*. He became a representative of the conservative rightists who opposed Communism politically since the 1950s. Although he purposefully diminished Mao Zedong's thoughts in this paper due to his political stand, Wittfogel did put forward some systematic and original ideas about the relation between Mao Zedong's thought and teachings of Marx and Lenin. This is partly because he was once a member of the Communist Party of Germany and was familiar with the theories of Marx and Lenin and the history of the Communist International. After Wittfogel published his paper, Schwartz replied him by publishing a paper "The Legend of *the Legend of 'Maoism'*," in which he restated the opinions he had argued in his book *Chinese Communism and the Rise of Mao*: "Mao Zedong was first of all a Chinese, and his original theoretical creation had been proved by his theory and practice in guiding the Chinese revolution."

The second debate was between the leftists represented by Richard M. Pfeffer and Andrew G. Walder and the liberal school scholars including Benjamin Schwartz, Stuart Schram and Maurice Meisner in the mid-1970s. They have argued their studies through *Modern China*, an international quarterly published in England.

Richard M. Pfeffer, assistant professor of politics in Johns Hopkins University, had published the paper "Mao and Marx in the Marxist-Leninist Tradition: A Critique of 'The China Field' and a Contribution to a Preliminary Re-appraisal" in *Modern China*, Volume 2, in October 1976. Focusing on how to comprehend Mao's thought by correctly understanding the relationship between Mao's thought and Marxism-Leninism, Pfeffer had criticized the academic viewpoints of the liberal school scholars in "the China studies." He had criticized three well-known scholars in the field of Mao studies.

The first scholar he criticized was Benjamin Schwartz, who was then a history and politics professor at Harvard University and the vice-director of the university's Center for East Asian Researches. Schwartz's *Chinese*

Communism and the Rise of Mao had dominated Chinese studies in the U.S. for ten years. According to this book, Mao's interpretation of Marxism-Leninism was based on Leninism but had deviated from Leninist tradition. Schwartz has reached this conclusion because he thought Marxism alone could not directly help the Chinese intellectuals to understand their situations during the period of the May 4th Movement in 1919, and it was Lenin's theory of imperialism that integrated Marxism with Asian conditions. However, the Chinese Communist movement had developed along the path of Maoism and eventually deviated from Leninism. In fact, both Lenin and Mao had deviated from Marxism because they both believed that Marx's works did not apply to the specific historical conditions, political problems and urgency for change in their countries. Schwartz had further developed this idea in his book *Communism and China* (1968), in which he advanced that although the term "Marxism" was kept in China, its content had changed greatly.

The second scholar Pfeffer criticized was Stuart Schram, an American professor in University of London. Stuart Schram was well-known for his book *Mao Tse-tung*, which was first published in 1966, the book was republished in 1967 after a revision and had seen eight reprints. Pfeffer had criticized that Stuart Schram, like Benjamin Schwartz, believed the Chinese Communist revolution originated from Leninism, and not Marxism. Schram had basically accepted the opinion that "Asian Marxism" was based on Leninism and Mao Zedong's thought had deviated more from Marxism and less from Leninism. In addition, in his book *The Political Thought of Mao Tse-tung* published in 1969, Schram had advanced that Mao's thought was the result of his vigorous personality, China's environment and Mao's revolutionary experience. Mao's voluntarist ideas and his emphasis on people's will and military strength had overweighed his "natural Leninism." In this way, Mao had become an incompetent Marxist.

The third scholar Pfeffer criticized was Maurice Meisner, history professor in the University of Wisconsin. Maurice Meisner had published the paper "Leninism and Maoism: Some Populist Perspectives on Marxism-

Leninism in China" in 1971. Pfeffer had criticized Meisner for associating Maoism with Populism and who had stressed their similarities, saying that doing so will lead people to consider Maoism an abstract thought instead of a Marxist method of dealing with practical problems in China. Pfeffer had also criticized Meisner for regarding Maoism as Utopianism in his paper titled "Utopian Socialist Themes in Maoism." According to Meisner, both Marxism and Maoism and even all great revolutions and civilizations primarily have emerged from utopian assumptions, and Mao's utopianism had originated from Marx's highly utopian vision of a society without classes and of complete equality. Mao Zedong did not have any utopian ideas before the founding of New China and during the first five years after its founding. But he began to develop utopian ideas in 1955, and the Great Leap Forward was a typical example of utopianism. Meisner had also pointed out that utopianism in Marxism had certain limits in then prevalent historical conditions, while Mao's utopianism seemed free of any restraints. Pfeffer had disputed Meisner's above ideas. According to Pfeffer, Mao had tirelessly examined how China's revolution was determined inevitably by the country's social, economic, political and historical realities. In his text, Pfeffer had developed the idea of "permanent revolution." Mao had considered a society of material abundance as the prerequisite for achieving communism ld not be taken before entering such a society of material abundance. This idea may seem not orthodox, but it was obviously not a utopian assumption. Pfeffer defended the Great Leap Forward and the "cultural revolution." In short, Pfeffer believed that Mao Zedong's thought is a development of Marxism and the strategy guiding the Chinese revolution, and definitely not "heretical" Marxism.[1]

Following Richard M. Pfeffer, Andrew G. Walder, professor in Department of Sociology at the University of Michigan, had also criticized the academic opinions of the liberal school scholars. His paper "Marxism, Maoism, and Social Change" was published in two issues of *Modern China*

---

[1] For Pfeffer's ideas, see Xiao Yanzhong et al. (eds.), *The Legend of the "Legend,"* Vol. IV of *Assessments of Mao Zedong by Foreign Scholars*, China Workers Publishing House, Beijing, 1997, pp. 279-314.

(No. 1 and 2, Volume 3) in 1977. In this paper, he had criticized the idea of associating Mao Zedong's thought with voluntarism in Chinese studies. According to him, this incorrect association was due to misunderstanding of Marxism by some researchers in Chinese studies, who had distorted Marxist tenets on basis of a simple cause-and-effect relationship between the economic base and the superstructure and exaggeratedly regarded Marx as an economic determinist and thus evaluated Mao who stressed the importance of the superstructure as a voluntarist, and he criticized them as distorting Marxist tenets on stages of historical development, who rigidly considered a full development of capitalism as the prerequisite for achieving socialism, and consequently regarded Mao who advocated building a socialist society on the basis of a pre-capitalist economic structure as a voluntarist. In dealing with the above distortions, Walder had quoted from Marx and Engels to stress that Marx was not an economic determinist although he did stress the importance of the economic base. Terms "the superstructure," "the economic base" and "relations of production" are indispensable to each other and should not be understood in isolation. In Marx's view, these terms describe various aspects of a thing, and they together constitute a complicated, ever-changing organic whole. In this case, the economic base is closely connected and restricted by various aspects of the superstructure and is not an objective force that can "pre-determine history." Therefore, in no way could Marx logically formulate a theory of "stages" in world history or a theory of "timing" of revolution universally applicable to all times and all circumstances. But it is often incorrectly believed by some scholars that Marx had indeed formulated this kind of a theory, which leads to the conclusion that Mao was a voluntarist. Walder then pointed out that many important documents about Mao Zedong had exaggerated Mao's emphasis on human factors, and that this exaggeration was an important reason behind the idea that Mao was a voluntarist who had deviated from the Marxist tenets that the consciousness of men is dependent on the relations of production and that Mao instead advocated that change in men's consciousness determines changes in the relations of production. In fact, both Marx and Mao insisted that relations of production are an important component of the economic base and have a profound influence on men's activities and consciousness. Mao was not a voluntarist because he believed that change in the superstructure and ideology cannot last long without a change in relations of production and vice versa. Mao's revolutionary strategy is definitely not a voluntarist theory that attempts to bring about a reform in the social system by solely or mainly changing men's consciousness and the superstructure.[1]

Pfeffer's and Walder's criticism of the liberal school scholars was supported by some scholars in Chinese studies. For instance, Mark Selden from Washington University had stated, "Pfeffer and Walder have opened a significant new path for interpreting Mao Zedong and the Chinese revolution in Marxist and in world historical perspective. They correctly criticize the virtual unanimity in the field of Chinese studies in ignoring or distorting Mao's contributions as a Marxist philosopher, teacher, and revolutionary."[2] Stephen Andors, research associate in Columbia University East Asian Institute, had also published papers in *Modern China* to support the opinions of Pfeffer and Walder.

Liberal school scholars wrote back articles to refute the leftist criticism. Benjamin Schwartz published the paper "The Essence of Marxism Revisited: A Response" to defend his idea that Maoism is "heretical" Marxism. According to him, it is more meaningful to see Mao within the context of the Chinese cultural heritage and see his thought as a creative original response to the concrete revolutionary experience of China in the twentieth century. He pointed out, "to the extent that there is a Western dimension in Mao's thought, it may be fruitfully related to more general notions of eighteenth- and nineteenth-century Western thought rather than simply to Marxism. Thus, to assess that Mao belongs within the boarder stream of the history of

---

[1] For Walder's ideas, see Xiao Yanzhong et al. (eds.), *The Legend of the "Legend,"* Vol. IV of *Assessments of Mao Zedong by Foreign Scholars*, China Workers Publishing House, Beijing, 1997, pp. 315-362.

[2] Mark Selden, "Karl Marx, Mao Ze-dong, and the Dialectics of Socialist Development," p. 409.

socialist-communist ideas is not the same as to identify him as a Marxist."[1] Schwartz had compared the difference between Marx's and Mao's ideas on socialism and communism, theory and practice, and on the dictatorship of the proletariat. He did not deny the connection between Mao and Marx, but in his view this connection was not sufficient to prove whether or not Mao is the true disciple of Marx. He restated his idea that Mao was not a Marxist.

Following Schwartz, Frederic Wakeman, professor of history in University of California, Berkeley, also published papers in *Modern China* to refute the ideas of the leftists. His book *History and Will: Philosophical Perspectives of Mao Tse-tung's Thought* published in 1973 was very influential among American scholars in Chinese studies. Arguing that no researcher should attempt to define any thought before fully understanding its origin and course of development, he had analyzed Mao's thought by focusing on several theoretical viewpoints that had influenced Mao's theoretical exploration. His paper published in *Modern China* was targeted at Walder, who undermined Marx's theory of economic determinism. Wakeman argued that both Marx and Lenin and even Stalin were believers in economic determinism. He also disputed the interpretation on the nature of the "cultural revolution" made by Walder, who believed that China's mass movements, including the "cultural revolutions," are a reform of both the superstructure and the relations of production. Wakeman had pointed out that according to Mao's view, the superstructure is the stage for class struggle and the "cultural revolution" is a class struggle in the superstructure.

Maurice Meisner, who had published some influential books and writings on the relationship between Mao Zedong's thoughts on the one hand and utopian socialism and Russian Populism on the other since the late 1960s, had also published papers in *Modern China* to answer the criticism of the leftists. He pointed out, "Pfeffer and Walder have chosen to ignore the major historical point presented in the writings they attack. And that point is not that Mao was a 'heretic' or an 'infidel' who violated timeless truths and orthodoxies. In attempting to explore the relationship between

---

[1] Xiao Yanzhong et al. (eds.), *op. cit.*, p. 364.

Maoism and the Marxist-Leninist tradition, however inadequately, nowhere have I suggested that Mao 'sinned' against some sacred body of canonical texts. The point is precisely the opposite. And that, briefly put, is that revolutionaries who adhered to orthodox Marxist-Leninist teachings proved politically irrelevant in the modern Chinese historical environment, whereas it was precisely Mao's departure from many of the premises of Marxism and Leninism (and the departures are enormous) that formed the essential intellectual-ideological prerequisites for a revolution to be made in a country where a revolution was desperately needed." In order to prove his statement, Meisner had quoted a passage from Mao Zedong's talk when he read the *Soviet Union's Political Economy, Textbook*. Mao had said, "Lenin's dictum, 'The more backward the country, the more difficult its transition from capitalism to socialism' was incorrect. As a matter of fact, the more backward the economy, the easier, and not more difficult, the transition from capitalism to socialism." Meisner consequently stated that Mao himself was far more explicit and candid than Pfeffer and Walder in recognizing how far his own thought had moved from the theories of Marx and Lenin. Meisner further criticized Pfeffer for ignoring Marxist conception of the relationship between state and society in the discussion on the dictatorship of the proletariat. He stated, "Marx, after all, had viewed the state as a form of alienated social power, and it was from that perspective (in large measure) that he set forth his conception of socialism and the transition to communism." Meisner had stressed that at the very heart of the Marxist concept on the dictatorship of the proletariat was a time when the social powers usurped by the state would be returned to society as a whole. Meisner further pointed out, if Pfeffer really had taken seriously the study on Marxist theory, he might "have been moved to ask whether the masses of producers in China have the political means to determine the conditions under which they work and to control the products of their labor. That, after all, is the first and essential condition of socialism. He might have posed the question of whether the bureaucratic state apparatus in the People's Republic is really under popular control. He might even have pondered the question of how a presumably socialist society could have produced so extreme a form of alienated social power as the cult of Mao."[1]

Stuart Schram had also published papers in *Modern China* to criticize some ideas and opinions of the leftists. According to him, Pfeffer's idea that Mao accorded with Marx was vague, and Pfeffer had overlooked the connection between Mao's thoughts and the traditional Chinese culture that had great influence on Mao. Schram criticized the leftists for imposing criticism on the liberal school scholars like Don Quixote tilting at windmills. With regard to Walder's accusation that he had attempted to prove the inevitability of capitalism in non-European countries by quoting some of Marx's isolated and ambiguous ideas, Schram defended that he had long ago discussed the possibility that Asian countries might by-pass the stage of capitalism. Although he did have written that Marxism had first made its influence effectively felt in China in the form of Leninism, but this is not to "reduce" Mao's thought to Leninism, but merely to indicate the most important among the many sources from which Mao drew his ideas. Schram further disputed Walder's idea that Marx was not an economic determinist, saying that Marx had definitely stated that among all the assumptions and conditions in the interaction between the economic base and the superstructure, the economic ones are ultimately decisive. Schram expressed strong dissatisfaction with the leftists who used the far left theory of the "cultural revolution" to criticize the liberal school scholars, and argued that Yao Wenyuan's (who belonged to Gang of Four) article contained many absurdities. He scornfully stated that although he does not regard everything he has written previously as correct, he did not go too far in the wrong direction under the influence of the ultra-leftist tendencies in the "cultural revolution."[2]

Following Stuart Schram, John Bryan Starr, assistant professor of

---

[1] For Meisner's ideas, see Xiao Yanzhong et al. (eds.), *The Legend of the "Legend,"* Vol. IV of *Assessments of Mao Zedong by Foreign Scholars*, China Workers Publishing House, Beijing, 1997, pp. 382-386.

[2] For Schram's ideas, see Xiao Yanzhong et al. (eds.), *The Legend of the "Legend,"* Vol. IV of *Assessments of Mao Zedong by Foreign Scholars*, China Workers Publishing House, Beijing, 1997, pp. 394-408.

political studies in the University of California, had also joined the debate. His book *Continuing the Revolution: The Political Thought of Mao* published in the late 1970s was regarded by Western scholars as the only book published during 1976-1984 that exclusively focused on studying Mao Zedong's thought. His paper "On Mao's Self-Image as a Marxist Thinker" published in *Modern China* in 1977 (Vol. 3, No. 4) stated that one important facet of the question of the relationship of Mao's thought to that of Marx is "Mao's own perception of that relationship." Starr did not completely deny the relationship between Mao and Marx, but he at the same time pointed out that both Pfeffer and Walder have ignored the thrust of Mao's own tendency to emphasize the discontinuities rather than the consonance of his theoretical conclusions with those of Marx. Starr cited the example of the concept of alienation to support his idea. Mao ignored the Marxist concept of alienation not because the relevant works were belatedly translated into Chinese, but because this concept was foreign both to Chinese practice at the time and to Chinese modes of conceptualizing that practice.[1]

Edward Friedman, professor at Political Science Department in University of Wisconsin, also joined the debate by publishing the paper "Marx and Mao and ..." The paper begins with "so much of vitally important facts were omitted or distorted if Mao is comprehended as Marx." In the paper, Friedman stated, "Mao emerges as a great revolutionary innovator and creator, perhaps the greatest ever. In place of the ethno-centric and anachronistic tendency to measure the truth of Mao's revolutionary practice against Marx's strategic conclusions, I would opt for discovering some of the flaws in Marx's strategies by comparing them to the actual revolutionary practice of Mao and other twentieth-century third world revolutionaries. Here again Schwartz was right being earliest in calling our attention to Mao's so-called heresies in practice. We were asked to pay more attention to what Mao and his colleagues and followers did than to what they said."[2]

At the invitation of editor-in-chief of *Modern China*, John G. Gurley,

---

[1] For Schram's ideas, see Xiao Yanzhong et al. (eds.), *The Legend of the "Legend,"* Vol. IV of *Assessments of Mao Zedong by Foreign Scholars*, China Workers Publishing House, Beijing, 1997, pp. 425-431.

[2] *Ibid.,* p. 388.

professor of economics at Stanford University, published the paper "The Symposium Papers: Discussion and Comments" in the quarterly (Vol. 3, No. 4) to give a summary of this debate.

The paper had first analyzed the theory of Marx and Engels. As pointed out by Gurley, inasmuch as all of the papers in the symposium analyze the problem of the relation of Mao to Marx and Engels, and because none of them explained exactly what Marx and Engels had stood for, it seems essential to begin with their theory of history and revolution. Marx and Engels analyzed historical development with three broad categories: the productive forces, the relations of production, and the superstructure. Accumulated changes in the productive forces will ultimately cause a qualitative change in the relations of production. Such changes in the economic base will sooner or later cause changes in the superstructure. As productive forces develop, they increasingly come into conflict with the relations of production. A revolution is usually necessary to resolve the conflict, and the revolution is of course carried out by human beings—by a rising class that is associated with the new productive forces. Whatever the causal relationships postulated among Marx's and Engels' three historical categories, the agency of change is human being. Since Marx and Engels believed that men make their own history, albeit under a definite set of circumstances not chosen by themselves, they would have been puzzled by the modern argument between voluntarist and determinist versions of historical change. Changes in productive forces, they thought, are the bases for historical change, but these forces include human beings, whose actions, necessary for change, have determinate causes.

Next, Gurley had reviewed the complete process of development from "original Marxism" to "Maoism." In his view, Marx and Engels were wrong about socialism in Europe. They had believed that the proletarian revolutions would very likely occur first in the most advanced capitalist countries, more or less simultaneously, where the productive forces had sufficiently developed to be in serious conflict with the relations of production and where, consequently, class struggles were acute. In reality, however, they had underestimated the growing strength of the bourgeoisie and declining revolutionary zeal of the proletariat. As a matter of fact, outside the center of global capitalism, Marxism took the new revolutionary form as Leninism, which had successfully guided the revolution in less-developed Russia into victory. The later Stalinism was Leninism in the age when the Soviet Union was in isolation and within a sea of imperialism. Stalin succeeded in rapidly building up country's socialist productive forces. Maoism was formed in the Chinese revolution. Mao, based on the theory and practice of his Marxist predecessors, became the architect of a socialist society that serves as a model for many of the world's poor. But the path to this success was also the path to the split of the world Marxist movement; within success lurked the failure.

The third part of the paper had commented on the symposium papers. Gurley was in general accord with Pfeffer's argument that "understanding the thought of Mao Zedong in theory and practice requires seeing it as a revolutionary development strategy evolved from within the Marxist-Leninist tradition to achieve Marx's communist goals in China." He also declared agreement with Pfeffer, that there has been a strong tendency in the field of Chinese studies to separate "Maoism" from its rich Marxist background.

Gurley agreed with Schwartz that the thought of Mao Zedong is not the same as Marx's own thought, but at the same time, he opposed Schwartz's idea that Maoism represents a departure from or deconstruction of Marxism.

Gurley had argued that Schram should free himself from the metaphysical pattern that A is A and B is B and adopt a dialectical materialist way of thinking to give a definite answer to the question whether Mao, who is both related to and different from Marx, is a Marxist or not. In Gurley's view, if one takes a Marxist—that is, dialectical materialist—view of Marxism itself, Mao could differ significantly from Marx and still be solidly within Marxism.

Gurley had also commented on Meissner: "Meisner's central idea is that Mao did not "sin" against Marx, but he has certainly departed from him."

Gurley generally agreed with Friedman and Starr that Mao was "a great revolutionary innovator and creator" and "a creative and audacious Marxist."

Gurley had also disapproved Walder's idea that Marx was not an economic determinist and Mao was not a voluntarist. On the contrary, he in general agreed with Wakeman's and Schram's contention that Marx was more determinist than Walder thinks. While Mao was a materialist, his world was somewhat disorderly. Mao did not consistently think in terms of historical laws, and in this respect alone he differed markedly from his predecessors.

Gurley had also commented on the ideas of Selden and Andors. In his view, Selden's conclusion that "Mao has created the preconditions for the ultimate achievement of communism within the Marxian tradition" needs further discussion. Gurley pointed out that Andor's predominantly idealist view of Marxism reminded him of a resolution by the establishment of the Fabian Society: "A human association to be formed whose ultimate aim should be the reconstruction of society in accordance with the highest moral possibilities."

Finally, Gurley summarized the similarities and differences between Mao and Marx that had been emphasized in the above debating papers. On the side of similarities, Mao thought in terms of Marx's categories on historical materialism and had Marx's revolutionary outlook; he carried out socialist programs, which emphasized collectivism, the reduction of social differences, planning, and the development of the productive forces, all in all accord with Marx's theories; and his ultimate aim was communism, the same as Marx. On the side of differences, Mao did not carry out a proletarian revolution against a fully-matured bourgeoisie in the "Marxist way." Instead, he fomented a revolution by means of base areas defended militarily and supported by the peasantry, against landlords and various hues of the bourgeoisie. He greatly emphasized class struggles and social transformation in the building of a socialist society, and he had new approaches to the transition from socialism to communism. Lastly, Mao's world was not as "tight" as Marx's; there were more gaps in it for surprises and upsets.[1]

This debate in the 1970s has attracted more scholars and discussed

---

[1] Xiao Yanzhong et al. (eds.), *The Legend of the "Legend,"* Vol. IV of *Assessments of Mao Zedong by Foreign Scholars*, pp. 455-473.

more issues than the one in the 1960s. However, the focus and fundamental issue in the debate was still the relationship between Mao Zedong Thought and Marxism-Leninism. Chinese researchers such as Li Junru has given an analytical summarization of this debate as follows:

The liberal school scholars have focused too much on the discontinuities between Marx and Mao, while the "New Left" scholars overemphasized their consonance. This, however, does not mean that the liberal school scholars deny the existence of a continuity from Marx to Mao or that "New Left" scholars totally ignore the discontinuity between Mao and Marx. From the perspective of their fundamental stand and viewpoint, Mao Zedong Thought is a continuation of Marxism. In fact, the liberal school scholars have recognized this continuity to some degree, but they have focused more on the discontinuity by stressing the fact that Mao was not an ordinary Marxist, but "a creative and audacious Marxist" (John Bryan Starr). In terms of content, Mao Zedong Thought and Marxism are naturally different because the former deals with problems in China while the latter had taken shape in Europe. In the same sense, the "New Left" scholars in principle have accepted the existence of the discontinuity between Mao and Marx, but at the same time they have emphasized the continuity because Mao's thought is "a revolutionary development strategy evolved from within the Marxist-Leninist tradition to achieve Marx's communist goals in China" (Richard M. Pfeffer).

Some liberal scholars have emphasized too much on the discontinuity between Mao and Marx and eventually came to the conclusion that Maoism is a heresy of Marxism. They have argued that Mao Zedong was not a true Marxist and his thought represents a departure from and heresy of Marx. They have gradually developed a commonly accepted idea that Mao carried on Marxism not merely by restating the Marxian tradition, but by integrating Marxism with traditional Chinese culture. In this sense, the debate between liberal scholars and New Left scholars was an argument over whether Maoism is a heresy of Marxism or an integration of Marxism with traditional Chinese Culture.[1]

---

[1] Li Junru et al., *Study of Mao Zedong in Foreign Countries*, pp. 122-123.

Of course, it should be noted that, the above idea that Mao's thought was an integration of Marxism with traditional Chinese culture and philosophy, which stresses its "national feature," is different from today's universally accepted conclusion that Mao Zedong Thought is the result of the integration of the basic tenets of Marxism-Leninism with the concrete realities of China's social revolution. That idea of integration was novel but at the same time still not comprehensive enough. Although Mao did draw ideas from China's traditional culture, it is more accurate and more desirable to replace traditional Chinese culture with the experience of China's social revolution.

1.3.2 Studies in Japan

Japan was only second to the United States in the studies on Mao Zedong Thought in the 1960s and 1970s. In addition to Matsumura Kazuto who had began to study Mao's thought in the 1950s, scholars including Minoru Takeuchi, Atsuyoshi Niijima, Hidemi Nagano, Tsutomu Nakanishi and Koichi Yamura were also very influential during this period.

Minoru Takeuchi, professor at the Department of Oriental Studies in Institute for Research in Humanities in Kyoto University and director of the university's Center for Asian Documents, published *Notes on Mao Zedong*, *Mao Zedong Thought: On Men's Conscious Dynamic Role* and *On the Origin of Mao's "On Contradiction."* In his view, Mao Zedong's two philosophical essays "On Contradiction" and "On Practice" had originated from the Soviet philosophy in the "Lenin period" from the late 1920s to the early 1930s. Mao had borrowed many philosophical ideas from the textbooks and dictionaries edited by Soviet philosophers during Lenin's period and had applied them to the Chinese conditions. Men's conscious dynamic role is an important idea in Mao Zedong's thought.

Atsuyoshi Niijima, professor at Japanese Rikkyo University, published *Mao Zedong's Philosophy, Mao Zedong's Thought, My Study on Mao Zedong, Mao Zedong in History, Some Issues in Mao Zedong's Theory of Dialectics* and *Formation and Development of Mao Zedong Thought*. He had conducted a systematic study of Mao Zedong Thought. According to him, Mao Zedong's philosophy is a philosophy of war because his thought was formed and developed on battlefield and had guided China's revolutionary war. Of the three types of revolutionaries—technician, craftsman and scholar, Mao was a technician who tirelessly works hard to discover, reflects and creates superior thoughts that meet the demands of the times in a truth-seeking manner, while a craftsman has blind faith in experience, rejects novelty and acts in strict line with the established codes, and a scholar strives only to comprehend and interpret his own theory. He has summarized the main content of Mao Zedong Thought into six aspects: theories during the period of its formation and development; theory of building rural revolutionary bases and the Party organization; theory of the rectification movements; "On Practice"— a summary of traditional philosophy of practice; "On Contradiction"—a unique theory of contradictions; "Serve the People," "The Foolish Old Man Who Removed the Mountains" and "In Memory of Norman Bethune"— which reflect the relations between Mao Zedong and tradition. Atsuyoshi Niijima has advanced that Mao's philosophy has two prominent features: it theoretically starts from people's social experience and not from an individual thing; and it adopts both short- and long-term ideological methods in observing a thing or an object. He has further pointed out that Mao's philosophy had drawn ideas from both Marxist-Leninist philosophy and traditional Chinese philosophical ideas such as dualism in yin and yang, unity of theory and practice, the doctrine of making academic study serve reality, and the theory of making Western technology serve China.

Atsuyoshi Niijima had especially focused on studying Mao Zedong's two philosophical essays. He agreed with Mao's definition of "practice" that it includes material production, class struggle and scientific practice, and called this a "unique creation" of Mao Zedong. He then compared material production and class struggle with scientific practice, holding that they are all practice activities and consequently are all opposite to theory but at the same time they are subject to different formulas: the formula for material production and class struggle is practice-theory-practice; the formula for scientific practice is theory-practice-theory. Although the two formulas have different starting and ending points and intermediate link, they are fundamentally the same because the theory as the starting point of a scientific test still comes from practice. He has also stressed that the practice here means social practice and not the acts of individuals, which is what distinguishes pragmatist epistemology from the Marxist theory of knowledge. He further used two formulas to explain the difference between Mao's philosophy of knowledge and pragmatist epistemology: the former undergoes through a formula of practice-knowledge-practice while the latter, a formula of perceptual knowledge-rational knowledge-practice. He has specially discussed Mao Zedong's "On Contradiction" in his book *Mao Zedong's Philosophy* and paid close attention to Mao's statement "difference itself is a contradiction," which in his view represents the development of materialist dialectics from Marx to Lenin and to Stalin. At the same time, he held that Mao was very different from other Marxists because he took every difference as contradiction, and that "On Contradiction" Mao has advocated absolute contradiction and struggle. He has even commented that: the reason that armed struggles occurred during the "cultural revolution" was because Mao's "On Contradiction" had silently taught China's seven hundred million population to do so.[1]

Atsuyoshi Niijima had produced some novel and ingenious ideas such as the three types of revolutionaries, the main content of Mao Zedong Thought, and analysis on Mao's philosophy. But, it was not fair to relate Mao's essay "On Contradiction," which in his view advocated absolute contradiction, with the armed struggles during the "cultural revolution."

Koichi Yamura, also professor at Japanese Rikkyo University, has published *Culture and Revolution: China in the Era of Mao Zedong*, *Development and Progress in the Chinese Revolution*, *Components and Features of Mao Zedong Thought* and *Mao Zedong*. The book *Mao Zedong* published in 1978 was his representative work and expressed a high opinion on Mao Zedong Thought. Koichi Yamura has stressed that Mao Zedong had always adhered to and armed himself with Marxism-Leninism in the

---

[1] Bi Jianheng et al., *A Review of Study on Mao Zedong in Foreign Countries*, p. 117.

Chinese revolution. Mao Zedong Thought, which stressed application of Marxism-Leninism in line with concrete realities, has embodied the living soul of Marxism—concrete analysis of concrete conditions. Figuratively speaking, Mao Zedong Thought had emerged out of the magnetic field or soil of traditional Chinese thoughts and developed around the axis of Marxism-Leninism. Koichi Yamura believed that the features of Mao Zedong Thought manifests in the following three aspects: (1) Liberation, which is the fundamental feature, and the line is "To rebel is justified." (2) Practice in the subjective and objective world—carrying out theoretical research starting from practice and stressing the importance of men's conscious dynamic role in practice. (3) Education to transform people—changing people's ideology by educating them on class consciousness and class struggle.

Although he tended to generalize directly from part to a whole conclusion, Koichi Yamura has indeed made a lively, succinct and enlightening analysis on the features of Mao Zedong Thought and the interaction between Marxism and traditional Chinese thoughts in it.

Hidemi Nagano, professor at Tokyo Metropolitan University, has focused on studying Mao's thought in his early years and during the Great Revolution between 1924-1927 and his ideas about Party building. His books in this regard included *Mao Zedong during the Northern Expedition: On the Formation of Mao's Line*, *Mao Zedong and the Line of the Communist International*, and *Mao Zedong's Thought in the 1920s*. Hidemi Nagano has argued that Mao Zedong was a agrarian populist—like Narodnists in Russia—in the 1920s. He has offered four facts to support his idea. First, Mao had published the essay "The Great Union of the Popular Masses" in *Xiangjiang Review* in 1919 and put forward the idea of "self-determination of Hunan people" and "Hunan Republic" in the Hunan Autonomous Movement in the early 1920s. Second, Mao had always attached great importance to peasants and supported their movements. Third, Mao had judged the attitude of rural classes and strata toward revolution by how much rice they had in the low season and reached the conclusion that the lesser rice they have, the more they participate the revolution. This was not a Marxist method of class analysis, but a populist idea of Mikhail Bakunin. Hidemi Nagano has pointed out that Mao's above idea was similar to Bakunin's idea that the so-called lumpen-proletariat has the ability to inaugurate and could triumph the socialist revolution, the peasants were unconscious socialists, and the primary goal of the revolution is to guarantee the life of the people. Fourth, Mao had rather attached more importance to handle men and men relations and eradicating the system of exploitation and stressed ideological struggles rather than to liberate and develop the productive forces. In his view, Mao did not take liberating the productive forces as a prerequisite for moving to socialism, but defined socialism as a system in which exploitation has been eradicated among humans and all people other than those who abuse power to exploit others can play a dynamic role in promoting the progress of society and history. Hidemi Nagano has concluded that Mao Zedong was a populist in the 1920s, specifically during the period from the summer of 1920 to the Autumn Harvest Uprising in 1927. At the same time, he has stressed that Mao Zedong has not followed this populist idea temporarily but had kept it throughout his life.

Hidemi Nagano has analyzed Mao Zedong's thought in the 1920s from a unique perspective and produced some novel results. However, he ignored lots of material in his study. Consequently, his conclusion that Mao was a populist in the 1920s is quite questionable.

Tsutomu Nakanishi, different from Hidemi Nagano who has focused on studying Mao Zedong's early thoughts, devoted most of his attention to Mao Zedong's later thoughts. His representative work is *The Chinese Revolution and Mao Zedong Thought* published in 1969. He divided the development of Mao Zedong Thought into two periods: the new-democratic revolution and the socialist revolution. During the period of the new-democratic revolution, Mao Zedong had prepared his theory during the First Great Revolution and the Soviet revolution period; his thought began to develop rapidly after the Xi'an Incident in 1936 and was formally named Mao Zedong Thought at the Seventh Congress of the CPC in 1945. The socialist revolution period can be further divided into two periods: before and after 1957-1958. According to Tsutomu Nakanishi, Mao Zedong's thought formulated during the new-democratic revolution and formally accepted by the CPC at its Seventh Congress and his thought about socialist revolution formulated before 1957-1958 and formally accepted by the CPC at its Eighth Congress had all been proved correct by history. However, his thoughts after 1957-1958, which mainly included ideas on the general line in the transition period, Great Leap Forward, people's commune and the "cultural revolution," had deviated from the previous correct direction. Tsutomu Nakanishi termed Mao's thought after 1957-1958 "today's Mao Zedong Thought," which, in his view, was due to the conflict between China's new socialist mode of production and Mao's old ways of thinking and was a regress to Mao's early thoughts. Tsutomu Nakanishi disapproved and criticized the term "today's Mao Zedong Thought" and consequently concluded that Mao Zedong was a great national liberator but was not a true socialist. It was quite fair by Tsutomu Nakanishi to differentiate Mao's later thought from his previous thought, but at the same time it was equally one-sided to assert that Mao Zedong had not become a socialist.

Like their American and British counterparts, Japanese scholars have also staged two debates in the field of studies on Mao Zedong Thought in the 1960s and 1970s. The first debate was between the left scholars led by Kyuichi Tokuda and liberal scholars led by Hiroshi Jono over how to assess Mao Zedong's theory on national liberation. The second debate was between the left scholars led by Kazuto Matsumura and right-wing scholars led by Sotaro Ozaki over Mao Zedong's "On Contradiction" and "On Practice." From today's perspective, the anti-communist ideas of the right-wing scholars should be refuted, and the left scholars' criticism leveled at the liberal scholars was also questionable because they were profoundly influenced by the ultra-leftist tendency in the "cultural revolution" and consequently deified Mao Zedong, extolled Lin Biao and supported the Gang of Four.

It should be noted that Japanese scholars have always attached great importance to collect and investigate documents and material about Mao Zedong. In particular, the *Complete Collection of Mao Zedong's Works* compiled by Minoru Takeuchi et al. was highly valued by scholars around the world. This collection was printed in Chinese character in ten of volumes and was faithful to Mao Zedong's original works and ideas. Its first ten volumes printed in 1972 has collected Mao Zedong's 429 works from 1917 to 1949. Another nine volumes were printed in 1983, making it a grand 19-volume work. In addition, in compiling the collection, compilers have carefully compared different editions of Mao Zedong's works. They have strived to collect the original edition or at least the earliest edition and annotated all the discrepancies between secaral editions, including big or small changes. However, it does not include some essays that are published in *Selected Works of Mao Zedong* and *Selected Readings of Mao Zedong's Works* printed in China. They have purposefully prefered that, as they have declared: "this collection will not include works that can only be found in *Selected Works of Mao Zedong* and *Selected Readings of Mao Zedong's Works*." To put it bluntly, they did not believe in the authenticity of collections of Mao Zedong's works published in China. Consequently, they have not included those works until they find evidence for their existence, but at the same time they have included essays that they believed were Mao's works even though these essays did not bear Mao's signature. This is obviously too subjective and biased and cannot guarantee the veracity of works included in the collection.

In addition, Japanese scholars have also collected Mao Zedong's works after the founding of the People's Republic. The book *Long Live Mao Zedong Thought* popular during the "cultural revolution" in China was also published in Japanese.

1.3.3 Studies in Other Countries

Scholars in other countries such as Germany, France and India have also studied Mao Zedong and his thoughts and produced some research results in the 1960s and 1970s.

Study on Mao Zedong and his thought in Germany was undertaken mainly by two types of bodies: government-funded research institutions collecting and studing newest materials about the CPC and New China and on Mao Zedong; and those institutes in universities who focus studies on Chinese language, Asian, China and East Asian socio-political studies. Many professors and scholars have produced a large number of research results. For instance, Peter J. Opitz, professor at the University of Munich, published *Maoism* (Stuttgart, W. Kohlhammer, 1972) and *The Sons of the Dragon* (List Verlag, München, 1974), and Jürgen Domes, professor at the Saarland University, published *Twenty Years of Tyranny: Communist China 1949-1969* (1971) and *China after the Cultural Revolution: Politics between Two Party Congresses* (1975). German scholars have also attached great importance to collecting, sorting out and publishing documents and material about Mao Zedong. For instance, H. Martin began in 1979 to compile a seven-volume Chinese-German *Selection of Mao Zedong's Works*, which included Mao's essays, speeches, talks and telegraphs from 1949 to 1976.

French scholars began to translate and publish *Selected Works of Mao Zedong* in the 1950s. Jean Chesneaux, theoretician of the French Communist Party, had published the paper "Mao Zedong and Creative Development of Marxism in China" in periodical *La Pensée* (*The Thought*) in November and December 1955 to greet the publication of Volume One of the French edition of *Selected Works of Mao Zedong* in Paris. He had a high opinion of Mao Zedong's works in the paper. And, professor Michelle Loi wrote a preface to the French edition of Mao Zedong's "On Practice" in 1973. He had comprehensively analyzed and assessed this philosophical essay and concluded that Mao's theory of practice has removed mysticism from philosophy and is a theory of knowledge on transforming the world.

India was among the neighboring countries of China that has studied Mao Zedong intensively and broadly. *In the Image of Mao Tse-Tung, Mao Tse-tung Conquered China* and some other books was published in the 1950s. In the 1960s and 1970s Indian researchers have produced a large number of works such as *The Political Philosophy of Mao Tse-tung* (1978) by Manoranjan Mohanty, *The Socio-Political Essence of Maoism* (1975) by Lev Petrovich Deliusin, *Foundations of Maoism* (1966) by Ram Swarup, and *Maoism: Slogans and Practice* (1979) by Vladimit Glebov.

Studies in the Soviet Union also deserve to be noted. As the CPC and CPSU began to openly dispute with each other in the 1960s, Sino-Soviet relations had worsened and eventually came to a split. In this process, Soviet scholars have changed their assessment on Mao Zedong Thought completely. Their essays and works on Mao Zedong Thought in this period were far from objective and were tainted with political bias and anti-China ideas. For instance, in his book *Political Essence of Maoism* Sladkovsky Mikhail Iosifovich, director of the Far East Institute of the Soviet Union Academy of Sciences, and also other scholars have repudiated their original high opinion on Mao Zedong's two philosophical essays—"On Practice" and "On Contradiction"—in the 1950s. They have reversely argued that Mao Zedong's aim of writing "On Practice" was to indicate that only those who directly or frequently participate in the Chinese revolution are qualified to discuss it. Mao Zedong's aim in those essays was to instigate doubts and resistance to the instructions from the Communist International, and that "On Contradiction" was aimed to split the CPC and oppose Marxism-Leninism. There were many books in Soviet Union attacking and distorting Mao Zedong Thought which was published during this period, such as *Mao's Pseudo Socialism* (1968), *Maoism: Ideological and Political Enemy of Marxism-Leninism* (1974) and *Reactionary Nature of Maoism* (1975), whose names point to their quality or content. This tendency did not change until the mid-1980s when the Sino-Soviet relations were normalized.

1.4 The Period of Reflection, Decrease and Silence

This period has continued from the 1980s to the 1990s.

In the 1980s, studies on Mao Zedong Thought in foreign countries has decreased greatly and in the 1990s, only a few foreign scholars have studied Mao Zedong Thought, thus influential research works were rarely produced.

The Third Plenary Session of the Eleventh CPC Central Committee in December 1978 had opened a new page in China's history, which marked the beginning of a new era as reform and opening up and later a new path termed as building socialism with Chinese characteristics. The Resolution on Certain Questions in the History of Our Party since the Founding of the People's Republic of China passed at the Sixth Plenary Session of the Eleventh CPC Central Committee in 1981 completely negated the Great Proletarian Cultural Revolution and its theories and pointed to the mistakes Mao Zedong made in his later years. This great turning point in the CPC's theory and practice and its reassessment of leaders and the history after the founding of the People's Republic caused quite a stir among foreign scholars who were studying Mao Zedong Thought. Some of them felt confused and could not understand this change. Other scholars, after reflecting on this change, have realized that their previous study had been superficial and one-sided. On this basis, they have adjusted their stand, viewpoint and method in studying Mao Zedong Thought in the hope of understanding it more comprehensively and thoroughly.

More importantly, foreign scholars studying China and especially modern China also advise their governments on relations with China, and multinational corporations in their countries on business strategies in China, so they should know China well, keep a close eye on China's changes and study new trends and issues. Besides studies on Mao Zedong is an important part of modern Chinese studies in foreign countries. In the 1960s and 1970s Mao Zedong was at the center of world focus because, as a leader of the CPC and the Chinese people, he had launched the "cultural revolution" that shocked the world and greatly changed China's political and social circumstances. In the 1980s, however, as the CPC's second generation of central collective leadership with Deng Xiaoping at the core was established and consolidated, China's reform and opening up policy has progressed rapidly, and the theory of building socialism with Chinese characteristics was formulated, Western scholars shifted their focus to Deng Xiaoping and China's reform and opening up. Roderick Mac Farquhar, well-known American specialist in the "cultural revolution," had discussed this change with CPC history teachers at Renmin University of China in the spring of 1998 during his trip to China. Australian scholar Nick Knight wrote: "At the tenth anniversary of Mao's death, the analysis of his life and work, which was once popular in both China and Western countries, is not as urgent and as important as before. He is no longer a leader admired by Western young people and his position in China has dropped greatly due to his policies in his later years. This means Mao studies in the future will interest only a small number of scholars, whose study will become increasingly more academic because their object of study has become less important politically." Stuart Schram had expressed similar ideas. In his paper "Mao Studies: Retrospect and Prospect" published in *China Quarterly* in March 1984, Schram stated, "Even today, Mao Zedong, though he does not loom so large as he did in the 1960s, both in China and in the world, has not receded far enough on the horizon so that we can view him in true historical perspective." Japanese scholars also expressed similar ideas that, after the "cultural revolution" was put to an end and especially after it was completely negated in China, the number of scholars interested in Mao Zedong has decreased sharply, and they began to conduct in-depth study on Mao Zedong Thought. In short, study on Mao Zedong Thought in foreign countries had decreased greatly in the 1980s, but still a group of academic books and papers were published and some newcomers have joined the studies.

Compared to scholars in other Western countries, American, British and Australian scholars were more active in the study of Mao Zedong Thought and produced some influential works in the 1980s.

Well-known scholar Stuart Schram published his new book *The Thought of Mao Tse-tung* in 1989. This book was highly assessed by American scholars: "The book made an in-depth analysis of the development of Mao Zedong Thought by fully utilizing the texts of Mao's works found recently. It will provide a general standard for the textual study of Mao's works in the foreseeable future."[1] In the book, Schram has argued that the development of Mao Zedong Thought was a process of interaction between the subjective and objective factors, between theory and practice, between

---

[1] Brantly Womack, "Review of *The Thought of Mao Tse-tung* by Stuart R Schram," Chin. ed., *Research of Mao Zedong Thought*, 1991 (2).

traditional Chinese thought and imported thoughts, and between rationality and personality, and that Mao Zedong Thought is a dialectical unity of the opposites, the complex interactions between them were also discussed. This book did not rash to make generalizations like many other books did, but adopted a multi-dimensional analytical method to explore the true meaning of Mao Zedong Thought. However, while focusing on studying how Western culture, Marxism, traditional Chinese culture and nationalism had influenced the formation and development of Mao Zedong Thought, Schram did not pay enough attention to China's concrete revolutionary practice, which was a deficiency making some ideas in the book dubious.

Brantly Womack, assistant professor of politics at Northern Illinois University, has published *The Historical Shaping of Mao Zedong's Political Thought* (1982), *The Foundations of Mao Zedong's Political Thought, 1917-1935* (1982) and *Politics in China* (1986). The most well-known was *The Foundations of Mao Zedong's Political Thought, 1917-1935*, which made a correct, steady, profound and insightful analysis of Mao Zedong's political thought. This book was praised as one of the best books published in recent years discussing Maoism by Stuart Schram in his paper "Mao Studies: Retrospect and Prospect." Womack has strived to find out the political nature and background in Mao Zedong's works, combined Mao's political ideas with their corresponding realities, and discussed how Mao had reacted to urgent and major issues at critical political moments. After studying the complete process in which Mao Zedong Thought took shape and developed before 1935, he has concluded that the integration of theory and practice with the goal of effective revolutionary action is not only a basic feature in the development of Mao's thought but also a fundamental feature of Mao's political thought. In his view, Mao Zedong's political movements before 1935 were manifested in a three-in-one mode—individual model, revolutionary strategy and political model, which embodied the policy of egalitarian re-distribution of financial resources, the principle that cadres should maintain close ties with the masses, and the political strategy of transforming the support of masses to military forces. This mode has great historical significance because it has embodied a political concept suitable to China's conditions and removed the bottleneck in the country's historical progress. At the same time, Womack pointed out that this mode functions well only when it is put in suitable circumstances, so it will be no longer applicable after it has successfully changed the circumstances.

Raymond F. Wylie, another influential scholar in the field of Mao studies in the United States, began in the 1970s to publish papers about Mao's thoughts in the 1930s and 1940s and published his well-known book *The Emergence of Maoism: Mao Tse-tung, Ch'en Po-da, and the Search for Chinese Theory, 1935-1945* in 1980. This book splendidly integrated the theoretical disputes within the CPC with the political struggles both within and without the Party. Wylie had systematically discussed the content and meaning of Maoism and its relation with Mao Zedong by focusing on the ideological and political course in which Mao Zedong Thought was gradually established as the Party's guiding ideology. His analysis has involved both Marxism and traditional Chinese thought. In his view, the principle of "integrating Marxism with Chinese practice" is of vital importance for the establishment of Mao Zedong Thought as the CPC's guiding ideology because it means applying, improving or abandoning theoretical viewpoints of Marxism-Leninism and urges the Chinese Communists to create new theories suitable to the country's new situations. In this process, Marxism has guided the Chinese revolution and benefited from the traditional Chinese culture, which in return judged or tested Marxism's effectiveness in guiding China's revolutionary struggle. Wylie consequently asserted that Maoism is sinified Marxism and is a brand new theory for the Chinese revolution. In short, Wylie made a comparatively thorough analysis on Maoism by tracing the process of how Marxism was applied in China and discussing both Marxism-Leninism and traditional Chinese thought. His analysis would be more comprehensive and convincing if he had also discussed China's revolutionary practice.

Australia leads the newest studies:

In the 1980s, the center of Mao studies in foreign countries has moved from Europe and the United States to Australia. Mao studies in Australia had started later than that in the United States, England and Japan, but has developed rapidly. After the CPC has assessed Mao Zedong at the Sixth Plenary Session of its Eleventh Central Committee in 1981, many foreign scholars studying Mao Zedong had either ceased their study or began to reflect on their previous study. However, a large number of Australian scholars has appeared conducting new Mao studies, such as Graham Young from Contemporary China Centre at the Australian National University, Frederick C. Teiwes, senior lecturer at University of Sydney, and Nick Knight, senior lecturer at Modern Asian Institute of Griffith University. They have published many papers in the mid-1980s to express their opinions in the debate over "Good Mao" and "Bad Mao."

The Australian Journal of Chinese Affairs published many papers on the theme of "Good Mao" and "Bad Mao" in July 1986. They were: "'Good Mao,' 'Bad Mao': Mao Studies and the Re-Evaluation of Mao's Political Thought" by John Bryan Starr, "Empiricism and Discourse in the Field of Mao Studies" by Nick Knight, "Where Mao Went Wrong: Epistemology and Ideology in Mao's Leftist Policies" by Brantly Womack, "Mao Zedong and the Class Struggle in Socialist Society" by Graham Young, "Peng Dehuai and Mao Zedong" by Frederick C. Teiwes, and "Ten Years after Mao" by Lowell Dittmer. It should be noted here that the debate between "Good Mao" and "Bad Mao" was conducted on the basis of a consensus that Mao Zedong's contributions should be fully affirmed and his contributions outweigh his mistakes. At the core of the debate was a key question: how to differentiate between his correctness and mistakes.

Nick Knight has argued that the reason behind the debate lies in the empiricist epistemology of Western scholars. According to empiricism, sense-data and the facts of observation are most commonly designated as the evidential basis of knowledge, and the experience of the human subject is thus the ultimate court of appeal in the determination of what constitutes knowledge. First, consequence of this illogical empiricist procedure has been a poverty of theory within the field of Mao studies. Second, because empiricism "can say nothing to explain why some people's experiences are to be preferred to those of others," some empiricist Mao scholars find no alternative but to reiterate dogmatically the validity of their own interpretations as opposed to those of others. Third, from the empiricist perspective, the Mao texts constitute a neutral realm whose function is the validation of the objectivity of a particular interpretation; the reader, the passive recipient of the text's message, has merely to read the text to comprehend the authorial intent. This involves an assumption that a literal reading of the surface message of the text is sufficient to disclose authorial intention. As a result, the true intention of the author is often obscured because a text represents a complex structure constituted by a number of possible levels of meaning, and the reader can correctly understand the authorial intention only when comprehending all the levels of the meaning as a complex structure. Fourth, empiricism tends to raise a presumptuous banner of objectivity. This, in Knight's view, is impossible because there is and can be no objective or ideologically neutral reading of the Mao texts, which, instead, should be read on an ideological basis. An important factor contributing to the meaning drawn from a text is the personal ideological perspective of the reader. Such is the case even when the reader is not aware of this. In this sense, how Mao scholars read, study and assess the essence of Mao's works is up to their theoretical and ideological standpoint and not to their empirical "correctness," precision of argument or number of reinforcing quotations. Fifth, empiricism tends to reduce complex texts to an "essence" in order to make the text accessible to the experience of the reader. Consequently, contradictions and lacunae within the text are glossed over or swept aside as the text is interpreted as containing an essential message. This is clearly illogical and unscientific. As a matter of fact, there is an interaction between reader and text. The readers are not and cannot be a passive recipient of the text's surface message; instead, the readers will interrogate the text from their perspective and move beyond the initial surface, reading to grasp the text's deeper levels of meaning.

According to Nick Knight, the reason behind the vociferous debates in the field of Mao studies is that Mao scholars are adopting empiricist procedures in their study. Then, what measures should be taken to overcome this empiricist epistemology and assess Mao and his thought more scientifically? Nick Knight has advanced the method of "personal ideological perspective," which features the combination of "theoretical framework," "methodological procedures" and "protocols of evidence." First, reading Mao texts should cease to be a quest to arrive at definitive comprehension of authorial intention and become instead a process in which the reader imposes his or her own framework for understanding on the text. Doing so will activate the text and help the reader understand the deep meaning of Mao. In this process, Mao scholars, as readers, are no longer passive recipients of the author's message and become an active, dominant principle. Second, Mao scholars should formulate methodological procedures in line with their theoretical framework. An admission and elaboration of the discursive assumptions which underpin reading is an important step forward in this process. Third, the discourse of Mao scholars which provides the theoretical framework should be the protocols of evidence for the assessment of the validity of interpretation. In short, the protocols of evidence can be found only in their theoretical framework and not in the seemingly neutral Mao texts. And there are no other neutral realms that can assess the validity of interpretation.[1]

Lowell Dittmer has opposed Nick Knight's opinions. He has pointed out, "Knight's argument would lead to a bootless solipsism where few would wish to follow; it is perhaps useful to remind us of the ineluctable subjectivity of the search for truth and the ambiguity of the corroborating evidence. Actually, there is a surprising degree of accord in the descriptive accounts of Mao's contribution in such discussions."

John Bryan Starr has also opposed Nick Knight's opinions. He has commented that Knight's prescription calls for a potentially solipsistic atmosphere and is therefore futile from the outset.

---

[1] Xiao Yanzhong et al. (eds.), *The Legend of the "Legend,"* Vol. IV of *Assessments of Mao Zedong by Foreign Scholars*, pp. 117-140.

Brantly Womack advanced his own novel ideas. In his view, Mao scholars should comprehend the dichotomy between the "good" and the "bad" Mao by investigating how Deng Xiaoping and his colleagues assessed Mao. He agrees with the CPC's Resolution on Certain Questions in the History of Our Party since the Founding of the People's Republic of China that the year 1957 represented a turning point in Mao's politics and thought. In addition, he put forward that not all of Mao's ideas after 1957 were bad—Mao had scored achievements as well as made mistakes. The image of "bad" Mao was typical in 1957, and the Great Leap Forward and the "cultural revolution" were mistakes which characterized Mao's new track. At the same time, however, it is not fair to impose the image of "bad" Mao on Mao himself because the disruption and famine caused by the Great Leap Forward were certainly not his intension, and the same can be said of the "cultural revolution." Womack has further pointed out that the commonly accepted mistakes of Mao were in essence a step in the structural weakening of a correct ideology and were attributable to the dogmatic construal of Marxism-Leninism. Therefore, Mao should not be solely blamed for the mistakes.

Lowell Dittmer has disputed Womack's above ideas. He has criticized that Womack failed to efficiently describe Mao's ambivalence in thinking and practice after 1957. While Mao was clearly unrealistically euphoric during the heyday of the Great Leap Forward, his motive for launching the "cultural revolution" seems to have reflected profound anxiety and even pessimism about the future of the revolution. As a matter of fact, Mao had frequently showed such ambivalence. Dittmer has further pointed out, although Womack strived to regard Mao as a good Maoist, he still regarded Mao as a "heretical" Marxist or even an equivalent of Soviet dictator Stalin. In fact, however, Mao was not like Stalin, which can be proved by a comparison of the posthumous fate of Mao's legacy to that of Stalin. Stalin was completely denied, while Mao's ideas about seeking truth from facts, the mass line and self-reliance continued to operate as the living soul of Mao Zedong Thought.

Approaching from a perspective different from that of other scholars, Graham Young has discussed the theoretical reasons behind "bad Mao" by a thorough analysis of Mao's three theories of class struggle. The first was based on a conception of "remnant" classes before the founding of New China and throughout the 1950s. The second was based on the notion that classes could re-generate themselves under socialism by taking advantage of such superstructural relics as "bourgeois rights" The third embraced the idea that a "new class" could arise on the basis of the power and privileges accruing to the Communist political elite. In the view of Graham Young, these three theories of class, each had somewhat different political implications, the contradictions among which remained veiled until the "cultural revolution" drew them out. The first theory is targeted at remnant classes, namely the former "five black" classes—landlords, rich farmers, anti-revolutionists, bad elements and rightists—and their offspring. The second theory is targeted at the new bourgeois elements. The third theory is targeted at bourgeois ideas of revolutionary cadres and other emergent beneficiaries of the revolution. According to Graham Young, Mao and his colleagues did not realize the conflicts among the three theoretical orientations, which had led to the failure of the "cultural revolution," and it is clear that such a theoretical framework prevented Mao from taking unified measures to accomplish socialist revolution and prevent comeback of capitalism.

Both Starr and Dittmer had a high opinion of Graham Young's above analysis. At the same time, Dittmer pointed out that the distinction between the second and third theories did not appear to him altogether clear.

In some sense, this debate in *The Australian Journal of Chinese Affairs* was a symbol that Australia was becoming the center of Western Mao studies. Australian scholars had also introduced some new, prominent academic analytical methods and approaches, which were conducive to deepening the studies on Mao Zedong Thought.

After entering the 1980s, foreign scholars of Mao studies increased exchange with Chinese researchers. Scholars such as Stuart Schram, Roderick Mac Farquhar, Nick Knight, Frederick C. Teiwes and Minoru Takeuchi have all visited China for academic exchange—some of them have visited China several times or have become visiting professors in Chinese universities.

By expanding and deepening academic exchange with Chinese researchers, they became to know the viewpoints of Chinese scholars more directly and comprehensively and have easier access to documents and materials about Mao Zedong. All this has greatly helped their study.

In the 1990s, foreign studies on Mao Zedong and his thought was at a low ebb. The small number of books and papers on Mao studies published in the early 1990s were actually research results of the late 1980s. From the mid-1990s to present, few books are published to study Mao Zedong Thought, and available information indicates that no influential books in this field have been published. But, some papers on Mao Zedong Thought were published, and some books about contemporary China or Deng Xiaoping have also studied Mao Zedong's thought.

Books about Mao Zedong and his thought published in the 1990s were: *The Saga of Anthropology in China: from Malinowski to Moscow to Mao* (M.E. Sharpe, Inc., 1994) by Gregory Eliyu Guldin, *Role of Ch'i in Mao Tse-Tung's Leadership Style* (San Francisco: Mellen Research University Press, 1994) and *Mao Tse-Tung's Purposive Contention with the Superpowers: The Theory of Ch'i* (New York: Mellen Research University Press, 1994) by Lai Sing Lam, *The New Emperors: China in the Era of Mao and Deng* (Little Brown & Co., 1992) by Harrison E. Salisbury, *Modern China's Politics and Mao Zedong* (Japan Law and Culture Publications, 1991) by Teiichi Ikegami, *China's Reform and Democratization* (Japan Contemporary Publications, 1992) by Ryosei Kokubun, and *Mao Zedong and Deng Xiaoping* (NTT Publications, 1994) by Toshio Watanabe and Tomoyuki Kojima. Papers about Mao studies were mainly published in journals such as *China Quarterly* and *Modern China* in the 1990s. For instance, *China Quarterly* published "Comment: Mao, the Comintern and the Second United Front" (No. 129, 1992) by John W. Garver, "The Most Respected Enemy: Mao Zedong's Perception of the United States" (No. 137, 1994) by He Di, and "Mao Zedong a Hundred Years on: The Legacy of a Ruler" (No. 137, 1994) by Stuart Schram.

It deserves to be noted that Australian scholars were still very interested in Mao studies and produced many papers in the 1990s. In particular, Nick Knight published "Contrasting Perspectives on Causation and Social Change in the Thought of Mao Zedong," "Soviet Philosophy and Mao Zedong's 'Sinification of Marxism'," "The 'Orthodoxy' of Mao Zedong's Handling of the Law of the 'Negation of the Negation'" and some other papers. Paul Healy published "Mao and Classical Marxism: Epistemology, Social Formation, Classes and Class Struggle in Mao Zedong's Post-1955 Thought" and some other papers. In recent years, Nick Knight is devoting himself to studying Mao Zedong's philosophy. He has analyzed how the Soviet Marxist philosophy in the 1930s had influenced Mao's two philosophical essays written in 1937—"On Practice" and "On Contradiction." According to him, the Soviet Marxist philosophy had greatly influenced Mao's philosophical thought. However, it should be stated clearly that Mao's Marxism was neither a reproduction of thoughts of Soviet predecessors nor a heresy of Marxism. Mao Zedong has laid the theoretical and ideological foundation for Chinese Marxism by publishing a large number of influential philosophy textbooks and essays. At the same time, Nick Knight has admitted that Mao's Marxist theory was formed on the basis of the Marxist philosophy textbooks of the Soviet Union in the 1930s.[1] Nick Knight especially stressed the importance of Mao's "Dialectical Materialism-Notes of Lectures," where "On Practice" and "On Contradiction" originated, and Mao's original annotations to Soviet and Chinese philosophy textbooks. His aim of doing so is to oppose the arbitrary idea that Mao's philosophical works had simply copied ideas from Soviet philosophy textbooks as well as the one-sided idea that Mao had deviated from orthodox Marxism.

Nick Knight, Paul Healy and other Australian scholars have also reflected and assessed Western Mao studies in the 1990s. Nick Knight published the paper "Mao Zedong's Thought and Chinese Marxism: Recent Documents and Interpretations" in the *Bulletin of Concerned Asian Scholars* (Vol. 25, No. 2) in 1993 to assess books about Mao studies such as *The*

---

[1] Nick Knight, "Soviet Philosophy and Mao Zedong's 'Sinification of Marxism'," Chin. ed., *Research of Mao Zedong Thought*, 1991 (3).

Thought of Mao Tse-tung by Stuart Schram in 1989, *Philosophy and Politics in China: The Controversy over Dialectical Materialism in the 1930s* by Maurice Meisner in 1990, and *The Secret Speeches of Chairman Mao: From the Hundred Flowers to the Great Leap Forward* edited by Roderick Mac Farquhar. Nick Knight has criticized empirical research methods in Western Mao studies, which often overlooked Marxism's influence on Mao's theory and tended to conclude that Mao's thought and works were the result of needs of class struggle and inner-Party struggle. Paul Healy has also criticized empirical research methods of Western scholars in his long paper "Mao and Classical Marxism: Epistemology, Social Formation, Classes and Class Struggle in Mao Zedong's Post-1955 Thought." In order to dispute the idea that Mao Zedong was not an orthodox Marxist, Healy has analyzed Mao's statements about the economic base and superstructure, about class and class struggle, and about theory of knowledge and dialectics to prove that Maoism did not deviate from the basic tenets of Marxism, and reached the conclusion that Maoism is a development of orthodox Marxism in China.[1]

In 1993, at the centenary of the birth of Mao Zedong, Japanese journal *Chinese Studies Daily* specially published a series of papers to assess Mao Zedong's life and thought. Tadayoshi Murata, professor at Yokohama National University, wrote that Mao Zedong had the following historical achievements: (1) he did not rigidly follow Stalin, but created a unique revolutionary road of encircling the cities from the countryside; (2) he openly criticized the Soviet Union for practicing social imperialism and clearly stated that the Chinese people should take a path of socialist construction different from the Soviet model; and (3) he spread the idea of opposing hegemony across the world.

Finally, the five collections of Mao Zedong's works published in the United States in the 1990s deserve to be mentioned. The first book is *Mao Zedong on Dialectical Materialism: Writings on Philosophy* edited by Nick Knight and published by M.E. Sharpe, Inc. Armonk in 1990. It included

---

[1] For details, see *Research of Mao Zedong Thought*, 1996 (2), 1997 (2).

the complete text of "Dialectical Materialism—Notes of Lectures," the earliest texts of "On Practice" and "On Contradiction," Mao's excerpts from and annotations to Ai Siqi's *Philosophy and Life*, and his marginal notes to two Soviet philosophy works. The second book is *Mao's Road to Power: Revolutionary Writings 1912-1949* Vol. 1 edited by Stuart Schram and published by M.E. Sharpe, Inc. Armonk in 1992. The third book is *The Writings of Mao Zedong, 1949-1976* edited by John K. Leung et al. and published by M.E. Sharpe, Inc. Armonk in 1992. The fourth book is *Report from Xunwu by Zedong Mao* translated by Roger R. Thompson and published by Stanford University Press. The fifth book is *The Secret Speeches of Chairman Mao: From the Hundred Flowers to the Great Leap Forward* edited by Roderick MacFarquhar et al. and published by Harvard University Press in 1989. This book, containing one hundred pages of high quality introductory papers, produced great influence in the field of Mao studies and was published in Japanese in the 1990s. Well-known scholar Brantly Womack wrote a paper to introduce the above five books in *China Quarterly* in March 1994.

Chapter 2

Focuses in Mao Studies

Foreign scholars have studied Mao Zedong's thought for decades. They have studied many issues in Mao's thought and their focuses are on its sources, its key components and features, and Mao's methodology. Below is an introduction of their novel and penetrating ideas in this regard.

2.1 The Sources of Mao Zedong's Thought

Foreign scholars of Mao studies have always attached close attention to and disputed much over the sources of Mao Zedong's thought, which was a focus in the two debates in the 1960s and 1970s. In general, they have the following opinions in this regard.

First, Mao Zedong's thought is a heresy of Marxism, and its true sources are Leninism and traditional Chinese thought and not Marxism. Mao Zedong was not a true Marxist, although he had developed Marxism creatively. This idea was popular among Western scholars, especially the liberal school scholars such as Benjamin Schwartz, in the 1960s and 1970s. Of course, by saying Mao's thought is a heresy of Marxism, Western scholars are not defaming Mao Zedong or his thoughts, but are stressing the creativity and novelty of Mao's thought.

Second, Mao Zedong's thought had originated from Chinese tradition and does not belong to the theoretical system of Marxism-Leninism. This opinion is based on the following facts. First, the Chinese culture and philosophy has always been fundamentally different from the rest of the world due to the unique Chinese language structure, and Mao's thought has carried on the tradition of Chinese culture and philosophy in language structure. So, it is a Chinese thought. Second, Chinese philosophy does not discuss ontology, neither did Mao Zedong. Therefore, Mao's thought belongs to and is a development of traditional Chinese culture and philosophy. Third, Chinese tradition has always stressed the integration of culture and politics, and Mao Zedong had also stressed that culture and philosophy are an important part of politics and should serve it. Therefore, Mao Zedong's thought originates mainly from traditional Chinese culture and philosophy, although it does have something in common with Marxism.[1] Representatives of this opinion are Japanese scholar Yoshimi Takeuchi and French scholar Roger Garaudy.

Third, Mao Zedong's thought is a development of Marxism. Mao's thought is a revolutionary development strategy evolved from within the Marxist-Leninist tradition to achieve Marx's communist goals in China. It is dogmatic to decide whether Mao Zedong's thought originated from Marxism by solely comparing Mao's texts with Marx's texts. On the contrary, researchers should take Marxism as an analytical method for human society and not a dogma and study how Mao Zedong had applied Marxism in line with China's particular conditions. Then, they will reach the conclusion that neither Mao's emphasis on the superstructure nor his statement about the peasant problem had deviated from Marxism. Besides, Mao Zedong wrote many works to discuss Marxist concepts such as the economic base and superstructure, the productive forces and relations of production, and class

---

[1] Bi Jianheng et al., *A Review of Study on Mao Zedong in Foreign Countries*, p. 237.

and class struggle. These also indicate that Mao's thought had originated from the theory of Marxism. This opinion is mainly held by left-wing scholars such as Americans Richard M. Pfeffer and Andrew G. Walder, French Michelle Loi and Australian Nick Knight.

Fourth, Mao Zedong's thought was influenced by both Marxism and traditional Chinese culture. Scholars holding this opinion still disagree with each other on whether Marxism or traditional Chinese culture had produced greater influence. Some of them have argued that Chinese culture outweighed Marxism; others believed they were equally important and together constituted a unity; still others held that Marxism produced greater influence than Chinese tradition did. Major representatives of this opinion are American scholar John G. Gurley, German scholar Peter J. Opitz and Japanese scholar Kazuto Matsumura. This opinion is being accepted by more and more scholars and has become the "majority opinion."

The first two opinions seem one-sided because they both focus too much on some aspects while ignoring others. On the contrary, the last two opinions are more objective and quite fair. In fact, we believe that Mao Zedong Thought has two theoretical sources: Marxism-Leninism, which is the primary source, and fine traditions of Chinese thought and culture. In addition, we should attach close attention to the concrete realities of the Chinese revolution when studying the theoretical source of Mao Zedong Thought because the Thought is not a theory of pure imagination, but a theoretical system grounded in the Chinese revolution.

2.2 Key Components and Features of Mao Zedong's Thought

Foreign Mao scholars have always strived to define the focuses and features of Maoism. Their opinions in this regard are different greatly due to their different social and cultural background and study perspectives.

According to Japanese scholar Koichi Yamura, there are three features in Mao's thought: first, it was fundamentally created to liberate the Chinese people; second, it consciously focused on drawing theories from the Chinese revolution; third, it emphasized the need to change society and transform people's thinking through class struggles. Koichi Yamura has pointed out that Mao Zedong was determined to liberate China and consequently strived to bring victory to the Chinese revolution. As he put it, "Only the revolutionary practice of numerous Chinese people can bring victory to the revolution. In this sense, Mao's thought was created to guide that revolutionary practice, and its validity was tested and proved in the revolution. From this perspective, Mao had purposefully paid close attention to the revolutionary practice when developing his thought." It should be said that "Mao had focused on practice and given the highest priority to practice."[1]

Japanese scholar Atsuyoshi Niijima expressed similar ideas. In his view, Mao's thought was formed on battlefield and dealt with action, because Mao believed that practice produces knowledge and is the criterion for testing truth.[2]

American scholar Brantly Womack has pointed out that Mao's sinification of Marxism was also based on practice. In other words, it was an issue about revolutionary practice. Conditions in the Chinese revolution had changed from time to time, so Mao should apply Marxism to the specific revolutionary realities in a flexible and realistic way. Mao had never created theories for mere theoretical purposes; instead, he created theories only to deal with actual problems, and he never purposefully attempted to create a complete system of theories that is in accord with his innovation and progress in practical politics.[3]

In fact, practice has been considered as the basic feature of Mao's thought by most foreign Mao scholars, who either put it at the core of Maoism or regard it as an important notion in Mao's ideological system.

---

[1] *Mao Zedong Thought in the Eye of Japanese Scholars*, Chin. ed., translated and compiled by the CPC Party Literature Research Center, the Central Party Literature Press, Beijing, 1988, pp. 66-67.

[2] *Ibid.*, pp. 33, 47.

[3] Brantly Womack, *The Foundations of Mao Zedong's Political Thought*, Chin. ed., in *Research of Mao Zedong's Philosophical Thought*, 1989 (6).

At the same time, a number of scholars have also paid close attention to Mao's emphasis on peasants and rural areas. As Japanese scholar Mineo Nakajima put it, "Mao's thought contains the idea that the peasantry is the main force in the country's revolution" and "the idea of the Agrarian Revolution is the pillar of Mao's military thinking." As he saw it, victory of Mao's line in China's revolution was due to Mao's creativity, which allowed him to recruit peasants into the revolutionary forces, expand rural base areas and make revolution around base areas more rapidly. That revolutionary experience "is still the source of strength in the CPC's actions and has become an essential factor in defining the nature and character of the CPC." "Mao's idea of the Agrarian Revolution soon developed into a theory of worker-peasant alliance participated mainly by poor peasants and workers, different from Lenin's theory of dictatorship of workers and peasants." Lenin, on the one hand, had recognized that the peasantry can carry the revolution through to the end and stressed that the working class should win their support. On the other hand, Lenin had pointed to the limitations of peasants—they belong to the land-owning class and consequently are unsteady in revolutionary struggles. On the contrary, Mao, starting from the statement that without the poor peasants there would be no revolution, pointed out that the peasants will sweep all the imperialists, warlords, corrupt officials, local tyrants and evil gentry into their graves, and every revolutionary party and every revolutionary comrade will be put to the test, to be accepted or rejected as they decide. Mineo Nakajima then concluded, "It could be said that Mao had from the very beginning noticed the readiness of the peasants to make revolution, and he had maintained this understanding throughout China's revolution. Different from Lenin's theory of dictatorship of workers and peasants which relied mainly on workers, Mao's theory of worker-peasant alliance had always regarded the peasantry as the mainstay." Of course, this difference is partly due to the different specific realities in the two countries. "Capitalism in then China was far more underdeveloped than that in Russia under the Czars; the number of industrial workers in then China was negligible compared to the country's population." In conclusion,

"From the perspective of theoretical development, Mao's theory of worker-peasant alliance is a continuation of Lenin's theory of dictatorship of workers and peasants."

Mineo Nakajima also pointed out that Mao's creations concerning peasants' revolutionary movements and experience there from were related to China's traditional agricultural society. In his view, China's agricultural civilization had cultivated unique utopian, equalitarian ideas. The well-field system and the equal-field system in ancient China, the land system in the Taiping Heavenly Kingdom in the 19th century, and Dr. Sun Yat-sen's thesis of "equalization of peasant lands" and "land to the tiller" in modern China all more or less embodied China's tradition of rural society. He has then concluded, "Mao's creation was effective because he consummately mobilized the Chinese peasants' awareness of tradition."[1]

American scholar Maurice Meisner has also discussed how Mao Zedong had stressed the importance of the peasants and concluded that there is a tendency of utopian socialism and a populist tendency in Maoism. He has listed three levels of evidence to support his conclusion that there is a tendency of utopian socialism in Maoism. First, Maoism rejects the Marxist premise that modern industrial capitalism is a necessary and progressive stage in historical development and a prerequisite for socialism. As Meisner has put it, the modern Chinese historical situation was hardly conducive to the acceptance of this Marxist faith in the progressive nature of capitalism. Modern capitalist industrialism was not an indigenous development, but one that came to China under the aegis of foreign imperialism. Insofar as industrial capitalism had developed in twentieth-century China, it had created all the social evils associated with early industrialism in the West, and in more extreme forms. If a perception of capitalism as alien and evil is a general response to the effects of early industrialization, it was a perception that the modern Chinese historical experience served to intensify that. The Chinese situation did not encourage holding to a faith in the socialist potential

---

[1] *Mao Zedong Thought in the Eye of Japanese Scholars*, Chin. ed., translated and compiled by the CPC Party Literature Research Center, pp. 9-12.

of a capitalism so alien in origin and so distorted in form. The general tendency, as it found expression in Maoism, was to identify capitalism with imperialism, to see both as external impingements, and to look elsewhere for the socialist regeneration of Chinese society. In other words, Maoism denies "that China's socialist future rested on the social and material results of modern capitalist forces of production—or that the relative absence of such forces constituted a barrier to the pursuit of revolutionary socialist goals."[1]

Second, Maoism "denies—implicitly in theory and most explicitly in practice—the Marxist belief that the industrial proletariat is the bearer of the socialist future."[2] On the contrary, Maoism tends to find the sources of socialism in the peasants. As pointed out by Meisner, in Marx's analysis on the transition from feudalism to capitalism in the West, the major class struggle is between the newly arisen bourgeoisie and the old feudal aristocracy; the peasants, though victims of that historical transition, are not major historical actors in the process. According to Maoist theory, by contrast, in Chinese feudal society the main contradiction was between peasants and landlords. It seems that Mao paid much more attention to the potential and creativity of the peasantry than to the bourgeoisie and the proletariat, the two Marxian-defined revolutionary classes in modern history. Of course, Mao did repeatedly stress upholding the leadership of the proletariat. However, "the 'leadership of the proletariat' meant no more than the leadership of the Communist Party, or more precisely, revolutionary activists deemed to possess the appropriate proletarian socialist consciousness."[3]

Third, Maoism replaces the Marxist belief in objective laws of history with a voluntaristic faith in the consciousness and the moral potentialities of men as the decisive factor in socio-historical development. "In Maoism, as in utopian socialism, economic backwardness was not seen as an obstacle to the achievement of socialist goals but rather was converted into

---

[1] Maurice Meisner, *Marxism, Maoism, and Utopianism*, Chin. ed., the Central Party Literature Press, Beijing, 1991, p. 54.

[2] *Ibid.*, p. 60.

[3] *Ibid.*, p. 58.

a socialist advantage. It was thus that Mao proclaimed the special Chinese revolutionary virtues of being 'poor and blank'.... To celebrate the 'advantage of backwardness' is to abandon the Marxist faith in the objective determining forces of history, to deny, in a word, that socialism is immanent in the progressive movement of history itself. Rather the historical outcome turns on 'subjective factors'—the consciousness, moral values, and the actions of dedicated men. Maoism shares with the utopian socialist tradition the view that socialism rests, not on the development of material productive forces, but rather on the moral virtues of 'new men'."[1]

Maurice Meisner has also discussed the populist tendency in Maoism. Meisner stated, "In the most general sense, the Populist strain in Maoism manifested itself as a strong tendency to view 'the people' as an organic whole and to celebrate their spontaneous revolutionary actions and collective potentialities." "The much celebrated Maoist 'faith in the masses' was, of course, essentially a faith in the peasant masses, the great majority of the Chinese people and the principal actors in the Chinese Communist revolution. Although Mao's successful revolutionary experiences in the countryside had undoubtedly served to reinforce his rural orientation, he was of course drawn to the peasantry long before they proved their revolutionary value. For a half century Maoist thought was characterized by a deep emotional attachment to the rural ideal of 'the unity of living and working' and the rural traditions of 'plain living' and 'hard work'." Though Mao never argued that the peasantry was socialist by tradition, he did celebrate the revolutionary traditions of the Chinese peasantry. "Mao's proclivity to look the countryside and the rural masses for the sources of revolutionary creativity was quite naturally accompanied by a perception of the urban areas as sources of social and ideological impurities." Meisner has pointed out that Mao's hostility to the cities was closely related to the fact that the Chinese revolution relied mainly on the peasantry and rural areas, and the almost total political apathy of the urban working class after 1927 intensified this tendency of Mao, who

---

[1] Maurice Meisner, *Marxism, Maoism, and Utopianism*, Chin. ed., the Central Party Literature Press, Beijing, 1991, p. 59.

consequently showed contempt for the urban intelligentsia and distrust of the revolutionary capacities of the urban proletariat. "These agrarian orientations remained dominant in the Maoist mentality in the post-revolutionary era. While Mao was consistently eloquent about the revolutionary virtues of the peasantry, he had remained remarkably silent on the political role of China's rapidly growing urban working class. Indeed, urban people were sent to the countryside to become 'proletarianized' and learn from the peasants the 'proletarian virtues' of struggle, hard work and plain living. Maoist economic policies, at least since the Great Leap era, had emphasized more the industrialization of the countryside than the industrial growth of the potentially 'revisionist' cities."[1]

In addition, Mao had adopted extreme Populist hostility to all forms of bureaucracy—a phenomenon he condemned throughout his revolutionary career as the greatest of social evils. He knew well that the "accompanying emergence of social patterns and value orientations" will threaten to increase the economic and cultural gulf between the intelligentsia and the masses, especially the peasantry, and at the same time increase the separation between the cities and the countryside. For this reason, he launched rectification movements and even the "cultural revolution" to root out bureaucracy.

After analyzing the populist tendency in Maoism, Meisner has pointed out that although there are certain remarkable similarities between Maoism and classical Russian Populism, Maoism is scarcely the twentieth-century resurrection of the nineteenth-century Russian creed. "The Populist strain in Maoism is an indigenous Chinese phenomenon." "The Maoist combination of Marxism and populism appears as a not illogical outcome of the history of Marxism in an economically backward and largely peasant land threatened by foreign capitalist political and economic forces." It is aimed to promote revolutionary social change to "realize a future egalitarian socialist society."[2]

It is undoubtedly true that Mao Zedong had highly emphasized the

---

[1] Maurice Meisner, *Marxism, Maoism, and Utopianism*, Chin. ed., the Central Party Literature Press, Beijing, 1991, pp. 100-102.

[2] *Ibid.*, pp. 113-114, 117.

position and role of peasants in China's revolution and socialist construction, and his theory of the peasantry is an important component of his thought. He had greatly developed and transcended Marx's and Lenin's understanding of the peasant problem. This was intimately related to the fact that China was a big agricultural country and the Chinese revolution was in essence an agricultural revolution led by the Communist Party of China. Foreign scholars have ingeniously and insightfully analyzed Mao's ideas in this aspect. However, it was one-sided to conclude that Mao Zedong was a populist. We believe that Mao Zedong was overall a Marxist and a proletarian political leader although he did develop some populist ideas in his later years.

Unlike most foreign scholars who attached close attention to discussing how and why Mao Zedong emphasized practice and the peasant problem and have produced varying opinions, scholars represented by James C. F. Wang and Edward Hammond have focused on discussing the important, or even central, position of the mass line in Mao's thought. According to them, Mao had always given top priority to the mass line both in practice and in theory. As Mao saw it, correct theory and practice do not come from not people's thinking, but from the mass line. The mass line, as a complete theory, is intimately related to every component of Mao's thought and has solved a series of knotty problems such as the relationship between those who lead and those who are led, between theory and practice, and between policy and mass movement. Then, how should we correctly comprehend the mass line that had played such an important role? According to James C. F. Wang and Edward Hammond, the true mass line should be understood from three aspects. First, the mass line is a sociological definition. It denies the existence of any superman or super-natural power or the idea of technological determinism; it believes that the people create leaders, machines and the God and not vice versa. Second, the mass line is a methodology. It advocates the method of concrete analysis of concrete problems. Third, the mass line is a theory of knowledge. It allows the people to change from being subject to or driving historical progress to creating history through their perceptual practices.

Other scholars have concluded that the mass line is an expression of self-determination and self-governance of the masses. Obviously, they have reached this conclusion, which generally contradicts with real the essence of Mao's mass line thought, because they have borrowed the Western example of "self-governing communities" to interpret it.

Scholars who put the mass line at the core of Mao's thought have further pointed out that Mao had led the masses in surmounting all difficulties and obstacles by arousing their will and determination and mobilizing their creativity that was suppressed by ignorance and superstition in the past centuries.[1]

Although foreign Mao scholars have argued much over the focuses and features of Mao Zedong's thought, they generally agree that the core component of Mao's thought should meet two qualifications: first, it should have influenced Mao's ideas and theories in every stage of his career as a politician and thinker; second, it should be able to effectively define the logical extension and connotation of Mao's thought.

2.3 On Mao Zedong's Methodology

During the 1970s, Western scholars have began to discuss Mao Zedong's methodology and produced a number of books and papers in this regard. The book *Mao Tse-tung's Theory of Dialectic* written by American scholar Francis Y. K. Soo had produced great influence. According to him, Mao's methodology, in essence, is a theory of dialectic. It consists of four essential elements: synthetic perspective, historical perspective, concrete objectivity, and praxiological perspective. The synthetic perspective follows a "whole-part-whole" approach. Mao had always understood reality as the whole rather than as parts. That is, he had never viewed any situation or event in terms of isolated aspects, but always in its totality, and he had stressed that the parts are subordinate to the whole. The historical perspective follows a "past-

---

[1] Bi Jianheng et al., *A Review of Study on Mao Zedong in Foreign Countries*, pp. 256-259.

present-future" approach. According to Mao, since the present had grown out of the past, we should not distance ourselves from history but rather we should know it. In a sense, Mao considered history as a "mirror" by which we can know our past as well as our present. At the same time, Mao did not unconditionally emphasize the importance of history. On the contrary, he had always insisted that we should study history critically, learning what is beneficial and rejecting whatever "harmful" is. He had also stressed that it is necessary to study history—the China of today and the China of yesterday—to learn from historical experience, and thereby to guide the present and the future correctly. The concrete objectivity perspective follows an "objective-subjective-objective" approach. That is, one should first start with objective reality, collect specific facts or data, and analyze and critically evaluate them to form ideas and conclusions. Then, one should return to objective reality to verify those ideas and conclusions. The praxiological perspective follows a "practice-theory-practice" or "social practice-theory-social practice" approach. Francis Y. K. Soo has asserted that Mao has elaborated this element most comprehensively. In Mao's view, men should begin with social practice in order to initiate the process of cognition. After two distinct but inseparable movements—perceptual and rational, men form theories and subject them to be tested by social practice. Thus, the first cycle of human cognition is completed. There are endless cycles in the whole process of human cognition, and with each cycle the content of practice and knowledge rises to a higher level.

According to Francis Y. K. Soo, Mao's methodology has three basic features. First, it is flexible. It is flexible in its choice of methods; that is, it is not restricted to any single method, but rather is receptive to all methods. In addition, its flexibility is manifested in its four multi-dimensional processes of triple movements. Second, it is dynamic. It focuses on the multi-dimensional movements and proceeds from the whole to its parts and back to the whole, and from the objective to the subjective and back to the objective. Furthermore, all these movements are not isolated but interrelated. All this constitutes a very dynamic way of knowing reality. Third, it is practical.

This practicability results from a twofold function of social practice, which not only serves as the staring point of synthetic praxis but also verifies the validity of any decision or policy made.

At the same time, Francis Y. K. Soo has pointed out the two difficulties in Mao's methodology. First, Mao's methodology is hard to understand and employ in practice because it is not systematically and logically presented. As pointed out by him, Mao's methodology, scattered throughout his writings, does not provide any concrete or tangible guidance in its application. How could one know which particular method is useful and necessary in a concrete situation? What happens when different, even conflicting opinions or views concerning the same situations arise? What is the criterion in such a case? It is difficult to use Mao's synthetic praxis to answer these questions. Second, it has limitations in dealing with problems that are abstract or metaphysical in nature. Mao's methodology proves highly effective and realistic in dealing with concrete issues or problems related to men and society. But when dealing with abstract or metaphysical problems, it becomes difficult to employ. On this point, Mao would say that his synthetic praxis is not geared for such abstract questions; nor was he interested in them. Mao was totally occupied throughout his life with the concrete problem of the Chinese revolution and had no time left to improve the theoretical structure. In addition, being a Marxist, Mao did not believe in anything supernatural or transcendental. Thus he tended to view the universe, society and man in pragmatic terms and regarded the spiritual dimension of human life as religion or abstract science.

Francis Y. K. Soo has also compared Mao's methodology with the method of Chinese philosophy and reached the conclusion that Mao's methodology is essentially Chinese. According to Francis Y. K. Soo, the Chinese way of thinking has four features. First, it is synthetic laying emphasis on the whole rather than its parts. This is its most distinctive feature. Mao also always thinks and solves problems from a synthetic perspective. Second, intuition is another dimension of the Chinese way of thinking. However, "intuition" here should not be understood as a primitive or instinctive hunch. On the contrary, it refers to a direct, immediate apprehension of the totality of the thing or situation concerned, resulting from reflection upon life experience. Third, the Chinese way of thinking involves a constant reference to history and tends to begin with the past and move to the present; only in the light of the past and present is the future dealt with. Fourth, the Chinese way of thinking is "practical," which should be understood in the following three aspects. One, the Chinese mind tends to adopt a very pragmatic world view—an orientation toward what is useful or beneficial to man and human relationships. Two, the Chinese mind tends to perceive reality by relying heavily on the five senses, especially vision by eyes and stress the concrete rather than the abstract. Three, the Chinese mind puts great emphasis on the unity of theory and practice, or conformity of word and action. On the basis of the above analysis, Francis Y. K. Soo haconcluded that there is a perfect similarity between Mao's way of thinking and the Chinese way of thinking. The four features in the Chinese way of thinking can also be found in Mao's way of thinking; the only major difference seems to be that Mao's methodology lacks the emphasis on the intuitive nature of Chinese thinking.[1]

American scholar Chu Don-chean has also studied Mao Zedong's methodology. He stated, "Mao's theories move away from mere metaphysical abstractions; they are, in fact, the social-philosophical justification of methods. Maoism can be considered as a theory of logic or a system of ways of doing. Mao Tse-tung thought has derived from life, work, war and revolution, is more methodological than philosophical." Then, how did Mao think about a scientific method?

Firstly, "it involves dealing with matter in their original phenomena, whatever they are. It is a system of deliberate planning, factual analysis, objective observation and orderly procedure, and it is characterized by

---

[1] Francis Y. K. Soo, *Mao Tse-tung's Theory of Dialectic,* Chin. ed., in *Research of Mao Ze-dong's Philosophical Thought,* 1986(4); "Philosophical Analysis of Mao Zedong's Theory of Dialectic," see Xiao Yanzhong et al. (eds.), *Immortality of the Thought,* Vol. III of *Assessments of Mao Zedong by Foreign Scholars,* China Workers Publishing House, Beijing, 1997, pp. 240-268.

preciseness, conciseness and simplicity."

Secondly, "it requires us to examine its fundamental basis in accordance with Mao's view. Work begins with reality. Understanding present, concrete and specific facts is the basis of the goal and the key for problem solving. Mao had asserted: '…in doing a thing, if one does not understand its circumstances, its characteristics and its relation to other things, then one cannot know its laws, cannot know how to do it, and cannot do it well'."

Thirdly, "Mao's idea regarding the steps of the scientific process can be analyzed as follows: Step one is investigation, the starting point of scientific work, and the prerequisite for solving problems." "The second step in the scientific process is to analyze what has been observed and explored. What is to be analyzed is not merely the 'concrete,' the 'quantitative,' or the 'superficial,' in accordance with Mao's thinking." Furthermore, Mao thought that the true causes behind the development of things should be analyzed. When we consider something, we should discard the dross and select the essential, eliminate the false and retain the true, and proceed from one to the other and from the outside to the inside. On this basis, we can make up our mind and formulate plans. "The last step in the scientific process is experimentation. The terms 'experiment,' 'test' and 'practice' were used by Mao interchangeably. Experiment is the application of theory to certain circumstances, developing and verifying the theory by doing; it is the means of gathering more knowledge about the characteristics of a social condition or physical object. Experimentation is a continuation of the whole process in search of knowledge." "Deep understanding, wise judgment and sound proposals are strengthened by objective evidence." "No knowledge is complete until it is in practice."[1]

In addition to Francis Y. K. Soo and Chu Don-chean, some other American scholars have also studied Mao's methodology, such as Geroge Thomson in his *From Marx to Mao Tse-tung: A Study in Revolutionary Dialectics*, Steve S. K. Chin in his *The Thought of Mao Tse-tung: Form and*

---

[1] Xiao Yanzhong et al. (eds.), *Immortality of the Thought*, Vol. III of *Assessments of Mao Zedong by Foreign Scholars*, pp. 381, 387-391.

Content, and Andreas Arndt in his *The Synthesis of Chinese and Western Philosophy in Mao Tse-Tung's Theory of Dialectic*.

Foreign Mao scholars have adopted many novel approaches and analytical methods to study Mao Zedong's methodology and have produced many ideas and opinions that Chinese researchers can learn from to facilitate their study in this regard.

Chapter 3

Study Approaches and Methods

O ne of the most prominent features in Mao studies by foreign, and especially Western scholars is their adoption of a variety of study approaches and methods. In the field of study on Mao Zedong's thought, the well-known approaches and methods are: "comparative study," "dynamic study," "static study," "combination of continuity and discontinuities," and "psycho-historical analysis." The book *A Review of Study on Mao Zedong in Foreign Countries* by Bi Jianheng et al, has systematically introduced the first four methods. The following is a brief introduction to those five methods.[1]

3.1 Comparative Studies

This method is most often used by foreign scholars to conduct comparative study on Mao Zedong's thought. It should be introduced in the following aspects.

First, they have compared Mao's thought with traditional Marxism.

---

[1] Bi Jianheng et al., *A Review of Study on Mao Zedong in Foreign Countries*, pp. 191-198.

Western Mao scholars have staged two debates on how Mao Zedong had carried on Marxism and how his thought was related to European and Soviet Marxism. Conservative scholars represented by Karl A. Wittfogel has compared Mao's thought with Marxism, and especially with the thought of Lenin and Stalin, and concluded that Mao did not make any original creation in problems of the peasants, the Agrarian Revolution and the new-democratic revolution and his thought was only a reproduction of thoughts produced by his Soviet predecessors. He has also concluded that the Chinese revolution was the result of an international plot manipulated by Moscow and Mao's thought was the result of mechanical application of Stalin's orthodox Marxism in China.

Liberal scholars represented by Benjamin Schwartz and Stuart Schram have argued that Mao's thought was related to and at the same time different from traditional Marxism. Both Mao's thought and Marxism had aimed to realize communism. However, Mao, paying close attention to realities in China's revolution, regarded the peasants as the mainstay or "vanguard" of the revolution, stressed political and ideological work, created strategies and tactics for a guerilla war, and emphasized the importance of people and their practice. Comparatively speaking, generally liberal scholars have stressed the difference between Mao's Marxism and orthodox Marxism and concluded that Maoism was a heresy of Marxism. They have argued that China's revolution was unique, and Mao's thought was only applicable to China and was a heresy of Marxism-Leninism.

Leftist scholars represented by Richard M. Pfeffer and Andrew G. Walder have focused on stressing the consonance between Mao's thought and Marxism. Mao Zedong had written many works to discuss Marxist concepts, and his emphasis on the superstructure and his statements on the peasant problem represent his application and development of Marxism in China's specific conditions.

Second, they have compared Mao's thought with traditional Chinese culture. Liberal scholars have paid close attention to discuss how traditional Chinese culture had influenced Mao Zedong. John King Fairbank has earlier realized that the efforts to study China's modern history should be integrated with the efforts to study its traditional culture. In comparing Mao's thought with traditional Chinese culture, Fairbank has advanced that the CPC's idea of self-criticism easily reminds people of the Confucian idea of self-contemplation and self-examination and also especially the ideas of Wang Yangming, an idealist philosopher of the sixteenth century in China. Benjamin Schwartz and Stuart Schram have also pointed out that Mao had drawn ideas from China's Confucian tradition when developing his idea of moral education and practice. John Bryan Starr, after comparing Mao's theory on contradictions with Chinese and Western philosophy, has concluded that Mao's stress on the problem of contradiction was due to the influence of China's yin-yang theory and his emphasis on the struggle of opposites was influenced by Marx.

Although it is commonly believed that Mao's theory and practice contain many traditional Confucian ideas, this does not mean that Mao's thought was a regression. As Fairbank put it, "this helps Mao to apply communism to China," so he has asserted that Mao was a creative Marxist. In the opinion of leftist scholars, many old maxims quoted by Mao to analyze dialectical movement of things and people's feelings should not be regarded as an evidence that Mao had unconditionally accepted China's ancient traditions, and especially Confucianism. In fact, Mao had clearly opposed Confucianism. Leftist scholars have also pointed out that Mao had always applied Marxism to China and integrated it with realities in the country while criticizing Chinese traditions. Japanese scholars such as Yoshimi Takeuchi and Koichi Yamura have focused more on stressing the unity between Mao's thought and traditional Chinese culture. They have studied the language structure and philosophical and political features of Mao's thought and concluded that it was mainly rooted in traditional Chinese culture and philosophy.

Third, foreign scholars have compared Mao's thought with trends of thoughts in Europe with his contemporaries. They have compared Mao's thought not only with the thoughts of the three main representatives of

Western Marxism—Georg Lukacs, Karl Korsch and Antonio Gramsci, but also with the ideas of Trotsky, Bukharin and Marcuse, and even with Max Weber's organizational theory and Russian populism. After a comparative study on Mao's thought and Western Marxism, they have found both similarities and differences. On the side of similarities, both Maoism and Western Marxism have evaluated historical materialism as a praxis philosophy and Marxism as a guide to action and not dogma; both had stressed that people should study Marxism by applying it to solve practical problems; and attached great importance to the role of human and spiritual factors and the superstructure. On the side of differences, Western Marxism had stressed relying on the "new-left" intellectuals, while Mao stressed relying on the peasants and his thought could be named "peasants Marxism." Japanese scholars have analyzed why Mao Zedong had paid so much attention to peasants in his works "Analysis of the Classes in Chinese Society" and "Report on an Investigation of the Peasant Movement in Hunan" and have concluded that, what was manifested in Mao's works from 1926 to 1927 was not Marxism-Leninism, but rather Russian populism, which had influenced Mao all along his works. Maurice Meisner has also compared Russian populism and Leninism with China's modern age political thoughts in his book *Marxism, Maoism, and Utopianism*. He has concluded that Mao's thought was very closely related to classical Russian populism in many aspects.

In conclusion, the above comparative studies are undoubtedly reasonable in some sense but at the same time, we can say that they have focused too much on certain issues in Mao's thought while overlooked some others.

3.2 Dynamic Study

This method, also called the "method of continual study", investigates Mao's thought as an ever-changing process and studies every particular period in which those ideas and theories were raised or formulated. This method was first introduced and applied by Brantly Womack in his book titled *The Foundations of Mao Zedong's Political Thought, 1917-1935*. He has stressed that, "Mao's theoretical development has never been simply an explication of earlier convictions; developing experience and shifting political contexts have led to continual re-castings of his thinking. Hence a study of any particular period in Mao's thought cannot reveal all the roots for his whole thought; to be comprehensive, therefore, this study would have to continue till to 9 September 1976."[1] It should be noted that this continuous, dynamic study method does not mean simply tracing the source of Mao's thought; it strives to discover the course of dialectical development of Mao's thought by focusing on Mao's political practice and observing the development of Mao's thought and its relations with other thoughts and doctrines. This method was praised by Stuart Schram and was affirmed in some sense by Frederic E. Wakeman who wrote the book *History and Will: Philosophical Perspectives of Mao Tse-tung's Thought*.

3.3 Static Study

This method takes Mao's thought as an "integrated whole" and focuses on studying Mao's ideas that were permanent or static and which had not changed over time and tries to analyze Mao's theory and practice in over fifty years from the 1920s to the 1970s.

John Bryan Starr has used this method in his book *Continuing the Revolution: The Political Thought of Mao*. In preface to the book, he wrote, "In this book, the choice of a thematic presentation, rather than a historical one, on Mao's political ideas was a carefully considered one ... a fundamental concept in Mao's theory of knowledge is that there is a necessary, dialectical relationship between revolutionary theory and revolutionary practice.... There is a certain illegitimacy in treating his theoretical conclusions in isolation

---

[1] Brantly Womack, *The Foundations of Mao Zedong's Political Thought, 1917-1935*, Honolulu: University Press of Hawaii, 1982, p. xii.

from their practical context."[1] In his view, taking Mao's works as an abstract whole would be conducive to understanding the theme and essence of Mao's thought. He has then concluded that the practice guided by the theory of the "cultural revolution" was the goal that Mao had strived for all his life, and among his theoretical contributions—the idea that order can only be achieved from chaos and the idea of never ceasing to fight against the bourgeoisie— were the most important. In fact, this method of taking Mao and his works as an "integrated whole" has been adopted by many other scholars in different ways. For example, American scholar Richard H. Solomon, in his book *Mao's Revolution and the Chinese Political Culture,* has discussed the continuity in Mao's ideas during different periods from a psychological viewpoint. Raymond L. Whitehead, the author of *Love and Struggle in Mao's Thought* has stressed the consistency in Mao's thoughts when discussing his ethical thought. Starr has reached the conclusion that the essence of Mao's political thought did not change in greatest part of his life, because Mao had given too much emphasis on the continuity of his thought and had failed to systematically integrate his political thought with his political practice. Stuart Schram has criticized him for that conclusion and commented that essentially Starr's study method had not paid enough attention to historical development. On the one hand, Schram has recognized the rationality of Starr's study method and stated that Mao and his life should be discussed from the perspectives of both periods and topics and no scholar should oppose the perspective of topical or thematic study. On the other hand, he has stressed that it is very necessary to make it clear in which particular period Mao's which idea was formulated, but Starr rarely did this.[2]

---

[1] Bi Jianheng et al., *A Review of Study on Mao Zedong in Foreign Countries*, p. 196.

[2] Xiao Yanzhong et al. (eds.), *The Legend of the "Legend,"* Vol. IV of *Assessments of Mao Zedong by Foreign Scholars*, pp. 16-17.

3.4 The Method of Combining Continuity and Discontinuity

This method was mainly adopted by Stuart Schram, who has suggested that Mao's ideas on some issues embody continuity and on other issues, discontinuities. While acknowledging that some factors in Mao's thought did not change all along, Schram has pointed out that the political practice and background against which Mao formulated his ideas should be analyzed. He has affirmed Brantly Womack's assessment that Mao's thought had always been developing and therefore should be studied under concrete historical backgrounds. In addition, he has pointed out that Mao's thought did develop in a certain format and had basically taken shape after the Long March and especially in the Yan'an period. He further argued that the development of Mao's thought and practice can be divided into periods, which was proposed by many Mao scholars. For example, Australian scholar Nick Knight had used this method to divide Mao's revolutionary career into six periods: before the Yan'an period; the Yan'an period; the War of Liberation period; period of cooperatives; the "cultural revolution" period; and after the "cultural revolution." Nick Knight has argued that the central themes in Mao's thought embody continuity and consistency and did not change through these periods, but it had different focuses in different periods.[1]

Objectively speaking, this method is conducive to understanding Mao's thought as a whole and may offer qualitative study on its development in various periods, but it needs a tiring investigation and effort to properly combine continuity with discontinuities. Brantly Womack, after analyzing some of Schram's papers and ideas, concluded that Schram's above method was in fact a method of discontinuities which attempts to divide Mao's mature thought from his early thought and later thought in the "cultural revolution" period. Ross Terrill has criticized Schram for evaluating Mao's whole revolutionary career as a consistent course. Although the above

---

[1] Nick Knight, "Western Mao Studies: Analysis and Critique," Chin. ed., *Research of Mao Zedong Thought*, 1989 (2).

Schram critics were somewhat one-sided in their analyses, it is undoubtedly true that Schram could not combine continuity and discontinuities so skillfully.

3.5 The Method of Psycho-Historical Analysis

This method, also called the "restoration method," restores Mao's thought and practice to his psychology. According to Mao scholars adopting this method, the method and feature of the Chinese revolution as well as Mao's thought were after all determined by Mao's personality. They have criticized that most Mao scholars have focused on results but overlooked causes and consequently could not discover Mao's way of thinking and psychological process. They have argued that the formation and development of Mao's thought was always largely subject to a subjective, psychological factor. Thus, they have attempted to explain Mao's though and political practice by investigating his psychological experience. Representative scholars who have adopted this method were American scholars Lucian W. Pye, Robert Jay Lifton and Richard H. Solomon. Some Soviet scholars have also studied Mao and his thought by adopting this method.

Lucian W. Pye, professor of political psychology at the Massachusetts Institute of Technology, has written the book *Mao Tse-tung: The Man in the Leader*, which was quite influential among Western Mao scholars. Pye has attempted to discover Mao's world of emotions and his way of mind to mind communication with others, in order to find out how he could successfully arouse the passion of the Chinese people and peoples of other countries. In his view, Mao had shouldered both public and private roles: he had played the public role as a politician and played the private role when forming his psychological structure and personality in his early years. Pye strived to reveal the interaction between the public and private roles and concluded that Mao had formed his whole personality when playing the private role.

Robert Jay Lifton, professor of psychology at Yale University, is another well-known scholar who had employed this study method. His book *Revolutionary Immortality: Mao Tse-tung and The Chinese Cultural Revolution* has proposed two conceptions—immortality symbol and revolutionary immortality—in attempt to analyze Mao and his thought and especially focused on his deep psychological motivation for launching the "cultural revolution." According to Lifton, immortality and eternal life as a whole constitute the cultural foundation of men's internal psychological structure, and they should be realized or expressed through a practical symbol. Mao knew well that the length of his life was limited, but he as a revolutionary wanted to conquer this limitation by maintaining a symbol of immortality for his revolutionary cause and thought, and people's extremely flexible and tolerant faith has made this possible. In this way, after his death, his orthodoxy would continue and the revolution would become eternal. The "cultural revolution" was exactly an attempt made by Mao in his later years to surmount death and make the revolution immortal.

Richard H. Solomon, professor of politics at University of California, has also analyzed Mao's thought from the psychological perspective in his representative book *Mao's Revolution and the Chinese Political Culture*. In his view, analysis of modern Chinese politics, thoughts and practice should start with discovering the Chinese people's attitude toward authority and power, because their common attitude, emotions and moral norms, namely their culture, are in essence is an "integrated social practice." But, Mao's personality resists authority and expresses strong self-confidence. Then, how had Mao used his personality to arouse the revolutionary enthusiasm of the masses, especially the poor peasants, in the above circumstances of China's traditional politics and culture? Solomon argues that, there was wide spread resentment in Chinese society, because the Chinese people had long lived in extreme hardships and had no say in political affairs due to China's economic situation and political system and also had been humiliated by foreign invasions. That resentment was exactly the fundamental impetus and force for revolution and rebellion. Even, people's minimum demands for conditions of living was ruthlessly suppressed by the old authority and their hope for a responsible and trustworthy government was snuffed out, their trust had developed into hatred and they earnestly expected to be protected by a new authority that can provide them with what they live with—power-related responsibility.

Soviet scholars have disputed the individualistic psycho-historical analysis method. It should be noted that Soviet scholars, different from Western scholars, have studied Mao and his thought from a socio-psychological perspective. Soviet scholars have published many papers in the quarterly journal *Far Eastern Affairs* in the late 1970s to challenge the psycho-historical analysis method. Ekimova's long paper "Psychological Concepts of Maoism in Chinese Studies in the United States" published in the journal (No. 1) in 1982 had given a concentrated manifestation of Soviet scholars' opinions. According to the paper, American scholars, by adopting the psycho-historical analysis method, have misunderstood the essence of the social emotions in Chinese society and overlooked the masses' enthusiasm for democratic revolution and social liberation. Although Mao's subjectivity had played an important role in China's modern history, his thought was not the result of his personal emotions and psychology. In this sense, scholars should study not only Mao's personal psychology and emotions but also the social and class psychology in order to distinguish the period in which the leader represents historical progress and his practice accords with the demands of the times and social psychology. And also distinguish the periods in which he represents historical regression, places his emotions and psychology over the people, and lead the people into darkness. Ekimova pointed out that the major defect of the psycho-historical analysis method is its tendency to simplify issues. She had commented, "American scholars adopting the psycho-historical analysis method have regarded Mao's subjective, psychological practice as absolute because they have reduced all social factors to psychological reasons and exaggerated the importance of Mao's personality. Their study neglects the objective conditions under which Mao had developed his personality and has not considered Mao's process of accumulating his knowledge." As a result, many of their conclusions were unreliable.[1] The paper had further pointed out that the grave mistake American scholars made was confusing some permanent social psychological phenomena with leader's personal emotions and psychology. As a result, "they have failed to offer an all-round analysis on the relationship between social and individual psychological phenomena and neglected various numerous social relationships. Ekimova had developed a comprehensive, three-in-one study method which combines three relations in a Marxist sociological analysis. The three relationships are: between individual and social psychology; between individual psychology and the social and historical context; and a third relation, between psychological and historical development and the effect of unconscious motives on conscious behavior. The "one" is the study system of Marxist sociology integrates them in an all-round analysis.

Of course, it would be quite discouraging to simply reject the method of psycho-historical analysis adopted by foreign and especially American Mao scholars, who have developed original ways of thinking and reasoning. At the same time, I can say that the method does have many noticeable deficiencies. For instance, many scholars adopting it have made many subjective inferences or even pure suppositions, without mentioning their concrete basis. Besides, some have expressed racial and political prejudices in their books,which should be opposed.

In over half a century, Mao studies in foreign countries have produced an abundance of fruits, and many of them offer Chinese researchers thought provoking ideas they can learn from. For instance, foreign Mao scholars have always stressed collecting, sorting out and proving primary sources of information, pay close attention to the newest academic trends, and constantly broaden their study methods, perspectives and approaches. Of course, they have deficiencies as well. For example, they often overlook the influence of objective social realities on Mao's thought and rather focus on the historical backgrounds, and sometimes pay little attention to theoretical

---

[1] Li Junru et al., *Study of Mao Zedong in Foreign Countries*, p. 176.

preconditions and content and rather focus their research to prove historical facts. In addition, they generally have insuffcient knowledge on Marxist theories and often regard them as a closed, fixed theoretical pattern, thus they often fail to notice the internal relationship between Mao Zedong Thought and Marxism. For researchers in China, it is also necesarry to draw lessons from their deficiencies.

References

Stuart Schram, *Mao Tse-tung*, Chin. ed., Hongqi Publishing House, Beijing, 1987.

Stuart Schram, *The Thought of Mao Tse-tung*, Chin. ed., the Central Party Literature Press, Beijing, 1990.

Maurice Meisner, *Marxism, Maoism, and Utopianism*, Chin. ed., the Central Party Literature Press, Beijing, 1991.

Jerome Ch'en, *Mao and the Chinese Revolution*, Chin. ed., the Central Party Literature Press, Beijing, 1992.

Frederic Wakeman, *History and Will: Philosophical Perspectives of Mao Tse-tung's Thought*, Chin. ed., the Central Party Literature Press, Beijing, 1992.

John Bryan Starr, *Continuing the Revolution: The Political Thought of Mao*, Chin. ed., the Central Party Literature Press, Beijing, 1992.

Taijun Takeda and Minoru Takeuchi, *Mao Tse-tung as a Poet*, Chin. ed., the Central Party Literature Press, Beijing, 1993.

Dick Wilson, *Mao Tse-tung in the Scales of History*, Chin. ed., the Central Party Literature Press, Beijing, 1993.

Mao Zedong Thought in the Eye of Japanese Scholars, Chin. ed., the Central Party Literature Press, Beijing, 1988.

Paul A. Cohen, *Discovering History in China: American Historical Writing on the Recent Chinese Past*, Chin. ed., Zhonghua Book Company, Beijing, 1989.

Ross Terrill, *Mao Tse-tung (Revision),* Chin. ed., Hebei People's Publishing House, Shijiazhuang, 1994.

Roderick MacFarquhar, *The Origins of The Cultural Revolution* (Vol. 1-2), Chin. ed., Hebei People's Publishing House, Shijiazhuang, 1989.

Benjamin I. Schwartz, *Chinese Communism and the Rise of Mao*, Harvard University Press, 1951.

Brantly Womack, *The Foundations of Mao Zedong's Political Thought, 1917-1935*, Honolulu: University Press of Hawaii, 1982.

Dick Wilson (ed.), *Mao Tse-tung in the Scales of History*, Cambridge University Press, 1975.

Frederick C. Teiwes, *Leadership, Legitimacy and Conflict in China: From a Charismatic Mao to the Politics of Succession*, M.E. Sharpe, Inc., 1984.

Lucian W. Pye, *Mao Tse-tung: The Man in the Leader*, Harvard University Press, 1985.

Raymond F. Wylie, *The Emergence of Maoism: Mao Tse-tung, Ch'en Po-ta, and the Search for Chinese Theory, 1935-1945*, Stanford University Press, 1980.

Richard H. Solomon, *Mao's Revolution and the Chinese Political Culture*, Berkeley, University of California Press, 1971.

Robert Jay Lifton, *Revolutionary Immortality: Mao Tse-tung and the Chinese Cultural Revolution*, New York, Random House, 1968.

Xiao Yanzhong et al. (eds.), *Assessments of Mao Zedong by Foreign Scholars*, Vol. I-IV, China Workers Publishing House, Beijing, 1997.

Li Junru et al., *Study of Mao Zedong in Foreign Countries*, Henan People's Pubilshing House, Zhengzhou, 1993.

Bi Jianheng et al., *A Review of Study on Mao Zedong in Foreign Countries*, Zhejiang People's Publishing House, Hangzhou, 1993.

Part Three

Authoritative Assessments and Documents on Mao Zedong and Mao Zedong Thought

Introduction to Leaders' and Party Assessments

In this chapter , we would like to present a part of numerous assessments made by the leaders of the CPC, and Mao Zedong himself and speeches or documents prepared as reports to several important meetings of the Party. These speeches or documents contain assessments on Mao Zedong and the Mao Zedong Thought made by leaders themselves or assessments by collective organs of the Party. Mao Zedong's role and Mao Zedong Thought is also incorporated in the General Introduction part—theoretical part—of the CPC program and defines Mao Zedong Thought as the major ideological guideline of the Party. These evaluations and definitions reflect study results made by several generations of researchers, theoreticians and Party leaders on Mao Zedong and Mao Zedong Thought. As we have mentioned in previous parts of the book, the assessments made by leaders or authoritative bodies have also greatly effected the orientation of the studies and researches.

Readers will have a better understanding on the studies in China after a review of those assessments and documents in this chapter. They are just to give an idea on the content of the assessments, and due to space restrictions, we could not include the whole text or the historical context of these speeches, so they are presented as excerpts from original texts or speeches. In the following six chapters we have classified the excerpts under six important aspects of the Mao Zedong Thought. Researchers and political leaders generally agree that Mao Zedong Thought is the result of the first historical leap in integrating Marxism with China's realities and Deng Xiaoping Theory has opened a new era in integrating Marxism with China's realities. Although we have covered all those aspects and ideas in previous chapters their complete terming and presentation by leaders will give the reader an idea on the Marxist political discourse or political literature in China, their style of debating and commenting on issues.

The political discourse in China like in every nation have some peculiarities and also reflects the changes in the society and advances by assimilating time features. For example since 90ies the term "generation of the collective leadership of the CPC" was introduced; and related to that term another term as "the leader at the core" is widely seen in texts or speeches. According to researches in China the CPC built in 1921 could only start to shape a mature collective leadership in about 1930s especially in Zunyi meeting in 1935, and this leadership included Mao Zedong, Liu Shaoqi, Zhou Enlai, Zhu De, Ren Bishi with Mao Zedong at the core of leadership. The prominent Party leaders before, Chen Duxiu, Qu Quibai, Zhiang Zhongfa, Li Lisan and Wang Ming, could not form such a qualified, mature leadership. And Chen Yun had replaced Ren Bishi after his death and was included in the first generation of the collective leadership. In the 8th Party Congress in 1956 Deng Xiaoping was included in the standing committee of the Political Bureau of the CPC, meaning that he had become member of the first generation of the collective leadership. Later in 1960s Lin Biao was included as a member in the first generation. In 1976, in the same year CPC has lost its three very important leaders, the "gang of four" was defeated and the "cultural revolution" was ended. In that critical point of time veteran communists Li Xiannian, Ye Jianying including others and Deng Xiaoping, Hua Guofeng had played an important role to restore the Party and political atmosphere. After Third Plenary Session of the Eleventh Central Committee of the CPC in 1978, the second generation had started to shape with Deng Xiaoping at the core. Deng Xiaoping was the first in the history of the CPC and supposedly in the World socialist movement to reform the old tradition of life-long leadership in proleterian parties and strived for retirement in his older age. After him Jiang Zemin suggested by Deng Xiaoping and elected by the Party became the core leader of the third generation of the collective leadership in 1989. And in 2002 Hu Jintao was elected as the core leader of the fourth generation. Below the reader will find assessments made by several members of those three generations in the political history of new China.

Mao Zedong Thought Is the Result of the First Historic Leap in Integrating Marxism with China's Realities

Mao Zedong Thought is the theory which integrates Marxist-Leninist theories with the practice of the Chinese revolution. It is communism and Marxism applied to China.

Mao Zedong Thought is the development of Marxism with regard to the national-democratic revolution in the colonial, semi-colonial and semi-feudal country of the present period. It is an outstanding example of how Marxism is applied to a given nation. It has taken shape and developed in the course of the long revolutionary struggles of the Chinese nation and people which include the three great revolutionary wars (the Northern Expedition, the Agrarian Revolutionary War and the present War of Resistance Against

Japan). It is at once Chinese and thoroughly Marxist. It has evolved through the application of the Marxist world outlook and social outlook, specifically, dialectical materialism and historical materialism. In other words, it has evolved through careful, scientific analysis of the exceedingly rich experience of all modern revolutions. This includes, of course, the experience gained by the Chinese Communist Party in directing the revolutionary struggle of the Chinese people in the light of the characteristics of the Chinese nation and on the solid foundation of Marxist-Leninist theories. As theories and politics for achieving the emancipation of the Chinese nation and people, Mao Zedong Thought has developed by applying the scientific method of Marxism-Leninism to a synthesis of China's history, social conditions and entire revolutionary experience with a view to furthering the interests of the proletariat and consequently the interests of the entire people. These are, therefore, the only correct theories and policies with which the proletariat and all the working people of China fight for their emancipation.

"On the Party," *Selected Works of Liu Shaoqi*, **Eng. ed., FLP, Beijing, 1984, Vol. I, pp. 331-332.**

*****

In the twenty-four years since its birth, Mao Zedong Thought has developed and matured. It has stood the test of innumerable bitter struggles of millions upon millions of people and has been proved to be objective truth and embody the only correct theories and policies for saving China.... Comrade Mao Zedong has exactly effected the integration of the Marxist-Leninist theories with the practice of the Chinese revolution. This has given rise to Chinese communism—Mao Zedong Thought—which has guided, and is still guiding, the Chinese people towards complete emancipation and which has made useful contribution to the cause of emancipation of the people all over the world, particularly people in the East.

"On the Party," *Selected Works of Liu Shaoqi*, **Eng. ed., FLP, Beijing, 1984, Vol. I, pp. 332-333.**

*****

Because of the distinctive characteristics of China's social and historical development and its backwardness in science, it is a unique and herculean task to apply Marxism systematically to China, to transform it from its European form into a Chinese form and thereby to solve the various problems in the contemporary Chinese revolution from the Marxist standpoint and with the Marxist method. Many of our problems have never been considered or approached by the world's Marxists because, unlike the conditions in other countries, in China the main sections of the masses are not workers but peasants and the fight is directed not against domestic capitalism but against foreign imperialist oppression and feudal practices. This can never be accomplished, as some people seem to think it can, by memorizing and reciting Marxist works or by just quoting from them. It requires a high level of the combination of scientific and revolutionary spirit. It requires profound historical and social knowledge, rich experience in guiding the revolutionary struggles and skill in using Marxist-Leninist methods to make an accurate, scientific analysis of social and historical conditions and their development. It further requires boundless and tenacious loyalty to the cause of the proletariat and the people, faith in the strength, creative power and future of the masses and skill in crystallizing the experience, ideas and will of the masses and in bringing what is crystallized back to the masses for application. Only thus, is it possible to make original and brilliant additions to Marxism-Leninism in the light of the historical development of each specific period and the concrete economic and political conditions in China, to express Marxism-Leninism in plain language easily understood by the Chinese people, to adapt it to the new historical environment and China's special conditions and to make it a weapon in the hands of the Chinese proletariat and the working people. No one but our Comrade Mao Zedong has so splendidly and successfully performed the extremely difficult task of adapting Marxism to China. This constitutes one of the greatest achievements in the history of the Marxist movement all over the world, and the dissemination of Marxism—

the best of all truths—in a nation of 475 million people, is unprecedented.

"On the Party," *Selected Works of Liu Shaoqi,* **Eng. ed., FLP, Beijing, 1984, Vol. I, pp. 333-334.**

*****

We cannot conceive of survival of our Party without controlling big cities and the economy or without a developed industry and regular army. Some say Marxism does not work in China because it cannot solve these problems. In fact, this is because we are not applying the Marxist stand, viewpoint and method to solve these problems.

"Closing Speech at the Seventh National Congress of the Communist Party of China," *Collected Works of Mao Zedong,* **in 1945 , Chi. ed., People's Publishing House, Beijing, 1996, Vol. III, p. 396.**

*****

Chairman Mao's orientation is the correct orientation for the Chinese people. He has time and again pointed out the truth and upheld the truth. And that is why we often say that Chairman Mao has applied the truth of world revolution—the universal truth of Marxism-Leninism—to China and has integrated it with China's revolutionary practice to create Mao Zedong Thought. Mao Zedong is a man who points out the truth and upholds and develops it. His orientation has been correct at the many crucial historical junctures of the Chinese revolution over the past thirty years.

"Learn from Mao Zedong," *Selected Works of Zhou Enlai,* **Eng. ed., FLP, Beijing, 1981, Vol. I, pp. 373-374.**

*****

This is an ideology that integrates the universal truth of Marxism-Leninism with the concrete practice of China's revolution and development.

Its correctness has been borne out by history. It was the guidance of Mao Zedong Thought, not that of any other ideology, that led the Chinese revolution to victory. In the years following that victory, it has also been thanks to the guidance of Mao Zedong Thought that we have been able to achieve such noticeable successes in socialist construction and to continue on our triumphant advance.

"Speech Delivered at an Enlarged Working Conference of the Party Central Committee," *Selected Works of Deng Xiaoping*, **Eng. ed., FLP, Beijing, 1995, Vol. I, p. 295.**

*****

It is right, not to say that Mao Zedong Thought is a development of Marxism-Leninism in all its aspects or that it represents a new stage of Marxism. But we ought to recognize that Mao Zedong Thought is the application and development of Marxism-Leninism in China. In the course of applying it to the solution of China's practical problems, our Party has indeed developed Marxism-Leninism in many respects. This is an objective reality and a historical fact.

"Remarks on Successive Drafts of the 'Resolution on Certain Questions in the History of Our Party since the Founding of the People's Republic of China'," *Selected Works of Deng Xiaoping*, **Eng. ed., FLP, Beijing, 1995, Vol. II, p. 298.**

*****

Throughout the period of the new-democratic revolution, as well as during the early period of the socialist revolution and construction, Comrade Mao Zedong's ideas were correct, and we should not discard them. During this long period Comrade Mao Zedong successfully integrated the universal principles of Marxism-Leninism with the realities in China, proposing the creative strategy of encircling the cities from the countryside and taking the path of the October Revolution while adopting different methods. Because we paid close attention to the realities in China and proceeded from those realities in everything we did, we accomplished the new-democratic revolution and moved smoothly into the socialist period.

"We Are Undertaking an Entirely New Endeavour," *Selected Works of Deng Xiaoping*, **Eng. ed., FLP, Beijing, 1994, Vol. III, p. 250.**

*****

Anyone who fails to carry Marxism forward with new thinking and a new viewpoint is not a true Marxist.

Lenin was a true and great Marxist because it was not books that enabled him to find the revolutionary road and to accomplish the October socialist revolution in backward Russia but realities, logic, philosophical thinking and communist ideals. It was not by reading the works of Marx and Lenin that the great Marxist-Leninist Mao Zedong learned how to accomplish the new-democratic revolution in backward China. Could Marx predict that the October Revolution would take place in backward Russia? Could Lenin foresee that the Chinese revolutionaries would win by encircling the cities from the countryside?

"Let Us Put the Past behind Us and Open Up a New Era," *Selected Works of Deng Xiaoping*, **Eng. ed., FLP, Beijing, 1994, Vol. III, pp. 284-285.**

*****

The Chinese Communists, with Comrade Mao Zedong as their chief representative, created Mao Zedong Thought by integrating the basic tenets of Marxism-Leninism with the concrete practice of the Chinese revolution. Mao Zedong Thought is Marxism-Leninism applied and developed in China; it consists of a body of theoretical principles concerning the revolution and construction in China and a summary of experience therein, both of which have been proved correct by practice; and it represents the crystallized, collective wisdom of the Communist Party of China.

"Constitution of the Communist Party of China (Adopted at the Twelfth National Congress of the Communist Party of China on September 6, 1982)," *Selected Collection of Important Documents Since the Twelfth National Congress of the Communist Party of China*, **Chin. ed., People's Publishing House, Beijing, 1986, p. 64.**

*****

Chinese Communists, with Comrade Mao as their chief representative, made a theoretical synthesis of China's long experience in revolution and construction to formulate a scientific guiding ideology that is in line with basic tenets of Marxism-Leninism and suitable for China's conditions, namely, Mao Zedong Thought. Comrade Mao integrated basic tenets of Marxism-Leninism with the concrete realities of China to firmly plant the roots of Marxism-Leninism in China. Mao Zedong Thought is a complete system of scientific ideology. Its creative theories enriched and developed Marxism-Leninism in many areas, including the new-democratic revolution, the socialist revolution, socialist construction, building a revolutionary army, military strategy, national defense development, policy and tactics, ideological and political work, cultural work, and Party building.

Jiang Zemin, "Speech at a Meeting to Celebrate the Centenary of Comrade Mao Zedong's Birth," the *People's Daily*, **Dec. 27, 1993.**

*****

The Communist Party of China takes Marxism-Leninism, Mao Zedong Thought, and Deng Xiaoping Theory as its guide to action.

Marxism-Leninism brings to light the laws governing the development of the history of human society, analyzes the unsolvable, inherent contradictions in capitalist system, and points out that socialism will inevitably supplant capitalism and develop into communism. The history over a century since the publication of *The Communist Manifesto* has proved that the theory of scientific socialism is correct and socialism has tremendous vitality. The nature of socialism is to liberate and develop the productive forces and eliminate exploitation and polarization in order to eventually achieve prosperity for all. The development and improvement of the socialist system is a long historical process, and there will be twists and turns in this process. However, it is irreversible and inevitable that socialism will supplant capitalism, and the road of socialism is chosen by people of each country of their own accord, is suited to their specific conditions, and will therefore be crowned with final victory.

The Chinese Communists, with Comrade Mao Zedong as their chief representative, created Mao Zedong Thought by integrating the basic tenets of Marxism-Leninism with the concrete practice of the Chinese revolution. Mao Zedong Thought is Marxism-Leninism applied and developed in China; it consists of a body of theoretical principles concerning the revolution and construction in China and a summary of experience therein, both of which have been proved correct by practice; and it represents the crystallized, collective wisdom of the Communist Party of China.

"Constitution of the Communist Party of China (Amended and adopted at the Fifteenth National Congress of the Communist Party of China on September 18, 1997)," *Documents of the Fifteenth National Congress of the Communist Party of China*, **Chin. ed., People's Publishing House, Beijing, 1997, pp. 54-55.**

*****

The Chinese Communist Party attaches great importance to the guiding role of theory. Since the Chinese people found Marxism-Leninism, the Chinese revolution has taken on an entirely new look. The integration of Marxism-Leninism with China's reality has experienced two historic leaps, resulting in two great theories. The result of the first leap was a correct theory, a body of correct principles and a summary of experience that have been confirmed in the practice of the Chinese revolution and construction. Its principal founder being Mao Zedong, our Party has called it Mao Zedong Thought. The result of the second leap was the theory of building socialism with Chinese characteristics. Its principal founder being Deng Xiaoping, our Party has called it Deng Xiaoping Theory. These two great theories so achieved are the crystallization of the practical experience and collective wisdom of the Party and the people.

Jiang Zemin, "Hold High the Great Banner of Deng Xiaoping Theory for an All-round Advancement of the Cause of Building Socialism with Chinese Characteristics to the Twenty-First Century— Report to the Fifteenth National Congress of the Communist Party of China," *Documents of the Fifteenth National Congress of the Communist Party of China***, Chin. ed., People's Publishing House, Beijing, 1997, p. 9.**

Mao Zedong Thought as the Crystallization of the Collective Wisdom of the CPC and the People

My thought is still not mature, and I am still learning Marxism-Leninism. So it is still not the time to advocate my thought. Maybe, some of my essays can be advocated, for example, the essays for the rectification movement. But my thought as a whole should not be advocated because it still has not formulated a complete theoretical system.

"Letter to He Kaifeng," *Collected Works of Mao Zedong*, **Chin. ed., Vol. III, p. 15.**

*****

I should say that it is not fair to put all the achievements under my name. It is fine to say I am the representative; after all, I alone can not make a party.

"Principles for Our Party's Work at the Seventh National Congress of the Communist Party of China," *Collected Works of Mao Zedong,* **Chin. ed., Vol. III, p. 297.**

*****

Our Comrade Mao Zedong is not only the greatest revolutionary and statesman in Chinese history, but also the greatest theoretician and scientist. He has had the prowess to lead the whole Party and the entire Chinese people to wage struggles that shook the world and, what is more, he has been the best-versed and the sternest challenger to theories. In the theoretical field, he has been bold in blazing the trail. He has discarded certain specific Marxist principles and conclusions that are outmoded or incompatible with the concrete conditions in China and replaced them with appropriate new ones. For this reason he has been able to successfully carry out the difficult and monumental task of sinifying Marxism.

"On the Party," *Selected Works of Liu Shaoqi,* **Eng. ed., FLP, Beijing, 1984, Vol. I, p. 334.**

*****

The cause and the thought of Comrade Mao Zedong are not his alone: they are likewise those of his comrades-in-arms, the Party and the people. His thought is the crystallization of the experience of the Chinese people's revolutionary struggle over half a century. The case of Karl Marx was similar. In his estimation of Marx, Frederick Engels said that it was only thanks to Marx that the contemporary proletariat became conscious for the first time of its own position and demands and of the conditions necessary for its own liberation. Does this mean that history is made by any one individual?

History is made by the people, but this does not preclude the people from respecting an outstanding individual. Of course, this respect should not turn into blind worship. No man should be looked upon as a demigod.

"Uphold the Four Cardinal Principles," *Selected Works of Deng Xiaoping*, **Eng. ed., FLP, Beijing, 1995, Vol. II, p. 181.**

*****

Answer: For most of his life, Chairman Mao did very good things. Many times he saved the Party and the state from crises. Without him the Chinese people would, at the very least, have spent much more time groping in the dark. Chairman Mao's greatest contribution was that he applied the principles of Marxism-Leninism to the concrete practice of the Chinese revolution, pointing the way to victory. It should be said that before the sixties or the late fifties many of his ideas brought us victories, and the fundamental principles he advanced were quite correct. He creatively applied Marxism-Leninism to every aspect of the Chinese revolution, and he had creative views on philosophy, political science, military science, literature and art, and so on. Unfortunately, in the evening of his life, particularly during the "Cultural Revolution", he made mistakes—and they were not minor ones—which brought many misfortunes upon our Party, our state and our people. As you know, during the Yan'an days our Party summed up Chairman Mao's thinking in various fields as Mao Zedong Thought, and we made it our guiding ideology. We won great victories for the revolution precisely because we adhered to Mao Zedong Thought. Of course, Mao Zedong Thought was not created by Comrade Mao alone—other revolutionaries of the older generation played a part in forming and developing it—but primarily it embodies Comrade Mao's thinking. Nevertheless, victory made him less prudent, so that in his later years some unsound features and unsound ideas, chiefly "Left" ones, began to emerge....

Question: You mentioned that there are others who made contributions to Mao Zedong Thought. Who were they?

Answer: Other revolutionaries of the older generation, for example Premier Zhou Enlai, Comrades Liu Shaoqi and Zhu De—and many others. Many senior cadres are creative and original in their thinking.

Question: Why did you leave your own name out?

Answer: I am quite insignificant. Of course, I too have done some work. Otherwise, I wouldn't be counted as a revolutionary.

"Answers to the Italian Journalist Oriana Fallaci," *Selected Works of Deng Xiaoping*, **Eng. ed., FLP, Beijing, 1995, Vol. II, pp. 342-343; pp. 348-349.**

Mao Zedong Thought Took Shape and Developed in the Chinese Revolution and in the Struggle against Erroneous Ideas and Trends of Thought in and outside the Party

Only after having carried out democratic revolution for so long a period of time, fought so many battles and made so many mistakes, did we formulate a series of correct political, military and organizational lines and know how to deal with inner-Party relationship, how to balance the interests of Party members and non-Party people, how to establish united front, and how to implement the mass line. This means we cannot write papers before getting related experience. I could not have written these essays without the experience of the Northern Expedition, the Agrarian Revolutionary War and the War of Resistance against Japan. Failures and defeats can educate us and drive us to correct mistakes.

"On the Problem of Election of the Eighth Central Committee of the Communist Party of China," *Collected Works of Mao Zedong*, **Chin. ed., People's Publishing House, Beijing, 1999, Vol. VII, p. 101.**

*****

During the period of the democratic revolution, it was only after experiencing first victory, then defeat, victory again and again defeat, and after comparing the two [victories and defeats], that I came to understand this objective world of China. On the eve of the War of Resistance to Japan and during that war I wrote a number of articles, such as "Strategic Problems of China's Revolutionary War," "On Protracted War," "On New Democracy," and "Introducing *The Communist*," and I drafted a number of documents on policy and strategy for the Central Committee. All these served to summarize revolutionary experience. These articles and documents could only have been produced at that time, and not before, because until I had been through these great storms and had been able to compare our two victories with our two defeats, I did not yet have sufficient experience, and could not yet fully understand the laws of the Chinese revolution.

"Talk at an Enlarged Work Conference Convened by the Central Committee of the Communist Party of China," *Collected Works of Mao Zedong*, **Chin. ed., People's Publishing House, Beijing, 1999, Vol. VIII, p. 299.**

*****

It was not until the period of the Resistance to Japan that we formulated a general line for the Party and a complete set of concrete policies which were appropriate to the actual situation. By this time we had been making revolution for more than twenty years. For so many years previously we were working very much in the dark. If anyone were to claim that any comrade, for example any member of the Central Committee, or I myself, completely understood the laws of the Chinese revolution right from the beginning, then that comrade would be talking through his hat. He should definitely not be believed. It was not like that at all. In the past, and especially at the beginning, all our energies were directed toward revolution, but as for how to make revolution, what we wanted to change, which should come first and which later, and which should wait until the next stage—for a fairly long time none of these questions were properly understood, or we could say they were not thoroughly understood. When I explain how our Party during the period of democratic revolution, after much difficulty successfully came to understand the laws of the Chinese revolution, my aim in bringing up these historical facts is to help our comrades to appreciate one thing: that understanding the laws of socialist construction should pass through a process. It should take practice as its starting-point, passing from having no experience to having some experience; from having little experience to having more experience; from the construction of socialism, which is in the realm of necessity as yet not understood, to the gradual overcoming of our blindness and the understanding of objective laws, thereby attaining freedom, achieving a flying leap in our knowledge and reaching the realm of freedom.

"Talk at an Enlarged Work Conference Convened by the Central Committee of the Communist Party of China," *Collected Works of Mao Zedong*, **Chin. ed., People's Publishing House, Beijing, 1999, Vol. VIII, p. 300.**

*****

At that time (the days in the Jinggang Mountains), some comrades named me a fanatic in the barrel of a gun because I said "Political power grows out of the barrel of a gun." They criticized that how can political power grow out of the barrel of a gun? They said I was making a mistake because Marx did not say that and Marxist works did not say that. It is true that Marx did not say it exactly that way, but he did stress seizing state power by armed force. That is exactly what I meant. Of course I did not mean that political power could literally come out from the barrel of a rifle or a machine gun. Later they renamed me "always opportunism." Then I was ridiculed as "narrow empiricism." In my essay "Strategic Problems of China's Revolutionary War," I criticized those who scorned the "narrow empiricism." They thought "narrow empiricism" is not Marxism, and Marxism can be found in cities and not in mountains. They forgot that they had come to mountains too, and we were in cities before. They thought we had been in mountains for two or three years and did not have Marxism any longer; they were just arriving in mountains and still had Marxism.... They seemed to believe that they can have a monopoly of Marxism and no others can have Marxism except for them. Then, can others also have Marxism? I know no foreign language and have never been in foreign countries; I have only read some books that had been translated into Chinese. But I always said to other comrades that we can learn Marxism-Leninism, more or less.

"On the Problem of Election of the Eighth Central Committee of the Communist Party of China," *Collected Works of Mao Zedong*, **Chin. ed., People's Publishing House, Beijing, 1999, Vol. VII, pp. 105-106.**

*****

It (Mao Zedong Thought) has taken shape and developed in the course of the long revolutionary struggles of the Chinese nation and people which include the three great revolutionary wars (the Northern Expedition, the Agrarian Revolutionary War and the present War of Resistance against Japan)....

Mao Zedong Thought—the theory and practice of communism applied to China—has come into being and developed not only in the course of the revolutionary struggles against domestic and foreign enemies but also in the course of the principled struggles against various erroneous opportunist ideas within the Party, such as, Chen Duxiuism, the Li Lisan line and the subsequent "Left" deviationist line, capitulationist line, dogmatism and empiricism. It is our Party's only correct guiding ideology and its only correct general line.

"On the Party," *Selected Works of Liu Shaoqi*, **Eng. ed., FLP, Beijing, 1984, Vol. I, p. 332.**

*****

Where does dogmatism come from? Does it come from the works of Marx, Engels, Lenin or Stalin? The answer is definitely no.

They have repeatedly reminded us in their works that their doctrines are guide to action and not dogma. Still, we read their works as dogmas. This means that we did not understand their ideas thoroughly. Can we blame them for that?

"Closing Speech at the Seventh National Congress of the Communist Party of China," *Collected Works of Mao Zedong*, **Chin. ed., People's Publishing House, Beijing, 1996, Vol. III, p. 418.**

*****

Ever since the time Comrade Mao Zedong joined the communist movement and helped to found our Party, he always conducted investigations and studies of the objective social conditions and urged others to do likewise. He always fought resolutely against the erroneous tendency to divorce theory from practice and to act unrealistically, according to wishful thinking, or mechanically, according to books and instructions from above regardless of the actual conditions. In 1929, in the resolution he drafted for the Gutian Meeting, he sharply opposed subjectivism in the guidance of work, pointing out that this would "inevitably result either in opportunism or in putschism." In 1930 he wrote the essay "Oppose Book Worship," in which he advanced the scientific thesis, "no investigation, no right to speak." He firmly opposed the misguided mentality of those who, in discussions within the Communist Party, could not open their mouths without citing a book, as if whatever was written in a book was right....

After the defeat of the "Left" line of Wang Ming which had caused serious setbacks to the Chinese revolution, Comrade Mao Zedong summed up the lessons from this struggle and wrote, in 1936 and 1937, a series of immortal works including "Problems of Strategy in China's Revolutionary War," "On Practice" and "On Contradiction." In these he laid the ideological and theoretical foundation for our Party....

However, some opponents of Mao Zedong Thought within our Party did not change their stand in the light of Comrade Mao's teachings. Therefore, he initiated the great rectification movement of 1941-1942. Among the main documents guiding that movement were his works "Preface and Postscript to *Rural Surveys*," "Reform Our Study," "Rectify the Party's Style of Work" and "Oppose Stereotyped Party Writing." In the movement, he repeatedly emphasized the need for the fundamental principle and attitude of seeking truth from facts and proceeding from reality.... Comrade Mao Zedong admonished all comrades in the Party not to "regard Marxist theory as lifeless dogma" or to "regard odd quotations from Marxist-Leninist works as a ready-made panacea which, once acquired, can easily cure all maladies." For this would "impede the development of theory and harm themselves as well as other comrades." He declared that "there is only one kind of true theory in this world, theory that is drawn from objective reality and then verified by objective reality." Basing himself on this fundamental tenet of Marxism, Comrade Mao Zedong, in his report to the Seventh National Congress of the Party, defined integration of theory with practice as the first of the three major features of our Party's style of work.

Comrade Mao Zedong frequently explained this tenet and this style of work on subsequent occasions.

"**Speech at the All-Army Conference on Political Work,**" *Selected Works of Deng Xiaoping*, Eng. ed., FLP, Beijing, 1995, Vol. II, pp. 125-127.

Chapter 5

Mao Zedong Thought Has Creatively Enriched and Developed Marxism-Leninism

Mao Zedong Thought, in terms of world outlook and style of work, is Marxism being developed and improved through its application in China. It constitutes the comprehensive theories of revolution and national reconstruction for the Chinese people. These theories are to be found in Comrade Mao Zedong's writings and in many works of our Party literature. They include Comrade Mao Zedong's analysis of the present world situation and China's conditions and his theories and policies with regard to New Democracy, the emancipation of the peasantry, the revolutionary united front, revolutionary wars, revolutionary bases, the establishment of a new-democratic republic, Party building, culture, etc. These theories and policies are at once thoroughly Marxist and thoroughly Chinese. They are the highest expression of the wisdom of the Chinese people and the most succinct of theoretical generalizations.

"On the Party," *Selected Works of Liu Shaoqi*, **Eng. ed., FLP, Beijing, 1984, Vol. I, p. 333.**

*****

In making these remarks, of course I have not introduced to you all of Chairman Mao's merits or all of his principal doctrines. I've only taken up a very small part of Mao Zedong Thought. Chairman Mao's achievements in founding a people's army, his military strategy and tactics; his political writings *On New Democracy* and *On Coalition Government*; his articles on economics; in culture, his *Talks at the Yan'an Forum on Literature and Art*; his new contributions to philosophy and his Marxist ideological system; and all the rest—his achievements are enormous. They are not only wide-ranging, but specialized, profound. I don't intend to say more about them here.

"Learn from Mao Zedong," *Selected Works of Zhou Enlai*, **Eng. ed., FLP, Beijing, 1981, Vol. I, pp. 380-381.**

*****

Why were we able to achieve victory in the Chinese revolution? Because the Chinese Communists led by Comrade Mao Zedong thought independently and, by integrating the universal principles of Marxism-Leninism with specific Chinese conditions, found the revolutionary road, forms and methods suited to China.

"We Are Building a Socialist Society with Both High Material Standards and High Cultural and Ethical Standards," *Selected Works of Deng Xiaoping*, **Eng. ed., FLP, Beijing, 1994, Vol. III, p. 37.**

*****

Throughout the period of the new-democratic revolution, as well as during the early period of the socialist revolution and construction, Comrade Mao Zedong's ideas were correct, and we should not discard them. During this long period Comrade Mao Zedong successfully integrated the universal principles of Marxism-Leninism with the realities in China, proposing the creative strategy of encircling the cities from the countryside and taking the path of the October Revolution while adopting different methods. Because we paid close attention to the realities in China and proceeded from those realities in everything we did, we accomplished the new-democratic revolution and moved smoothly into the socialist period.

"We Are Undertaking an Entirely New Endeavour," *Selected Works of Deng Xiaoping*, **Eng. ed., FLP, Beijing, 1994, Vol. III, p. 250.**

*****

We all agree that much was achieved during the first seven years of the People's Republic. China's socialist transformation was a success—a truly remarkable success—and it represented a major contribution by Comrade Mao Zedong to Marxism-Leninism. Even today, we need to elaborate upon it in terms of theory. Of course there were shortcomings. Sometimes, in certain spheres, we were a bit too impetuous in our work.

"Remarks on Successive Drafts of the 'Resolution on Certain Questions in the History of Our Party Since the Founding of the People's Republic of China'," *Selected Works of Deng Xiaoping*, **Eng. ed., FLP, Beijing, 1995, Vol. II, pp. 300-301.**

*****

Today I should like to discuss briefly the theory of Party building, which is a component part of Mao Zedong Thought. Marx and Engels did not say much on this subject, but Lenin had a comprehensive theory concerning it. It was precisely because Lenin built such a fine party that the October Revolution triumphed and that the first socialist country was created. And it was Comrade Mao Zedong who developed Lenin's theory of Party building most comprehensively. Even in the period of revolutionary struggle in the Jinggang Mountains, that is, in the period of the formation of the Chinese Red Army, his ideas on Party building were already well defined. You can see this by reading the resolution adopted at the Ninth Party Congress of the Fourth Army of the Red Army. His comprehensive theory on the subject took shape, on the basis of practice, in the Yan'an rectification movement. He developed an integral theory on the type of party to be built and its guiding ideology and style of work. By creating a comprehensive theory of Party building in the Yan'an rectification movement—and by educating the whole Party, army and people in this theory—he made it possible for us to build a fine party; that was why we were able to win complete victory in the War of Resistance Against Japan (1937-1945) and in the War of Liberation (1946-1949). After the founding of the People's Republic of China our Party continued to be vigorous and dynamic. Later, Comrade Mao Zedong's theory of Party building was developed further. In 1957 he summed up our aim as follows: "Our aim is to create a political situation in which we have both centralism and democracy, both discipline and freedom, both unity of will and personal ease of mind and liveliness, and thus to promote our socialist revolution and socialist construction, make it easier to overcome difficulties, build a modern industry and modern agriculture more rapidly and make our Party and state more secure and better able to weather storm and stress." Of course, Comrade Mao Zedong was discussing a political situation that should prevail not only in the Party but also in the army and among the people of the whole country. To repeat, this kind of political situation should prevail in the whole Party, in the whole army and among the whole people.

Let us recall that it is precisely according to Comrade Mao Zedong's theory of Party building that this fine party of ours has been built. After the rectification movement in Yan'an, people in both the front and rear areas were active and buoyant, their minds were at ease and they were united as one. The Party built by Comrade Mao Zedong was able to encourage a broad spirit of democracy and of voluntary observance of discipline among those working at the lower levels and, on this basis, it established a high level of centralism. Who then would not willingly obey the orders and answer the calls of Chairman Mao and the Central Committee? Without this style of work in the Party, how could we have defeated an enemy so much stronger than we, and how could we have gone on from victory to victory after the founding of the People's Republic?

"Mao Zedong Thought Should Be Correctly Understood as an Integral Whole," *Selected Works of Deng Xiaoping*, **Eng. ed., FLP, Beijing, 1995, Vol. II, pp. 56-57.**

*****

As we see it, the whole series of concepts concerning Party building defined by Comrade Mao Zedong has immensely expanded on Lenin's principles on Party building. The fine work style of the Party should be carried on by our successors. We attach particular importance to spreading Mao Zedong Thought in order that it will take root among the masses. As for what kind of party we should build, this is a question not only for our generation, but also for the next generation and the generation after that. The party is the key element in a country's revolution. Only a good party can steer revolution towards victory, after which a good party is still essential to the building of socialism if it is to succeed.

"Build a Mature and Combat-Effective Party," *Selected Works of Deng Xiaoping*, **Eng. ed., FLP, Beijing, 1995, Vol. I, p. 340.**

*****

It is now even clearer to everyone how brilliant and far-sighted was the strategy of differentiating the three worlds formulated by Comrade Mao

Zedong in the evening of his life. It is also clearer how brilliant and far-sighted were his policy decisions on this issue, namely, that China should side with the third-world countries and strengthen its unity with them, try to win over the second-world countries for a concerted effort against hegemonism, and establish normal diplomatic relations with the United States and Japan. This strategic principle and these policies have been invaluable in rallying the world's people to oppose hegemonism, changing the world political balance, frustrating the Soviet hegemonists' arrogant plan to isolate China internationally, improving China's international environment, and heightening its international prestige.

From the international point of view, Mao Zedong Thought is inseparably linked with the struggle against hegemonism; and the practice of hegemonism under the banner of socialism is a most obvious betrayal of socialist principles on the part of a Marxist-Leninist party after it has come to power. As I have already mentioned, in the evening of his life Comrade Mao Zedong formulated the strategy of differentiating the three worlds and personally ushered in a new stage in Sino-American and Sino-Japanese relations. By so doing he created new conditions for the development of the worldwide struggle against hegemonism and for the future of world politics. While conducting our modernization program in the present international environment, we cannot help recalling Comrade Mao's contributions.

"Uphold the Four Cardinal Principles," *Selected Works of Deng Xiaoping*, **Eng. ed., FLP, Beijing, 1995, Vol. II, pp. 170, 180.**

*****

Comrade Mao's greatest historical achievement was to apply the basic tenets of Marxism-Leninism to the concrete realities of China in leading the Party and people in finding a correct path in the new-democratic revolution, completing the task of combating imperialism and feudalism, ending China's history as a semi-colonial, semi-feudal society, founding the People's Republic of China, and setting up a socialist system. He then began exploring the path of socialist construction based on China's actual conditions.

After the socialist transformation was basically completed, Comrade Mao borrowed from the experience of the Soviet Union in actively working out China's own path for building socialism. In 1956, he published "On the Ten Major Relationships," in which he emphasized that it was our basic policy to mobilize all positive factors, internal and external, to serve the cause of socialism. In 1957, he published "On the Correct Handling of Contradictions Among the People," in which he pointed out that the basic contradictions in socialist society are still those between the relations of production and the productive forces and between the superstructure and the economic base. He went on to say that our basic task had changed from liberating the productive forces to protecting and expanding them in the context of the new relations of production. He also introduced the strategic ideas of strictly differentiating between and correctly handling the two different types of contradictions, and uniting with the people of all our ethnic groups to develop our economy and culture and build China into a strong socialist country. These were two very significant documents for the Party when it was first delineating the path of socialist construction. In these and other documents, Comrade Mao introduced many important ideas about China's socialist construction involving politics, economics, culture, national defense and foreign affairs.

Jiang Zemin, "Speech at a Meeting to Celebrate the Centenary of Comrade Mao Zedong's Birth," the *People's Daily*, Dec. 27, 1993.

Chapter 6

The Living Soul of Mao Zedong Thought

A s for Chairman Mao's attitude towards study, his own motto is "seek truth from facts". He is most honest, unequivocal about what is right and what is wrong.... So in order to learn from him to seek truth from facts, we should have an honest attitude and style of work and should not acquire habits of superficiality, conceit or impetuosity.... We should rid ourselves of impetuosity, arrogance, dejection, discouragement and demoralization; we should learn from Mao Zedong's style of study and style of work, be honest, seek truth from facts, work conscientiously and advance steadily and courageously.

"Learn from Mao Zedong," *Selected Works of Zhou Enlai*, **Eng. ed., FLP, Beijing, 1981, Vol. I, p. 381.**

*****

Seeking truth from fact is an old saying. Comrade Mao Zedong has made a new interpretation of it, which has come to represent one of his principal tenets. Although it is very terse phrase, it is rich in meaning. What is the best way to put it into practice? The first thing is to conduct detailed investigations and studies.... To make successful social investigations we have to maintain close contacts with the masses.

"Speak the Truth, Make Genuine Efforts, Do Real Work and Strive for Practical Results," *Selected Works of Zhou Enlai*, **Eng. ed., FLP, Beijing, 1989, Vol. II, p. 363.**

*****

I think that the principles of following the mass line and seeking truth from facts are of fundamental importance in the style of work advocated by Comrade Mao Zedong. Of course, the relationships between democracy and centralism and between freedom and discipline are also very important. But in view of the existing state of affairs in our Party, I believe that following the mass line and seeking truth from facts take on special importance. Comrade Mao Zedong was a thoroughgoing materialist. He had complete faith in the masses and always opposed any act that was not in keeping with trust in the masses and reliance on them. He listened particularly to what the masses had to say. Our comrades certainly remember how the production campaign was launched in the Yan'an days. What were the reasons for that production campaign? One was that we had requisitioned too much grain from the masses, so that there were complaints among them, which made many Party members unhappy. But Comrade Mao Zedong saw things differently. He said that the complaints were justified and were the voice of the masses. He was indeed great and different from the rest of us in that he was able to discern the problems behind the complaints of the masses and formulate the principles and policies required to deal with them. He paid great attention to the opinions, ideas and problems of the masses.

"Mao Zedong Thought Should Be Correctly Understood as an Integral Whole," *Selected Works of Deng Xiaoping*, **Eng. ed., FLP, Beijing, 1995, Vol. II, p. 58.**

*****

We should have a correct and comprehensive understanding of Mao Zedong Thought as a system. Apparently, there are people who object to my posing this issue. It is common knowledge that Marxism-Leninism as a system should be understood correctly and comprehensively. Shouldn't the same thing apply to Mao Zedong Thought? Of course it should, otherwise mistakes will be inevitable. Comrade Mao Zedong wrote the four-word motto "Seek truth from facts" for the Central Party School in Yan'an, and these words are the quintessence of his philosophical thinking.

"Setting Things Right in Education," *Selected Works of Deng Xiaoping*, **Eng. ed., FLP, Beijing, 1995, Vol. II, p. 80.**

*****

Comrade Mao Zedong always maintained that in raising, analyzing and solving problems we should adhere to the Marxist-Leninist stand, viewpoint and method. He always discussed problems in the context of time, place and conditions. He once said that in writing articles he himself seldom quoted from Marx and Lenin, and that he felt uneasy when his own words were quoted again and again by the newspapers. People should learn to write in their own words. This, of course, does not mean that they should refrain from quoting others altogether. Rather, it means they shouldn't quote others all the time. The important thing is to adhere to the Marxist stand, viewpoint and method in analyzing and solving problems. Concrete analysis of concrete conditions is the living soul of Marxism. Marxism-Leninism and Mao Zedong Thought lose their vitality if they are not integrated with actual conditions. When we are analysing and solving problems, it is our duty as leading cadres to integrate the instructions from higher levels, up to and including the Central Committee of the Party, with the actual conditions in our own units. We should not just function like a "relay station", simply receiving and transmitting instructions.

Comrades, let's think it over: Isn't it true that seeking truth from facts, proceeding from reality and integrating theory with practice form the fundamental principle of Mao Zedong Thought? Is this fundamental principle outdated? Will it ever become outdated? How can we be true to Marxism-Leninism and Mao Zedong Thought if we are against seeking truth from facts, proceeding from reality and integrating theory with practice? Where would that lead us? Obviously, only to idealism and metaphysics, and thus to the failure of our work and of our revolution.

"Speech at the All-Army Conference on Political Work," *Selected Works of Deng Xiaoping*, **Eng. ed., FLP, Beijing, 1995, Vol. II, p. 128.**

*****

The fundamental point of Mao Zedong Thought is seeking truth from facts and integrating the universal truth of Marxism-Leninism with the concrete practice of the Chinese revolution. Comrade Mao Zedong wrote a four-word motto for the Central Party School in Yan'an: "Seek truth from facts." These four words are the quintessence of Mao Zedong Thought. In the final analysis, Comrade Mao's greatness and his success in guiding the Chinese revolution to victory rest on just this approach. Marx and Lenin never mentioned the encirclement of the cities from the countryside— a strategic principle that had not been formulated anywhere in the world in their lifetime. Nonetheless, Comrade Mao Zedong pointed it out as the specific road for the revolution in China's concrete conditions. At a time when the country was split up into separatist warlord domains, he led the people in the fight to establish revolutionary bases in areas where the enemy's control was weak, to encircle the cities from the countryside and ultimately to seize political power. Just as the Bolshevik Party led by Lenin made its revolution at a weak link in the chain of the imperialist world, we made our revolution in areas where the enemy was weak. In principle, the two courses were the same. But instead of trying to take the cities first, we began with the rural areas, then gradually encircled the cities. If we had not applied the fundamental principle of seeking truth from facts, how could we have raised and solved this problem of strategy? How could the Chinese revolution have been victorious?

After the founding of the People's Republic of China, Comrade Mao Zedong continued to lead us forward by applying the principle of seeking truth from facts. Of course, at that time many questions could not be raised because the necessary conditions were absent. If we are to hold high the banner of Mao Zedong Thought, we should always proceed from current reality when handling questions of principle and policy.

"Hold High the Banner of Mao Zedong Thought and Adhere to the Principle of Seeking Truth from Facts," *Selected Works of Deng Xiaoping,* **Eng. ed., FLP, Beijing, 1995, Vol. II, pp. 137-138.**

*****

Marx and Engels propounded the ideological line of dialectical and historical materialism, a line which Comrade Mao Zedong summarized in the four Chinese characters "Seek truth from facts". To seek truth from facts, we should proceed from reality in all things, link theory with practice and hold practice to be the touchstone of truth—that is the ideological line of our Party.... But still, it should be remembered that this ideological line was laid down by Comrade Mao Zedong, and that he adhered to it through most of the years during which he led the Chinese revolution.... The principle we advocate—seeking truth from facts—is a basic component of Marxism-Leninism and Mao Zedong Thought. Therefore, our advocacy of it can in no way be construed to mean that we can separate ourselves from the basic tenets of Marxism-Leninism and Mao Zedong Thought, or that we can neglect the great contribution Comrade Mao Zedong made in formulating this principle.

"Adhere to the Party Line and Improve Methods of Work," *Selected Works of Deng Xiaoping,* **Eng. ed., FLP, Beijing, 1995, Vol. II, p. 277.**

*****

The road to socialism in China has been full of twists and turns. But the experience of the last 20 years has taught us one very important principle: to build socialism we should adhere to Marxist dialectical materialism and historical materialism or, as Comrade Mao Zedong put it, in everything we do we should seek truth from facts—in other words, we should proceed from reality.

"We Should Expand Political Democracy and Carry Out Economic Reform," *Selected Works of Deng Xiaoping*, **Eng. ed., FLP, Beijing, 1994, Vol. III, p. 124.**

*****

If we have learned anything from our achievements in these years, it is that we were right to reaffirm the principle of seeking truth from facts, as advocated by Comrade Mao Zedong. The Chinese revolution owed its success to Comrade Mao Zedong, who blazed a Chinese road by integrating Marxism-Leninism with Chinese realities. In our present development program we should do likewise.

"We Should Follow Our Own Road in Economic Development as We Did in Revolution," *Selected Works of Deng Xiaoping*, **Eng. ed., FLP, Beijing, 1994, Vol. III, p. 101.**

*****

In studying Marxism-Leninism we should grasp the essence and learn what we need to know.... The essence of Marxism is seeking truth from facts. That's what we should advocate, not book worship.... Practice is the sole criterion for testing truth. I haven't read too many books, but there is one thing I believe in: Chairman Mao's principle of seeking truth from facts. That is the principle we relied on when we were fighting wars, and we continue to rely on it in construction and reform. We have advocated Marxism all our lives. Actually, Marxism is not abstruse. It is a plain thing, a very plain truth.

"Excerpts from Talks Given in Wuchang, Shenzhen, Zhuhai and Shanghai," *Selected Works of Deng Xiaoping*, **Eng. ed., FLP, Beijing, 1994, Vol. III, pp. 369-370.**

*****

When in Yan'an, I carefully studied the documents and telegrams drafted by Chairman Mao. I discerned that the basic guiding ideology running through these was to seek truth from facts. But how does one seek truth from facts? At that time, my answer to this question was that we should not blindly follow the instructions of superiors or what we have read; rather, we should value only that information which has been ascertained through exchange, comparison and reconsideration.

However, I do not mean that we should disobey the instructions of the higher authorities nor that we should lay documents and books aside. By valuing only certain information I mean that we should proceed from actual conditions in studying and handling problems. This is the most reliable method. By the term exchange I mean that we should exchange ideas.... By the term comparison I mean that we should make comprehensive comparisons.... By reconsideration I mean that we should not settle a question in haste but should allow time for reconsideration....

The first part of the title of this article concerns materialism, the second part concerns dialectics, and the integration of the two is what is meant by the term materialist dialectics.

"Not Blindly Following the Instructions of Superiors or What Has Been Read; Considering Only Information Which Has Been Ascertained Through Exchange, Comparison and Reconsideration," *Selected Works of Chen Yun*, **Eng. ed., FLP, Beijing, 1999, Vol. III, pp. 362-363.**

*****

The living soul of Mao Zedong Thought is the stand, viewpoint and method that permeate all these areas. This stand, viewpoint and method consist in three basic points: seeking truth from facts, the mass line, and self-reliance. Seeking truth from facts means constantly deepening understanding of conditions in China, studying and fully understanding the objective laws governing social development, finding a path for the revolution and construction suited to China's circumstances, and deciding upon the Party's strategy and tactics to lead the people in transforming and developing China in order to achieve the objective of moving history forward. The mass line is the Party's fundamental working line formulated by systematically embodying in all of the Party's activities the Marxist-Leninist theory that it is the people who make history. The Party does everything for the masses, believes in them, relies on them, pools their wisdom, and organizes their strength so it can overcome all types of difficulties and perform all manner of wonders. Self-reliance means unswervingly safeguarding national independence, protecting state sovereignty, basing our efforts on our own strength while actively seeking foreign assistance, developing international economic and cultural exchanges, and learning from all advanced aspects of other countries that could be beneficial for China.

Jiang Zemin, "Speech at a Meeting to Celebrate the Centenary of Comrade Mao Zedong's Birth," the *People's Daily*, Dec. 27, 1993.

Mao Zedong Thought as the Banner Guiding the People's Revolution and Construction under the Leadership of the CPC

Because of inadequate theoretical preparation, our Party and many Party members have been confused about how to do their work and so have suffered a lot, making quite a few unnecessary detours. Now, thanks to Comrade Mao Zedong's painstaking work and brilliant creativity, the theoretical groundwork has been fully laid for our Party and the Chinese people. This will greatly enhance our self-confidence and our ability to fight and speed the Chinese revolution to victory. Therefore, the important task now is to mobilize the entire Party membership to study and disseminate Mao Zedong Thought and to arm our membership and the revolutionary people with it, so that it may become a living, irresistible force. For this purpose, all Party schools and training classes should adopt Comrade Mao Zedong's writings as basic teaching material, and the cadres should study these writings systematically. Our entire Party press should propagate Mao Zedong Thought in a systematic way. The propaganda departments of the Party should edit Comrade Mao Zedong's important works into popular reading matter suited to the level of the average Party member.

"On the Party," *Selected Works of Liu Shaoqi*, Eng. ed., FLP, Beijing, 1984, Vol. I, pp. 334-335.

*****

Mao Zedong Thought has nurtured our whole generation. All comrades present here may be said to have been nourished by Mao Zedong Thought. Without Mao Zedong Thought, the Communist Party of China would not exist today, and that is no exaggeration either. Mao Zedong Thought will forever remain the greatest intellectual treasure of our Party, our army and our people. We should understand the scientific tenets of Mao Zedong Thought correctly and as an integral whole and develop them under the new historical conditions.

"Emancipate the Mind, Seek Truth from Facts and Unite as One in Looking to the Future," *Selected Works of Deng Xiaoping*, Eng. ed., FLP, Beijing, 1995, Vol. II, p. 158.

*****

On no account can we discard the banner of Mao Zedong Thought. To do so would, in fact, be to negate the glorious history of our Party. On the whole, the Party's history is glorious.... Our country would still be in its old plight were it not for our Communist Party, our new-democratic revolution, our socialist revolution and the establishment of our socialist system. What we have achieved cannot be separated from the leadership of the Chinese Communist Party and Comrade Mao Zedong. It is precisely this point that many of our young people don't sufficiently appreciate.

The appraisal of Comrade Mao Zedong and the exposition of Mao Zedong Thought relate not only to Comrade Mao personally but also to the entire history of our Party and our country. We should keep this overall judgment in mind…. It's not merely a theoretical question that is involved but also and especially a political question of great domestic and international significance.

"Remarks on Successive Drafts of the 'Resolution on Certain Questions in the History of Our Party Since the Founding of the People's Republic of China'," *Selected Works of Deng Xiaoping*, Eng. ed., FLP, Beijing, 1995, Vol. II, pp. 297-298.

*****

Affirmation of the historical role of Comrade Mao Zedong and explanation of the necessity to uphold and develop Mao Zedong Thought. This is the most essential point. We should hold high the banner of Mao Zedong Thought not only today but in the future…

Mao Zedong Thought was set as the guiding thought for our whole Party at its Seventh National Congress. The Party educated an entire generation in Mao Zedong Thought, and that is what enabled us to win the revolutionary war and found the People's Republic of China. The "Cultural Revolution" was really a gross error. However, our Party was able to smash the counter-revolutionary cliques of Lin Biao and the Gang of Four and put an end to the "Cultural Revolution" and it has continued to advance ever since. Who achieved all this? Is it not the generation educated in Mao Zedong Thought? Now, when we speak of setting things right, we mean that we should undo the damage done by Lin Biao and the Gang of Four, criticize the mistakes Comrade Mao Zedong made in his later years, and put things back on the right track of Mao Zedong Thought. In short, if we fail to include in the resolution a section concerning Mao Zedong Thought, which, since it has been proved correct in practice, ought to serve as the guideline for our future work, we will diminish the practical and historical significance of the revolution and construction we have engaged in and will continue to engage in. It would be a grave historical mistake not to expound Mao Zedong Thought in the resolution or to cease to adhere to it.

"Remarks on Successive Drafts of the 'Resolution on Certain Questions in the History of Our Party Since the Founding of the People's Republic of China'," *Selected Works of Deng Xiaoping*, **Eng. ed., FLP, Beijing, 1995, Vol. II, p. 290 and 299.**

*****

We should never sully the glorious image of Comrade Mao Zedong in the entire history of the Chinese revolution, and never waver on the principle of holding high the banner of Mao Zedong Thought. We should understand this and bear it in mind. For it serves the interests not only of the Chinese Communist Party and the Chinese nation but also of the international communist movement.

"Adhere to the Party Line and Improve Methods of Work," *Selected Works of Deng Xiaoping*, **Eng. ed., FLP, Beijing, 1995, Vol. II, p. 277.**

*****

What does holding high the banner of Mao Zedong Thought mean here? It means proceeding from present realities and making full use of all favourable conditions to attain the objective of the four modernizations as defined by Comrade Mao Zedong and proclaimed by Comrade Zhou Enlai. If we could only act as Comrade Mao suggested, what could we do now? We have to develop Marxism and also Mao Zedong Thought. Otherwise, they will become ossified.

"Hold High the Banner of Mao Zedong Thought and Adhere to the Principle of Seeking Truth from Facts," *Selected Works of Deng Xiaoping*, **Eng. ed., FLP, Beijing, 1995, Vol. II, pp. 138-139.**

*****

The "Cultural Revolution" was a blunder and a failure because it ran completely counter to the scientific tenets of Mao Zedong Thought. These tenets, which have been tested and proved correct through long years of practice, not only guided us to victory in the past but will remain our guiding ideology in the years of struggle ahead. It is incorrect and against the fundamental interests of the Chinese people to have any doubt or to waver to any degree on this important principle of our Party.

"On the Reform of the System of Party and State Leadership," *Selected Works of Deng Xiaoping*, **Eng. ed., FLP, Beijing, 1995, Vol. II, pp. 332-333.**

*****

We will continue to adhere to Mao Zedong Thought, which represents the correct part of Chairman Mao's life. Not only did Mao Zedong Thought lead us to victory in the revolution in the past; it is—and will continue to be—a treasured possession of the Chinese Communist Party and of our country.

"Answers to the Italian Journalist Oriana Fallaci," *Selected Works of Deng Xiaoping*, **Eng. ed., FLP, Beijing, 1995, Vol. II, p. 344.**

*****

Mao Zedong Thought, which has been proved correct through practice, remains our guiding ideology. We should adhere to it and develop it in the light of specific conditions, and we should disseminate it with full confidence, permitting no slackening of effort. Mao Zedong Thought should be differentiated from Comrade Mao's mistakes in his later years so that there is no confusion. Of course, this does not mean that in the evening of his life Comrade Mao never put forth any correct ideas.

"Implement the Policy of Readjustment, Ensure Stability and Unity," *Selected Works of Deng Xiaoping*, **Eng. ed., FLP, Beijing, 1995, Vol. II, p. 361.**

*****

I have discussed the dissemination of Mao Zedong Thought in Shandong and Tianjin and later discussed the subject with other comrades of the central leading bodies. Yesterday I mentioned this matter to Chairman Mao and he agreed with the following views. First, the major problem at present is that Mao Zedong Thought has been vulgarized. Every success is being attributed to Mao Zedong Thought. For instance, when a shop does a greater volume of business, people say it is a development of Mao Zedong Thought, and Mao Zedong Though is even said to be applicable to table tennis. Second, people say little about Marxism-Leninism. This tendency can be found to varying degrees in more than a few newspapers. Why do we need to raise this question? Because Mao Zedong Though, if we understand it correctly, involves two aspects: one, upholding and safeguarding Marxism-Leninism, and the other, developing Marxism-Leninism. Mao Zedong Thought and Marxism-Leninism are one and the same thing. Mao Zedong Though not only adheres to the universal truth of Marxism-Leninism, but also adds much new content to the treasure house of Marxism-Leninism. Therefore, we should not separate Mao Zedong Thought from Marxism-Leninism as if the two were different things.

"Correctly Disseminate Mao Zedong Thought," *Selected Works of Deng Xiaoping*, **Eng. ed., FLP, Beijing, 1995, Vol. I, p. 280.**

*****

I always feel that there is a big problem we have to solve: How should we spread Mao Zedong Thought? Comrade Luo Ronghuan was the first to express his disapproval of Lin Biao's vulgarization of Mao Zedong Thought. He said that when we study Chairman Mao's works we should study their essence. At that time, the Secretariat of the Central Committee discussed Comrade Luo Ronghuan's views and concurred with them. Lin Biao urged people to study only the "three constantly read articles" (later, after two more were added, they became the "five constantly read articles"). This was a way of fragmenting Mao Zedong Thought. Mao Zedong Thought is rich in content and constitutes an integral whole. How can one designate only the "three constantly read articles" or the "five constantly read articles" as Mao Zedong Thought, while brushing aside Comrade Mao's other works? How is it possible to propagate Mao Zedong Thought lopsidedly and merely pluck one or two sentences or one or two ideas out of context? The problem of fragmenting Mao Zedong Thought actually remains unsolved.... I'm afraid that the problem of how to study, propagate and implement Mao Zedong Thought systematically exists in quite a few fields. Mao Zedong Thought is closely bound up with practice in every sphere, with the principles, policies and methods in every line of work. We should study, propagate and implement it in its totality and not base our conclusions on a partial understanding or an erroneous interpretation by others.

"Things Should Be Put in Order in All Fields," *Selected Works of Deng Xiaoping*, **Eng. ed., FLP, Beijing, 1995, Vol. II, pp. 49-50.**

*****

We cannot mechanically apply what Comrade Mao Zedong said about a particular question to another question, what he said in a particular place to another place, what he said at a particular time to another time, or what he said under particular circumstances to other circumstances.... In my letter of April 10 to the Central Committee, I had proposed that "from generation to generation, we should use genuine Mao Zedong Thought taken as an integral whole in guiding our Party, our army and our people, so as to advance the cause of the Party and socialism in China and the cause of the international communist movement". I also told them that I had made this proposal after considerable thought. Mao Zedong Thought is an ideological system. Comrade Luo Ronghuan and I struggled against Lin Biao, criticizing him for vulgarizing Mao Zedong Thought instead of viewing it as a system. When we say we should hold high the banner of Mao Zedong Thought, we mean precisely that we should study and apply Mao Zedong Thought as an ideological system.

"The 'Two Whatevers' Do Not Accord with Marxism," *Selected Works of Deng Xiaoping*, **Eng. ed., FLP, Beijing, 1995, Vol. II, pp. 51-52.**

*****

In saying that we should use as our guide genuine Mao Zedong Thought taken as an integral whole, I mean that we should have a correct and comprehensive understanding of Mao Zedong Thought as a system and that we should be proficient at studying it, mastering it, and applying it as a guide to our work. Only in this way can we be sure that we are not fragmenting Mao Zedong Thought, distorting or debasing it. We can then see that what Comrade Mao Zedong said with regard to a specific question at a given time and under particular circumstances was correct, and that what he said with regard to the same question at a different time and under different circumstances was also correct, despite occasional differences in the extent of elaboration, in emphasis and even in the formulation of his ideas. So we should acquire a correct understanding of Mao Zedong Thought as an integral system instead of just citing a few specific words or sentences. But the Gang of Four, and especially their so-called theoretician Zhang Chunqiao, distorted and adulterated Mao Zedong Thought. They tried to fool people or intimidate them by quoting a phrase or two from Comrade Mao Zedong. We need to have a true grasp of Mao Zedong Thought and a correct understanding of it as an integral whole, even when dealing with a particular sphere or one aspect of a particular problem.... Mao Zedong Thought has developed Marxism-Leninism in many spheres, not just in some individual aspects. It constitutes an integral system and is a further development of Marxism. For this reason I suggest that in addition to editing and publishing the works of Mao Zedong, comrades doing theoretical work should endeavour to expound Mao Zedong Thought as a system from various perspectives. We should educate our Party in Mao Zedong Thought as a system so that it can continue to guide us forward.

"Mao Zedong Thought Should Be Correctly Understood as an Integral Whole," *Selected Works of Deng Xiaoping*, **Eng. ed., FLP, Beijing, 1995, Vol. II, pp. 55-56.**

*****

One of the key points of our struggle against Lin Biao and the Gang of Four was opposition to their falsification, doctoring and fragmenting of Marxism-Leninism and Mao Zedong Thought. Since the smashing of the Gang, we have restored the scientific character of Marxism-Leninism and Mao Zedong Thought and have guided ourselves by them. This is a resounding victory for the whole Party and people.... What we consistently take as our guide to action are the basic tenets of Marxism-Leninism and Mao Zedong Thought or, to put it another way, the scientific system formed by these tenets. When it comes to individual theses, neither Marx and Lenin nor Comrade Mao could be immune from mis-judgements of one sort or another. But these do not belong to the scientific system formed by the basic tenets of Marxism-Leninism and Mao Zedong Thought.

This is why we have often repeated that it is necessary to emancipate our minds, that is, to study new situations and solve new problems by applying the basic tenets of Marxism-Leninism and Mao Zedong Thought.

We have said that by studying in depth the new conditions and new problems encountered in realizing the four modernizations, and by working out solutions to those problems—solutions that will serve as guidelines for our action—our ideological and theoretical workers will be making a major contribution to Marxism and a genuine effort to hold high the banner of Mao Zedong Thought.

"Uphold the Four Cardinal Principles," *Selected Works of Deng Xiaoping*, **Eng. ed., FLP, Beijing, 1995, Vol. II, pp. 180, 187.**

*****

I think we should launch a movement to study the works of Marx, Lenin and Comrade Mao Zedong. This study should be integrated with study of the history of the Chinese revolution so as to help people understand how the Party led the revolution, how Comrade Mao contributed to it and how it succeeded.

"On Opposing Wrong Ideological Tendencies," *Selected Works of Deng Xiaoping*, **Eng. ed., FLP, Beijing, 1995, Vol. II, p. 375.**

*****

Marxism should be developed. We do not take Marxism as a dogma; rather, by combining Marxism with the concrete practice in China, we formulate our own principles. That is why we have achieved successes. Our revolution triumphed because we encircled the cities from the rural areas, although that strategy is not to be found in Marxist-Leninist books. Today we still uphold Marxism-Leninism and Mao Zedong Thought, part of which we have inherited and part of which we have developed ourselves. We are building socialism, or to be more precise, we are building a socialism suited to conditions in China. In this way we are truly adhering to Marxism.

"We Should Unite the People on the Basis of Firm Convictions," *Selected Works of Deng Xiaoping*, **Eng. ed., FLP, Beijing, 1994, Vol. III, p. 191.**

*****

Since the defeat of the Gang of Four and the convocation of the Third Plenary Session of the Party's Eleventh Central Committee, we have formulated correct ideological, political and organizational lines and a series of principles and policies. What is the ideological line? To adhere to Marxism and to integrate it with Chinese realities—in other words, to seek truth from facts, as advocated by Comrade Mao Zedong, and to uphold his basic ideas.

"Building a Socialism with a Specifically Chinese Character," *Selected Works of Deng Xiaoping*, **Eng. ed., FLP, Beijing, 1994, Vol. III, p. 72.**

*****

Mao Zedong Thought is the application and development of Marxism-Leninism in China and the crystallization of the collective wisdom of the CPC. Mao Zedong Thought will always be a theoretical treasure trove for Chinese Communists and a spiritual pillar of the Chinese nation and will always serve as a guide to action for developing China into a modern socialist country...

... Comrade Mao was a great Marxist, proletarian revolutionary, strategist and theorist and a great patriot and national hero in modern Chinese history. During the protracted and bitter revolutionary period, he demonstrated the political farsightedness of a revolutionary leader, unswerving belief in the revolution, proficiency in the art of struggle, and his ability to control the overall situation. Comrade Mao was a great leader who grew up among the masses and always belonged to the people. His revolutionary spirit had the power to bring people together, he had great charisma, and his scientific thinking had great appeal. The great achievements Comrade Mao and his comrades-in-arms made shine through history and are respected by all people of integrity throughout the world... His name, his thought and his spirit will forever serve as an inspiration to Chinese Communists and the people of all our ethnic groups and will continue to drive Chinese history forward. As a great historical figure, Comrade Mao belongs to both China and the whole world. He will always live among us. We should diligently study his scientific writings and draw strength and wisdom from them. The fact that China produced a man like Mao Zedong is a matter of pride for the Party, the country and the Chinese nation. We will always have a deep love and respect for Comrade Mao.

Jiang Zemin, "Speech at a Meeting to Celebrate the Centenary of Comrade Mao Zedong's Birth," the *People's Daily*, Dec. 27, 1993.

*****

Correctly assessing the historical achievements and mistakes of Comrade Mao and confirming the historical position of Mao Zedong Thought have a bearing on how to judge how well the Party and country did in the last few decades of struggle, on the unity of the Party and the stability of the country, and on the future development path of the Party and country. This was a comprehensive, pressing and crucial issue that the Party faced following the death of Comrade Mao. Comrade Deng, in leading the Party and the country in recovering from the profound disaster caused by the Cultural Revolution and restoring order to the guiding ideology, exerted great efforts in resolving the issue of how to correctly assess Comrade Mao and Mao Zedong Thought. He pointed out that without Chairman Mao, the Chinese people would, at the very least, have spent more time groping in the dark. Mao Zedong Thought is a scientific system. We should fully and accurately understand it and apply it in guiding our entire Party, our whole army and all our people in order to make progress in the cause of the Party and socialism. Comrade Deng took the lead in opposing and criticizing the erroneous principle of the "two whatevers," supported the debate throughout the Party and the country about whether practice is the sole criterion for testing truth and led the whole Party in smashing through the restraints of "Left" ideology. Comrade Deng pointed out that Comrade Mao's contributions are primary and the mistakes of his later years are secondary, and that he made them only because he acted contrary to his own correct ideas. His mistakes were those of a great revolutionary and a great Marxist. Comrade Deng resolutely criticized the erroneous tendency to use the mistakes Comrade Mao made in his later years as a pretext to fundamentally negate his contributions and Mao Zedong Thought. He said that it is precisely because we have abided by Mao Zedong Thought that we have achieved such magnificent success in the Chinese revolution. We cannot lower the banner of Mao Zedong Thought; to do so would be a huge historical mistake. Fixing Comrade Mao's position in history and upholding and developing Mao Zedong Thought are of central importance. We should hold high the banner of Mao Zedong Thought both today and for a long time to come. These important views of Comrade Deng formed the basic thinking underlying the Resolution on Certain Questions in the History of Our Party Since the Founding of the People's Republic of China, the writing of which he personally directed and which was passed at the Sixth Plenary Session of the Eleventh Central Committee. This resolution upheld Marxism, and it truthfully, fairly and objectively analyzed the Party's historical experience and assessed its leaders, once again demonstrating that the Party is a strong, Marxist party that is politically and theoretically mature. The resolution eliminated "Left" and Right interference, united ideology throughout the Party, strengthened Party unity and encouraged all Party members and all our people to march confidently into the future.

Jiang Zemin, "Speech at a Meeting to Celebrate the Centenary of Comrade Mao Zedong's Birth," the *People's Daily*, Dec. 27, 1993.

*****

Ever since it was founded, our Party has taken Marxism-Leninism as its guiding ideology. After the Zunyi Meeting and the Yan'an Rectification, the Party decided at its Seventh Congress to take Mao Zedong Thought— the integration of the theory of Marxism-Leninism with the practice of the Chinese revolution—as its guiding ideology. This historic decision was based on a summary of the experience of twenty-four years after the founding of the Party. On the basis of the Third Plenary Session of the Eleventh Central

Committee and the Twelfth, Thirteenth and especially Fourteenth Congresses of the Party, the Central Committee has proposed that the Party, at its Fifteenth Congress, establish Deng Xiaoping Theory as its guiding ideology by stipulating in its Constitution that the Communist Party of China takes Marxism-Leninism, Mao Zedong Thought and Deng Xiaoping Theory as its guide to action. This historic decision has been made by our Party after nearly twenty years of successful practice of the reform, opening up and the socialist modernization drive.

Jiang Zemin, "Hold High the Great Banner of Deng Xiaoping Theory for an All-Round Advancement of the Cause of Building Socialism with Chinese Characteristics to the Twenty-First Century— Report to the Fifteenth National Congress of the Communist Party of China," *Documents of the Fifteenth National Congress of the Communist Party of China*, **Chin. ed., People's Publishing House, Beijing, 1997, pp. 9-10.**

*****

Marxism is a science, which is firmly based on objective facts. Actual life, however, is always changing and the changes over the past century and more have been so drastic and profound that our predecessors could hardly have conceived them. Hence, Marxism will necessarily advance along with the development of the times, practice and science; it cannot remain unchanged. There is a question concerning the style of study of Marxism: whether we should indulge in book worship, or use the Marxist stand, viewpoint and method to study and solve the practical problems in China. During the rectification movement in Yan'an, Mao Zedong emphasized, "A policy should be established of focusing on the study of the practical problems of the Chinese revolution and using the basic principles of Marxism-Leninism as the guide, and the method of studying Marxism-Leninism statically and in isolation should be discarded."... We should never discard Marxism-Leninism and Mao Zedong Thought. If we did, we would lose our foundation. Meanwhile, centering on the practical problems in the reform, opening up and the modernization drive and on the things we are doing, we should emphasize the application of the Marxist theory, the theoretical study of practical problems, and new practice and development. It is meaningless to talk about Marxism in isolation from a given country's reality and the development of the times. We would get nowhere if we studied Marxism statically and in isolation, and separated it from its vigorous development in actual life, or set them against each other. In present-day China, Marxism-Leninism, Mao Zedong Thought and Deng Xiaoping Theory constitute a unified scientific system imbued with the same spirit. Adhering to Deng Xiaoping Theory means genuinely adhering to Marxism-Leninism and Mao Zedong Thought; holding high the banner of Deng Xiaoping Theory means genuinely holding high the banner of Marxism-Leninism and Mao Zedong Thought.

Jiang Zemin, "Hold High the Great Banner of Deng Xiaoping Theory for an All-Round Advancement of the Cause of Building Socialism with Chinese Characteristics to the Twenty-First Century—Report to the Fifteenth National Congress of the Communist Party of China," *Documents of the Fifteenth National Congress of the Communist Party of China***, Chin. ed., People's Publishing House, Beijing, 1997, pp.13-14.**

Appendix

Resolution on Certain Questions in the History of Our Party Since the Founding of the People's Republic of China (abridged)

Editor's note: The below document was prepared after numerous studies and discussions at various levels in and outside the CPC which took about two and half years work and adopted by the Sixth Plenary Session of the Eleventh Central Committee of the Communist Party of China on June 27, 1981. The document includes 7 parts or sub-titles and 37 points altogether. Included in the appendix are parts 2,3,4 and 6. Part 6 directly includes evaluation of Mao Zedong and Mao Zedong Thought. Later an annotations document was added to this document and issued by the CPC.

Part 2 The Seven Years of Basic Completion of the Socialist Transformation

9. From the inception of the People's Republic of China in October 1949 to 1956, our Party led the whole people in gradually realizing the transition from new democracy to socialism, rapidly rehabilitating the country's economy, undertaking planned economic construction and in the main accomplishing the socialist transformation of the private ownership of the means of production in most of the country. The guidelines and basic policies defined by the Party in this historical period were correct and led to brilliant successes.

10. In the first three years of the People's Republic, we cleared the mainland of bandits and the remnant armed forces of the Kuomintang reactionaries, peacefully liberated Tibet, established people's governments at all levels throughout the country, confiscated bureaucrat-capitalist enterprises and transformed them into state-owned socialist enterprises, unified the country's financial and economic work, stabilized commodity prices, carried out agrarian reform in the new liberated areas, suppressed counter-revolutionaries, and unfolded the movements against the "three evils" of corruption; waste and bureaucracy and against the "five evils" of bribery, tax evasion, theft of state property, cheating on government contracts and stealing of economic information, the latter being a movement to beat back the attack mounted by the bourgeoisie. We effectively transformed the educational, scientific and cultural institutions of old China. While successfully carrying out the complex and difficult task of social reform and simultaneously undertaking the great war to resist U.S. aggression and aid Korea, protect our homes and defend the country, we rapidly rehabilitated the country's economy which had been devastated in old China. By the end of 1952, the country's industrial and agricultural production had attained record levels.

11. On the proposal of Comrade Mao Zedong in 1952, the Central

Committee of the Party advanced the general line for the transition period, which was to realize the country's socialist industrialization and socialist transformation of agriculture, handicrafts and capitalist industry and commerce step by step over a fairly long period of time. This general line was a reflection of historical necessity.

(1) Socialist industrialization is an indispensable prerequisite to the country's independence and prosperity.

(2) With nationwide victory in the new-democratic revolution and completion of the agrarian reform, the contradiction between the working class and the bourgeoisie and between the socialist road and the capitalist road became the principal internal contradiction. The country needed a certain expansion of capitalist industry and commerce which were beneficial to its economy and to the people's livelihood. But in the course of their expansion, things detrimental to the national economy and the people's livelihood were bound to emerge. Consequently, a struggle between restriction and opposition to restriction was inevitable. The conflict of interests became increasingly apparent between capitalist enterprises on the one hand and the economic policies of the state, the socialist state-owned economy, the workers and staff in these capitalist enterprises and the people as a whole on the other. An integrated series of necessary measures and steps, such as the fight against speculation and profiteering, the readjustment and restructuring of industry and commerce, the movement against the "five evils", workers' supervision of production and state monopoly of the purchase and marketing of grain and cotton, were bound to gradually bring backward, anarchic, lopsided and profit-oriented capitalist industry and commerce into the orbit of socialist transformation.

(3) Among the individual peasants, and particularly the poor and lower-middle peasants who had just acquired land in the agrarian reform but lacked other means of production, there was a genuine desire for mutual aid and co-operation in order to avoid borrowing at usurious rates and even mortgaging or selling their land again with consequent polarization, and in order to expand production, undertake water conservancy projects, ward off

natural calamities and make use of farm machinery and new techniques. The progress of industrialization, while demanding agricultural products in ever increasing quantities, would provide stronger and stronger support for the technical transformation of agriculture, and this also constituted a motive force behind the transformation of individual into co-operative farming.

As is borne out by history, the general line for the transition period set forth by our Party was entirely correct.

12. During the period of transition, our Party creatively charted a course for socialist transformation that suited China's specific conditions. In dealing with capitalist industry and commerce, we devised a whole series of transitional forms of state capitalism from lower to higher levels, such as the placing of state orders with private enterprises for the processing of materials or the manufacture of goods, state monopoly of the purchase and marketing of the products of private enterprise, the marketing of products of state-owned enterprises by private shops, and joint state-private ownership of individual enterprises or enterprises of a whole trade, and we eventually realized the peaceful redemption of the bourgeoisie, a possibility envisaged by Marx and Lenin. In dealing with individual farming, we devised transitional forms of co-operation, proceeding from temporary or all-the-year-round mutual-aid teams, to elementary agricultural producers' co-operatives of a semi-socialist nature and then to advanced agricultural producers' co-operatives of a fully socialist nature, always adhering to the principles of voluntariness and mutual benefit, demonstration through advanced examples, and extension of state help. Similar methods were used in transforming individual handicraft industries. In the course of such transformation, the state-capitalist and co-operative economies displayed their unmistakable superiority. By 1956, the socialist transformation of the private ownership of the means of production had been largely completed in most regions. But there had been shortcomings and errors. From the summer of 1955 onwards, we were over-hasty in pressing on with agricultural co-operation and the transformation of private handicraft and commercial establishments; we were far from meticulous, the changes were too fast, and we did our work in a

somewhat summary, stereotyped manner, leaving open a number of questions for a long time. Following the basic completion of the transformation of capitalist industry and commerce in 1956, we failed to do a proper job in employing and handling some of the former industrialists and businessmen. But on the whole, it was definitely a historic victory for us to have effected, and to have effected fairly smoothly, so difficult, complex and profound a social change in so vast a country with its several hundred million people, a change, moreover, which promoted the growth of industry, agriculture and the economy as a whole.

13. In economic construction under the First Five-Year Plan (1953-1957), we likewise scored major successes through our own efforts and with the assistance of the Soviet Union and other friendly countries. A number of basic industries, essential for the country's industrialization and yet very weak in the past, were built up. Between 1953 and 1956, the average annual increases in the total value of industrial and agricultural output were 19.6 and 4.8 per cent respectively. Economic growth was quite fast, with satisfactory economic results, and the key economic sectors were well-balanced. The market prospered, prices were stable. The people's livelihood improved perceptibly. In April 1956, Comrade Mao Zedong made his speech On the Ten Major Relationships, in which he initially summed up our experiences in socialist construction and set forth the task of exploring a way of building socialism suited to the specific conditions of our country.

14. The First National People's Congress was convened in September 1954, and it enacted the Constitution of the People's Republic of China. In March 1955, a national conference of the Party reviewed the major struggle against the plots of the careerists Gao Gang and Rao Shushi to split the Party and usurp supreme power in the Party and the state; in this way it strengthened Party unity. In January 1956, the Central Committee of the Party called a conference on the question of the intellectuals. Subsequently, the policy of "letting a hundred flowers blossom and a hundred schools of thought contend" was advanced. These measures spelled out the correct policy regarding intellectuals and the work in education, science and culture

and thus brought about a significant advance in these fields. Owing to the Party's correct policies, fine style of work and the consequent high prestige it enjoyed among the people, the vast numbers of cadres, masses, youth and intellectuals earnestly studied Marxism-Leninism and Mao Zedong Thought and participated enthusiastically in revolutionary and construction activities under the leadership of the Party, so that a healthy and virile revolutionary morality prevailed throughout the country.

15. The Eighth National Congress of the Party held in September 1956 was very successful. The congress declared that the socialist system had been basically established in China; that while we must strive to liberate Taiwan, thoroughly complete socialist transformation, ultimately eliminate the system of exploitation and continue to wipe out the remnant forces of counter-revolution, the principal contradiction within the country was no longer the contradiction between the working class and the bourgeoisie but between the demand of the people for rapid economic and cultural development and the existing state of our economy and culture which fell short of the needs of the people; that the chief task confronting the whole nation was to concentrate all efforts on developing the productive forces, industrializing the country and gradually meeting the people's incessantly growing material and cultural needs; and that although class struggle still existed and the people's democratic dictatorship had to be further strengthened, the basic task of the dictatorship was now to protect and develop the productive forces in the context of the new relations of production. The congress adhered to the principle put forward by the Central Committee of the Party in May 1956, the principle of opposing both conservatism and rash advance in economic construction, that is, of making steady progress by striking an over-all balance. It emphasized the problem of the building of the Party in office and the need to uphold democratic centralism and collective leadership, oppose the personality cult, promote democracy within the Party and among the people and strengthen the Party's ties with the masses. The line laid down by the Eighth National Congress of the Party was correct and it charted the path for the development of the cause of socialism and for Party building in the

new period.

Part 3 Ten Years of Initially Building Socialism in All Spheres

16. After the basic completion of socialist transformation, our Party led the entire people in shifting our work to all-round, large-scale socialist construction. In the ten years preceding the "cultural revolution" we achieved very big successes despite serious setbacks. By 1966, the value of fixed industrial assets, calculated on the basis of their original price, was 4 times greater than in 1956. The output of such major industrial products as cotton yarn, coal, electricity, crude oil, steel and mechanical equipment all recorded impressive increases. Beginning in 1965, China became self-sufficient in petroleum. New industries such as the electronic and petrochemical industries were established one after another. The distribution of industry over the country became better balanced. Capital construction in agriculture and its technical transformation began on a massive scale and yielded better and better results. Both the number of tractors for farming and the quantity of chemical fertilizers applied increased over 7 times and rural consumption of electricity 71 times. The number of graduates from institutions of higher education was 4.9 times that of the previous seven years. Educational work was improved markedly through consolidation. Scientific research and technological work, too, produced notable results.

In the ten years from 1956 to 1966, the Party accumulated precious experience in leading socialist construction. In the spring of 1957, Comrade Mao Zedong stressed the necessity of correctly handling and distinguishing between the two types of social contradictions differing in nature in a socialist society, and made the correct handling of contradictions among the people the main content of the country's political life. Later, he called for the creation of "a political situation in which we have both centralism and democracy, both discipline and freedom, both unity of will and personal ease of mind and liveliness". In 1958, he proposed that the focus of Party and government work be shifted to technical revolution and socialist construction. All this was the continuation and development of the line adopted by the

Eighth National Congress of the Party and was to go on serving as a valuable guide. While leading the work of correcting the errors in the Great Leap Forward and the movement to organize people's communes, Comrade Mao Zedong pointed out that there must be no expropriation of the peasants; that a given stage of social development should not be skipped; that equalitarianism must be opposed; that we must stress commodity production, observe the law of value and strike an over-all balance in economic planning; and that economic plans must be arranged with the priority proceeding from agriculture to light industry and then to heavy industry. Comrade Liu Shaoqi said that a variety of means of production could be put into circulation as commodities and that there should be a double-track system for labour as well as for education in socialist society. Comrade Zhou Enlai said, among other things, that the overwhelming majority of Chinese intellectuals had become intellectuals belonging to the working people and that science and technology would play a key role in China's modernization. Comrade Chen Yun held that plan targets should be realistic, that the scale of construction should correspond to national capability and considerations should be given to both the people's livelihood and the needs of state construction, and that the material, financial and credit balances should be maintained in drawing up plans. Comrade Deng Xiaoping held that industrial enterprises should be consolidated and their management improved and strengthened, and that the system of workers' conferences should be introduced. Comrade Zhu De stressed the need to pay attention to the development of handicrafts and of diverse undertakings in agriculture. Deng Zihui and other comrades pointed out that a system of production responsibility should be introduced in agriculture. All these views were not only of vital significance then, but have remained so ever since. In the course of economic readjustment, the Central Committee drew up draft rules governing the work of the rural people's communes and work in industry, commerce, education, science and literature and art. These rules which were a more or less systematic summation of our experience in socialist construction and embodied specific policies suited to the prevailing conditions remain important as a source of reference for us to this very day.

In short, the material and technical basis for modernizing our country was largely established during that period. It was also largely in the same period that the core personnel for our work in the economic, cultural and other spheres were trained and that they gained their experience. This was the principal aspect of the Party's work in that period.

17. In the course of this decade, there were serious faults and errors in the guidelines of the Party's work, which developed through twists and turns.

1957 was one of the years that saw the best results in economic work since the founding of the People's Republic owing to the conscientious implementation of the correct line formulated at the Eighth National Congress of the Party. To start a rectification campaign throughout the Party in that year and urge the masses to offer criticisms and suggestions were normal steps in developing socialist democracy. In the rectification campaign a handful of bourgeois Rightists seized the opportunity to advocate what they called "speaking out and airing views in a big way" and to mount a wild attack against the Party and the nascent socialist system in an attempt to replace the leadership of the Communist Party. It was therefore entirely correct and necessary to launch a resolute counter-attack. But the scope of this struggle was made far too broad and a number of intellectuals, patriotic people and Party cadres were unjustifiably labelled "Rightists", with unfortunate consequences.

In 1958, the Second Plenum of the Eighth National Congress of the Party adopted the general line for socialist construction. The line and its fundamental aspects were correct in that it reflected the masses' pressing demand for a change in the economic and cultural backwardness of our country. Its shortcoming was that it overlooked objective economic laws. Both before and after the plenum, all comrades in the Party and people of all nationalities displayed high enthusiasm and initiative for socialism and achieved certain results in production and construction. However, "Left" errors, characterized by excessive targets, the issuing of arbitrary directions, boastfulness and the stirring up of a "communist wind", spread unchecked throughout the country. This was due to our lack of experience in socialist construction and inadequate understanding of the laws of economic development and of the basic economic conditions in China. More importantly, it was due to the fact that Comrade Mao Zedong and many leading comrades, both at the centre and in the localities, had become smug about their successes, were impatient for quick results and overestimated the role of man's subjective will and efforts. After the general line was formulated, the Great Leap Forward and the movement for rural people's communes were initiated without careful investigation and study and without prior experimentation. From the end of 1958 to the early stage of the Lushan Meeting of the Political Bureau of the Party's Central Committee in July 1959, Comrade Mao Zedong and the Central Committee led the whole Party in energetically rectifying the errors which had already been recognized. However, in the later part of the meeting, he erred in initiating criticism of Comrade Peng Dehuai and then in launching a Party-wide struggle against "Right opportunism". The resolution passed by the Eighth Plenary Session of the Eighth Central Committee of the Party concerning the so-called anti-Party group of Peng Dehuai, Huang Kecheng, Zhang Wentian and Zhou Xiaozhou was entirely wrong. Politically, this struggle gravely undermined inner-Party democracy from the central level down to the grass roots; economically, it cut short the process of the rectification of "Left" errors, thus prolonging their influence. It was mainly due to the errors of the Great Leap Forward and of the struggle against "Right opportunism" together with a succession of natural calamities and the perfidious scrapping of contracts by the Soviet Government that our economy encountered serious difficulties between 1959 and 1961, which caused serious losses to our country and people.

In the winter of 1960, the Central Committee of the Party and Comrade Mao Zedong set about rectifying the "Left" errors in rural work and decided on the principle of "readjustment, consolidation, filling out and raising standards" for the economy as a whole. A number of correct policies and resolute measures were worked out and put into effect with Comrades Liu Shaoqi, Zhou Enlai, Chen Yun and Deng Xiaoping in charge. All this constituted a crucial turning point in that historical phase. In January 1962, the enlarged Central Work Conference attended by 7,000 people made a preliminary summing-up of the positive and negative experience of the Great Leap Forward and unfolded criticism and self-criticism. A majority of the comrades who had been unjustifiably criticized during the campaign against "Right opportunism" were rehabilitated before or after the conference. In addition, most of the "Rightists" had their label removed. Thanks to these economic and political measures, the national economy recovered and developed fairly smoothly between 1962 and 1966.

Nevertheless, "Left" errors in the principles guiding economic work were not only not eradicated, but actually grew in the spheres of politics, ideology and culture. At the Tenth Plenary Session of the Party's Eighth Central Committee in September 1962, Comrade Mao Zedong widened and absolutized the class struggle, which exists only within certain limits in socialist society, and carried forward the viewpoint he had advanced after the anti-Rightist struggle in 1957 that the contradiction between the proletariat and the bourgeoisie remained the principal contradiction in our society. He went a step further and asserted that, throughout the historical period of socialism, the bourgeoisie would continue to exist and would attempt a comeback and become the source of revisionism inside the Party. The socialist education movement unfolded between 1963 and 1965 in some rural areas and at the grass-roots level in a small number of cities did help to some extent to improve the cadres' style of work and economic management. But, in the course of the movement, problems differing in nature were all treated as forms of class struggle or its reflections inside the Party. As a result, quite a number of the cadres at the grassroots level were unjustly dealt with in the latter half of 1964, and early in 1965 the erroneous thesis was advanced that the main target of the movement should be "those Party persons in power taking the capitalist road". In the ideological sphere, a number of literary and art works and schools of thought and a number of representative personages in artistic, literary and academic circles were subjected to unwarranted, inordinate political criticism. And there was an increasingly serious "Left" deviation on the question of intellectuals and on the question of education, science and culture. These errors eventually culminated in the "cultural revolution". but they had not yet become dominant.

Thanks to the fact that the whole Party and people had concentrated on carrying out the correct principle of economic readjustment since the winter of 1960, socialist construction gradually flourished again. The Party and the people were united in sharing weal and woe. They overcame difficulties at home, stood up to the pressure of the Soviet leading clique and repaid all the debts owed to the Soviet Union, which were chiefly incurred through purchasing Soviet arms during the movement to resist U.S. aggression and aid Korea. In addition, they did what they could to support the revolutionary struggles of the people of many countries and assist them in their economic construction. The Third National People's Congress, which met between the end of 1964 and the first days of 1965, announced that the task of national economic readjustment had in the main been accomplished and that the economy as a whole would soon enter a new stage of development. It called for energetic efforts to build China step by step into a socialist power with modern agriculture, industry, national defence and science and technology. This call was not fulfilled owing to the "cultural revolution".

18. All the successes in these ten years were achieved under the collective leadership of the Central Committee of the Party headed by Comrade Mao Zedong. Likewise, responsibility for the errors committed in the work of this period rested with the same collective leadership. Although Comrade Mao Zedong must be held chiefly responsible, we cannot lay the blame for all those errors on him alone. During this period, his theoretical and practical mistakes concerning class struggle in a socialist society became increasingly serious, his personal arbitrariness gradually undermined democratic centralism in Party life and the personality cult grew graver and graver. The Central Committee of the Party failed to rectify these mistakes in good time. Careerists like Lin Biao, Jiang Qing and Kang Sheng, harbouring ulterior motives, made use of these errors and inflated them. This led to the inauguration of the "cultural revolution".

Part 4 The Decade of the "Cultural Revolution"

19. The "cultural revolution", which lasted from May 1966 to October 1976, was responsible for the most severe setback and the heaviest losses suffered by the Party, the state and the people since the founding of the People's Republic. It was initiated and led by Comrade Mao Zedong. His principal theses were that many representatives of the bourgeoisie and counter-revolutionary revisionists had sneaked into the Party, the government, the army and cultural circles, and leadership in a fairly large majority of organizations and departments was no longer in the hands of Marxists and the people; that Party persons in power taking the capitalist road had formed a bourgeois headquarters inside the Central Committee which pursued a revisionist political and organizational line and had agents in all provinces, municipalities and autonomous regions, as well as in all central departments; that since the forms of struggle adopted in the past had not been able to solve this problem, the power usurped by the capitalist-roaders could be recaptured only by carrying out a great cultural revolution, by openly and fully mobilizing the broad masses from the bottom up to expose these sinister phenomena; and that the cultural revolution was in fact a great political revolution in which one class would overthrow another, a revolution that would have to be waged time and again. These theses appeared mainly in the May 16 Circular, which served as the programmatic document of the "cultural revolution", and in the political report to the Ninth National Congress of the Party in April 1969. They were incorporated into a general theory—the "theory of continued revolution under the dictatorship of the proletariat"— which then took on a specific meaning. These erroneous "Left" theses, upon which Comrade Mao Zedong based himself in initiating the "cultural revolution", were obviously inconsistent with the system of Mao Zedong Thought, which is the integration of the universal principles of Marxism-Leninism with the concrete practice of the Chinese revolution. These theses must be clearly distinguished from Mao Zedong Thought. As for Lin Biao, Jiang Qing and others, who were placed in important positions by Comrade Mao Zedong, the matter is of an entirely different nature. They rigged up

two counter-revolutionary cliques in an attempt to seize supreme power and, taking advantage of Comrade Mao Zedong's errors, committed many crimes behind his back, bringing disaster to the country and the people. As their counter-revolutionary crimes have been fully exposed, this resolution will not go into them at any length.

20. The history of the "cultural revolution" has proved that Comrade Mao Zedong's principal theses for initiating this revolution conformed neither to Marxism, Leninism nor to Chinese reality. They represent an entirely erroneous appraisal of the prevailing class relations and political situation in the Party and state.

(1) The "cultural revolution" was defined as a struggle against the revisionist line or the capitalist road. There were no grounds at all for this definition. It led to the confusing of right and wrong on a series of important theories and policies. Many things denounced as revisionist or capitalist during the "cultural revolution" were actually Marxist and socialist principles, many of which had been set forth or supported by Comrade Mao Zedong himself. The "cultural revolution" negated many of the correct principles, policies and achievements of the seventeen years after the founding of the People's Republic. In fact, it negated much of the work of the Central Committee of the Party and the People's Government, including Comrade Mao Zedong's own contribution. It negated the arduous struggles the entire. people had conducted in socialist construction.

(2) The confusing of right and wrong inevitably led to confusing the people with the enemy. The "capitalist-roaders" overthrown in the "cultural revolution" were leading cadres of Party and government organizations at all levels, who formed the core force of the socialist cause. The so-called bourgeois headquarters inside the Party headed by Liu Shaoqi and Deng Xiaoping simply did not exist. Irrefutable facts have proved that labelling Comrade Liu Shaoqi a "renegade, hidden traitor and stab" was nothing but a frame-up by Lin Biao, Jiang Qing and their followers. The political conclusion concerning Comrade Liu Shaoqi drawn by the Twelfth Plenary Session of the Eighth Central Committee of the Party and the disciplinary

measure it meted out to him were both utterly wrong. The criticism of the so-
called reactionary academic authorities in the "cultural revolution" during
which many capable and accomplished intellectuals were attacked and
persecuted also badly muddled up the distinction between the people and the
enemy.

(3) Nominally, the "cultural revolution" was conducted by directly
relying on the masses. In fact, it was divorced both from the Party
organizations and from the masses. After the movement started, Party
organizations at different levels were attacked and became partially or
wholly paralysed, the Party's leading cadres at various levels were subjected
to criticism and struggle, inner-Party life carne to a standstill, and many
activists and large numbers of the basic masses whom the Party has long
relied on were rejected. At the beginning of the "cultural revolution", the vast
majority of participants in the movement acted out of their faith in Comrade
Mao Zedong and the Party. Except for a handful of extremists, however, they
did not approve of launching ruthless struggles against leading Party cadres
at all levels. With the lapse of time, following their own circuitous paths, they
eventually attained a heightened political consciousness and consequently
began to adopt a sceptical or wait-and-see attitude towards the "cultural
revolution", or even resisted and opposed it. Many people were assailed
either more or less severely for this very reason. Such a state of affairs could
not but provide openings to be exploited by opportunists, careerists and
conspirators, not a few of whom were escalated to high or even key positions.

(4) Practice has shown that the "cultural revolution" did not in fact
constitute a revolution or social progress in any sense, nor could it possibly
have done so. It was we and not the enemy at all who were thrown into
disorder by the "cultural revolution". Therefore, from beginning to end, it
did not turn "great disorder under heaven" into "great order under heaven",
nor could it conceivably have done so. After the state power in the form of
the people's democratic dictatorship was established in China, and especially
after socialist transformation was basically completed and the exploiters
were eliminated as classes, the socialist revolution represented a fundamental

break with the past in both content and method, even though its tasks remained to be completed. Of course, it was essential to take proper account of certain undesirable phenomena that undoubtedly existed in Party and state organisms and to remove them by correct measures in conformity with the Constitution, the laws and the Party Constitution. But on no account should the theories and methods of the "cultural revolution" have been applied. Under socialist conditions, there is no economic or political basis for carrying out a great political revolution in which "one class overthrows another". It decidedly could not come up with any constructive programme, but could only bring grave disorder, damage and retrogression in its train. History has shown that the "cultural revolution". initiated by a leader labouring under a misapprehension and capitalized on by counter-revolutionary cliques, led to domestic turmoil and brought catastrophe to the Party, the state and the whole people.

21. The "cultural revolution" can be divided into three stages.

(1) From the initiation of the "cultural revolution" to the Ninth National Congress of the Party in April 1969. The convening of the enlarged Political Bureau meeting of the Central Committee of the Party in May 1966 and the Eleventh Plenary Session of the Eighth Central Committee in August of that year marked the launching of the "cultural revolution" on a full scale. These two meetings adopted the May 16 Circular and the Decision of the Central Committee of the Communist Party of China Concerning the Great Proletarian Cultural Revolution respectively. They launched an erroneous struggle against the so-called anti-Party clique of Peng Zhen, Luo Ruiqing, Lu Dingyi and Yang Shangkun and the so-called headquarters of Liu Shaoqi and Deng Xiaoping. They wrongly reorganized the central leading organs, set up the "Cultural Revolution Group Under the Central Committee of the Chinese Communist Party" and gave it a major part of the power of the Central Committee. In fact, Comrade Mao Zedong's personal leadership characterized by "Left" errors took the place of the collective leadership of the Central Committee, and the cult of Comrade Mao Zedong was frenziedly pushed to an extreme. Lin Biao, Jiang Qing, Kang Sheng, Zhang Chunqiao

and others, acting chief ly in the name of the "Cultural Revolution Group",
exploited the situation to incite people to "overthrow everything and wage
full-scale civil war". Around February 1967, at various meetings, Tan
Zhenlin, Chen Yi, Ye Jianying, Li Fuchun, Li Xiannian, Xu Xiangqian, Nie
Rongzhen and other Political Bureau members and leading comrades of
the Military Commission of the Central Committee sharply criticized the
mistakes of the "cultural revolution". This was labelled the "February adverse
current", and they were attacked and repressed. Comrades Zhu De and Chen
Yun were also wrongly criticized. Almost all leading Party and government
departments in the different spheres and localities were stripped of their
power or reorganized. The chaos was such that it was necessary to send in the
People's Liberation Army to support the Left, the workers and the peasants
and to institute military control and military training. It played a positive role
in stabilizing the situation, but it also produced some negative consequences.
The Ninth Congress of the Party legitimatized the erroneous theories and
practices of the "cultural revolution", and so reinforced the positions of
Lin Biao, Jiang Qing, Kang Sheng and others in the Central Committee of
the Party. The guidelines of the Ninth Congress were wrong, ideologically,
politically and organizationally.

(2) From the Ninth National Congress of the Party to its Tenth National
Congress in August 1973. In 1970-1971 the counter-revolutionary Lin
Biao clique plotted to capture supreme power and attempted an armed
counterrevolutionary coup d'etat. Such was the outcome of the "cultural
revolution" which overturned a series of fundamental Party principles.
Objectively, it announced the failure of the theories and practices of the
"cultural revolution". Comrades Mao Zedong and Zhou Enlai ingeniously
thwarted the plotted coup. Supported by Comrade Mao Zedong, Comrade
Zhou Enlai took charge of the day-to-day work of the Central Committee and
things began to improve in all fields. During the criticism and repudiation of
Lin Biao in 1972, he correctly proposed criticism of the ultra-Left trend of
thought. In fact, this was an extension of the correct proposals put forward
around February 1967 by many leading comrades of the Central Committee

who had called for the correction of the errors of the "cultural revolution". Comrade Mao Zedong, however, erroneously held that the task was still to oppose the "ultra-Right". The Tenth Congress of the Party perpetuated the "Left" errors of the Ninth Congress and made Wang Hongwen a vice-chairman of the Party. Jiang Qing, Zhang Chunqiao, Yao Wenyuan and Wang Hongwen formed a Gang of Four inside the Political Bureau of the Central Committee, thus strengthening the influence of the counter-revolutionary Jiang Qing clique.

(3) From the Tenth Congress of the Party to October 1976. Early in 1974 Jiang Qing, Wang Hongwen and others launched a campaign to "criticize Lin Biao and Confucius". Jiang Qing and the others directed the spearhead at Comrade Zhou Enlai, which was different in nature from the campaign conducted in some localities and organizations where individuals involved in and incidents connected with the conspiracies of the counterrevolutionary Lin Biao clique were investigated. Comrade Mao Zedong approved the launching of the movement to "criticize Lin Biao and Confucius". When he found that Jiang Qing and the others were turning it to their advantage in order to seize power, he severely criticized them. He declared that they had formed a "gang of four" and pointed out that Jiang Qing harboured the wild ambition of making herself chairman of the Central Committee and "forming a cabinet" by political manipulation. In 1975, when Comrade Zhou Enlai was seriously ill, Comrade Deng Xiaoping, with the support of Comrade Mao Zedong, took charge of the day-to-day work of the Central Committee. He convened an enlarged meeting of the Military Commission of the Central Committee and several other important meetings with a view to solving problems in industry, agriculture, transport and science and technology, and began to straighten out the work in many fields so that the situation took an obvious turn for the better. However, Comrade Mao Zedong could not bear to accept systematic correction of the errors of the. "cultural revolution" by Comrade Deng Xiaoping and triggered the movement to "criticize Deng and counter the Right deviationist trend to reverse correct verdicts", once again plunging the nation into turmoil. In January of that year, Comrade Zhou

Enlai passed away. Comrade Zhou Enlai was utterly devoted to the Party and the people and stuck to his post till his dying day. He found himself in an extremely difficult situation throughout the "cultural revolution". He always kept the general interest in mind, bore the heavy burden of office without complaint, racking his brains and untiringly endeavouring to keep the normal work of the Party and the state going, to minimize the damage caused by the "cultural revolution" and to protect many Party and non-Party cadres. He waged all forms of struggle to counter sabotage by the counter-revolutionary Lin Biao and Jiang Qing cliques. His death left the whole Party and people in the most profound grief. In April of the same year, a powerful movement of protest signalled by the Tian An Men Incident swept the whole country, a movement to mourn for the late Premier Zhou Enlai and oppose the Gang of Four. In essence, the movement was a demonstration of support for the Party's correct leadership as represented by Comrade Deng Xiaoping. It laid the ground for massive popular support for the subsequent overthrow of the counter-revolutionary Jiang Qing clique. The Political Bureau of the Central Committee and Comrade Mao Zedong wrongly assessed the nature of the Tian An Men Incident and dismissed Comrade Deng Xiaoping from all his posts inside and outside the Party. As soon as Comrade Mao Zedong passed away in September 1976, the counterrevolutionary Jiang Qing clique stepped up its plot to seize supreme Party and state leadership. Early in October of the same year, the Political Bureau of the Central Committee, executing the will of the Party and the people, resolutely smashed the clique and brought the catastrophic "cultural revolution" to an end. This was a great victory won by the entire Party, army and people after prolonged struggle. Hua Guofeng, Ye Jianying, Li Xiannian and other comrades played a vital part in the struggle to crush the clique.

22. Chief responsibility for the grave "Left" error of the "cultural revolution", an error comprehensive in magnitude and protracted in duration, does indeed lie with Comrade Mao Zedong. But after all it was the error of a great proletarian revolutionary. Comrade Mao Zedong paid constant attention to overcoming shortcomings in the life of the Party and state. In his later

years, however, far from making a correct analysis of many problems, he confused right and wrong and the people with the enemy during the "cultural revolution". While making serious mistakes, he repeatedly urged the whole Party to study the works of Marx, Engels and Lenin conscientiously and imagined that his theory and practice were Marxist and that they were essential for the consolidation of the dictatorship of the proletariat. Herein lies his tragedy. While persisting in the comprehensive error of the "cultural revolution", he checked and rectified some of its specific mistakes, protected some leading Party cadres and non-Party public figures and enabled some leading cadres to return to important leading posts. He led the struggle to smash the counter-revolutionary Lin Biao clique. He made major criticisms and exposures of Jiang Qing, Zhang Chunqiao and others, frustrating their sinister ambition to seize supreme leadership. All this was crucial to the subsequent and relatively painless overthrow of the Gang of Four by our Party. In his later years, he still remained alert to safeguarding the security of our country, stood up to the pressure of the social-imperialists, pursued a correct foreign policy, firmly supported the just struggles of all peoples, outlined the correct strategy of the three worlds and advanced the important principle that China would never seek hegemony. During the "cultural revolution" our Party was not destroyed, but maintained its unity. The State Council and the People's Liberation Army were still able to do much of their essential work. The Fourth National People's Congress which was attended by deputies from all nationalities and all walks of life was convened and it determined the composition of the State Council with Comrades Zhou Enlai and Deng Xiaoping as the core of its leadership. The foundation of China's socialist system remained intact and it was possible to continue socialist economic construction. Our country remained united and exerted a significant influence on international affairs. All these important facts are inseparable from the great role played by Comrade Mao Zedong. For these reasons, and particularly for his vital contributions to the cause of the revolution over the years, the Chinese people have always regarded Comrade Mao Zedong as their respected and beloved great leader and teacher.

23. The struggle waged by the Party and the people against "Left" errors and against the counter-revolutionary Lin Biao and Jiang Qing cliques during the "cultural revolution" was arduous and full of twists and turns, and it never ceased. Rigorous tests throughout the "cultural revolution" have proved that standing on the correct side in the struggle were the overwhelming majority of the members of the Eighth Central Committee of the Party and the members it elected to its Political Bureau, Standing Committee and Secretariat. Most of our Party cadres, whether they were wrongly dismissed or remained at their posts, whether they were rehabilitated early or late, are loyal to the Party and people and steadfast in their belief in the cause of socialism and communism. Most of the intellectuals, model workers, patriotic democrats, patriotic overseas Chinese and cadres and masses of all strata and all nationalities who had been wronged and persecuted did not waver in their love for the motherland and in their support for the Party and socialism. Party and state leaders such as Comrades Liu Shaoqi, Peng Dehuai, He Long and Tao Zhu and all other Party and non-Party comrades who were persecuted to death in the "cultural revolution" will live for ever in the memories of the Chinese people. It was through the joint struggles waged by the entire Party and the masses of workers, peasants, PLA officers and men, intellectuals, educated youth and cadres that the havoc wrought by the "cultural revolution" was somewhat mitigated. Some progress was made in our economy despite tremendous losses. Grain output increased relatively steadily. Significant achievements were scored in industry, communications and capital construction and in science and technology. New railways were built and the Changjiang River Bridge at Nanjing was completed: a number of large enterprises using advanced technology went into operation; hydrogen bomb tests were successfully undertaken and man-made satellites successfully launched and retrieved; and new hybrid strains of long-grained rice were developed and popularized. Despite the domestic turmoil, the People's Liberation Army bravely defended the security of the motherland. And new prospects were opened up in the sphere of foreign affairs. Needless to say, none of these successes can be attributed in any

way to the "cultural revolution", without which we would have scored far greater achievements for our cause. Although we suffered from sabotage by the counter-revolutionary Lin Biao and Jiang Qing cliques during the "cultural revolution", we won out over them in the end. The Party, the people's political power, the people's army and Chinese society on the whole remained unchanged in nature. Once again history has proved that our people are a great people and that our Party and socialist system have enormous vitality.

24. In addition to the above-mentioned immediate cause of Comrade Mao Zedong's mistake in leadership, there are complex social and historical causes underlying the "cultural revolution" which dragged on for as long as a decade. The main causes are as follows:

(1) The history of the socialist movement is not long and that of the socialist countries even shorter. Some of the laws governing the development of socialist society are relatively clear, but many more remain to be explored. Our Party had long existed in circumstances of war and fierce class struggle. It was not fully prepared, either ideologically or in terms of scientific study, for the swift advent of the new-born socialist society and for socialist construction on a national scale. The scientific works of Marx, Engels, Lenin and Stalin are our guide to action, but can in no way provide ready-made answers to the problems we may encounter in our socialist cause. Even after the basic completion of socialist transformation, given the guiding ideology, we were liable, owing to the historical circumstances in which our Party grew, to continue to regard issues unrelated to class struggle as its manifestations when observing and handling new contradictions and problems which cropped up in the political, economic, cultural and other spheres in the course of the development of socialist society. And when confronted with actual class struggle under the new conditions, we habitually fell back on the familiar methods and experiences of the large-scale, turbulent mass struggle of the past, which should no longer have been mechanically followed. As a result, we substantially broadened the scope of class struggle. Moreover, this subjective thinking and practice divorced from reality seemed

to have a "theoretical basis" in the writings of Marx, Engels, Lenin and Stalin because certain ideas and arguments set forth in them were misunderstood or dogmatically interpreted. For instance, it was thought that equal right, which reflects the exchange of equal amounts of labour and is applicable to the distribution of the means of consumption in socialist society, or "bourgeois right" as it was designated by Marx, should be restricted and criticized, and so the principle of "to each according to his work" and that of material interest should be restricted and criticized; that small production would continue to engender capitalism and the bourgeoisie daily and hourly on a large scale even after the basic completion of socialist transformation, and so a series of "Left" economic policies and policies on class struggle in urban and rural areas were formulated; and that all ideological differences inside the Party were reflections of class struggle in society, and so frequent and acute inner-Party struggles were conducted. All this led us to regard the error in broadening the scope of class struggle as an act in defence of the purity of Marxism. Furthermore, Soviet leaders started a polemic between China and the Soviet Union, and turned the arguments between the two Parties on matters of principle into a conflict between the two nations, bringing enormous pressure to bear upon China politically, economically and militarily. So we were forced to wage a just struggle against the big-nation chauvinism of the Soviet Union. In these circumstances, a campaign to prevent and combat revisionism inside the country was launched, which spread the error of broadening the scope of class struggle in the Party, so that normal differences among comrades inside the Party came to be regarded as manifestations of the revisionist line or of the struggle between the two lines. This resulted in growing tension in inner-Party relations. Thus it became difficult for the Party to resist certain "Left" views put forward by Comrade Mao Zedong and others, and the development of these views led to the outbreak of the protracted "cultural revolution".

(2) Comrade Mao Zedong's prestige reached a peak and he began to get arrogant at the very time when the Party was confronted with the new task of shifting the focus of its work to socialist construction, a task for which the

utmost caution was required. He gradually divorced himself from practice and from the masses, acted more and more arbitrarily and subjectively, and increasingly put himself above the Central Committee of the Party. The result was a steady weakening and even undermining of the principle of collective leadership and democratic centralism in the political life of the Party and the country. This state of affairs took shape only gradually and the Central Committee of the Party should be held partly responsible. From the Marxist viewpoint, this complex phenomenon was the product of given historical conditions. Blaming this on only one person or on only a handful of people will not provide a deep lesson for the whole Party or enable it to find practical ways to change the situation. In the communist movement, leaders play quite an important role. This has been borne out by history time and again and leaves no room for doubt. However, certain grievous deviations, which occurred in the history of the international communist movement owing to the failure to handle the relationship between the Party and its leader correctly, had an adverse effect on our Party, too. Feudalism in China has had a very long history. Our Party fought in the firmest and most thoroughgoing way against it, and particularly against the feudal system of land ownership and the landlords and local tyrants, and fostered a fine tradition of democracy in the anti-feudal struggle. But it remains difficult to eliminate the evil ideological and political influence of centuries of feudal autocracy. And for various historical reasons, we failed to institutionalize and legalize inner-Party democracy and democracy in the political and social life of the country, or we drew up the relevant laws but they lacked due authority. This meant that conditions were present for the over-concentration of Party power in individuals and for the development of arbitrary individual rule and the personality cult in the Party. Thus, it was hard for the Party and state to pre-vent the initiation of the "cultural revolution" or check its development.

Part 6 Comrade Mao Zedong's Historical Role and Mao Zedong Thought

27. Comrade Mao Zedong was a great Marxist and a great proletarian

revolutionary, strategist and theorist. It is true that he made gross mistakes during the "cultural revolution", but, if we judge his activities as a whole, his contributions to the Chinese revolution far outweigh his mistakes. His merits are primary and his errors secondary. He rendered indelible meritorious service in founding and building up our Party and the Chinese People's Liberation Army, in winning victory for the cause of liberation of the Chinese people, in founding the People's Republic of China and in advancing our socialist cause. He made major contributions to the liberation of the oppressed nations of the world and to the progress of mankind.

28. The Chinese Communists, with Comrade Mao Zedong as their chief representative, made a theoretical synthesis of China's unique experience in its protracted revolution in accordance with the basic principles of Marxism-Leninism. This synthesis contributed a scientific system of guidelines befitting China's conditions, and it is this synthesis which is Mao Zedong Thought, the product of the integration of the universal principles of Marxism-Leninism with the concrete practice of the Chinese revolution. Making revolution in a large Eastern semi-colonial, semi-feudal country is bound to meet with many special, complicated problems which cannot be solved by reciting the general principles of Marxism-Leninism or by copying foreign experience in every detail. The erroneous tendency of making Marxism a dogma and deifying Comintern resolutions and the experience of the Soviet Union prevailed in the international communist movement and in our Party mainly in the late 1920s and early 1930s, and this tendency pushed the Chinese revolution to the brink of total failure. It was in the course of combating this wrong tendency and making a profound summary of our historical experience in this respect that Mao Zedong Thought took shape and developed. It was systematized and extended in a variety of fields and reached maturity in the latter part of the Agrarian Revolutionary War and the War of Resistance Against Japan, and it was further developed during the War of Liberation and after the founding of the People's Republic of China. Mao Zedong Thought is Marxism-Leninism applied and developed in China; it constitutes a correct theory, a body of correct principles and a

summary of the experiences that have been confirmed in the practice of the Chinese revolution, a crystallization of the collective wisdom of the Chinese Communist Party. Many outstanding leaders of our Party made important contributions to the formation and development of Mao Zedong Thought, and they are synthesized in the scientific works of Comrade Mao Zedong.

29. Mao Zedong Thought is wide-ranging in content. It is an original theory which has enriched and developed Marxism-Leninism in the following respects:

(1) On the new-democratic revolution. Proceeding from China's historical and social conditions, Comrade Mao Zedong made a profound study of the characteristics and laws of the Chinese revolution, applied and developed the Marxist-Leninist thesis of the leadership of the proletariat in the democratic revolution, and established the theory of new-democratic revolution—a revolution against imperialism, feudalism and bureaucrat-capitalism waged by the masses of the people on the basis of the worker-peasant alliance under the leadership of the proletariat. His main works on this subject include: *Analysis of the Classes in Chinese Society, Report on an Investigation of the Peasant Movement in Hunan, A Single Spark Can Start a Prairie Fire, Introducing "The Communist", On New Democracy, On Coalition Government and The Present Situation and Our Tasks.* The basic points of this theory are: a) China's bourgeoisie consisted of two sections, the big bourgeoisie (that is, the comprador bourgeoisie, or the bureaucrat-bourgeoisie) which was dependent on imperialism, and the national bourgeoisie which had revolutionary leanings but wavered. The proletariat should endeavour to get the national bourgeoisie to join in the united front under its leadership and in special circumstances to include even part of the big bourgeoisie in the united front, so as to isolate the main enemy to the greatest possible extent. When forming a united front with the bourgeoisie, the proletariat must preserve its own independence and pursue the policy of "unity, struggle, unity through struggle"; when forced to split with the bourgeoisie, chiefly the big bourgeoisie, it should have the courage and ability to wage a resolute armed struggle against the big bourgeoisie, while

continuing to win the sympathy of the national bourgeoisie or keep it neutral. b) Since there was no bourgeois democracy in China and the reactionary ruling classes enforced their terroristic dictatorship over the people by armed force, the revolution could not but essentially take the form of protracted armed struggle. China's armed struggle was a revolutionary war led by the proletariat with the peasants as the principal force. The peasantry was the most reliable ally of the proletariat. Through its vanguard, it was possible and necessary for the proletariat, with its progressive ideology and its sense of organization and discipline, to raise the political consciousness of the peasant masses, establish rural base areas, wage a protracted revolutionary war and build up and expand the revolutionary forces. Comrade Mao Zedong pointed out that "the united front and armed struggle are the two basic weapons for defeating the enemy". Together with Party building, they constituted the "three magic weapons" of the revolution. They were the essential basis which enabled the Chinese Communist Party to become the core of leadership of the whole nation and to chart the course of encircling the cities from the countryside and finally winning countryside victory.

(2) On the socialist revolution and socialist construction. On the basis of the economic and political conditions for the transition to socialism ensuing on victory in the new-democratic revolution, Comrade Mao Zedong and the Chinese Communist Party followed the path of effecting socialist industrialization simultaneously with socialist transformation and adopted concrete policies for the gradual transformation of the private ownership of the means of production, thereby providing a theoretical as well as practical solution to the difficult task of building socialism in a large country such as China, a country which was economically and culturally backward, with a population accounting for nearly one-fourth of the world's total. By putting forward the thesis that the combination of democracy for the people and dictatorship over the reactionaries constitutes the people's democratic dictatorship, Comrade Mao Zedong enriched the Marxist-Leninist theory of the dictatorship of the proletariat. After the establishment of the socialist system, Comrade Mao Zedong pointed out that, under

socialism, the people had the same fundamental interests, but that all kinds of contradictions still existed among them, and that contradictions between the enemy and the people and contradictions among the people should be strictly distinguished from each other and correctly handled. He proposed that among the people we should follow a set of correct policies. We should follow the policy of "unity-criticism-unity" in political matters, the policy of "long-term coexistence and mutual supervision" in the Party's relations with the democratic parties, the policy of "let a hundred flowers blossom, let a hundred schools of thought contend" in science and culture, and, in the economic sphere the policy of over-all arrangement with regard to the different strata in town and country and of consideration for the interests of the state, the collective and the individual, all three. He repeatedly stressed that we should not mechanically transplant the experience of foreign countries, but should find our own way to industrialization, a way suited to China's conditions, by proceeding from the fact that China is a large agricultural country, taking agriculture as the foundation of the economy, correctly handling the relationship between heavy industry on the one hand and agriculture and light industry on the other, and attaching due importance to the development of the latter. He stressed that in socialist construction we should properly handle the relationships between economic construction and building up defence, between large-scale enterprises and small and medium-scale enterprises, between the Han nationality and the minority nationalities, between the coastal regions and the interior, between the central and the local authorities, and between self-reliance and learning from foreign countries, and that we should properly handle the relationship between accumulation and consumption and pay attention to over-all balance. Moreover, he stressed that the workers were the masters of their enterprises and that cadres must take part in physical labor and workers in management, that irrational rules and regulations must be reformed and that the three-in-one combination of technical personnel, workers and cadres must be effected. And he formulated the strategic idea of bringing all positive factors into play and turning negative factors into positive ones so as to unite the whole Chinese people and build a powerful socialist country. The important ideas of Comrade Mao Zedong concerning the socialist revolution and socialist construction are mainly contained in such major works as *Report to the Second Plenary Session of the Seventh Central Committee of the Communist Party of China, On the People's Democratic Dictatorship, On the Ten Major Relationships, On the Correct Handling of Contradictions Among the People* and *Talk at an Enlarged Work Conference Convened by the Central Committee of the Communist Party of China.*

(3) On the building of the revolutionary army and military strategy. Comrade Mao Zedong methodically solved the problem of how to turn a revolutionary army chiefly made up of peasants into a new type of people's army which is proletarian in character, observes strict discipline and forms close ties with the masses. He laid it down that the sole purpose of the people's army is to serve the people whole-heartedly, he put forward the principle that the Party commands the gun and not the other way round, he advanced the Three Main Rules of Discipline and the Eight Points for Attention and stressed the practice of political, economic and military democracy and the principles of the unity of officers and soldiers, the unity of army and people and the disintegration of the enemy forces, thus formulating by way of summation a set of policies and methods concerning political work in the army. In his military writings such as *On Correcting Mistaken Ideas in the Party, Problems of Strategy in China's Revolutionary War, Problems of Strategy in Guerrilla War Against Japan, On Protracted War* and *Problems of War and Strategy*, Comrade Mao Zedong summed up the experience of China's protracted revolutionary wars and advanced the comprehensive concept of building a people's army and of building rural base areas and waging people's war by employing the people's army as the main force and relying on the masses. Raising guerrilla war to the strategic plane, he maintained that guerrilla warfare and mobile warfare of a guerrilla character would for a long time be the main forms of operation in China's revolutionary wars. He explained that it would be necessary to effect an appropriate change in military strategy simultaneously with the changing

balance of forces between the enemy and ourselves and with the progress of the war. He worked out a set of strategies and tactics for the revolutionary army to wage people's war in conditions when the enemy was strong and we were weak. These strategies and tactics include fighting a protracted war strategically and campaigns and battles of quick decision, turning strategic inferiority into superiority in campaigns and battles, and concentrating a superior force to destroy the enemy forces one by one. During the War of Liberation, he formulated the celebrated ten major principles of operation. All these ideas constitute Comrade Mao Zedong's outstanding contribution to the military theory of Marxism-Leninism. After the founding of the People's Republic, he put forward the important guideline that we must strengthen our national defence and build modern revolutionary armed forces (including the navy, the air force and technical branches) and develop modern defence technology (including the making of nuclear weapons for self-defence).

(4) On policy and tactics. Comrade Mao Zedong penetratingly elucidated the vital importance of policy and tactics in revolutionary struggles. He pointed out that policy and tactics were the life of the Party, that they were both the starting-point and the end-result of all the practical activities of a revolutionary party and that the Party must formulate its policies in the light of the existing political situation, class relations, actual circumstances and the changes in them, combining principle and flexibility. He made many valuable suggestions concerning policy and tactics in the struggle against the enemy, in the united front and other questions. He pointed out among other things: that, under changing subjective and objective conditions, a weak revolutionary force could ultimately defeat a strong reactionary force; that we should despise the enemy strategically and take him seriously tactically; that we should keep our eyes on the main target of struggle and not hit out in all directions; that we should differentiate between and disintegrate our enemies, and adopt the tactic of making use of contradictions, winning over the many, opposing the few and crushing our enemies one by one; that in areas under reactionary rule, we should combine legal and illegal struggle and, organizationally, adopt the policy of

assigning picked cadres to work underground; that, as for members of the defeated reactionary classes and reactionary elements, we should give them a chance to earn a living and to become working people living by their own labor, so long as they did not rebel or create trouble; and that the proletariat and its party must fulfil two conditions in order to exercise leadership over their allies: a) Lead their followers in waging resolute struggles against the common enemy and achieving victories; b) Bring material benefits to their followers or at least avoid damaging their interests and at the same time give them political education. These ideas of Comrade Mao Zedong's concerning policy and tactics are embodied in many of his writings, particularly in such works as *Current Problems of Tactics in the Anti-Japanese United Front, On Policy, Conclusions on the Repulse of the Second Anti-Communist Onslaught, On Some Important Problems of the Party's Present Policy, Don't Hit Out in All Directions* and *On the Question of Whether Imperialism and All Reactionaries Are Real Tigers.*

(5) On ideological and political work and cultural work. In his *On New Democracy*, Comrade Mao Zedong stated: Any given culture (as an ideological form) is a reflection of the politics and economics of a given society, and the former in turn has a tremendous influence and effect upon the latter; economics is the base and politics the concentrated expression of economics. In accordance with this basic view, he put forward many important ideas of far-reaching and long-term significance. For instance, the theses that ideological and political work is the life-blood of economic and all other work and that it is necessary to unite politics and economics and to unite politics and professional skills, and to be both red and expert; the policy of developing a national, scientific and mass culture and of letting a hundred flowers blossom, weeding through the old to bring forth the new, and making the past serve the present and foreign things serve China; and the thesis that intellectuals have an important role to play in revolution and construction, that intellectuals should identify themselves with the workers and peasants and that they should acquire the proletarian world outlook by studying Marxism-Leninism, by studying society and through practical work. He

pointed out that "this question of 'for whom?' is fundamental; it is a question of principle" and stressed that we should serve the people whole-heartedly, be highly responsible in revolutionary work, wage arduous struggle and fear no sacrifice. Many notable works written by Comrade Mao Zedong on ideology, politics and culture, such as *The Orientation of the Youth Movement*, *Recruit Large Numbers of Intellectuals*, *Talks at the Yan'an Forum of Literature and Art*, *In Memory of Norman Bethune*, *Serve the People* and *The Foolish Old Man Who Removed the Mountains*, are of tremendous significance even today.

(6) On Party building. It was a most difficult task to build a Marxist, proletarian Party of a mass character in a country where the peasantry and other sections of the petty bourgeoisie constituted the majority of the population, while the proletariat was small in number yet strong in combat effectiveness. Comrade Mao Zedong's theory on Party building provided a successful solution to this question. His main works in this area include *Combat Liberalism*, *The Role of the Chinese Communist Party in the National War*, *Reform Our Study*, *Rectify the Party's Style of Work*, *Oppose Stereotyped Party Writing*, *Our Study and the Current Situation*, *On Strengthening the Party Committee System* and *Methods of Work of Party Committees*. He laid particular stress on building the Party ideologically, saying that a Party member should join the Party not only organizationally but also ideologically and should constantly try to reform his non-proletarian ideas and replace them with proletarian ideas. He indicated that the style of work which entailed integrating theory with practice, forging close links with the masses and practicing self-criticism was the hallmark distinguishing the Chinese Communist Party from all other political parties in China. To counter the erroneous "Left" policy of "ruthless struggle and merciless blows" once followed in inner-Party struggle, he proposed the correct policy of "learning from past mistakes to avoid future ones and curing the sickness to save the patient", emphasizing the need to achieve the objective of clarity in ideology and unity among comrades in inner-Party struggle. He initiated the rectification campaign as a form of ideological education in Marxism-

Leninism throughout the Party, which applied the method of criticism and self-criticism. In view of the fact that our Party was about to become and then became a party in power leading the whole country, Comrade Mao Zedong urged time and again, first on the eve of the founding of the People's Republic and then later, that we should remain modest and prudent, guard against arrogance and rashness and keep to plain living and hard struggle in our style of work, and that we should be on the lookout against the corrosive influence of bourgeois ideology and should oppose bureaucratism which would alienate us from the masses.

30. The living soul of Mao Zedong Thought is the stand, viewpoint and method embodied in its component parts mentioned above. This stand, viewpoint and method boil down to three basic points: to seek truth from facts, the mass line, and independence. Comrade Mao Zedong applied dialectical and historical materialism to the entire work of the proletarian party, giving shape to this stand, viewpoint and method so characteristic of Chinese Communists in the course of the Chinese revolution and its arduous, protracted struggles and thus enriching Marxism-Leninism. They find expression not only in such important works as *Oppose Book Worship, On Practice, On Contradiction, Preface and Postscript to "Rural Survey", Some Questions Concerning Methods of Leadership* and *Where Do Correct Ideas Come From?* but also in all his scientific writings and in the revolutionary activities of the Chinese Communists.

(1) Seeking truth from facts. This means proceeding from reality and combining theory with practice, that is, integrating the universal principles of Marxism-Leninism with the concrete practice of the Chinese revolution. Comrade Mao Zedong was always against studying Marxism in isolation from the realities of Chinese society and the Chinese revolution. As early as 1930, he opposed blind book worship by emphasizing that investigation and study is the first step in all work and that one has no right to speak without investigation. On the eve of the rectification movement in Yan'an, he affirmed that subjectivism is a formidable enemy of the Communist Party, a manifestation of impurity in Party spirit. These brilliant theses helped people

break through the shackles of dogmatism and greatly emancipate their minds. While summarizing the experience and lessons of the Chinese revolution in his philosophical works and many other works rich in philosophical content, Comrade Mao Zedong showed great profundity in expounding and enriching the Marxist theory of knowledge and dialectics. He stressed that the dialectical materialist theory of knowledge is the dynamic, revolutionary theory of reflection and that full scope should be given to man's conscious dynamic role, when it is based on and is in conformity with objective reality. Basing himself on social practice, he comprehensively and systematically elaborated the dialectical materialist theory on the sources, the process and the purpose of knowledge and on the criterion of truth. He said that as a rule, correct knowledge can be arrived at and developed only after many repetitions of the process leading from matter to consciousness and then back to matter, that is, leading from practice to knowledge and then back to practice. He pointed out that truth exists by contrast with falsehood and grows in struggle with it, that truth is inexhaustible and that the truth of any piece of knowledge, namely, whether it corresponds to objective reality, can ultimately be decided only through social practice. He further elaborated the law of the unity of opposites, the nucleus of Marxist dialectics. He indicated that we should not only study the universality of contradiction in objective existence, but, what is more important, we should study the particularity of contradiction, and that we should resolve contradictions which are different in nature by different methods. Therefore, dialectics should not be viewed as a formula to be learned by rote and applied mechanically, but should be closely linked with practice and with investigation and study and should be applied flexibly. He forged philosophy into a sharp weapon in the hands of the proletariat and the people for knowing and changing the world. His distinguished works on China's revolutionary war, in particular, provide outstandingly shining examples of applying and developing the Marxist theory of knowledge and dialectics in practice. Our Party must always adhere to the above ideological line formulated by Comrade Mao Zedong.

(2) The mass line means everything for the masses, reliance on the

masses in everything, and "from the masses, to the masses". The Party's mass line in all its work has come into being through the systematic application in all its activities of the Marxist-Leninist principle that the people are the makers of history. It is a summation of our Party's invaluable historical experience in conducting revolutionary activities over the years under difficult circumstances in which the enemy's strength far outstripped ours. Comrade Mao Zedong stressed time and again that as long as we rely on the people, believe firmly in the inexhaustible creative power of the masses and hence trust and identify ourselves with them, no enemy can crush us while we can eventually crush every enemy and overcome every difficulty. He also pointed out that in leading the masses in all practical work, the leadership can form its correct ideas only by adopting the method of "from the masses, to the masses" and by combining the leadership with the masses and the general call with particular guidance. This means concentrating the ideas of the masses and turning them into systematic ideas, then going to the masses so that the ideas are persevered in and carried through, and testing the correctness of these ideas in the practice of the masses. And this process goes on, over and over again, so that the understanding of the leadership becomes more correct, keener and richer each time. This is how Comrade Mao Zedong united the Marxist theory of knowledge with the Party's mass line. As the vanguard of the proletariat, the Party exists and fights for the interests of the people. But it always constitutes only a small part of the people, so that isolation from the people will render all the Party's struggles and ideals devoid of content as well as impossible of success. To persevere in the revolution and advance the socialist cause, our Party must uphold the mass line.

(3) Independence and self-reliance are the inevitable corollary of carrying out the Chinese revolution and construction by proceeding from Chinese reality and relying on the masses. The proletarian revolution is an internationalist cause which calls for the mutual support of the proletariats of different countries. But for the cause to triumph, each proletariat should primarily base itself on its own country's realities, rely on the efforts of its own masses and revolutionary forces, integrate the universal principles of

Marxism-Leninism with the concrete practice of its own revolution and thus achieve victory. Comrade Mao Zedong always stressed that our policy should rest on our own strength and that we should find our own road of advance in accordance with our own conditions. In a vast country like China, it is all the more imperative for us to rely mainly on our own efforts to promote the revolution and construction. We must be determined to carry the struggle through to the end and must have faith in the hundreds of millions of Chinese people and rely on their wisdom and strength; otherwise, it will be impossible for our revolution and construction to succeed or to be consolidated even if success is won. Of course, China's revolution and national construction are not and cannot be carried on in isolation from the rest of the world. It is always necessary for us to try to win foreign aid and, in particular, to learn all that is advanced and beneficial from other countries. The closed-door policy, blind opposition to everything foreign and any theory or practice of great-nation chauvinism are all entirely wrong. At the same time, although china is still comparatively backward economically and culturally, we must maintain our own national dignity and confidence, and there must be no slavishness or submissiveness in any form in dealing with big, powerful or rich countries. Under the leadership of the Party and Comrade Mao Zedong, no matter what difficulty we encountered, we never wavered, whether before or after the founding of New China, in our determination to remain independent and self-reliant and, we never submitted to any pressure from outside; we showed the dauntless and heroic spirit of the Chinese Communist Party and the Chinese people. We stand for the peaceful co-existence of the people of all countries and their mutual assistance on an equal footing. While upholding our own independence, we respect other people's right to independence. The road of revolution and construction suited to the characteristics of a country has to be explored, decided on and blazed by its own people. No one has the right to impose his views on others. Only under these conditions can there be genuine internationalism. Otherwise, there can only be hegemonism. We will always adhere to this principled stand in our international relations.

31. Mao Zedong Thought is the valuable spiritual asset of our Party. It

will be our guide to action for a long time to come. The Party leaders and the large group of cadres nurtured by Marxism-Leninism and Mao Zedong Thought were the backbone forces in winning great victories for our cause; they are and will remain our treasured mainstay in the cause of socialist modernization. While many of Comrade Mao Zedong's important works were written during the periods of new-democratic revolution and of socialist transformation, we must still constantly study them. This is not only because one cannot cut the past off from the present and failure to understand the past will hamper our understanding of present-day problems, but also because many of the basic theories, principles and scientific approaches set forth in these works are of universal significance and provide us with invaluable guidance now and will continue to do so in the future. Therefore, we must continue to uphold Mao Zedong Thought, study it in earnest and apply its stand, viewpoint and method in studying the new situation and solving the new problems arising in the course of practice. Mao Zedong Thought has added much that is new to the treasure-house of Marxist-Leninist theory. We must combine our study of the scientific works of Comrade Mao Zedong with that of the scientific writings of Marx, Engels, Lenin and Stalin. It is entirely wrong to try to negate the scientific value of Mao Zedong Thought and to deny its guiding role in our revolution and construction just because Comrade Mao Zedong made mistakes in his later years. And it is likewise entirely wrong to adopt a dogmatic attitude towards the sayings of Comrade Mao Zedong, to regard whatever he said as the immutable truth which must be mechanically applied everywhere, and to be unwilling to admit honestly that he made mistakes in his later years, and even try to stick to them in our new activities. Both these attitudes fail to make a distinction between Mao Zedong Thought—a scientific theory formed and tested over a long period of time—and the mistakes Comrade Mao Zedong made in his later years. And it is absolutely necessary that this distinction should be made. We must treasure all the positive experience obtained in the course of integrating the universal principles of Marxism-Leninism with the concrete practice of China's revolution and construction over fifty years or so, apply and carry forward this experience in our new work and enrich and develop Party theory with new principles and new conclusions corresponding to reality, so as to ensure the continued progress of our cause along the scientific course of Marxism-Leninism and Mao Zedong Thought.

Printed in P.R.C. by order of Canut-Berlin.